Rave reviews for th  es!

"**I nearly died laughing …**" – Sylvain Moreau, China.

"**Best damn thing I've read in years…**" – Geoff Hughes, ex-US Navy.

"**It is so funny, and horrifying. Laughed like a drain … there should be a warning on the cover not to read it in airports. You are inclined to snort with laughter and get funny looks from fellow travellers.**" – Liz Davies, Manila.

"**Still laughing my ass off!**" – Paul Nugnes, Florida USA.

"**Had a great laugh reading your first two books ... bring on the next two!**" – David Ellis-Jones, Vietnam.

"**Your stories are a constant source of entertainment for me and my buddies. Keep up the great work.**" – Brad Carpenter, US Air Force.

"**This reviewer rates his asides into history on a par with his unqualified enjoyment of sex.**" – Bernard Trink, The Bangkok Post.

"**Captures the lifestyle of the sinful expat male with terrifying accuracy!**" – Nury Vittachi, author 'The Feng Shui Detective'.

"**A mighty collection of tales. The bawdy humour comes thick and fast throughout. A rib-tickling read for the not-so-faint-hearted.**" – The Expat Magazine, Singapore.

"**A no-holes-barred romp through Asia. You're in for a great laugh.**" – Nexus Expatriate Magazine, UK.

"HARDSHIP POSTING"

True tales of expat misadventure in Asia.

Volume 3.

Compiled and edited by
Stu Lloyd.

Piston Broake Press
(An imprint of Captions)
"De gustibus non disputandum est."

All reference and likeness to persons living or dead is purely intentional.

Published by Captions of Industry Pty Ltd.
ACN 089 800 304
PO Box 350, Pymble, NSW, 2073, Australia.
Fax: 612-9499-5908
Trade enquiries: captions@bigpond.net.au
Editor: hardshipposting@hotmail.com
Colonel Ken: ColonelKen@hotmail.com

www.hardshipposting.com

© Copyright 2003 Captions of Industry Pty Ltd.

All rights reserved. Without limiting the rights of the copyright owner, no part of this publication may be reproduced, stored in or introduced into a retrieval system, or transmitted in any form or by any means (electronic, mechanical, photocopying, recording or otherwise), without the prior written permission of the copyright owner. Opinions and views of contributors are not those of the editor or publisher, nor are all activities described herein endorsed by the editor or publisher.

National Library of Australia Cataloguing-in-Publication:
Hardship Posting: true tales of expat misadventure in Asia volume 3.

ISBN 0 9578332 2 9

1. Businesspeople - Asia - Anecdotes. 2. Aliens - Asia -
Anecdotes. 3. Employment in foreign countries - Anecdotes.
4. Employment in foreign countries - Humor. 5. Asia -
Social life and customs - Humor. I. Lloyd, Stuart, 1962- .
II. Oathe, Ken.

950.00424

Cover photography of Colonel Ken by Shrimp Studios, Thailand.
Cover design by Stu Lloyd and Said Studios, Sydney.
Typeset by Q2A Solutions, India.

Printed in Australia

10 9 8 7 6 5 4 3

Dedicated to the victims of the Bali bombings, October 2002. Especially those members of the Singapore Cricket Club, ISCI Jakarta, Hong Kong RFC, and Taipei Baboons RFC.

Contents

Foreword

Guest in hotel to housekeeping: "I'm up on the wardrobe and this bloody great lizard has just knocked me coffee table over. Now it's under the bed and it's growling … do you have anything I can feed it?" This anecdote was told to me by a Scottish gent in Manila. It's a variation on the old 'Oh, geckos … everyone's got them!' story, and – apocraphyl as it is – underlines the fact that a) there are always two or three versions of a good story, and b) a good story grows with the retelling.

Hardship Posting deals in 'true tales', stories that are fundamentally grounded in factual occurence. Some call them 'sea stories': stories that have an element of truth in them. Whereas fairy tales start off with 'Once upon a time …' sea stories start are often prefaced with: 'This ain't no shit …'

The point is we make no effort to corroborate most of the stories that are contributed here. It's virtually impossible to. Plus, if it's a better story for the embellishment, so be it. No-one's reputation is going to come to grief because of our 'Kai Tak Accord' anonymity policy anyhow. We get a lot of mail from readers in places such as Singapore who say they have trouble believing some of the more extreme goings-on. Whilst others, in places like Cambodia, say all these things happen on a daily basis before breakfast! This highlights the infinite variety of the expat experience in Asia.

When I conceived 'Hardship Posting' as the title for this series, the tongue was firmly in cheek, for – with the exception of a couple of the frontier locations in Indochina – Asia was largely comfortable, enjoyable, economically rewarding, and you could watch your favourite sport live on satellite TV … a virtual paradise. Now in the wake of the Bali incident, the term 'Hardship Posting' rings a bit more true. Combined with economic rationalism, Western expats have become the unwitting front-line troops in this ill-defined amorphic war of attrition. A shift from colonialism, to neo-colonialism to … who knows what? … is undoubtedly afoot. No-one knows exactly. Hence all the more reason, I believe, to document the heady times of the last few decades in Asia.

Perhaps things have come full circle. Ferdinand Magellan, one of the first ever Europeans to set foot on South East Asian soil, was killed in 1521 by Chief Lapu Lapu on Mactan Island, Cebu, in the Philippines.

Whilst these books aim to be generally light and flippant, any story dealing with untimely demise is not necessarily humorous nor entertainment. Mark Twain, a famous writer who called Asia home for a while, would disagree as he saw tragedy as the source of potential levity and humour (60 million Filipinos can't be wrong, can they?). Rather, in our case, tragic events are included to capture the full spectrum of the expatriate experience and lifestyle. And death, you'll agree, is a very extreme form of life!

However, it is our job to provide lightness in these times often darkened by gathering storm clouds. Perhaps the best indication of this is the number of emails doing the rounds that have included funny stories extracted from Hardship Posting received by us.

Indeed we are not exempt from the odd frustration-turned-humourous event ourselves. Take the situation last year sometime when our distributors in Hong Kong placed a re-order for 500 copies of our books. These duly arrived from Singapore, at which point we got a frantic call from our distributor: "Why are there four pallets of books?" Ten thousand copies of Hardship Posting had arrived in their warehouse! There was no rational explanation. Suffice to say, we didn't pay the shipping company and we can afford to laugh about it. Now.

Despite our repeated threats to slash his expense account and rein in his outspoken opinions, Colonel Ken is back again this volume due to popular demand – mainly from him, it must be said.

Happy reading and good health until the next volume.

Cheers!

Stu Lloyd,
March 2003.

Acknowledgements

A full list of contributors to this volume is overpage. Thanks to you all for keeping us generously plied with your endless stories, humour and camaraderie.

One contributor in particular struck a real chord with me: one James R Folsom. James had been a sailor and spent nearly 50 years as an 'expat' in and around Asia, before retiring to northern Thailand. One day I received a handwritten letter in the mail from him, with a few stories and an apology as he "had no access to an English typewriter let alone a computer or fax". I wrote back, longhand, thanking him and taking him up on his offer of "I got more if you want 'em".

The next instalment I received months later was in different handwriting … he had got his dear young Thai wife, Pornsawan 'Am' Suksri, to transcribe his stories only days before passing away. To her eternal credit she had mailed them to us along with the sad news of his passing. Many others I'm sure would have just binned them, especially as it detailed a lot of his very personal antics and 'history'. "You couldn't call these 'misadventures', because I wouldn't have missed them for the world," he wrote. *Khop khun maak khrap*, Khun Am, for your unstinting efforts.

On a lighter note, I'm pleased to say that we have had an ever-increasing amount of contributors putting their material forward for consideration: a lot more from North Asia (Japan, Korea, India, China and Taiwan) this time, and more nationalities represented. Also, it's not just career expats. Contractors, military, long-term residents and die-hard colonials have all entered the fray willingly.

Perhaps somewhat surprisingly, we enjoy a strong following among some sectors of the female constituency, proven by the fact that we have more contributions from women and housewives than before. And in my research and promotional travels I haven't got a slap across the face. Yet! Frankly, I feel the world is undergoing a backlash against the oppressive political-correctness of the last decade or so. People are privately bored with its kill-joy constrictures.

I like to think we've achieved a good cross-sectional 'representation', given that 'balance' is not a word best used in the context of many of our contributors in Asia.

A very special note of thanks to the following who know what they have done to deserve a mention here: Alan Williams, Arjan van de Laak, Andrew Patterson, the Asia Books team, Barry Smit, Ben Knowles, Bill Percy and The Oasis Hotel folks, Carol Lo, Colin at Big Chilli magazine, Damien Horigan, Dave Rick, Duncan Smith, Imelda Talens and the Far East Media team, Hari Bedi, Heamakarn Sricharatchanya, Tom Danby and the INT Press team, Jack Corman, Jeffrey E Brunton, John and Jackie Lampert, John Oles, Johnson Lee and the Market Asia team, Jurgen Thorwirth, Katrina Mayer, Kenneth Wong and team at Times Newslink Singapore, Kerry Bielik, Khun Som, Michael Madac, Mike Double, Peter O'Donnell, Philip Strachan, Richard Oh and Ingrid Suriya at QB World Books, Sam at The Office, Bangkok, Stuart Jackets, the WH Smith team in Hong Kong, and Wika Menzies.

Contributors to Hardship Posting, Volume 3.

Adrian Barrett	Barry Smit
Albert Schmied	Ba-Thong Phan
Alex Chelleri	Bill Corbett
Allan Jackman	Bill Percy
Andrew Karam	Bill Panton
Andrew Kefford	Billy Thomas
Andrew Macguire	Brad Walker
Andrew Patterson	Brett Gorney
Andy Kaye	Brian Holgate
Annette Mossbacher	Bryan Leveinge
Anthony Lee	Bryan Payne
Anthony Ryder	Charlie Chamberlin
Anthony Varga	Chris Destrieux
Anthony Stapleton	Christian Oeljeschlager
Barbara Valente	Dave Brock
Barry Owen	David Collings

David Glass

David Wise

Des Pearson

Dick Murphy

Dominic Lavin

Don McEvoy

Doug Banker

Dougal Brown

Dreaded Fog

Eric McGaw

Ernie Purvis

Frank Land

Fred van den Bosch

Fred Whitaker

Garry Murrell

Geoff Hughes

Geoff Alexander

Gordon Keys

Graeme Baker

Graham Patton

Graham Ruby

Greg Harbutt

Greg Starr

Guy Evans

Hanoi Bill

Hanspeter Meier

Harry Bonning

Harry Howell

Holcombe Thomas

Ian Foster

Ian Mitchell

Jack Corman

Jackie Lampert

Jake Jacobs

James Hall

James Parsons

James R Folsom

Jason Meyeroff

Jeffrey Kuperus

Jerry Findley

Jesse Gump

Jim Anderson

Jim Butler

Jock Hill

Johan Olstenius

John Bruggen

John Duncan

John Ewing

John Kennedy

John Lampert

John O'Rourke

John Stall

John Wood

Joost Pannekeet

Kaizad Varsavandi

Keith Teacher

Ken Ginnett

Ken White

Kerry Bielik

Kevin Parnell

Kim Johnston

Leo Crohan

Leslie Staples

Liz Davies

Mal Lowson

Malcolm Lambert

Marc Bogard

Mark Kovalevsky

Mark Weingartner
Martin Slater
Marty Hanratty
Matt Marcus
Matthew Caddick
Max Martin
Michael Butler
Michael Keats
Mike Davies
Mike Frowens
Mike Gentleman
Mike Miall
Mike Van Niekerk
Mitchell Stein
Myles Glew
Nick Robertson
Niek Janssen
Nigel Miller
Nobby Clarke
Ofay
Ofer Rozen
Owen Dolan
Pat Brett
Patrick Gauvain
Paul Dempsey
Paul Fichter
Paul McDonnell
Paul Nugnes
Peter Banks
Peter Holmes
Peter O'Donnell
Peter Walt
Phil Riddell
Richard O'Brien

Rick Reid
Rick Stanford
Roland Bosshard
Ron Boon
Ross French
Russell Kelly
Scott Guthrie
Scott Terrey
Simon Durrant
Simon Ogus
Simon Wagstaff
Skinny Dipper
Slippery Beaver
Stephen Greenough
Steve Brentnall
Steve Puttock
Steve Rhodes
Steve Young
Sylvain Moreau
Tapeworm
Ted Royer
Terje Schau
Terry Clarke
Terry O'Toole
Tim Whisenand
Titch Callanan
Tjasa Boh
Tom Welch
Tommie Duncan
Tony Elliot
Tony James
Walter English
Colin Woods
Overlooked? Apologies.

Foreplay from Colonel Ken

Ladies and gentlemen, bastards and bargirls, it's an undisputed pressure, er, pleasure to be back in the hotseat again. My publishers tell me some sections of the reading public think that I am nothing more than a dirty old man who talks of nothing but sex in Asia. Entirely untrue … I can also talk about foreplay. OK, time's up!

For those who don't know, I have recently awarded the Nubile Piece Prize to a worthy recipient and am now embedded and sharing my hairy hot dog (or *chi zi wang* as the Chinese call it) with the delightful Khun Aei, whom readers might remember better as Miss October in our 2001 Hard-on Posting calendar. You've got to love this place – dig a hole and bury me, it doesn't get better than this.

That's the great thing about Asia: you can be fatter than Thailand's Miss Jumbo Queen, balder than a baboon's backside, older than the girls at Hong Kong's Red Lips bar, and uglier than a bucket of arseholes with all the pretty ones picked out, but – if you've got a dollar – you're still in the game. The ol' fiscal attraction never fails. A full wallet of crisp purple 500-baht notes is the human equivalent of a proud peacock strutting his stuff with his massive and colourful plumage fanned out. Fortunately I don't have a conscience but, if I did, it would probably bother me.

Of course, this great life in Asia is not for everyone. God knows there are some whingers who can't handle the excitement. But now, in the continuing list of those who have called Asia home over the years, a number of surprising entries: Earl Woods (Tiger's dad, did a tour of duty in Vietnam), David 'Campo' Campese (the legendary Wallaby winger was a coach in Singapore), Mark Twain (he spent three weeks in India to help pay off his debts), Freddie Mercury (of band Queen, was educated in India), Winston Churchill (was with the cavalry in India), Lord Louis Mountbatten (Viceroy of India), Engelbert Humperdinck (was born Arnold Dorsey in India), and Errol Flynn (gold prospecting and slave-trading in New Guinea). The list goes on, but more of that in the next instalment.

They say that great minds discuss ideas, average minds discuss events, and small minds discuss people. Speaking of which, one contributor – let's call him Gary – was preparing "20 or 30" stories for us when he was summarily busted by his wife, who shared access to his computer. Very soon he found himself alone while she was firmly ensconced in their house back in Australia. I never did get the stories.

Another – let's call him Baldrick – showed a sense of priorities of which I am weepingly proud: "I am currently getting rid of the next ex-Mrs Baldrick who, much to my annoyance, has my copy of Hardship Posting!" he wrote.

I also got a signal recently from my good friend Scott who pretends to work at Bangkok University. In return, he says, they pretend to pay him. He came across (not literally I hope!) our tome on the shelves of the University library. "I'm sure you will be proud to know that your words of wisdom are available to all the students at one of this nation's finest institutes of higher learning," he says. "Would it be possible for you to show up as a guest speaker one day? Maybe you could demonstrate the 'botty burp' for the class."

Speaking of small minds, I won't spoil the surprise for you, but you've got to hear what my good friends Dave, Pete and Barry have been up to lately.

So grab a gin and tonic, make yourself comfortable, and read on MacDuff.

Cop you later,

Colonel Ken

Col Kenneth B Oathe, DOM, SCB, VD (and bar).
Koh Samui, Thailand.

November 2002 [Received April 2003 –ed.] (Who's counting anyway? –The Col.) [Well, Ken, there is the small matter of missing the deadline for Christmas season –ed.] (Think of it as early for next Christmas! – The Col.) [Perhaps you could attend the next publishing meeting and propose that, Ken. Good luck! – ed] (Sure. I await my first-class ticket – The Col.)

❖ 1 ❖

Up, Up and Way-hey!
Or the Mile High Club

True tales of airports and flying experiences in Asia.

This Garuda airlines pilot was flying for the first time into the old Hong Kong airport. He'd been briefed on how it was the most treacherous approach in the world and the most difficult runway to land on bar none. He summoned all his experience and steered his craft masterfully between the apartment buildings with their washing hanging out, narrowly missing a few of the taller television antennae, dropped sharply to get the wheels on to the tarmac, then applied full reverse thrust and flaps. The plane shuddered and screeched to a halt, just centimetres from the end of the runway with the harbour water lapping at its edges.

"Phew!" he said to his co-pilot, wiping the sweat from his brow. "That's got to be the shortest runway in the world ... but, allah-mah, look how *wide* it is."

Yes, jetsetters, Asia's got more than its fair share of scarelines. Take Scare China for instance or, better still, don't take it. Or the Mongolian national carrier, MIAT. "Stands for Maybe I'll Arrive Tomorrow," Pete told me after a recent assignment up there. And domestic airlines in India are the absolute pits: there you are nicely ensconced at the pointy end of the plane, curtain firmly drawn between you and the great unwashed, when your meal is served ... and that's the cue for passengers in economy class to come and beg for their food from first class. But none could claim a worse track record – surely, hopefully! – than China Scarelines who have caused nearly 700 passenger deaths in the last decade.

No wonder I find the need to soothe the nerves with a tot or seventeen of brandy before boarding a plane. I'm not particularly proud of this, but I will share it with you: I got so plastered waiting to fly once that I ended up chatting up a life-size cardboard cut-out of the airline hostie in the first class lounge. You wouldn't blame me if you saw her – an absolute doll.

Speaking of which, the medical experts reckon they've stumbled on this new phenomena of Deep Vein Thrombosis. What a load of rot … it's been around for years. Ever since Malaysia-Singapore Airlines (as they were then known) introduced their new Pierre Cardin-designed *sarong kebaya* uniforms in 1968. That certainly caused a lot of thrombosis of the deep vein variety among the gentlemanly clientele of the day as they swished past in the aisles. A little tip for travellers who do feel a nasty thrombosis coming on … go for a therapeutic massage as soon as you land. Trained professional specialists like those at Darlings in Bangkok are experts I hold in the highest esteem at getting rid of all the accumulated clots from frequent fliers.

Here's a cocktail party gem for you: the first airmail service in Asia was between the USA and the Philippines in November 1935. A Pan Am clipper flying boat carried a letter from FDR to President Quezon, and – watched by all of Manila – the plane landed in the bay in front of the Manila Hotel. But, as it never contained any money nor a promise of marriage, they never wrote back [Check facts –ed.].

For flying stories, though, you can't beat Papua New Guinea. Mustar Pard was a World War One flying ace who ended up flying three-engined corrugated iron planes taking gold out of Bololo in the period before the Second World War. And Amelia Erhardt – the most famous aviator with a cockpit instead of a joystick – disappeared there in July 1937. If they'd had radar back then, she would've disappeared off the screen soon after take-off from Lae, and is presumed to have crashed but no wreckage was ever recovered. Then post-war, my good friend Lawrence Jones was a legendary mail pilot doing the rounds of PNG for years. (The good thing about being a mail pilot is that it's harder for the dogs to bite you.) Pard and Jones both wrote riveting books about their experiences, so you should've spent your money on those instead of this drivel. Stories? Those blokes make me look like a blushing wallflower.

How things have changed though through the years. Kansei Airport outside Tokyo is so big it can be seen from outer space (that and the Great Wall of China, so hopefully the shuttle pilots don't ever get them mixed up). But I loved the old Narita airport. Did you ever notice that in the middle of one of the runways was a patch of grass, about 10 metres by about 10 metres, fenced off? My good Japanese pal Fugu 'Terry' Aki tells me that when the airport was being developed there was one old farmer who just plain simply refused to sell his land. Not for any price. So this verdant testament to his stubbornness remains to this day. One for the good guys!

Had to laugh, my luggage was tagged for Kansei with its barcode and three-letter code: KIX. But it just got better when I flew to Fukuoka: FUK, seriously folks. I've always enjoyed the delicious irony of Singapore's SIN. And I learned a new one flying into Da Nang, Vietnam, again recently: DAD. Probably appropriate given the rampant hormones and wanton ways of the GIs over there before.

Nearby Burma have succumbed to the old third world 'build it and they will come' syndrome. Tin pot dictators should know by now that mantra only applies successfully to massage parlours and nothing else. The junta believed that by building one of the most elaborate state-of-the art airports in the world, their tourism business would really take off. Not only is the airport massive and super-equipped, but also a magnificent two-lane highway runs all the way from town straight to it. There's absolutely no traffic on the road out and car parking's not a problem.

One or two slight problems, though. Look, it's minor, minor stuff but let's mention it anyway. The runway is too bumpy so 747s are not able to land on it. Instead this white elephant serves about four domestic flights in great style and capaciousness on a busy day.

At busier airports, there's one thing that never fails to amuse me. All the young bucks will be standing at the luggage carousel, and strategically place themselves next to the young lovely they spotted earlier on their flight. Chances to maybe strike up a conversation while waiting. But the main reason is to show their gallantry … as her little suitcase comes along the belt, no less than three guys looking to impress her will fall over each other to have the honours of lifting her bag (which frankly could've been taken aboard as carry-on) onto her trolley. In return they get a sweet smile and a "thanks" and have created the impression that all expat guys are so kind, gentle, polite and chivalrous. Meanwhile, on the other side of the belt is some old grey-haired, gold-toothed, purple-pyjama-ed grandma from China who's just snapped a vertebra trying to lift her over-sized Samsonite off. But these same gallant gents will stand back and watch her struggle in a rally of indifference! Funny that.

The biggest suitcases in the world, though, must surely be manufactured in the Philippines. I'm not sure of the dimensions, but I think 'fucking huge' would be the technical description. Let's put it this way: the average maid carrying these things a) can't carry them herself with anything loaded inside because they're too heavy and b) all you see is the little black head protruding from the top of the handle and a couple of fancy shoes poking out from the bottom (the suitcase's not hers!). And they don't carry just one of these cavernous monstrosities. Oh, no. Three pieces, minimum. But suitcases are the least of their worries and – never mind the excess baggage – just carry it on board. That new 68 centimetre Sony TV and VCR, no problem … just stick in the overhead locker, or at your feet or in the aisle. Plus marker pen-labelled cardboard boxes the size of coffins or common two-door fridges. Maybe they are coffins and fridges, in which case I've got a suggestion: put the stiff inside the fridge to preserve it, and that way you only have to carry one package. How those overloaded planes ever take off, I'll never know, and don't say "they throttle the engines, Ken".

Is it just me or have you noticed that as a passenger you get this little lap strap to buckle around your not-insubstantial girth, while the crew – facing backward in larger, more comfortable and supportive seats – strap themselves in to those elaborate harnesses as used by your average Formula One racing team? Not that it makes a whole lot of difference when you slam into a mountain at a ground speed of 800 kilometres per hour.

Anyway, better fasten my bit of string for take-off. Not that I'm nervous but, gee, this runway does look hellishly wide.

Colonel Ken

A casual approach

We organised a charter flight for our sports group in India. We wanted a pilot that would let us have some fun en route and, fortunately, there was a pilot in our group who was more than keen to do the job and do something out of the ordinary himself.

After boarding, he came on the intercom: "Welcome on this flight from Bombay. Your destination is Goa. Bugger the altitude and the temperature outside … we can guarantee the beer's fucking cold. In fact as soon as we're airborne I'll put this sucker on autopilot and come back and get pissed with the rest of you!"

A few more classic interjections ensued, and then he left us with the following announcement as we came in to land: "As we will be landing shortly, please ensure your tray is stowed, your seat is upright, your seatbelt is fastened, and for fuck sake put your bloody trousers back on!"

East is east, and ...

Coming to Hong Kong one morning, Philippine Airlines' scheduled 07:45 departure took off punctually at 08:30 and climbed quickly to cruising altitude over San Fernando before turning left a bit to head out over the South China Sea. I had a very agreeable breakfast and – as the delightful, though somewhat overweight middle-aged, stewardess was collecting my tray – I just happened to mention that the sun was shining through my window. She promptly reached over and pulled down the blind. Though I hate to be a nuisance I suggested that it was in fact the *position* of the sun rather than the intensity that was causing me some concern. Being an amateur navigator I have noticed that when one is heading north in the morning, the sun is usually to be found somewhere to the right: I was sitting on the left-hand side of the aircraft. Either the sun had moved or we were heading south.

"Oh, sir, you hab noticed," she said with delight, "we are now going buk to Mayneela." I asked whether they intended to share this change of plan with their passengers at some stage. A sudden look of consternation, complete with dramatic knitting together of thinly-pencilled eyebrows, followed. "Poor a while, ser, I will ask de kaptane," after which she waddled off in the direction of the flight deck. Some minutes later, after several attempts at mastering the intricacies of the intercom, the 'kaptane' introduced himself and proceeded to recite what he could remember of the textbook announcement.

"Because we were habing some mekanikal froblem, and also some illektrykal, we hab decided to return to Mayneela poor some purther ebaluation ob de froblem." While the cabin crew busied themselves with straps on their safety harnesses between etching signs of the cross in the air in front of them, he proceeded to assure us, rather unconvincingly, that though "we don't know exaktly what is de froblem, but I tink dat eberyteeng should be OK and you don't need to worry dat because eberyteeng on de plight deck is under kontrol."

Back safely in Manila at 11:00 I decided not to wait for the next attempt scheduled at 14:30 and came up on the next day's flight.

Cunning de-skys

It was just another trip to Hong Kong for the head of corporate finance as he boarded his BA flight from London. Working on a major deal, all he was thinking of doing was putting his nose straight into a report. However, it happened to be his birthday and he saw a birthday card on his seat. This was from his wife, wishing him a happy birthday, and promising that the airline had a surprise for him.

However, no cakes or complimentary bottles of Dom were forthcoming. Then the lady next to him – wearing Yoko Ono-style glasses – asked him if he'd like a peanut. He accepted and began reading his report again. She then asked him if he'd like another peanut. He took another.

Eventually, the peanut lady took off her glasses. She then smiled and ripped off a wig. It was his wife! She'd arranged the whole surprise with the airline. His staff in Hong Kong could not believe that a man with his eye for detail could sit next to his wife for several hours without recognising her. However, they both had the last laugh when she turned up at a company cocktail party in her disguise, and walked around the room without anyone recognising her either.

Fly the unfriendly skies

Waiting for my flight in the Port Moresby terminal, all hell broke out. A full-on knock-down drag-out affair, like something out of Hollywood, which seemed to go for ages but was probably over in a few minutes. The shoot-out was between the police and a local *raskal* gang. When the smoke cleared, and the dust settled, three of the gang lay dead, plus one policeman, and two innocent airport staff, right next to me. I couldn't get out of there quick enough.

Dim sum

Fortunately for me the ground hostess at the check-in counter at Hong Kong where I was boarding an economy flight was not a maths whiz. I had two suitcases, one that weighed 14kg and the other 29kg. She took a piece of paper and wrote the numbers down and started adding, ending up with a total of 33kg. Phew! The real answer, 43kg, would have been way over the limit and cost me a fortune.

Auto pilot

I was flying from Chengdu back to Beijing with my Chinese business manager, when our B-737 was diverted to Tianjin due to weather conditions. My colleague and I were now running late as we had to do a presentation that afternoon at an international conference. We decided to leave the plane in Tianjin and take a taxi for the last 100km to Beijing, rather than wait indefinitely on the ground. But when the plane landed they opened the doors but would not bring stairs to the plane to allow anybody to leave: they did not have permission to disembark passengers there.

Shortly after the captain came out of the flight deck and, in my broken Chinese and English, I told him I was a 'Canadian pilot' – meaning a private pilot – to establish some camaraderie, and asked him about the stairs as I was in a hurry. Shortly after, a stair truck came racing to the airplane and they took only my colleague and I off, down the stairs, into an ambulance, which raced us to the street side, and put us in a taxi on our way to Beijing.

My Chinese colleague told me laughingly that the captain thought I was a pilot with Canadian Airlines and needed to get to Beijing so he arranged the hasty exit for us!

The bad old days

Back in the early days of China opening up to the outside world (mid-Eighties) my company opened up an office in Beijing. Developing the business necessitated a fair amount of internal travel, which, in those days, meant taking the only airline, CAAC ('Crashes And Always Cancels'). This led to some fairly hair-raising flights and a sudden great faith in St Christopher, or some other guardian angel. Threadbare tyres and chickens in the toilet were commonplace; a choc-ice for breakfast a little more bizarre, as was a gift of a fan – complete with live creepy crawlies in the bamboo frame. The piece de resistance, however, was the day when my seat refused to stay upright and remained permanently in the full recline position. This was fine until the meal arrived and it became impossible to reach my table. In a peak of frustration I grabbed the back of the seat and jerked it firmly forward, hoping to wedge it in place. Unfortunately in those days the tray of the person behind was anchored to the seat in front, rather than hanging independently. As a result, his meal was catapulted into the air, only to turn upside down and re-deposit itself in his lap!

Standing room only

Leaving Ho Chi Minh City in 1988 on Air Vietnam (never again), all the flights were full to overflowing. Plenty of cash was changing hands at check-in to secure any available seat on the plane, an old Russian monster. As we taxied off, I saw the flight attendant standing up, bracing herself against the wall for take-off. They had even sold her seat, too.

Air freshener

Soon after having taken my seat on a flight from Thailand to Hong Kong, it became obvious to me that a passenger had brought durian with him. And it became obvious to the flight attendants, too, because they started asking around and, when no-one admitted to it, began searching the overhead bins.

Problem is that the smell is so strong that it is difficult to locate the source. Finally came this announcement: "Hello ladies and gentlemen, this is your captain. The person who has brought durian on board, please identify your self. We will not take off until it has been taken out of the plane."

Waiting for God knows

I was on a domestic flight between Guangzhou and Zhangjiang, China. It was the end of July, about 40 degrees Celsius and at least 90 per cent humidity. We all boarded and the door closed. We waited for a while, then the pilot shut off the engines (and the air-con in the process) without making any announcement to the passengers.

The flight was 100 per cent booked and, with no air circulation and the plane baking on the runway, it started to get really stuffy. Soon it was just like being in an oven. Thirty minutes ... some old folks started to pass out and people started to shout to open the door. Still no announcement of any kind. Forty-five minutes. People are getting more and more restless. Wheels of fire are dancing in front of my eyes. I beg the staff for a glass of water. Sorry, we can't serve drinks, we might take off at any time (really? with the engines shut off?). Sixty minutes ... we're close to a full-fledged riot, those who haven't collapsed from the heat want to trash the plane.

The pilot, who no doubt opened the cockpit windows (yes, they do open!), still cannot be bothered to tell us what is happening. He may even have left the plane for all I know.

Eventually we took off (I wasn't looking at the time anymore) and I think that everyone survived. At destination I bought a 1.5 litre bottle of water and drank all of it in one shot. Then I phoned a friend to tell him the story. He answered his cellular phone swearing and before I could place a word, he went: "You won't believe what happened this afternoon ... I nearly died in a fucking plane, and the plane wasn't even moving!" It turned out he was in the same plane just behind me.

Immediately if not sooner

We were still a good 15-20 minutes from destination on this China Southern Airlines flight when the crew made the announcement: "Ladies and gentlemen, please fasten your seat belt, we will be landing *immediately*." Immediately?!? We had not even started our descent; we were still at cruising altitude, so how could we possibly land immediately (other than crashing)?

After a short discussion with the staff, I finally explained to them the difference between 'immediately' (right now) and 'shortly' (soon).

I took a dozen subsequent flights but the plane still lands 'immediately' from 25,000 feet.

Jumping to conclusion

In 1990, on an Air Vietnam flight, a bungling freedom fighter messed up his attempt to take over the plane. We were all horrified when he opened the door and jumped out of the plane, somewhere low over Ho Chi Minh City. All expats and foreigners on the flight who witnessed it were debriefed by authorities upon landing, and made to sign an agreement not to disclose the details of the incident or else our visas would be pulled. As I no longer live there, thought I'd share this part of the tale with you.

Air sickness

In China, passengers on a CAAC domestic flight were delayed at Guangzhou and told the aircraft was 'sick' so a replacement would be found. After a couple of anxious hours, a replacement was indeed found. However, they were put back on the original plane with the explanation: "New aircraft more sick than first one, so we take first one!"

Missing in action

In 1988 I was stranded in Xian, China, with a colleague. There was heavy snow and therefore all flights were cancelled for the next few days. When the weather cleared up we had to get new tickets (the old ones were not valid anymore). A guy from the export corporation happily said he could help us get tickets, which were hard to come by, as he had connections with people at the airline. We went that afternoon to the airline and, without any problems, got some tickets for the flight to Wuhan the next day.

The airport was totally chaotic as everyone was trying to get on a plane after having been stranded for a few days. We checked the flight departure board (just a blackboard with flight details scribbled manually onto it) but could not find our flight. Asking around, people looked at us with strange faces (no-one spoke sufficient English and our Chinese was also so-so) and we just pushed our way through gates and doors until we finally came to some kind of traffic control room where there was a person who spoke sufficient English.

He explained us that the plane that used to fly this route crashed three months before and was therefore taken out of the schedule. I hope next time they also inform the ticketing office.

Best seat in the house

Flying with Evergreen from Taipei to Kuala Lumpur I was seated near the toilets, which turned out to be a spot for some entertainment. We had a whole bunch of people from the countryside on board who had never been on a plane before. So when they had to go to the toilet they had big difficulties with handling the toilet door and the lock.

They just went in after they finally managed to open the door and did what they had to do, but they never locked the door. Several times other unsuspecting passengers who opened the door had a full frontal show. When the stewardesses realised what was going on, they would lock the toilet door from the outside (which can be done easily, just use a ballpoint). Now once the person inside was finished they had a new problem: how to get out? This resulted in many scary moments for the people inside until the stewardess 'unlocked' them.

Plane terror

We were about to board our flight to Jodhpur from Delhi, India, when I noticed a huge dent in the wing near the hull. The dent was over a metre wide and reasonably deep and scared the shit out of me. I said to my colleague, "Let's go back as I do not like the look of it and this 737 does not look very new either." He told me not to worry as in front of us a big group of foreigners were boarding the same plane and he overheard them saying that they were attending an aviation conference in Jodhpur. I pulled myself together and boarded the plane, the interior of which did little to reassure me – it looked like this plane was the first 737 ever built and since then never had any kind of maintenance.

I sat still in my chair during the flight with sweat pouring out of the palms of my hand during the whole flight, which fortunately lasted less than

45 minutes. Having arrived safely I decided not to fly back but take the night train.

A few months later a similar 737 crashed after it got stuck on a remote airport with technical problems for several days. As they could not solve the problems there, the pilot decided to take off with the troubled plane and fly it to a city where the necessary tools were available. He never made it.

Sticky situation

Taking the first shuttle flight in the morning (least chance for a delay) to Bandung, Indonesia, I was sitting in the row just behind the cockpit of this small turbo-prop plane. As usual the door of the cockpit was open and the pilot was going through the checklist (we are still at the tarmac). He notices that the light indicator for the front door indicates it is still open so he orders the flight attendant to close the door properly.

She goes to the door and closes it firmly but the indicator still says 'door open'. After trying a few times they decide to get a technician to have a look at the problem (in Indonesia this means five guys show up, one is doing something and the others are just looking). This technician opens and closes the door a few times with the same result. The technician then decides to push the button at the door-opening which is pressed by the door when properly closed (I assume the same way as with the light switch of a refrigerator) and the indicator in the cockpit says 'door closed'. So apparently the system works. He tries a few more times to close the door but to no avail – the indicator keeps saying 'door open'. Thinking for a few moments he gives one of the other guys some instructions and he runs off. A few minutes later he comes back with a roll of industrial-size scotch tape. He cuts off a piece and sticks it over the switch in the door – result: door wide open, indicator says 'door closed'. He now closes the door and tells the pilot everything is OK.

At that moment I decide to get off and wait for the next shuttle. It does not take long before the other passengers follow my lead.

No wheel danger

On a small plane coming into Bandung, we start circling the airport. Bandung is surrounded by mountains so it's not very comforting as you can easily just bang into one of them. As Bandung is a small airport we were amazed we had to wait in order to land, as this had never happened before. After 15 minutes it became clear to us … one of the pilots came out of his seat, opened a small hatch in the floor and started manually lowering the front landing gear that had refused to come down automatically. Luckily it was not a Boeing 747 – the landing gear would be a bit more heavy.

Air traffic control

En route in China with some directors of the Dutch head office we were flying into Wuhan to pay a visit to our rep office. I had instructed our driver to pick us up at the airport. We arrived at the local airport in the middle of the town and were guided to a little cabin where our luggage would arrive. The driver was there and he had managed to get the car near the tarmac and the luggage area as his cousin was working at the airport. This made it quite convenient for us to load the luggage immediately from the luggage belt into the boot of the car. After getting into the car the driver speeds off towards the landing strip, turns on to the landing strip itself and drives to the end of it on to the grass for a few hundred metres, and turns on to the normal road again.

Apparently he thought we were in a hurry and decided to take the short-cut. Fortunately no plane arrived at that time.

Not Russian back

The three of us, client, director/cameraman, and I were in the middle of our "six countries in four weeks" documentary on behalf of a large NGO. We were travelling light – the client carried his briefcase, the director/cameraman had the camera body and lens case, and I was responsible for 422kg of assorted film equipment. A few days earlier we had flown into Kathmandu on Royal Nepal and we were now headed to India ... over the highest mountain range in the world. While waiting in the terminal, I noticed an odd eastern-European looking couple. He was a burly guy in a white shirt with epaulets and was chain-smoking. She was also chain-smoking – wearing a ratty polyester suit with a skirt and sporting the most improbably red-coloured hair. Some time later, our flight was called and we headed out to the tarmac. Instead of the pristine Royal Air Nepal aircraft like the one in which we had arrived, we were led to a filthy plane with the words 'Air Yugoslavia' on it. At the bottom of the stairway was our red-headed lady, and at the top was the burly chain-smoker. Alongside the aircraft were several baggage carts full of baggage, and an empty conveyor belt was running up to the cargo hold. Natasha (by now, I had named the two of them Boris and Natasha) gestured vaguely at the conveyor belt. The client and my boss disappeared into the plane just as I figured out that the only way we would have our equipment in Mumbai would be if I got it onto the conveyor belt myself. Right about this time, the rest of the passengers figured this out. There was a mad rush for the baggage carts. I had the advantages of height, weight and desperation on my side as I got to the first cart and starting flinging all 400-plus kilograms of our equipment cases onto the conveyor belt. I crawled up the ladder into the aircraft.

A cardboard sign with the royal crest and 'Royal Nepal' printed on it was taped to the bulkhead. By now Boris was twiddling switches in the cockpit and Natasha was counting heads. The 'Please stow tray for takeoff and landing' notice in front of me was in French. The next one over was in German. Across the aisle were ones in Spanish and one in English. The seats were all different colours and models, and the red exit sign said 'YBZXZ' or something like that. The three of us realised that the aircraft that was about to take us over the Himalayas was in fact made up of spare parts – a wet lease from a country that no longer existed, crewed by a couple out of the twilight zone.

The view was spectacular, the flight uneventful, and I do not recall any food at all. Boris managed to get us onto the runway with only a couple of little bumps and, armed with our NGO documents, we were ready to brave Indian customs. I wonder whether Boris and Natasha ever made it home.

Handy weapon

In the airport in Goroka, Papua New Guinea, is a sign (and I have the photo to prove it) that reads: 'Carrying of more than fifty rounds of ammunition in hand luggage is prohibited'. One assumes that fifty rounds or less is OK, PNG being what it is.

That's telling them

At the New Delhi airport above the Air India ticket counter there is a sign advising that 'Hand grenades, and other explosives are not permitted aboard any Air India aircraft'. Well, thank you very much for that little tit-bit. If I ever have to travel on Air India again, I'll rest much more comfortably knowing that the terrorists had to find alternate transport.

Clouded judgment

I had a 7am flight ex-Manila to Hong Kong on New Year's Day. I got on board and we sat there and sat there … out the window was this thick cloud of smoke. Turned out to be from the fireworks the night before, leaving the area clouded in thick blackish haze. Funnily enough, the tail sections were above the cloud so all you could see were these coloured fins poking out above the smoke. Two hours later, it was deemed clear enough to take off in.

HARDSHIP POSTING

Re-rooted

I was once on a flight from London to Hong Kong, en route to Taiwan. As luck would have it, a typhoon came into Hong Kong, and the plane was detoured to Taiwan. Fantastic, that saves a bit of time and money, I thought. Not a bit of it. We were not allowed to exit in Taiwan, so once the typhoon had passed, it was back on the plane to Hong Kong, there to board a plane back to Taiwan. I hope this made sense to someone upstairs somewhere.

And pigs might fly

During the 80s, a cargo of poisonous snakes arrived from the south at Hanoi Noibai airport, Vietnam. Unfortunately, the crate broke and the little buggers escaped and crawled into the deep recesses on the old Antonov they used to fly. For days, a plane was seen circling over the airport, rocking its wings back and forth trying to shake and wake up the creepy crawlers. Eventually, all snakes were captured and the plane released for regular service.

Flying thirst class

I had to go back for an urgent official meeting in Bangkok, and the only direct flights from Cambodia in the 70s were chartered Red Cross Caravels. The alternative was on yet another WorldVision cargo flight from Phnom Penh into Singapore and then fly up to Bangkok by regular commercial craft.

There I was, badly-shaven and poorly-cleaned (hotels and constant water and power supply were not the best during the old days, with only the Samaki and Monorom Hotel to choose from) on a propeller-powered five-hour ear-blasting journey to Singapore. On arrival in Singapore, totally exhausted, I had to transfer from the military airport to the international terminal and realised there that all flights to Bangkok were fully booked and that I would miss my next day's meeting after all.

The only way out of Singapore was to go on BA first class. Imagine the expression on the face of the elderly English lady in her classy outfit sitting next to me – me still in my dirty, smelly jungle outfit, ignoring her looks and sneers – happily sipping my way through a string of G&Ts on a two-hour joy ride to Bangkok.

High and dry

Bombay, India. Mid-July or mid-monsoon, whatever you want to call it. I'm at the airport watching my Indian co-pilot walk out to our aircraft prior to departure, dressed in his pilot's costume. White shirt, bars, trench coat, umbrella, brief case, and dark blue pants rolled up to his knees. And, oh yes, barefoot. I'm not sure, but I think he had his shoes in his briefcase.

Well and truly pissed

Has anyone else noticed the water bubbler at Shanghai domestic airport which is labelled: 'Drinking Water. Hot and Cold. Passed by Quarantine Authorities'. I hope it hasn't been!

Pink elephants

In Kota Kinabalu in 1976, I was sitting in a bar when this Philippines Airline BAC-111 came flying over. Being an inveterate plane-spotter I remarked to my co-drinkers that it was a very unusual sighting ... PAL didn't fly this route. Sure enough, a few days later when we got back to civilisation, it had been reported that this domestic Philippines flight had been hi-jacked, and island-hopped its way across to Libya. So I wasn't seeing things after all.

Air bubbles

Just after September 11, crew and passengers were all a bit jittery, not helped by a swarthy dark-haired guy – looking very middle-eastern – who took a seat in first class on a Cathay flight out of Hong Kong. Oh shit! The crew debated who was going to serve him, and thought that if he's a Muslim terrorist he'll decline an alcoholic beverage. They went round with the tray.

"Champagne, sir?" asked the nervous hostie.

"Oh, absolutely!" he beamed in a broad Scottish accent. Phew!

Indian takeaway

On a flight to India, on which the stewardesses are mostly Indian, I was sitting in the cockpit talking with my friend, the pilot. In the middle of the flight one of the crew came up and told the captain that one of the Indian passengers was making a ruckus in the cabin, not wanting to be served by an Indian stewardess. The first officer, without missing a beat, looked at her and said: "Tell him that the only other stewardess we have on board is Pakistani!"

Fly me to the moon

Flying the old Chinese CAAC (Catch Another Air Craft) airline was always a test of your nerves. But on a flight from Beijing to Hong Kong once, the muzak played while we boarded summed it up perfectly: 'Please release me, let me go ...'

Double trouble

I was taking a small plane from Port Moresby to Goodenough Island, PNG. This little old kite probably seated no more than nine passengers. I went to check in. "Oh, you've already checked in, Mr Baker," the lady said. I was adamant that I hadn't. "You are Mr Graeme Baker?" Yes I was, in fact still am. "Yes, we already have you listed here as checked in." I looked at their passenger list, and sure enough there were two Mr Graeme Bakers on it. So I called my secretary and explained to her about the two passengers on the list. "If the plane crashes and Graeme Baker is reported killed, it's only a 50 per cent chance that it's me."

Losing attitude

On a British Airways flight in 1982, we flew into ash which had spewed from the Gallungung Volcano, Java. The 747 Jumbo lost power to all four engines and glided from the usual 37,000 feet to just 13,000. Needless to say, many prayers were being said, and trousers soiled, when the engines sputtered back to life. By the time we landed at Jakarta, the windshield had been sand-papered absolutely opaque, with the pilot having to lean out the window to see where he was going. I've never been happier to be back on the ground.

Life in the fast lane

An Australian agent flying with an Indonesian policeman friend (who was the pilot) and two children, walked away from the wreckage after their plane crashed on a highway near Jakarta. The plane crashed shortly after take-off, ploughing into lanes of vehicles queuing on the busy toll-way.

Carried away

I once had a Thai girlfriend called Oom. This is a typical Thai nickname and means 'to pick up and carry in one's arms', as one might do to a baby. I had to meet Oom when I arrived at Bangkok airport from London and, before leaving Bangkok, had her write out her name in Thai on a large card so she would not miss me in the foreseen melee in the arrivals hall. Unfortunately she stood me up, so there I was holding up a card in front of me for half an hour asking all and sundry to pick me up and carry me, a subject of high amusement judging by the tone of the comments around me.

Over and outta here

DC was an Air Force captain during the Vietnam War and swears this conversation actually took place between the control tower and an American fighter pilot with a Vietnamese trainee co-pilot:

Pilot to control tower: "This guy is acting a little funny, over."

CT to pilot: "What's the problem, over?"

"He is taking his helmet off and he is sweating, over."

CT to pilot: "What else? Over."

"He is taking his flight suit off. Over."

"What else? Over."

"He is naked, over."

"What's he doing now? Over."

"Shitting in his helmet, over."

"WHAT THE FUCK? Over."

And finally, a few recent flight itineraries that some road warriors have shared with us:

A Brit in Singapore: "Hong Kong/ Bangkok last week, Jakarta this week and Manila on Monday. I leave for Bangkok Tuesday morning, return Wednesday afternoon and leave for Seoul that same evening, back on Friday or Saturday. So you can guess how I am!"

From a Manila-based expat: "Just back from Fiji and Vanuatu, preceded by a week up-river in East Kalimantan. Perpetual motion. Now for four days at home, and then another trip to Germany – the second of five trips there this year. Good for the air miles though!"

If you have a good story about flying to or from or in Asia, please identify yourself to the cabin crew or email The Editor at hardshipposting@hotmail.com or fax 612-9499-5908.

Beer Group Pressure
Or Chew and Spew

*True tales from the bars, pubs, restaurants
and kitchens of Asia.*

#$@&%! Oh, my head … I don't remember any mule kicking me repeatedly last night. This is not going to happen today. Over and out …

Well, that was yesterday's pathetic attempt to meet this dashed deadline which I thought I'd preserve for posterior, er, prosperity … posthumous … well, for a long-time anyway as it sums it up around here, really. In airline parlance, Dave tells me they call it 'AOG' – Airplane On Ground, meaning not able to take off. I've pieced the puzzle together and worked out the offender: no aggressive mule was in fact seen in the area at the time; however, the drinks bills reflects a large number of mystery items called 'soju' consumed. Soju is a Korean product, rather vodka-like as I remember, and they seemed to slip down quite nicely. All too nicely, perhaps. Well, I'll have to put that up on the 'drink only in case of emergency' list with Absinthe. Absinthe knocks me around viciously, too, but makes me a lovable puppy dog with it. Guess that's why they say Absinthe makes the heart grow fonder? Maybe not.

As we've got two topics to tackle here, let's start with the food side of it, the mid-air refuelling, and then move on to the demon grog as I'm still a bit on the fragile side.

Asian food is revered the world over for its delicious taste and flavours. People try and decipher the recipe and ingredients to find out what the secret active ingredient is that sets it apart. I'll tell you here, now, for free … it's MSG, or monosodium gluteus maximus. Bucketfuls of the stuff. For perhaps centuries, Japanese cooks used seaweed called Sea Tangle to make starch. They noticed this seemed to draw out the flavour from their otherwise dull diet, and made dinner guests slobber like Pavlov's dog. However, according to my good friend Emily Sudhyadom at the esteemed Emory seat of learning in the States, it was mad professor Kikunae Ikeda of the University of Tokyo who first discovered the link between seaweed and glutamate in 1908. The Japs immediately set to producing this flavour enhancing substance, which they called *aji-no-moto* ('mmmmmm, not bad' in English). It was used heavily in the Japanese ration packs in the Second Big Bang, and finally made it to America in the late 40s. Heck, it could just about make a McDonalds burger taste good.

I remember Barry, when he first came to Hong Kong, took this young Shanghainese bird on a date to a fancy Chinese restaurant trying to do the old impress-the-pants-off-her routine. He was love-struck (I was going to say 'cunt-struck' but the editor won't allow that I'm sure) and within half an hour he was struggling with his breathing, his chest was tightening and he was tingling in parts that hadn't tingled for years. He thought this must be true love, and the dream continued when he awoke to find his Chinese lass in bed with him. But wait … she wasn't in bed at all. He was in hospital and she was leaning over him mopping his fevered brow. He'd collapsed on the floor of the restaurant apparently, and the doctors diagnosed a MSG allergic reaction. That was the last time he ate Chinese, or Chinese *food* I should specify!

MSG has been known to cause obesity and retina damage in humans, and brain lesions in laboratory animals. But doesn't it taste great? Researchers at Nottingham University in the UK also found that curries were mysteriously addictive … blood pressure rose when a vindaloo ring-sting was placed in front of addicts, and pulse rates shot up when the waft of a mutton masala was detected by devotees. Unfortunately, the researchers couldn't reach a conclusion on why these addictions were so strong as they had to leave the room shortly after, when attempts to open the windows failed.

However, some things are never enough for some. Did you hear the case recently involving the Beijing restaurateur whose house specialty was spicy fish. It was a huge hit. Soon, the punters were demanding he opened early and serve his spicy fish for breakfast as well. They couldn't understand their craving – which bordered on addiction – till the blackbeans were spilt in court: he was sprinkling ground opium poppies over the fish to ensure return visits. He was jailed for 18 months.

Another manic restaurateur in east China tried a slightly different tack – he poisoned his competitor's fast-food with rat poison. He polished off 49 potential customers, mainly children, through haemorrhaging.

The various 'delicacies' served up in the region make some newcomers – and old hands – recoil in horror. But fear not, readers, it's all in the mind: after all, snake's blood tastes just like, er, chicken's blood. But for all my jungle survival training, I must admit some countries put things in front of you that just don't seem right. There's not enough beer in the world, shall we say. Pete was telling me about the time he ate smoked bats in some far-flung Indonesian place. He said he'd rather not rekindle that particular memory, thanks very much, but he was OK with talking us through the delights of *sambal goreng saren:* this is basically the engine room of a goat – lungs, bladder, intestines – chop it up, throw in the goat's prick for a bit of zest, then mix the whole lot in a rich coconut cream with a chilli paste.

In China, I enjoyed a nice meaty stew called *Zhou* once … just dabbing the last drops from my moustache when I was told *zhou* is the Chinese word for what we know as Chow, those friendly little waggly-tailed puppies. Barf! Barry asked me how it tasted:

"Great, just a bit stringy," I said.

"You're not supposed to eat the leash as well!" He thought this was hilarious. Arsehole!

The other thing in China I just don't get is bird's nest soup. I mean it tastes perfectly acceptable, just like chicken soup, but who was the inventive soul that first had the lightbulb appear above their head and say: 'Eureka! I'll get a bunch of twigs, dirt and bird spit and dump it in my soup'? Furthermore, to get these bloody nests in the first place, collectors have to risk life and limb to climb wind-blown cliffs on remote islands of Asia to find a better class of bird spit.

But maybe that's better than in Laos where I've not yet brought myself to partake of *luk-andong*, a whole bird wrapped in banana leaves. Doesn't sound so bad, Colonel, you say. Well that's because I didn't yet mention the tiny fact of them leaving the whole lot to decompose nicely for a week or so to get the juices all blending nicely before cooking it. Now are you game to try it, smartarse?!?

Korea, of course, is famous as a nation of dog lovers. But when they say 'I'm just going to take the dog for a walk,' what they mean is they're full and are going to work off their meal with a little stroll. There's a gent called

Doctor Dogmeat – Professor Ahn Yong-keun of Chungchong University to his mum – who claims to have 350 *poshintang* (dogmeat) recipes. I prefer to eat *poontang* myself. And no truth in the rumour that McDonalds in Korea is about to launch a McFido burger into the local market. The other big delicacy there is Spam. I'm having trouble getting my head around the idea of Spam as a delicacy, but I guess when you consider dog as the culinary high point, perhaps Spam's got to be in the top ten somewhere, too. They even sell it in presentation packs of nine cans in the supermarket.

Give me the civilisation of Japan any day. Kobe Beef has got to be in my list of all-time favourites. They tell me these sacred cows down south are given beer and wine, get massaged twice a week, and have classical music played to them. Hell, that's better than my living conditions! They're even killed in a low-stress way in order to keep them tender. You can have your bloody smoked bats, goat's dick and whatnot – that's for the birds.

However, every now and then the Japanese get it oh-so-wrong … wandering home through Roppongi one night, Dave and I stumbled across a pizza joint. A bit of gut luggage wouldn't go astray to soak up the super-tanker of *sake* and assorted poisons we had ingested that night. A quick look at the menu had us in hysterics – most of the pizzas came with corn as a standard topping. Some had potatoes and boiled egg. Then we noticed a couple in the corner: their mouths and teeth and gums were black as if they were looking into the sump of a motor car when the damn thing exploded, pouring grease and oil over them. Turns out they were eating Squid Ink pizza.

I did try octopus at a rather nice restaurant in one of the hotels there, but it was a trifle underdone, in as much as it still seemed to be crawling across my plate.

"Waiter, this octopus tastes rubbery," I said.

"Oh, thank you, sir," he said, pleased as punch. Another satisfied customer.

There's no funnier place to be than Roppongi at 4am after a nice early night. You've never seen so many businessmen so completely arseholed in all your life, weaving their way home, hair a little dishevelled, tie a little crooked, lipstick on their collar, suit pants on back to front. But, cripes, the price of booze there is enough to drive you to drink. Dave and I managed to find one place where beer was below US$4 for a mug. The Gas Panic Bar I think it was. But there's a little catch: their house rule states you must constantly have a beer in your hand otherwise they'll ask you to leave. Crap or get off the pot in other words. Not a problem as far as I could see, which admittedly was not very far past my nose by that time of the night.

Had to laugh. There's another name for *sake* over there, called *kichigai mizu*, literally 'crazy water'. And 'Terry' Aki was telling me the several words that they have for pissheads in Japan: *O-zakenomi* is a serious booze-hound, and *Nondakure* is someone who's constantly bombed. Like a guy in my regiment in Australia we used to call Hanoi – he was bombed every night! And someone who's a constant guzzler is also called *Hidari-to*, meaning a 'left-handed drinker' because even when he's eating with the chopsticks in his right hand, he'll have a drink going in his other. All these guys you can tell by their glow-in-the-dark red faces.

Funnily enough, the Japs hit the hard stuff when they go out but, when they stay home, it's beer. Nearly three-quarters of Japan's beer consumption is drunk at home.

Now here's some technology that will change lives and make the world a better place: New Scientist magazine reports that a Japanese crowd have invented a glass that can tell when you're ready for another drink. Hell, I've got girls that can do that for me already, but never mind. A microchip in its base senses when the glass is empty and sends a 'refill' signal to the waiters through a small radio coil. That's all very well, but it takes the fun out of yelling "MORE PISS, MISS!" across the room.

That's apparently not the done thing in terms of etiquette and protocol at a *geisha* teahouse, as I discovered the hard way. In Ky-bloody-oto Dave and I went to this place in the backstreets somewhere. The girls were absolutely delightful, in their kimonos with emergency 'chute packs on their back, and little white socks with thongs (or sandals or slippers or whatever you call those open-toed things). Dave and I were assigned not one, not two, but three *geishas* apiece, so I told him I was going out for a 'FFP' – Fatal First Piss, that's where you break the seal and from then on you have to keep on going – slipped out to the wash room and threw down a little blue helper or Vitamin V or whatever you want to call Viagra. They gave us face towels, they bowed and scraped, they floated across the room ferrying hot tea and cold drinks. Like butterflies on the wind they were. Then one of them picked up this thing called the *shamisen*, like a Japanese ukulele with a few strings missing. Plunk, plunk, plunk, she went. Then we had some old teahouse standards, the girls joining in with some vocal work. I was waiting for the big chorus to kick in (like the national anthem at the rugby) but it never did. Then the girls did some dancing. All the time, of course, Dave and I were sitting on the floor at this low table. When the little one with the big tits got up to dance I swear the table levitated several inches (more at my end than Dave's, it must be said). This was all building to a wonderfully poetic climax and, when they ushered us to stand up, I thought 'Right-o Mr Wobbly your chance to dance' and … and … that was it. The girls bowed, smiled sweetly, and exited stage left. Mr Yakuza stepped in to present us the bill, which totalled 495 billion gazillion yen (give or take a few zeros). Seriously it was about US$3,000 for the pair of us, and we didn't get a leg over. Didn't even remotely look like it. The little blue helper had fully kicked in by this stage, so I had to walk out into the street holding a tourist map of Kyoto's limited attractions in front of my trousers. I had to repeatedly slam the damn thing in the door of the hotel just to get it down that night. Never before has so much been spent by so few on so little, to paraphrase my good friend Winston Churchill.

No wonder the bastards are going out of business. Some teahouses are – take a seat, sushi lovers – installing karaoke machines in order to attract more clientele. The Gion district alone used to have 265 professional *geisha* in 1959, now they are down to less than 100, because it's easier for the birds to slap on a leather mini-skirt and sell their arse in a downtown bar than go through this whole charade of making cups of tea and learning to master that damned three-stringed banjo thing. But hopefully it won't go full circle – the first *geisha* were actually men. It was only a couple of hundred years ago that females came on to the scene, probably because they looked better tip-toeing pigeon-toed across the room in a dressing gown. In the mid-70s Lisa Dalby, an anthropologist, became the first and only foreigner to become a full-fledged *geisha*. OK for a novelty night, I guess.

There's Russian birds everywhere across Asia these days, who are especially popular with the local gents … the arse is always cleaner on the other side of the fence, and all that. Talking of whisky tangos, British lass Lucy Blackman worked as a nightclub hostess in Tokyo. She was allegedly drugged and raped, then dismembered and cemented into a cave by a prominent Japanese businessman recently. The same man is allegedly responsible for the similar demise of an Australian hostess.

Here's an astounding statistic for you: if all the bargirls in Asia were laid end-to-end, nobody would be in the least bit surprised. And whoever said 'money can't buy you love' was obviously never in Patpong at midnight. Or lunchtime for that matter.

But, as I've always said, lead us not into temptation – just point us in the general direction and we'll find it from there. With that, I'm going to slope off into the hammock for a wee lie down. Got a big night ahead that I'm not ready for. Could be a couple of drinks then straight to bed, if you know what I mean.

Let's finish off with a quick funny: what's the difference between a drug dealer and a bargirl? The drug dealer wishes he could simply wash his 'crack' and re-sell it!

Colonel Ken

Silly sausage

At Jurong Country Club, Singapore, we went for breakfast. My colleague wanted bacon and eggs (which was on the menu) and I wanted bacon, eggs and sausage (which wasn't).

"No, sir, you can't have that," I was informed. "But you can have bacon and eggs and you can have sausage and eggs?" I queried. "Yes, sir, but we don't have bacon and eggs and sausage." Getting fed up, I ordered two plates of bacon and eggs and one plate of sausage and eggs. The girl looked seriously puzzled now – we have ordered three meals but there are only two diners.

The meals duly came out and I pointed. "Eggs and bacon there, egg and bacon here," then grabbed the sausages from the remaining plate, put them on mine, then said: "Right, now I've got what I want, you can do what the hell you like with the other eggs …"

As far as I know, she's still standing with that plate of eggs and a very puzzled look on her face.

In hot water

There was an Italian restaurant in Shanghai in 1998. I checked the menu and wanted to order an espresso. I saw that the price for double espresso and single espresso were the same. I was curious and asked the waitress why. She turned out to be very honest: the restaurant didn't want to ask customers to pay more because water didn't cost much in China.

Tastes like shit

Rihand Power Station in Uttar Pradesh, India, was five hours' drive from the nearest civilisation (no, much more – you can't call Varanasi civilised). It was also five hours' drive from the nearest telephone, hospital or airport. The food provided by the company on the site was free and usually reasonable, once your stomach had become Indianised (which takes about six weeks of constant diarrhoea), and you learnt not to reject food just because it was full of bugs that it was not used to seeing.

Once or twice a week, myself and a few colleagues used to eat out in different local restaurants for a change of scenery, to see some real local colour, and to break the week up. We had spotted one little restaurant that we hadn't been to and, in the light of previous experience, we sent one of our drivers to tell the restaurant owner that we would be dining there that night, to have lots of cold beer ready, and that we demanded the highest standards of hygiene ...

We were led to a table that was absolutely filthy. When we complained, the owner took an even filthier rag from the floor and started to wipe the table, at which point we told him not to bother (or words to that effect).

X had already had many drinks after finishing work to 'wash the dust down' so he felt the need to visit the toilets. He asked a staff member where the toilets were and they led him away. By the time X returned the food had turned up and we were all tucking into our Chilli Chicken Full Boneless, Chicken Tikka, Naan Breads, etc. After a few minutes we all noticed that X had sat back down but was eating nothing. We all stopped eating simultaneously and asked him: "What's up with you then?"

"Before you eat anything else I think you should see something," he said. He took us all out the back and up a little slope to the whitewashed wall with a trough at the bottom that he had been told was 'the toilet'. We could see that the contents of the trough were overflowing and running down the little slope – right into the pond of water where some of the restaurant staff were busy washing the dishes. We all lost our appetites instantly, paid our bill and departed – never to return.

Turning water in to whine

Entertaining a Swiss businessman in Pattaya, Thailand, we went to an Italian restaurant where they try hard in the service department but don't always succeed. On this occasion I ordered a bottle of red wine and the response was: "Certainly, sir, hot or cold?"

HARDSHIP POSTING

A little whine

Some years ago an ad appeared in the Bangkok Post inviting customers to a Thai restaurant where they would receive a free bottle of Mateus Rose wine with the meal for every 1,000 baht spent on food. On arrival we claimed our 'freebie', which turned out to be about ten centimetres high and containing just about one glassful. The waiter asked what we wanted him to do with it, assuming that perhaps we wanted to take it home as a souvenir, but I instructed him to pour it out for my wife and me in accordance with what the restaurant had advertised: oh, and don't forget to put it in an ice bucket for a few minutes.

I don't know which of the two parties lost most face – theirs or mine.

Let's do lunch

We have an annual pre-Christmas industry lunch in Bangkok, a tradition in our group for years. One year X arrived looking somewhat high. Impressively, he fell backwards off his chair during the *first* course. He then had a phone call from some woman (one of his two wives or another?) and excused himself. Later that night (the lunch went till 2:30am) he walked into a bar in Patpong and introduced himself to me (we've known each other for 16 years, let alone just had lunch together). Must have been a bad ice cube!

Something to crow about

While on one of my many business trips to Batam, Indonesia, I noticed this sign in Lucy's Oar House: 'Cocktails told here'. Under the blackboard menu, it says: 'Food untouched by human hand – chef is a gorilla!'

A real piss up

Up-country near the Laos border I was entertaining the in-laws one evening at the local beer bar. The toilet was a concrete shack with two cubicles over in a corner of the dirt yard. I used the cubicle that was nearest which was, of course, unlit except for what filtered in through the hole in the roof. I suddenly became aware that something was moving on the floor. It seemed that I was splashing a giant toad, about the size of a dinner plate. Next time I decided to use the other cubicle and leave the toad in peace. As my eyes became accustomed to the gloom it seemed to me that the walls were moving and, as I looked more closely, I realised that the walls and ceiling were covered in an army of ants. Next time I needed a leak I went round the back and peed in the bushes.

Singing for your supplier

During one of the lunches we had with some suppliers in the south of Malaysia, our buyer was forced to go out on stage and do some karaoke. Normally he was not the type of guy to get persuaded that easily but, as we had already finished several bottles of X.O. between the eight of us, his resistance was somewhat lowered. He chose one of the lesser-known English songs. From the start he was cheered and applauded wildly and, when he finished his song, everyone (at least the males in the restaurant) was shouting for an encore of the same song. He thought he was doing a great singing job but, in fact, it was the scenes on the screen we were applauding – shots of the beach near Nice in France with all the ladies being topless and stretching themselves in front of the camera.

Whenever we were in town, one of the suppliers would take us there and ask us to sing this particular song.

Tea for two

My Chinese girlfriend J and I went out for a meal in Shanghai. At the end she insisted she settle the bill, to which I agreed as my Mandarin was not good [As good a reason as I've ever heard! – Col. Ken]. She then started a furious row with the waitress, with lots of pointing at the bill and gesticulating. The point at issue was that they had charged us for four teas, and we had only had two. Total disputed amount was six *jiao* (about 6p). After much arguing she paid. In the end the restaurant had agreed to dock the two disputed teas from the bill, but had added a RMB 1.00 cover charge, which they had 'omitted in error'. Both sides saved face, and we paid exactly what we would have paid anyway.

Splashing out

In a restaurant in Hong Kong, we were enjoying a good celebratory lunch. All the more because we were away from the office and a big sign said 'NO HANDPHONES' so we were blissfully incommunicado. However, at the next table a group of Chinese men sat, their hand-phones constantly ringing and loud conversations ensuing. I'd had enough. The next phone that rang, I went across, picked it up and promptly deposited it in the restaurant's fish tank and went back to the table. The Chinese gent came across all indignant and shaped to strike. I stood up, blocking him.

"I don't think so," I said. "*We* don't think so," said the group of lunching *gweilos*, all rising as one.

Put your money where your mouth is

I was taken out to the back-of-beyond somewhere in southern Taiwan by some local colleagues. We went into a restaurant where they ordered us an excellent meal. I noticed that the waiters kept looking at me and were doing what looked like laying bets. After we left, my colleagues asked me if I understood what the waiters had been saying. Of course I hadn't a clue. Apparently they had taken bets on whether I would use the chopsticks better than the last European they had had in there, seven months previously. As it happened I did, so someone must have won a bit of money on me.

Side order

At a street-side 'restaurant' in Bangkok one evening, a group of some out-of-town friends and I were enjoying a casual Thai meal. Our friends got excited when they saw one large and one baby elephant being led down the street to our table (we were the only *farangs* at the stall).

"So cute," gushed the ladies, grabbing their cameras. The elephant keeper asked for some money for bananas for the elephants, which they shelled out, and started feeding the baby elephant. With that the mother elephant turned around, depositing a huge pile of steaming elephant dung right next to our table.

Appetites somewhat diminished, we paid and left in a hurry. I'm not sure how the photos turned out!

Fresh fries

One day in Shejiazhuang, China, I was invited by the local corporation for dinner and was served a specially prepared fish. What they had done was deep-fried the whole fish, except for the head – that was kept out of the frying oil. The fish, however, was facing me and the mouth was still going open-and-close as if it was trying to breathe, and the eyes also looked as if it was still alive. In the meantime the other people at the table tucked their chopsticks into the fish's (fried) parts and started chomping away. I am not a choosy eater, but this sight made me too sick to eat.

A similar thing happens in Hong Kong when you go for the *tepan yaki* and order the lobster … in front of your eyes the live lobster goes on the hot plate and gets slowly cooked. The animal tries to escape often by jumping up but is quickly held down by the chef. It's the way it keeps looking at you that freaks me out.

Service by the book

In Hue, Vietnam, competition among restaurants was stiff and, judging by the prices, profits slim. Walking down the street, I was accosted by Li-Li, a slim and slender girl, with a mysterious scar which ran up her arm and into her shirt sleeve. On top of waitressing and kitchen work, her job was to drag customers into Xuan Trang Cafe by whatever means necessary.

After a while she came back, sat down at my table as if that were perfectly normal, fixed me with her fierce stare and demanded: "How old you think I am?" I still hadn't given her all my order. Somewhat taken aback by the directness, I studied her lineless face and girlish manner.

"Oh, I'll guess sixteen."

"Wrong!" she crowed, "Guess again." So we played the game, my guesses mounting higher, until finally I said, "Twenty one."

"Right!" she said, beaming, and slapped me smartly on the forehead with her order pad! What is going on here, I wondered, not quite sure how to respond to this strange woman. Next morning I went back and learned Li-Li had quite a following among expats around Hue as 'the waitress who hits you', sort of Vietnam's answer to the Seinfeld soup nazi. Vietnamese men wouldn't have tolerated her behaviour, but westerners are of course more used to it, a fact Li-Li found hugely amusing. Xuan Trang's owner completely ignored these antics, apparently satisfied enough with the flow of customers she produced. And so she plied her trade with great enthusiasm and, to my amazement, everyone seemed to take it good-naturedly.

One evening I'd had enough and decided to look for a quiet, abuse-free meal. Crossing the street and walking quickly away, I began to slip down an alley. From fifty yards Li-Li spotted me and came charging out across the intersection, grabbing me by the arm.

"Why you not come my restaurant? Very bad!" Her tone was commanding, but she wore a smile. "You eat now!" What could you do? The woman had radar that picked up everything and everyone within a 100-yard radius. She was hard to say 'no' to and not feel like a shit.

The next evening she carried a small aluminium mallet. "Why you not come my restaurant this morning?" she chirped. "Must come every morning!" She was lightning-quick and I took a rap on the hand, but with the other I snatched the mallet away from her. "You can't do that!" she squealed and came at me with a hand raised to slap. "I can hit you but you can't hit me."

Later she came and sat next to me again. "My work finished at ten, you want go karaoke with me and my friends?"

"Maybe," I said, mulling the appropriateness.

"I don't like maybe – yes or no?" she boomed. So much for the myth of compliant Asian woman.

MacWongs

We were in a touring party visiting Guangzhou, China. The guide told us that we would be eating at a 'renowned restaurant'. Sounded good. However we were a bit alarmed when the bus drew into town … outside MacDonald's! We were not a little relieved when instead of going in there we were taken into the building next door, which served us up a very enjoyable Chinese meal.

Catch of the day

In Hong Kong we went to a swanky restaurant. On the menu, 'Lips from Humphead Wrasse'. These were at the equivalent of US$225. I presume you got a *pair* of lips for that price.

Old dog, new tricks

I used to play a joke on visiting consultants while taking them out for dinner on their first night in Vietnam. Everybody was eager to sample local tradition and cuisine, and the local treat invariably was *thit cho* (dog meat). One night I took P, a visiting professor from a Bangkok university, out. Everything went normally but my guest's senses grew more and more weary, sitting on one-foot tall stools in a pretty dark and smoke-filled delicatessen stall along one of Hanoi's backstreets.

The main dish was eventually served, with the boiled dog tail standing erect in the middle of the plate (at my special request!) with little chunks of meat placed around in circles. It was not long before the question was asked: "What the fucking hell is that made of???"

Since canine meat in Asia is usually not considered regular food, P didn't believe me at all. Only after I made him walk back into the 'kitchen' and see the whole animal's carcass did the truth that he had just eaten dog meat finally work its way to his nervous system … and he emptied his stomach right there and then, much to the laughter of the cooks, other onlookers and, of course, yours truly.

Go figure

A group of us – all accountants – went out for an excellent lunch in Bangkok. Following several courses and many, many bottles of wine, we asked for the bill. When it arrived, we ran our beady eyes – honed by years of auditing experience – over the bill.

"It's wrong," I said to the waiter, and handed it back. Moments later, he reappeared.

"It's right, sir."

"No … it's wrong," I insisted. He went away again, disappearing for quite some time, checking with other staff and the kitchen, and reappeared somewhat nervously again.

"We have checked everything – it is correct, sir."

"No it's not … you've left out the desserts!" I said. He was gob-smacked. No-one had ever queried a bill that was too *low* before!

Lead in your pencil, sir?

In Asia food to boost virility is very important. My friend L was at a restaurant with two young and pretty 'girlfriends'. The waiter suggested something which was not on the menu but which would be indicated for the evening. L did not quite understand what this dish was until the waiter returned with a plate containing a whole deer penis.

Truth in advertising

At a restaurant in Puerto Gallera, Philippines, I ordered the 'chicken entrée'. Indeed, a whole chicken arrived on a tray for me.

All you can eat

It was my turn to host a group that convenes now and again for a posh dinner meeting. As it was in Bangkok, I thought the seedy Thermae club would be ideal, so invitations went out and everyone turned up on the night in their tuxedos. As it was early, we had the place to ourselves with a huge dinner table set up in the middle, waitresses fussing over the guests as we tucked into a feast fully catered by the Oriental Hotel, and some fine wines. Then gradually, movement in the dark shadows was noticed, as the working girls reported for work. By the end of the meal, the place was crowded with the regular complement of girls, who then became an integral part of the evening. It was declared a roaring success.

A bunch of fun

We'd had a huge lunch in Manila, after which Pete adjourned to the more adventurous upstairs section of this particular establishment. Noticing him missing in action for a while I went upstairs to find him. Opening one door, I found him alright … he was lying down and had one naked bargirl sitting on his face, one on each nipple, one sucking him furiously, and another ramming the largest banana I ve ever seen up his arse.

He doesn t remember any of this. Later, when he came to — I mean regained consciousness — he thought he d better take one of the girls home, and bar-fined her. We nicknamed him henceforth Plantain Pete. Till now I can t look at a bunch of bananas and not recall that episode.

Ripe and juicy

In Johor Bahru, Malaysia, was a bar called the Papaya Farm. Papaya was a nickname for tits. It was a rather small area, not too much light, and looked a bit sleazy with fake leather sofas and no proper decor. There were groups of girls standing everywhere but they were dressed wearing t-shirts and sports shorts. It wasn t how we had imagined it to be. We decided to sit down and order some beer, and immediately a group of girls swarmed to our sofa and kept standing there. Then the beer came and was being poured out and, the moment the waiter left, the girls all jumped towards us and started rubbing our crotches and wiggling their asses.

I strip, 10 ringgit, they said. With that, off came the tops and shorts and they sat stark naked on our laps, rubbing their titties in our face and more. Sir, you want blow job? 30 ringgit, I ask my sister to come. We had a lovely time over there, and every time I eat papaya I have to think back to that little bar with its girls.

Your head s familiar

Living in Jakarta and making the rounds through Java every fortnight I used to stay in the Hyatt in Surabaya whenever I was there. In those days there was not yet the Shangri La with the Desperado s bar so we mostly stayed in the hotel and, after dinner, took a massage in the room.

One time I had this nice lady called Andini, a cute, small lady with big breasts. I had the most wonderful massage I could imagine. Coming there next time I of course wanted her to come to my room again and called the health centre. Unfortunately she was not there, and this went on for several weeks when I was in Surabaya. Until, finally, one day she was on duty and came to my room.

You asked for me but I do not recognise you, she said. Anyway, she proceeds with her tantalising back massage and, when I turned over, she screamed: *Now* I recognise you!

That rings a bell-end

A guy was up-country in Thailand, went to a bar and took a nice little lass home for the night. Having got changed and hopped into bed, she said: "You were in Bangkok six weeks ago?" He was a bit surprised and puzzled by her question.

"Er, yes, I was," he said.

"I don't remember your face, but I remember *this one*," she said admiringly.

Coke sucker

Being with some Dutch colleagues and one of the local merchandisers for a three-day trip to Ipoh, Malaysia, we had a nice 'massage' at the health club of the hotel on the first day. We finished rather early on the last day and decided to go to the pool when a local guy went off to go to sleep for a while. As we did not believe that, one of my colleagues advised him to ask for the girl he had earlier at the health club because she was amazing.

When our guy came back an hour and a half later he also had a story to tell. The girl was rather amazed that he knew her name: he told her about his *gweilo* friend who had advised him. She then told him a few stories about the *gweilo* and the size and shape of his muscle. Since then the nickname of our *gweilo* colleague is 'Upside Down Coca Cola Bottle'.

On another trip to Hong Kong we went to a karaoke lounge called Cebu. The girls immediately wanted to start playing games and the one who lost the game had either to bottoms-up his/her drink or take off some clothing (more than half the bar was sitting in its underwear or less). The girl sitting next to Cola Bottle started feeling at his crotch and got shocked by what she felt: she then wanted to see the real thing but he only gave her a look at it while his crotch was covered with his jacket. She immediately called over the other girls to have a look at her trophy, leaving the rest of the guys sitting alone while the lucky bastard had the attention of all the girls in the bar.

Running aground

In the first three months of our Western Pacific deployment, M would start to drool every time he thought about our upcoming visit to the Philippines. When we pulled in, he was one of the first off the boat, practically sprinting to the gate. He went into the first bar he came to, picked out a likely-looking lass, paid her bar-fine, and headed for a hotel.

Half an hour later he was back, looking upset. When we asked him what was wrong, he said she pulled down his pants, saw how big he was, and backed away saying "No way," over and over again (he was black and apparently quite well-endowed). This event repeated itself over and over again for the next three days, with M becoming more and more depressed at being the only guy on board who couldn't get laid. Our last night in, he finally found someone brave enough, and came back to the boat with a very satisfied grin.

Falsetto tits

I was asked by a colleague to show his brother-in-law around Phuket as he would be going there on a holiday in the same period as we did. So we made an appointment the first evening to go to Patong Beach and show him the hidden dangers.

We go to the first roadside bar, which is full with lady-boys. They had not just had a sex change but had also transformed themselves to look like famous singers, so we had a Celine Dion, a Tina Turner and more like that. Our friend sat there with his beer and was talking to 'Celine Dion' about whom he was totally nuts. Despite telling him several times that they were actually all boys he did not want to believe us, and took her/him back to the hotel. He still shows his family the pictures of his pretty 'girlfriends' in Thailand.

Well-come to Malaysia

One of the buyers visited Malaysia for the first time and we decided to all go for a sauna and massage. When he went to the massage room the girl asked him what type of massage he wanted: Swedish, aroma or the traditional massage. Thinking that being in Malaysia he should take a 'traditional' Malaysian massage, he opted for that one. He was rather puzzled when he came out as to what sort of cultural tradition he had just experienced, the stiffness from *every* muscle in his body having been removed.

Whore d'ouevres

In the early days you were not even allowed to look at a girl in China or you would already have a police officer breathing down your neck. In 1988 a friend of mine took a girl back to his hotel. All of a sudden there was knocking at his door, and yelling. Before he could get to the door it was already opened and several police officers stormed into his room. They looked everywhere for the girl … under his bed, in the washroom, in the cabinets, in his desk drawers (I know Chinese girls are small but not that small) but could not find anything. He was interrogated and shouted at, then they left empty-handed.

Fortunately for him he had decided that a short-time quickie was enough and sent the girl off just before the authorities raided his room.

Blowing hot and cold

I had been to massage parlours before in China, but then you were laying with ten guys in a row, your body would be covered for the most part, and that was it. Recently one of my suppliers took me to one of the new-style massage parlours in China.

First we had to pick out the girl and were then guided to a room. Upon entering the girl asked in her best English: "Sir … hot tea, ice water?" I said OK not knowing what she had in mind. She took some of the hot tea in her mouth and started with the BJ. After a while she changed that for the ice water. I must say this was a nice new experience and it is good to know that China is making progress in every way they can.

Cock teas

During one of my first visits to the south of Malaysia I was invited by a supplier to go for a drink: he would pick me up from the hotel around eight. Indeed around eight he is there with some of his drinking buddies in tow. We took off in two cars and went to some strange place where there were all these girls sitting behind a glass wall with numbers pinned on their bras. This was my first time seeing such a 'fish tank' and several rows with chairs are set out so the guys can sit and choose. I was asked whether I wanted a drink. "Yes, a beer please." No beer available, only tea. So I say, "Then what the hell are we doing here?" My supplier misunderstood me and thought I didn't like the girls so he decided that we should see another fish tank.

After having visited several of these fish tanks with the same story going on, all of a sudden one of his buddies says, " I can't stand it anymore, I am too horny," and he called the number pinned on one of the girls and disappeared to the back. Within a very short time, he was back, and is now known as Two-Stroke Jack.

Blow me down

A friend of ours in Bangkok was a real eccentric, often dressed as a dandy gentleman. One time after returning from an overseas trip, he walked into the Napoleon Bar in Patpong wearing a life-jacket taken from the aeroplane. As he entered, he pulled the tabs and the damn thing inflated to the hoots and hollers from the patrons. Talk about a grand entrance!

HARDSHIP POSTING

Ejecting seamen

One night in my then-regular hangout, Hardy's in Lan Kwai Fong, Hong Kong, a group of American sailors came in. Judging by the volume of their talk and their rowdy behaviour, it was plain to see this was not the first bar they had visited that night. At one point one of these guys, around two metres tall, starts making a hell of a lot of noise to one of the waitresses, a mere five-foot 40-kilo Chinese lass. He says: "Come here and suck my dick," and starts opening his fly.

At that moment she takes off her shoe and directs the sharp pointy heel towards his groin and shouts: "You take it out and I will knife it on my shoe and put it on the BBQ … NOW GET OUT!!!" You've never seen a grown man turn into such a meek little lamb with his tail between his legs as he backed out of there.

Had a ball

After drinking a little too much at a snooker bar, I proceeded to try and chat up the girl on the till, suggesting she should come with me to my flat. She told me she was not a working girl and would not leave her job halfway through a shift for a quickie. Being very cheeky I told her my address, which was less than 500 metres away, and invited her to come along after her shift. She did not look very impressed so I left. I went to bed very drunk but I did not lock my door – just in case. I awoke at 6am with a terrible headache and remembered I had not locked the door. Before looking up from my bed I thought it quite likely I would find my flat had been robbed, but was pleasantly surprised. Everything was in its place including her. Asleep in my bed! After a look under the covers I was amazed to see my first leather g-string. I love Thailand.

Beer goggles

I owed a friend of mine, a Cathay Pacific pilot in Hong Kong, a big favour so I suggested I take him out for dinner, and we go for drinks and nibbles in Wanchai. The agreement was set: dinner from 8-9pm, then bars from 9-12midnight, and he could choose the lady of his liking which I would pay for. But there were some conditions … we'd have one beer in every bar and couldn't go back to a bar once we'd left it to retrieve a girl who earlier caught his eye. Long before midnight rolled around, we were both pissed as, and he still hadn't found Miss Universe. I reminded him the offer expired in a few minutes. In the last bar we came to, he pointed out a girl: "That's the one for me!" She was the shortest, oldest, fattest, ugliest woman I'd ever seen, even at that time of night. No, I told him, not her. He insisted: "No, she's perfect, that one." We almost came to blows over his considered lack of judgment. We compromised – I told him we needed a rematch of tonight so the favour was repaid another night.

Sour kraut

I was having a beer in Bangkok when a pretty girl started talking to me [Well, there's a turn up for the books! – Col Ken.]. It wasn't long before we were at a short time hotel just off Soi 22 on Sukhumvit. This hotel gives you a condom with your change! When she dropped her clothes I noticed a tattoo of a swastika on her leg. I pointed to it and said: "What the fuck is that?" She covered it up, embarrassed, and explained she had it done because she had a German boss and she thought he might like it. I asked if he had liked it. She said: "No, he went mental and demanded I never show it in his bar."

A flood of tears

I was in Bangkok with colleagues from three continents, trying to retrieve a project that was three months late and threatening to destroy my company's credibility in SE Asia. We had all been working for ten days, 7am to midnight, and at 11pm on the deadline day the computer system was finally working. I found the rest of the team had all gone back to their families, whereas I was still there in Bangkok, which was about to flood and be overrun with crocodiles. Being the only *farang* there, I felt exhausted and lonely, but thought I should see something of this exotic city before I went, so I asked a taxi driver to take me to the Golden Temple, and to find me a drink.

He took me into town, and we ended in a dark street, beside a building with 'Golden Temple night club' on the wall. Inside was a bar, loud music, girls dancing, and two Europeans drinking. I ordered a drink, and got cheap whiskey, but at least it was a drink. Then a young lady sidled up to me, and I bought us a drink. The barmaid then explained to me that the lady's price was 3,000 baht, and that we could either go upstairs, or I could take her back to my hotel. The price was cheap because all the tourists had left town because of the floods.

I was so exhausted I could not find the energy to get aroused at all and, after a couple more drinks, I tipped the girl and went back to my hotel alone, and just cried, feeling even more exhausted and lonely than ever, and thankful to be going back to Taipei next day. I then called my wife in England – whom I didn't expect to see for at least another month – and told the whole story to her. She laughed, and cheered me up, telling me that I was the only husband she knew who could be miserable in a brothel!

No such thing as a free lunch

The Napoleon restaurant and bar would put on a free Christmas lunch for us each year (God knows we spent enough at the place the other 364 days). On this special day we decided to buy all the girls in the house a drink. Mama got it slightly wrong ... she thought a drink from each of the ten of us for each girl, ie, each girl got ten drinks. One of our friends, T, was on a daily stipend from his wife of 150 baht (when that was actually worth something) and he could have lunch, two Bloody Marys and a taxi home with that.

Our bill for the free lunch came to 600 baht a head, so T was stuffed – he'd blown four days allowance – until I stepped in and covered it for him. For years his daily routine was two Bloody Marys at happy hour, then home, regardless of what the rest of us were doing.

Rear admiral

In Manila in the early 60s I went out at night for a couple of quiet beers and, as it happened, there was a US Navy vessel in the bay and the bars were pretty lively. Taking a seat, this guy came up and sat next to me. Soon enough, all these sailors with girls in tow kept on coming up to him and requesting salary advances for their drinks and tarts, which he was dishing out. Turns out he was the purser from the navy ship, and we got talking, told him where I was staying, and so on. After a while, I said goodbye to him, as I was turning in for the night.

"But I was hoping to fuck you tonight," he said, giving me this heart-broken look. I ran out of there, all the way back to my hotel and, once in the room, locked the door and put this bloody great chest of drawers across the entrance as well just in case. If I did sleep that night, it was with one eye open.

Stickman

This whorehouse in Singapore in the 70s used to serve great satays. So one day I thought I'd try and set a record. While two of the girls counted, I scoffed these things down, ending up with 101 sticks consumed in the hour.

A sour note

Down the old strip of Batu Rd in KL, Malaysia, a friend of mine would drink his gins and tonic (with a slice of lemon, of course). He'd always keep his first empty glass and pile up the lemons inside it as he went. As all the drinks were kept on a tab and totted up at the end of the night, he had a foolproof way of keeping them honest. Occasionally there'd be a dispute and he'd be counting his lemons out on the counter for them to set the record straight.

Sweet young thing

We were always trying to help out a single friend of mine by matching him up to whatever lasses we felt suitable. One of our friends, a beautiful blonde English lass, was passing through KL on her way to Vietnam. So we persuaded her to meet up with this friend of ours. He took her to the Selangor Club, and ordered a Drambui for her. Having not tried it before, he asked her what she thought of it. "That's lolly water," was her prognosis.

"Lolly water, eh?" said our friend, rising to the challenge. With that he calls the barman over and asks for the rest of the bottle to be put on the counter. Suffice to say they had breakfast together the next morning, were engaged within a matter of weeks afterward, and have now been married for several decades.

Open minded

On my last night of vacation in Chiang-Mai I decided to take a walk in the main street and check out the bars and nightclubs. As I was walking a cute Thai waitress invited me into this bar. The bar was totally empty. So I bought a beer and we began to chat, which proved to be quite challenging since her English was terrible. All this time I am examining her to determine if she is really a she. My conclusion was that this one was legit.

Then, out of the blue, she told me to wait until she closed the bar and then we could go to her place. Wow! So eventually she closes the bar and we start walking. After a few minutes we stray from the main street to a dark, creepy, abandoned smaller street which triggers some alarms in me, a first-timer in Asia: maybe she is leading me into a trap? Maybe I can get robbed, maybe even hurt? It was a classic case of 'think with my dick' or 'think with my mind'. Well, my dick won this time. After a few tense moments we reached her apartment building (which actually had a guard in the front). Her roommate just popped her head in to say hello and left after she saw me. And so that night I had my first Thai experience, and a freebie at that.

Some d-a-a-y-y-y never comes

The Vietnam Veterans of America bar in Angeles City, Philippines, has a sign which says: 'FREE BEER ALL DAY TOMORROW'.

Not overpromising

The Red Fox Too Bar in Lamai, Koh Samui, owned by an Irishman, has the following on its blackboard:

'BBQs at the drop of a hat
Fishing trips arranged
Bad jokes in a strange dialect'.
They're certainly right about the last part!

Out of pocket expenses

In Phuket a few years ago, I asked this girl if she wanted to go with me. Yes, she did, and duly called mama across. "How much is her bar fine, mama?" 300 baht. I dug through my pockets, turning up only 200 baht. "Sorry, sexy girl, I only got 200 baht … maybe next time."

"Here, I have 100 baht," she said, handing over her money. "I give to you. We go, no ploblem." Indeed, problem solved.

Out of the fire, and into Dante's inferno

Life here in Ban Chang, Rayong, Thailand is pretty quiet. There are numerous distractions, though. Notably numerous beer-bars, and leg-over joints. My friend D, drunk and horny, had just done the deed upstairs in the Wherehouse Bar (sic). Ambling down the stairs to the bar (with a spring in his step) he saw, to his horror, that his wife had entered the bar and was sitting at the bar with drink in hand, patiently waiting for his arrival.

Panicking, he crept back up the stairs, and pondered his next move. Unfortunately, beer had a large part in his decision-making, and he decided to leave the bar … through the window! Maybe inspired by Spiderman, he opened a window and crawled out onto a ledge. Looking through his beer-goggles (which make ugly girls seem attractive, and long distances seem jump-able) he tried to jump to an awning down below. He hung from the window ledge and kicked away into space … landed on the canopy, briefly, then crashed through it and hurtled the remaining storey to ground.

Obviously, D had some parachute-training as hitting the ground he immediately performed a forward-roll, stood up and dusted himself down. Appearing oblivious to the commotion from the window above, he nonchalantly entered the bar through the main door, and tried to appear innocently surprised at the presence of his darling wife, sat at the bar.

Sadly lacking any reflective surfaces to view his sorry self (cuts, abrasions, and blood all over) he attempted to converse with She Who Must Be Obeyed. Pandemonium ensued … he got a free drink in the face, and the girl who'd shared his delightful company upstairs came rushing down and embraced him – glad he was alive, having witnessed his Great Leap Backward.

He spent the next few days in the doghouse, obviously, and had to stump up for damages to property and person. Only problem with living in a small Thai town is that as *farang* we stick out like the proverbial sore thumb and wives have radar for errant husbands. Thai girls don't need the internet; gossip travels much faster here.

Spies unlike us

On our annual 'Asian tour of duty,' D and myself found ourselves in Krabi, southern Thailand. Tired of repeating the usual bar-patter of "My name is … I am 32, I come from London …" we decided to liven up the evening by posing as international arms dealers posing as tourists. The sweet young things had no idea what we were talking about, so mama (a great deal older and uglier) came over. It turned out that she was the bar owner and was fascinated to learn more about our dubious profession and how it was that two ordinary-looking blokes from London could be involved in purchasing rocket-propelled grenades, limpet mines, etc. Desperate to continue the charade and not lose face, we changed tack that we were not really arms buyers but in fact MI6 agents attempting to snare a notorious arms dealer who traded smuggled weapons from army bases in Malaysia and was believed to run his operations from a shop next to a 7-11 store in Krabi. Which particular store was our mission?

Some three hours later, mama had enthusiastically enlisted the help of her cousin and, without paying our bar tab, the four of us jumped into his Suzuki jeep and toured the streets of Krabi town with them pointing out and shouting "7-11, 7-11" every time a store came in sight. We responded by dismissing their claims as unprofessional, and eventually returned to the bar. We told them to make a list in Thai of each 7-11 store location and fax it to our London office (actually the Thai Airways Reservation department at Heathrow Airport).

Baffled Thai Airways staff may well have received such a fax, but one thing that is sure us that our bar tab remains unpaid to this day.

Missing in action

In Koh Samui, Thailand, I was sitting at an outside beer bar on Lamai Beach one evening watching the passing parade. A motorbike pulled up outside the karaoke bar opposite, the Thai pillion passenger dismounts, walks over to the doorman, pulls a gun and shoots him at point-blank range. Incredibly he misses, decides against another shot, remounts the waiting motorbike and is away into the night. Meanwhile, a tourist sitting at the next bar up falls off his stool clutching his shoulder. Hit, but not seriously, by the ricochet. Amazing Thailand? I would say so!

Getting a leg over

In Pattaya, I headed for the cheap and nasty shed bars in Soi Buhkao. Seeing a pretty little lass in tight denim, I knew my search for the evening was over. Terms were quickly negotiated and we headed for my room. As we changed I couldn't help noticing that my companion had only one leg ... in as much as she removed it and rested it up against the wardrobe.

Slightly shocked, and trying to make light of the situation, I cheekily asked for a fifty percent discount only to be told: "Price same same – pussy work okay!" I reluctantly agreed, but in fact the novelty actually added to the thrill.

Fever pitch

North of Hanoi is a brothel town called Phuc something or another, appropriately enough. I went into this one establishment that had no less than 200 birds on duty waiting to be pressed into action. What made it so interesting? They were all dressed in nurse's uniforms ... Russian disposals it turned out. Grrrrrowwwwl.

Dead drunk

In the good 'ole swinging days of KL, Molly was the legendary mama in one of the finer establishments. One evening, over a few drinks, she turned to me and said, "I don't feel well." So she ordered a coffee, and just fell over, dead on the spot. Similarly, an Irishman was driving up through Malaysia with his wife. They stopped at the Ipoh Club for lunch where he had two sandwiches and 'a hundred' Guinness's. His wife said "That's enough," but he insisted on one more for the road. He had a sip, put it down, and fell to the floor. Game over.

A marked man

Pattaya, early 80s. My friend – who lived there – had too much to drink and fell asleep whilst *standing* at the bar counter. Incredible. Proving unwakeable we thought we'd have some fun. So I unzipped his fly, leaving him hanging out for all to see. Then I asked the cashier for a black marker pen, and asked the girls to draw a smiley face on the end of his knob. They all wanted a go, so he ended up festooned with smiley faces. I decided to drag him home up the street at that point, making sure to tuck his dick back in before ringing his door bell. His wife answered and I pushed him forward and said: "Your husband."

Next day he woke up and his wife was staring daggers, demanding an explanation. He was in deep shit … only he's got absolutely no idea himself, let alone an explanation, for this body art. I turned up a bit later and explained all the sordid details and then asked, "Can S come out and play?" This melted the ice, she cracked up laughing, so we went out and got pissed again. This time he stayed awake, wide-awake!

Live by the gun …

In Angeles City, Philippines, in the early days, competition was stiff. We had recruited a lot of girls with particular talents from one bar in particular. One night its owner came into our bar, pulled out a gun, held it at my head and said: "I'm gonna kill you."

Being young and stupid I said, "You'd better, 'cause if you don't I'm gonna be really, really angry and fuck you up as well."

"I mean it," he said.

"So do I," I countered.

"I'm gonna shoot you," he threatened again. Just then I managed to get a fist onto his face, grabbed the gun, and flattened him. I threw the gun out over the back, picked him up and dumped him in his pick-up. The driver also had his gun drawn so I challenged him with the same treatment. He put it away and drove off at speed never to be seen again.

I heard years later that someone a little more violent than myself had killed this same guy.

Soldiers of misfortune

In Angeles in the early 80s, three GIs were causing trouble in my bar so I told them to pay up and piss off. They got ugly and turned on me. A scuffle ensued in, around, through the doorway and eventually outside. Net result: three GIs out cold. I told the managers to get someone to "pick up this garbage" and thought nothing more of it.

Next morning in the shower, singing away, when suddenly I notice three M-16 barrels sticking over the shower cubicle. "You're coming with us, sir." It was the US Forces MPs. The three guys I had taken out were on temporary assignment from Okinawa and, because I was a 'third party national' (meaning not American or Filipino), the matter was out of the Philippines' jurisdiction.

I was hauled in before a heavyweight colonel and about 40 or 50 others around the office. Luckily I knew him – he'd drunk in my bars occasionally.

"How soon can you leave?" he asked coldly. Fuck, this was my life … I had bars and businesses … I couldn't simply leave this behind. He explained the gravity of the situation. One of the guys was in hospital with his jaw wired. Another had been med-evacced to Tokyo. They were under intense pressure to deport me immediately. The Colonel was behaving as if he'd never met me before … he wanted to impress his troops.

"Now, anything else you can say in your defence?"

"Bloody oath. If those idiots hadn't come into my bar I wouldn't have beaten them up."

"Excellent," he said. "There's our defence …" He was showing signs of lightening up. I was still shaking. He mulled over it for a while.

"OK, we can agree that those people never set foot on your premises again and in return you promise not to physically harm them again."

It made sense to me. We shook on it, and I was ushered out of the room.

Company car

There was a Soi Nana bar owner who lived quite near the area, and was collected at the end of work each night in a wheelbarrow. "It just wasn't much fun when they forgot to kick the pig out first!" he remembers.

Dry spell

There's a hard-living resort manager who drinks like a fish, but goes off the grog every February. "I really hate leap years," he said.

Just looking thanks

A friend of mine and I stopped at a pub on the waterfront in Yokosaka, Japan, in the mid-50s. The main saloon was divided into two rooms separated by a rather flimsy partition. The front half was for serious drinkers, the back for the lovers. After throwing back a few, my friend said that he wanted to drink but watch the lovers at the same time. He then physically removed the partition, but no-one seemed to complain. Mamasan, however, called the police who soon arrived in force. My friend, mama and myself (for moral support) went down to the police station. After some discussion with the judge, the price of the damage was determined and paid, and mama, myself and my friend went back to the pub to drink and watch the lovers in action.

A family affair

While having a few beers in a pub in Sasebo, Japan, a crusty old chief bosun came in with a young sailor. After a chat, we ascertained they were father and son. The boy's mother had been with them until that day, when she had returned to the US, so they were now out on the town together. As they departed the pub, I heard the dad say: "Come on, son, let's go get a blow job."

Always thinking of the old fella

It was our seventh visit to Phnom Penh and this time we had X's father along. On the morning of day two of our trip X brought three gals from K11 back with him to the hotel. That afternoon he was relaxing in the room with his gals when his father came into the room. Sitting on the bed with the gals, Father X became interested in one. Being a good son, X told daddy to take her to his room, which he promptly did. Returning an hour or so later the gal handed X $5 which the father had given to her. X returned the money to the girl. Calling X a pimp for the rest of the trip, we could not help but wonder if X was thinking where his gal's mouth had been that night as he was kissing her.

Something for the weak end

There was a pub in Yokosuka, Japan, called the Cherry Center. There was only one cherry in the place – mama's seven-year-old daughter. The club gave its girls a three-day vacation each month at the time their usefulness on an *itami* mat was inhibited. On one visit, my regular girlfriend was on vacation so I took another who was not very good. I called her a 'bum fuck'. She said: "OK, but you don't get your money back."

At Christmas I bought her seven pairs (a week's worth) of bikini briefs and had 'Bum Fuck' embroidered on each pair. She wore them proudly, showing them off on any occasion she could.

Long distance love

In the heyday of the Del Pilar strip, the Firehouse was a beacon … it was possible to call ahead and let them know your flight arrival details, whereupon they would send a limo out to the airport replete with not just one, but two, of the Philippines' loveliest consorts to get the party started. They also had an ongoing honours board for the longest-distance 'bell ring' for girlie drinks. The record holder was some lovesick oilie who phoned in his instruction from Texas!

Straight shooter

I was drinking in one of the bars in the Nana complex. Feeling the need to use the toilet I made my way to the facilities. This bar, as is quite common in Bangkok, had no separate Ladies or Men's facilities, patrons and staff all sharing the one small room. While I was taking a pee at the urinal a girl came in, past me to go to the cubicle, which unfortunately was already occupied. Thinking she would wait, I shuffled forward in a semblance of modesty to spare the girl any embarrassment. Foolish me, the girl was completely unabashed and dropped her knickers, squatted and proceeded to pee straight down the floor drain.

Where's yer sense of adventure, Pete? This Thai food is as good as the stuff back home. Just give it a try!

Taken from behind

I was in a bar in, I think, Soi Cowboy. The place had a rather dark and dingy *khazi* and I was the only one in there, or so I thought. While I was in mid-stream I became aware that a Thai chap had appeared (I think he must have been sitting in one of the cubicles) and was now standing very close behind me – and I do mean close. All sorts of thoughts flashed through my mind as he put his hands on my neck. Fortunately, before I could panic, he started to give me a massage. This lasted for a few moments with me all the time trying to pretend that I was still having a pee and that this was the most normal thing in the world. He pulled on both my ear lobes so hard the bones in my ears cracked. Then he put his two arms through mine, locked his hands on the back of my neck and picked me up bodily from the ground. God knows how he managed it, as he must have been a good eight inches shorter than me [Now you're bragging! – Col Ken.]. He gave me a sudden twist and I swear that the sound of my backbone clicking was just like a line of dominoes being pushed over. At last he put me down and I re-buttoned my flies, gave him fifty baht and resolved never to drink in there again.

All in the family

In this bar in Bangkok, I was particularly taken with a cute young girl. However, toward the end of the night, she decided against coming home with me. Never mind, I took her brother home, who was actually much prettier!

Shootin' some pool

Playing pool in a Manila bar, a Filipino guy sunk the black ball accidentally. He then took it out the pocket and continued to play. "Hey, you can't do that!" said the British guy he was playing against. With that, a rusty revolver was pulled on him. The game carried on.

Hair-raising experience

Sitting in a bar one day, the girls were playing around, having some fun when one of our group suddenly had his rug – a fake hairpiece – pulled off his head. We were all surprised that it was a rug, and after an awkward silence, the girls started giggling and we had a jolly good laugh. "Wow, much better," said all the girls. True, it did take 20 years off him without it, and he's never worn it since.

One drink and out

A British engineer, unused to the ways of Japanese nightlife, dropped into a bar in Osaka for a quick drink. One glass of Scotch later he was presented with a bill for 18,000 Yen (nearly US$150). Turns out it was a hostess club.

The (w)hole truth?

Visiting one of my favourite massage parlours in Bangkok, which I had not frequented for some time, I enquired of the manager what the price was now. One thousand baht came the reply.

"What about that one sitting on her own outside the glass cage … can I have her?"

"Oh no," was the response, "unless you want to pay 5,000 baht."

"Why so high?" I enquired. "She's about 25 years old ... what's so special?"

"Ah, you see," said the manager, "she's half a virgin!"

"What the hell do you mean ... how can someone be *half* a virgin?"

"Because she hasn't had it for four years," he explained with a straight face.

Mirror mirror on the wall

Bottoms Up bar is a legend in Hong Kong, having featured in one of the James Bond movies. We fronted up there one evening to witness two memorable sights. The bars consist of a circular carousel where the near-naked girl sits and twirls herself around to dispense drinks. When we arrived we were treated to this sight of a rather portly gentleman, clad only in a brief pair of grundies, singing a song which will be engraved in my mind until the day I die ... it went along the lines of 'Tight as a drum, never been done, I'm the queen of the fairies ...'

However, the defining moment of the evening was the departure at some ungodly hour in the morning. As those who have been there will know, the walls are all mirrors. There was this old crow there who obviously thought that the next one would be her last and she had better not waste a minute. My friend, who hitherto in his life had never had much of a problem in pulling girls and thought that he could afford to be a little choosy, was suddenly espied by said crow, who started giving chase.

To see his valiant efforts to get out of the place by trying to find the one set of mirrors which doubled as a door must go down in the annals of history. By this time we were out on the street, and he eventually came popping out onto the street like a newly-released champagne cork to the still-resonant sounds of the stand-in barperson!

Lift shaft

H, a friend of mine, was in Bangkok for some meetings and – as these things go – ended up in Patpong one night with the boys to get really trashed. Alas – as these things go – he inevitably landed up with one of Patpong's finest who would accompany him back to his hotel. On the way there he bought her a dress to try and make her look a bit more decent. On arrival at the hotel, the petting in the elevator was so intense that he came in his pants before even reaching his floor. He paid the girl the amount owing and told her to go home so he could have a good night's sleep.

Call girl

A cautionary tale that booze, bar girls and cell phones do not mix. I was on a bit of R&R in Angeles City, from my home (and wife) in Manila. After a bit of bar-hopping and a large number of G&Ts I fell into the Tahitian Queen bar. Met with bargirl A who was a good friend of J, a long-term girl friend of mine. J was off duty and A asked to borrow my cell phone to send a text message to her. She sent the text message and, of course, it went something like: 'D has just arrived and is pissed and horny as usual, get your butt over here or he will go butterfly'. Just one snag, the silly bitch managed to send the text message to my wife's cell phone, probably using the 'last number dialled' feature.

The last call I had made was indeed to my wife, who incidentally thought I was in Puerto Gallera. Boy was I in the shit next day. This could have been avoided as A did have a cell phone herself, but it was in her locker. All GROs now seem to come fitted with cell phones and multiple e-mail addresses as standard.

A fine idea

A bunch of us walked into a bar in Olongapo, Philippines, and were immediately beset by bargirls. Being bargirls, of course, they were angling for bar-fines. What they didn't know is that I had about $100 on me, given to me by the wives of these particular friends, with instructions to keep their husbands 'honest' in the P.I. I had talked about this with my friends and we all agreed that, when in the bars, I would just keep buying pitchers of beer until they were all too drunk to do anything. Good in theory – harder to put into practice when a pretty young thing has her hands all over you. Finally, I just told the bargirls that the guy's wives would cut their dicks off if they fooled around. "That OK – you pay bar-fine now, you worry about dick later!"

The best thing is I was single ... I got my friends drunk, got them back to the barracks, and still had enough money left over to pay a bar-fine for myself! Good thing I never told the wives how cheap San Miguel was.

Thistle shock you

A group of expats were on a bar crawl through Wanchai, Hong Kong. In the group was a visitor from Scotland. One of the group, A, enjoyed the occasional blowjob [Define 'occasional'. Hourly? – Col Ken]. As the night went on the group got broken up, but with the intention to rendezvous in a certain downmarket bar at about 2:00am.

In that bar one group member bet the Scot HK$500 that within 60 seconds of A entering the bar, A would be getting a blowjob. The bet was taken on. Sure enough about 10 minutes later, in walks A, drunk but uncommitted and, lo and behold, after about 45 seconds A was in the corner getting the job done. The Scottish visitor was totally shocked and duly paid up the bet.

What he never knew was that one of the party had previously told the dirtiest bargirl that if she can get A into the required position with 60 seconds of his arrival she would get HK$250 for the job. So the girl got her HK$250, and the balance was used by us for drinking on another night.

Get well – away

In the Northern Thai town of Chiangmai I chatted one night with one of the bargirls. After a while, I raised the topic of AIDS. The reaction of that girl: "Uh, I do have AIDS, but only a little bit."

Blow dart

While in the navy, I had the luck to visit the wonderful and seedy port of Patong Beach, Phuket. There were about a dozen sailors on the stroll for an intriguing and educational evening of drinks, debauchery, and downright nastiness. While inside viewing an evening of these girls with an array of various objects – such as razor blades, sewing needles, fish hooks, ping pong balls, several kinds of fish and eels, even a cute little parakeet – placed in their nether regions, the infamous dart girl strolled out.

After strategically placing several balloons around the bar, she began her lessons on 'fire control' and 'radar accuracy' with little paper-finned darts. When she was shooting at one balloon, the dart popped the balloon, careened off a mirror and proceeded to bury itself into the back of my head. Luckily, the ship's doctor was sitting next to me and, with the skill of a surgeon, deftly removed what is probably the most unique West Pac souvenir any sailor could ever hope to place in a scrapbook.

This is a stick-up

Myself and another two expats, one of whom, X, is the general manager of the Asian division of one of Australia's largest companies, used to convene about four times a year in Bangkok for a few big nights on the company with a bit of work thrown in for good measure. One of our favourite hangouts in the Pong was Gold Finger, a bar owned by a fantastic American who used to let us play all the music we wanted, as well as give us free slammers and generally give us the run of his bar.

One night X was particularly hammered and had taken to wandering around the bar with a straw behind each ear like antennae and jumping up on stage with a broom to belt out a couple of tunes on the air guitar. Rather unfortunately a western girl and her partner, who had probably used all her courage to even enter the bar, had just arrived looking forward to a quiet drink together. No sooner had they ordered than X snuck up behind her and started prodding her fair up the arse with his broomstick. The girl spun around to see what the hell was going on … to be greeted by the sight of our senior company executive complete with antennae and broomstick propositioning her.

As long as I live I will never forget the look of surprise on the girl's face. The story has become the stuff of company legend, and even today still makes us snigger at the thought of it.

Monkey see, monkey do what?

I was dating this bird in Angeles who actually ran a bar and had a room out the back. She had an unhealthy sexual appetite which ran to handcuffs, leather, and so on. One night she brought a cage into the bar, pulled off the cover and in it was a monkey, your average rhesus. Big deal, we all thought.

Then she brought this sack through with a cat in it. She lifted the lid of the cage and threw the cat in. The monkey went ballistic and eventually got the cat in a wrestling grip, looking around with this manic stare as if he wanted us to dare him to go on with it, then proceeded to butt-fuck this cat. As he pumped it, the monkey looked for more encouragement from the crowd. Nearing his climax, the monkey's eyes started rolling back in his head and swirling around. Sated, he grabbed the cat's head and ripped it off, holding it valiantly up in the air, in a victory pose. The crowd, gob-smacked, went wild. "That's the best thing I've seen in my life," I said.

I decided that my mate needed to see this so I went to his place (it's 2am) and woke him. We kidnapped the neighbour's cat and headed back to the bar. The cat's introduced and the monkey repeats the performance on cue, ending with the victorious post-climactic head-snapping.

"Best fucking thing I've seen in my life," he too declares.

What worries me is that my girlfriend used to keep the monkey cage at the foot of her bed, which made me a little nervous. And I always wondered how she trained the monkey to do *that*?

Frack to bunt

While on shore leave in Sasebo, Japan, we stopped at the Black Rose, a notorious bar which was home to girls I hesitate to call 'wayward' as they always seemed to be going my way. After several drinks and an obligatory trip upstairs, we stepped out on to the street. My friend stopped me. "Buddy," he slurred, "did you ever drink so much your feet changed places?" Sure enough, his right shoe was now on his left foot and vice versa.

Bottle-to-throttle

In Vientiane, Laos, in 1976 the commies were cracking down on all the 'decadent' nightspots in the town. None was more decadent that the White Rose, a notorious knocking shop. On its last night of operation we were giving it a right royal send-off, going to the hilt till they literally started boarding the place up. There were a couple of other guys still in there and we got talking. Turns out they were airline guys, flying out the next morning. As it happened, so was I – in four hours' time, to be exact.

"I hope you're not the pilot," I joked.

"No, no, I'm just the co-pilot," he reassured me. "That," he said, pointing to a figure slumped on the bar counter, "is the captain."

If you have a good story about restaurants or bars in Asia, don't wait for happy hour. Email The Editor at hardshipposting@hotmail.com or fax 612-9499-5908 now. He'll shout you free beer all day tomorrow.

❖ 3 ❖

Snouts In the Trough
Or What's In It For Me?

*True tales of bribery, corruption, conmen
and slippery customers.*

Let's start in the way we plan to continue, by getting the cheap shots in.
What's the national tree of most South East Asian countries? The Greased
Palm (Palmus Asiatica also colloquially called the Open Palm) of course.

That's right, nary a chance for a little wage supplement or expansion of
turf goes begging. And the results can be either spectacularly enriching, or
downright disastrous. In Hangman's Point, my good friend Dean Barrett
points out the extent to which the British government of Hong Kong had got
on to the gravy train in 1857. There were scandals among officials in the territory to an extent that the governor was not on speaking terms with his own
attorney general, and they had to write notes to each other. The 'Protector of
Chinese' was found to be in league with the pirates, and a number of foreigners were beheaded in Hong Kong waters that year. The police commissioner
owned brothels, and the British fleet was shelling Canton just for the hell of
it. Having had a gutful of this, and not seeing much future in Hong Kong,
some Chinese bakers placed ten pounds of arsenic in the bread to be eaten by
foreigners living there. It was the only mass poisoning in history. Sounds like
a complete, er, bunfight.

Mind you, the Chinese learnt their lesson well and are now capable of
world-class corruption. In the year 2000, two in three China State firms were
found to have posted inaccurate financial statements, according to China
Connections magazine. One in ten companies listed faked profits. If you think
those figures are bad, you should see their other set of books!

In one particularly good case, a deputy chief of Air China's accounts department syphoned off roughly US$3,000,000. He was on the run for about four years (tiring, but it makes you very fit) before they collared him and gave him a bullet as a token of his diligence.

In Korea, they also seem to hire non-mathematicians to run their finance departments. Executives from the Daewoo Group distorted financial records and falsified financial documents. I love the word 'distorted' ... given that the 20 executives were fined a total of nearly US$20,000,000,000 I would say 'bent out of shape' might describe the picture more accurately. Five of them were also imprisoned, but the group's noble founder took it like a man and fled the country in 1999. Daewoo, which used to be South Korea's largest conglomerate, then collapsed into a smoking heap. Prosecutors called it Asia's largest fraud case ever. A big call indeed.

Asia also regularly takes the gold when it comes to credit card fraud. Statistics from major card merchants show that Malaysians are the main culprits in the world behind credit card fraud. Nearly 350 Malaysians were rounded up in 2001 for credit card offences, mainly in Asia, Australasia and Europe. The problem the prosecutors faced was in identifying their suspects ... each had wallets full of cards bearing different names!

But for barefaced bravery, you've got to hand it to the Moscow Philharmonic Orchestra ... or some people that look and act and sound exactly like them. The Moscow Phil toured Hong Kong a few years ago, heavily promoted by one of the local government departments. Tens of thousands forked over their hard-earned or ill-gotten money for the expensive tickets, and a successful series of concerts was staged. A little too late it was noted to be a bit strange that the Moscow Phil was touring Hong Kong at the same time as the Moscow Phil was engaged on a lengthy tour of southern Europe. Wait a minute, couldn't be ... yes, a bunch of unemployed freelancers had masqueraded as the real thing to many rapturous curtain calls and bouquets. Love it!

But were the Hong Kong government really that naïve? Corruption among civil servants there was often suspected but difficult to prove. So, Barry tells me, they brought in a new rule: if your personal assets exceeded your last ten years' salary (according to the tax office figures) you were busted and had to prove they were obtained by legal means. Ouch!

In Thailand they're a little more upfront with these things and it is now generally acknowledged by the Thai Engineering Institute that a full 20 per cent of the Thai national construction budget is swallowed by corruption. The big giveaway was that ten storey government buildings were only built eight storeys tall! Gosh, 20 per cent is really pushing it – bring back the good old days of a flat ten per cent. Or for that matter, say a lot of Filipinos, bring back Marcos. At least in his day you knew exactly who you had to pay to get the job done. Nowadays, every bastard's after a slice of the action, like the 12 traffic wardens who were extorting money from drivers. Along comes President Joseph Estrada in an unmarked car. They recognise him, flee in all directions, and were suspended from duty. Talk about going right to the top!

Bangladesh recently poo-poohed reports by a corruption watchdog that it was the world's most corrupt nation, two years in a row. This must have been a sore blow for the Indonesian government who felt they had worked hard for the award only to miss out so narrowly on the spoils. Bangladesh did the only honourable thing – blamed the previous administration.

And both of these nations of swaying palms must have had a close struggle to pip India out of the running. Let's look at just a few of the little transgressions that it has racked up in recent years: former prime minister Rao and a cabinet colleague were sentenced to three years' jail for vote-buying. My good Indian pal, Guvigotta Tummyrumble, tells me that most of his fellow citizens feel that politicians are crooks, so you may as well vote for the best crook. Let's talk about Jayalalitha for a while. She is the highest elected official (it doesn't say what her height is or whether she was wearing high heels at the time of measurement) in the state of Tamil Nadu and earns a salary equal to – I think I've got this right – two US cents per month. OK, let's cut her some slack and say it's $2 per month. Hell, let's call it $20, Colonel, you say. How then, the court would like to know, did she come to be in possession of five suitcases of jewellery? Just one of the items in these suitcases was a diamond-encrusted waistband. When I say encrusted, I think that's the best word to describe 2,389 individual diamonds!

Another good one out of India recently was the general in charge of ammunition procurement, famous for telling vendors and middlemen they needn't come to his house without a bottle of Blue Label scotch. The defence minister's lover was also in on the deal and allegedly took $200,000 on a multi-billion arms contract. She was also trying to haggle for an increase in the illegal commission. Late prime minister Rajiv Gandhi was outlived by a scandal in which it is alleged he took multi-million dollar bribes from western arms manufacturers.

Speaking of arms and legs, there are cases of loansharks in Japan forcing delinquent clients to sell body parts in order to repay the money. One employee of Japan Nichei Co Ltd was jailed for 20 months. You'd think they'd wheel in some cousin who's a sumo to be the standover man. But it seems that maybe they couldn't be trusted with the cash even if they did collect it. In the sacred sport, which has over 1,500 years of tradition, honour and sweaty jockstraps, it seems rubbery arms have made an appearance. University of Chicago analysts studied 32,000 sumo bouts and found that 40 per cent of final competition bouts are fixed. Despite the allegations dogging the sport for years, no action nor arrests have ever been made.

I tell you what, punters, I may have been involved in some shady schemes in the past. But these days when people come to me and say, "Colonel, what's the best way to double my money?" I tell them this:

"Fold it over and put it back in your wallet!"

Colonel Ken

What's mine is mine, what's yours is also mine

These two Australians had set up a business to develop a resort in Borocay, Philippines. They put in 100 per cent of the dollars but legally, on paper, only owned 40 per cent of the business. Their partners were high-profile Filipino business families in that area.

Just when everything was finally built and ready to go, they were told, "thanks, but you're no longer required." Bullshit, they thought, and flew to the Philippines thinking their wealth, acumen and contacts would assert and secure their rightful ownership. The brewing feud was written up in the local newspaper.

En route in Manila, one of the guys took a call from someone saying he was a journalist with a major daily newspaper and they'd like to interview him and get their side of the story. He immediately agreed. The following day two guys (a 'journalist' and a 'photographer') came up to his room, unpacked their briefcases, pencils and notebooks.

"Where's Mr Y?" they asked of his partner.

"He's down in Borocay already," he explained.

"Are you Mr X?" Yes, he was. "Mr John X?" Yes. BANG! They killed him on the spot and raced out of the back entrance of the hotel where a driver was waiting.

His partner in Borocay learned that the hit was on and called the Australian Embassy. Presumably for a sum of money, a helicopter was arranged to lift him out of Borocay and he was taken to a waiting plane in Cebu, and he was gone, out of the country, never to return.

White elephant

When the UN pulled out of Cambodia, they left behind about US$400 million worth of equipment. Our company won a contract to retrieve all the UN assets and centralise them at a base from where they could be inventoried and dispatched again to where they were next needed.

When the retrieval operation started, we were going up to Cambodian soldiers and saying, "Can we have our tank back please."

"No, it's ours," they'd say.

"But it's white, with a huge UN painted on it," we'd point out (a point obviously lost on them previously) and take it.

Not too long after, two young Cambodian boys were splashed by a UN-related person riding a motorbike along a muddy road. The boys shot him, so all UN personnel were ordered out of the country immediately. The UN just walked away from all this equipment, and reneged on our contract.

"Put in a compensation claim," said the disinterested liaison officer. Claim still pending, several years later.

Dicing with death

On holiday in Manila, I met these nice guys who invite me back to their place in 'the middle of nowhere' for some drinks. Why not? Once we got there, a non-descript suburban house, they asked if I liked gambling and card games. Yeah. They took me out the back where a makeshift 'casino' was set up … complete with a green baize table. We had just started when a shifty-looking Chinese customer came in. A few hands were played for small stakes, and I had a taste of winning. Then the Chinese guy started offering some tips ("Follow me, sure win"), which, incredibly, we did. The stakes were raised with each hand, and before I knew it I was sitting on a small fortune, with knowing winks from the Chinese guy.

Then, I started losing. The whole thing turned. I lost and lost and lost again. The Chinese guy was now very distant and trying his best to play innocent and ignorant (although he was obviously in on the whole set-up deal). Soon I was $1,000 in the red. I did exactly what I shouldn't have done – stood up and said, "This is bullshit … a complete scam!"

They demanded that I pay up. It got very tense, and I knew there was no way of getting out alive without paying up. So the guy (plus most of their extended family) accompanied me to the nearest ATM, where I was made to withdraw the $1,000, hand it over, then I scampered off quick as I could.

Gamekeeper turned poacher

A corrupt police official in a small village in central Java allegedly held a local Chinese Indonesian businessman hostage for five years because of his inability to pay the ransom demanded. Eventually his trustees arranged for him to be secretly freed. A crack squad of ex-SAS mercenaries was put together in New Zealand. They flew to Bali, ferried across to Java, then drove to a village south of Jogyakarta, and plucked the businessman out – with no bullets flying or injury caused to anyone. The businessman was taken directly to New Zealand, where an extended visitor's visa was arranged for him.

Blind drunk

When they introduced drink-driving laws in Malaysia in about 1995 it stopped us in our tracks. Well, for about two weeks, before the 'going rate' of 300 ringgit was established to turn the officer's blind-eye.

Tech wreck

A scam share-trading 'boiler room' – one of dozens in Bangkok – was busted, with the British and Australian bosses held for unlicensed security dealing and possible money laundering offences. They had about 100 backpackers working for them of various nationalities, cold-calling people around the world and conning them into investing in worthless tech stocks. The bosses face jail and fines if convicted: the workers, a slap on the wrist and a US$100 fine.

Return on investment

A Kiwi was working in Bangkok, allegedly running a 'boiler house' which operated illegal forex scams. Leaving his home one morning in Sukhumvit – in a flashy BMW, of course – he took five shots from someone on behalf of his disgruntled investors. Although a Kiwi, he claimed to have been a member of the Australian SAS. [SOS I think … Snake Oil Salesmen! – Col Ken.]

Kiss your baht goodbye

On my first trip to Thailand two very glamorous ladies driving in a top-of-the-range Mercedes stopped me. "We are performing at the Imperial Hotel but we are Taiwanese and have only just arrived. Can you direct us?"

"Yes," I said, "it's straight ahead about three kilometres." Fine, and would I like a lift in the direction in which I was walking? OK, so I hopped in the front passenger seat, the other lady sitting in the back holding on to their luggage.

After an extremely fast ride to my destination I requested them to stop, which they did, but – before I could exit – the driver gave me a real smoochy kiss full on the lips. Meanwhile, during this ecstasy, the other passenger was taking out 1,000 baht from my trouser pocket, leaving me with just five baht.

On reaching my guest house I discovered the loss and related my story to the sympathetic manager, pointing out that at least I got something pleasant from the encounter. He explained that the practice was well known and that they were in fact not Taiwanese ladies but Thai 'lady-boys'. I now catch buses instead.

Phnom de guerre

I had arrived in Cambodia without a visa and expected a bureaucratic shit-fight. But five minutes, $20, and maybe 10 or 12 peaked-capped customs officials later, I was in business.

On the straight and narrow

I am a competitive runner and needed to do a track session in Bangkok. I went to the National Stadium, and there was a soccer game going on. I had started my warm up when the groundskeeper tells me that I can stay and run, but not run on the home straight in front of the players. I went to my gear bag, took 200 baht and gave it to him. *Mai pen rai*! I can now use the full track.

Taken for a ride

My colleague X was a private contractor (quantity surveyor) working with us on the building of a large water treatment works at Din Daeng in Bangkok. He owned a car. One day going home from work he was stopped by a policeman – brown uniform, shiny black boots, but obviously short of cash.

"Your car insurance disc is one day out of date – you will have to go to court and will be fined 20,000 baht," said the scheming copper.

"But I haven't got that kind of money," protested X.

"We can make arrangement … maybe 3,000 baht."

"OK, but I have no money on me, I get it for you tomorrow – you come to my house in the morning and I will give it to you."

"How I know where you live?"

"You follow me now and see where I live, then come tomorrow."

X set off with the copper, on his motorcycle, in tow. As he neared his house, the policeman switched on his blue light, but no siren. X stopped and went back to the copper.

"Why did you flash your blue light?"

"That house is owned by our police general."

"Yes, I know, I rent it from him."

A roar of a twin-cylinder motorcycle engine as a policeman beats a rather hasty exit.

Not squeaky clean

H was a three-badge stoker (12 years service but no advancement) who disappeared every time our ship, the HMS Belfast, hit Hong Kong in the 60s. He went ashore and changed from greasy overalls into tux and patent leather shoes in the dockside toilets, emerging as a dashing and presentable figure who would've blended in to any level of HK society. The story went that he had a very beautiful girlfriend in HK, and he was only seen occasionally until a few minutes before sailing … except on occasion in the China Fleet Club.

I was playing tombola once in the Club and heard a 'pssst'. Looking around, I saw H peering through the curtains, and approached him. He borrowed the watch I had recently bought in Singapore. He then hocked it at a local pawnbroker for about HK$30, which kept him going for a day or two. Multiply this by about 10 guys after he had run out of his initial cash, and H could keep going for as long as we were in port (usually a week or two). He used to know when the ship was sailing and simply turn himself in as we were about to raise the gangway.

He would then be held in cells on board until we got to Singapore, and be sent to the military prison, Kinrara in Malaya (as it was then), for the term decided by the captain. All would be returned when he was released from the cells after each AWOL adventure. He would do exactly the same thing every time we returned to HK.

As a postscript, I went to a clairvoyant in 1988 and was told: "There is a man standing behind you – his name is H. He has passed on but said to give you his best wishes. He said you'll know who he is."

The one that didn't get away

J used to operate fishing boats out of Darwin, then apparently got bored and decided to move to Supang, West Timor, where his wife was from. He was going into a fish export business over there, and managed to get some business partners to invest, setting himself up nicely with boats, a sizeable house, and a four-wheel drive. Before long, the business was going bad and his business partners accused him of fraud and misconduct. He was shot at, and hit in the face with a tyre-lever one night. Soon after, he was arrested by Indonesian police. A court order saw all his possessions seized. He was put in jail for six months.

After his release, he stayed on and got involved with the Australian Federal Police as an 'informant' on people smuggling, for which he was reportedly well paid. However, just recently he was charged with being a people smuggler himself, and faces a possible 17-year jail sentence if found guilty.

Light fingered

In Cambodia we were dealing with the UN who had a huge area in downtown Phnom Penh – about five or six acres – which was a giant candy store full of cars, four-wheel drives, generators, you name it. The guy we were dealing with was a real crook and I asked others why we were dealing with him … he was handing out 4WD vehicles to UN police who'd just arrived from Bulgaria, who'd go to the border and sell the vehicles into Vietnam, then come back a couple of days later and say, "Sorry, we lost it, could we have another one please?" and he'd reissue it on the spot.

Going to his place once, I noticed his kitchen was filled with this huge white generator (45 Kva). I asked why he kept it in his kitchen. "That way, no-one will steal it at night," was his deadpanned ironic explanation. Whenever there was a brownout, he'd start the thing up, and it would roar to life, drowning out any conversation or music, and the air would fill with acrid diesel fumes and smoke. But at least his lights were on.

Head in the sand behaviour

We started a new venture in Nueva Ecija, Philippines … an ostrich farm. It was soon doing well, and the green eyes turned on us from competitors. One night our farmhouse and facilities were shot up, trying to scare us out of the area. We went above the local mayor to a senator, explained that we were not 'aliens' – my wife's great-grandmother had come from the area and was well known there – bought him a nice dinner and some drinks. The next day, a posse of security folks was posted on the farm, and the senator issued a 'hands off or else ...' to the other party. We've had no trouble since then.

Mine, not yours

An Australian couple was arrested in Laos on claims they were involved in a multi-million dollar sapphire smuggling and money laundering conspiracy. They were accused of stealing about US$6 million dollars worth of gems. Ironically, he was in charge of security at the mining company. The wife was arrested at a border post with her two children and US$50,000 in cash, reportedly. They were sentenced to seven years in jail, plus fines and 'compensation' of more than US$500,000 for tax evasion and embezzlement. The Laos authorities reportedly pocketed about $150,000 taken from the couple, before they were freed following an extended diplomatic wrangle that lasted nearly a year. Eventually the Laotian president signed a pardon.

Golden opportunity

A guy who'd lived in Hong Kong for many years retired to the Philippines. For whatever reason, possibly pocket money, he got involved in smuggling gold into India. It wasn't his gold ... he was just the courier. Anyone who knows India will tell you that they view gold smuggling as worse than drugs. He was immediately arrested with several kilograms in his bag. Because he was elderly and a bit frail, he successfully requested to be held under guard in a hospital rather than a prison. His wife flew up from the Philippines and used to take meals to him because the slop they served up was inedible.

He appealed to us all to help him out with the *baksheesh* money. Over the next 11 months we all sent him as much as we could spare (amounting to tens of thousands of US dollars) and he eventually bought his way out, got a fake passport, and made it back to the Philippines. He never fully recovered from the ordeal and died shortly after.

Bar-gain

My Thai girlfriend's next-door neighbour was a sweet young thing with a Thai boyfriend and an English boyfriend, the latter deciding to move to Phuket and set up business to be with his loved one. "What type of business will you do?" I asked. He wasn't sure yet.

Soon after, another girlfriend of mine was waiting to sell her bar for 800,000 baht, so I put two and two together. I told her I'd do her a deal; just leave it to me. So I approached the English guy and told him of this great opportunity … a Phuket bar for sale for only 1,200,000 baht. We could go 50/50 in the business. (The idea was he would put in 600,000 and I'd only have to pay 200,000 for my share.). First he got excited, then he got greedy. He didn't want a partner, so he started dealing direct with the bar owner, and was chuffed when he managed to bargain her 'down' from 1.2 million to 'only' 950,000, way over the odds.

Head over heels

I had been trying, without success, to obtain a US visa for my Indonesian girlfriend, A. We had applied, were turned down: I even had my congressman write a supporting letter and we were turned down again. And so finally, while in Bali, I called the consulate general in Surabaya and asked him what I needed to do to get the visa approved. He said that if I would appear in person in Surabaya, he would reconsider our request.

"We're going to Surabaya, get in the car," I said to A, but she insisted that it would be fruitless. So we made a bet that involved sexual favours.

When we got to the Gianiyar ferry we were informed that it was impossible to take rental cars off the island. Twelve thousand rupiah later it became possible after all, and off we went.

Upon arrival in Banyuwangi, Java, I got initiated into Javanese driving in a hurry, twice being run off the road by buses driving in our lane, despite my horns, screams and middle-finger salutes. So when we got to Surabaya after nine hours, my mood was not the best. And when we couldn't find the embassy it got worse.

It was dark and getting darker on the roads and it appeared that we had passed through Surabaya altogether. So A says, "OK, come back," meaning take a u-turn. So I crank the turn with-out slowing down — just in time to be broad-sided by a motor cyclist who literally flew over the hood and landed, motionless, on the curb. Dead?

About 20 people, all speaking Indonesian, surrounded the car. One big guy appointed himself spokesman and starts talking to me. As I can't understand Indonesian, I just tell A to offer the motorcyclist (now moving) US$100 to make the whole thing go away. The big guy communicates the offer and it is rejected. Now the police are called and visions of Indonesian jail start to dance in my head.

A police sergeant, also a rather large individual, arrives and A (all four-foot eight inches of her) steps between the two big guys and starts talking faster and louder than both. I have no idea what's being said, but it ends up with the sergeant getting in our car and driving us to the police station, all the while chatting with A. When we arrived, I ask A what she was saying and she said that she had convinced the police sergeant that the accident was the fault of the motorcyclist!

Finally, the police sergeant suggests we go to the hospital and see how the motorcyclist is doing. This we do and the sergeant comes out and reports that he's OK and that – if we wanted the whole matter to be dropped – 100,000 rupiah would do the trick. Since that was equal to about US$40 at the time, less than half of what I had originally offered the guy, I readily agreed, paid up, and left.

Oh yeah, we got the visa and this time A paid up.

Running on empty

Years ago we were shooting a TV commercial for a burger chain in Singapore. Their promotion was a 'scratch and win' opportunity to win running shoes, and other prizes. For the commercial we had to print up some mock winning tickets. Thousands of these were run off, and imprudently distributed among cast and crew and ad agency personnel and friends. The week after the promotion was launched, the client was a little intrigued and distressed as to how there were so many instant winners queuing up outside their stores to claim their free running shoes.

Caught with his pants down

I like to think I'm fairly worldly and, as seasoned as travellers go, awake to any tricks of the trade. However, I was caught with my pants down within two hours of reaching Chiangmai.

After the long overnight train journey from Bangkok, strolling around getting my bearings, the delightful girl on the motorcycle spoke great English and looked sensational. Her offer of a massage was just what my aching back needed. I accepted and she spun some convincing student/studying story as we drove.

Massage duly done, she drove me back downtown and promised to meet me in a certain bar that evening. Happy feelings soon vanished when I realised my wallet felt much lighter. She had removed about two thirds of the notes in my wallet, including Hong Kong and Taiwanese dollars, when my pants were off.

I didn't see her that night and, though I managed to backtrack the next morning and find the place, the police showed scant interest in my complaint. Furthermore, they informed me, 'she' was a he. Oops!

The truth, the whole truth …

On the new toll road from Ipoh to KL, Malaysia, an unmarked police car stopped me. The guy wanted to give me a ticket, but I said I was in a hurry to the airport in order to leave the country and had no time to go to the police station. I therefore asked whether we could settle it with a small payment that would save him paperwork and me time.

The only thing he asked was: "Are you sincere with this offer?" How sincere can a bribe be? I gave him 20 ringgit and sped off.

Flower power

I'd just arrived in Calcutta and was checking out one of the pubs recommended in the Rough Guide. Suddenly a plummy voice was heard alongside me; a well-dressed Indian, around 40 years of age, asking the usual questions of a tourist. While sinking a few beers together he told me he was a teacher in one of Mother Theresa's schools, and showed me some pamphlets that seemed to support his story.

He then said that his parents were celebrating their wedding anniversary the following day and his family would be very honoured to receive an Englishman into their home.

Eager to sample the local cuisine at the grassroots level, I accepted and asked what sort of gift might be appropriate for his parents. He suggested flowers and volunteered to buy them, on my behalf, the next morning at the market. He said 250 rupees should be enough to cover it. Having just come from the airport, I didn't have small change so gave him 500 rupees (about US$10). We arranged to meet at the Raj-style Fairlawns Hotel the next evening at 7pm, with my flowers and change.

As soon as I left the pub, I knew I had been done. I mused the next day about the positive side of human nature but, of course, he never showed up … probably busy at another pub inviting another Englishman to a non-existent wedding.

Will power-less

This guy's father had moved to the Philippines after his mum had died. After a little while his father had met a young lass and they set up a couple of bars, financed with his dad's money of course. They were run very successfully, and made quite a bit of money in the process.

Several years later, his father passed away, at a fairly ripe old age. The son dutifully flew to the Philippines to tie up all the loose ends and claim his inheritance, as the pubs had been willed to him. He passed condolences to his step-mum (around his own age), promising to take care of her and give her whatever money and support she needed.

"You don't understand, this is mine," she said.

"No, I have the documents here," he naively pleaded.

"No, these are mine. You should go home," she politely but firmly implied.

Seeing the impasse, he said, "I'll be speaking to my lawyer about this tomorrow," and walked out. Later at his hotel, there was a knock at the door and two men burst in.

"So, you will be leaving on the flight tonight?" they asked.

"Pig's arse. I'm not going anywhere till we sort everything out," he said.

"No, sir, you only have two options. You leave, sitting down, in tonight's plane … or you leave, lying down in a box, on tomorrow's plane."

He left, sitting down, on that night's flight, empty handed apart from a can of beer.

Crate expectations

I used to import premium beers into Vietnam … three containers a month. The supplier used to load in an extra 80 bottles – 40 for me, 40 for the customs guy – with each shipment. I don't believe we ever had a problem bringing a container in.

Losing my appetite

Living in Bangkok in the late 80s, I was stopped by a policeman after an illegal u-turn on my motorbike. After my usual "speak-to-me-in-English just let-me-go-because-it's-too-much-trouble" routine failed miserably, he was insistent that I go with him to the police station. With that I started speaking to him in Thai (which I actually spoke rather fluently). I said I didn't have much time, so let's just settle this here: how much did he want?

"Enough money for lunch," was his reply. "100 baht." I opened my wallet, which revealed only 270 baht. I then told him I wanted to have lunch with him, but as I was a big *farang* my lunch was going to cost more than his. So that only left 70 baht for him. He laughed and agreed to it. I paid up and then went to the bank.

Vanishing visa

The High Commission in Malaysia had organised a delegation of Australian businessmen to go on a study tour to Ho Chi Minh City, Vietnam. At the last minute, the group leader fell ill and I was asked to step in for him.

I knew about Vietnam's lengthy visa application procedure but was assured that, "not to worry, it's been arranged, collect it there." At the airport, no one knew anything about a visa to be collected. I was then taken into a side office where another official questioned my reason for visit, who was I, and what did I want? Then the 'police' took me in a van (for which I had to pay US$10!) to a nearby 'hotel' where further questioning ensued. No one was letting on anything to me, and I began to fear the worst and did indeed end up being kept overnight.

In the morning after a brief 'chat' I paid them US$100. "Oh, we *found* your visa, sir," said the smiling official who duly released me.

Life's a pitch

We had a major pitch coming up for the advertising account of the national tourism body of one of the major South East Asian countries. Big business, tens of millions of dollars at stake. As the big day drew nearer, I was worried that we hadn't really cracked the solution. I went into my boss's office – a local who owned the company – and said, "I don't know what to do."

"Do whatever you like," he said, "we have won the business."

I looked at him, not comprehending. "But we haven't even pitched yet," I said, thinking he'd lost his marbles.

"Who needs to pitch when you buy the minister's son a brand new BMW coupe?" he winked.

What's vat?

We were doing business with a big printing company in Thailand. They issued their invoice for jobs done and, when it came to payment time, we were told: "We have two accounts you can pay into. You can choose … with or without 7% VAT." I suspect the unofficial one was siphoned off quietly under a dead grandma's name or something.

Crooked but straight

I was with my Thai girlfriend driving through Bangkok when I made a u-turn. A policeman spotted me and waved me to pull over.

Knowing the system, I fumbled in my pocket for a 100 baht note for the 'fine'. I only had a 500 note, nothing smaller, so I resigned myself to the fact that this is still cheaper than arguing and going through the system. I slipped him the 500.

He told us to stay where we were and walked off, returning in a few minutes. Pushing his clipboard through the side window, he motioned me to lift the first sheet of paper. Underneath were four crisp 100 baht notes. He had gone to get change!

Out of pocket expenses

I arrived at Manila airport laden with gifts for the family after a long trip away. The customs officer gave me a sneering look and I swore I saw him rub his hands with potential he saw for searching my bags and levying some sort of 'import duty'. However, on spying a gold pen in my top pocket, he simply said, "Nice pen," reached for it and waved me on.

Hit or missing

There was a notoriously shifty German property dealer operating in Phuket. He got a lot of clients offside. At one point, a group of aggrieved clients got a Thai hit man to put a gun to his head as a warning. His body was found floating in the sea with concrete weights some time later.

Heard it all before

An Australian who'd lived in the Philippines for a while used to touch up unsuspecting expat businessmen and tourists with sob stories about his family in the province, fictitious accidents, etc, asking for a few thousand pesos each time. The Australian embassy was aware of his antics but could do nothing legally because borrowing money and being slow – like really, really slow – in paying it back is not actually a crime.

He came undone when he called a businessman to set up an 'urgent' appointment, without realising he'd hit that same guy up successfully before. When he arrived, the guy called security and told them to lock the doors and shoot him if he moved. Unfortunately he couldn't get hold of the police on the line, and the embassy was 'out to lunch' so he had to let him go.

A little later the con man went to the Manila Hotel and asked to inspect the Presidential Suite for a visiting dignitary's upcoming trip. While on the inspection, he allegedly stole a few items from the room and was subsequently brought to justice.

Black market

Three Canadians and a couple of African nationals were arrested in

Thailand after allegedly conning a South American into paying them 250,000 baht for a chemical which, they told him, would turn black money – blackened piecers of paper supposedly distributed secretly by the US government – into US dollars. He fell for it, but perhaps he wasn't the only one targeted as police also found several other bottles of the chemical and black-coated paper when searching their premises.

Innocence the first casualty

A former British school principal was busted for allegedly making a pornographic video in a Phnom Penh park with some under-aged girls. Taken to court, the case took on a whole new twist. He ranted and raved and even threw a chair in the courtroom. Protesting his innocence? No. Pissed off because he'd reportedly already paid the judge US$3,000 for an acquittal verdict.

Chinese checkers

A foreign insurance company keen to break into the China market had identified a Chinese man as their local facilitator. They visited Xian, China, four times during which he laid on Rolls Royces with military escorts and lavish banquets attended by generals of the People's Liberation Army. With their support, he said, business was assured. US$30 million was pumped into the joint venture. However, after over a year of operations, no board meetings, financial information or revenue was forthcoming. They decided to do a background check on their local partner, which soured the relationship when he got wind of it. The plug was eventually pulled, but US$4m was never retrieved. The local partner was banned as a director in China for 11 years.

Green with envy

I was running an Irish bar in Hanoi, and paid US$50 per month to a tax official to falsify tax forms as we had no license to operate. It was going well so the greedy landlord decided to take the business over. Soon after, the police raided it and confiscated the British manager's passport. He eventually got it back and beat a hasty retreat. The bar is now a shambles.

Don't judge a book …

In Thailand several years ago I was taken to court for producing a book with girlie pictures in it. The judge asked: "Did you take these photographs?" I acknowledged I did. I was duly fined 700 baht, plus 25 baht for stamp duty. "See you in my chambers," said the judge as I was dismissed. I went to his chambers, and he told me he wanted two extra copies of the book, which I duly sold to him at an extortionate price.

Very fishy business

During my military career I had created some high-level connections in Burma, so decided to take advantage of these and was running a fishing boat business out of there (although I am based in Australia). Fishing in Burma can be very lucrative because the area is not overly fished … in fact, it's the only place where fish actually die of old age! The waters are teeming with lobsters, etc.

I hired a Russian crew to run the boat, and the results were hugely disappointing. Checking it out further, it wasn't long before I discovered the crew were selling off the catch and transferring the fish to other boats before returning to harbour, and swapping the remaining petrol in the tank for vodka. I finally stepped in, told them I knew their scam, and they were all fired. They were indignant.

"But why didn't you say something? This is the way we operate and you didn't say anything so we assumed it was OK!" I told Boris to take a long walk off a short pier.

If you have a good story about bribery or corruption in Asia, slip a brown paper envelope under the door or email The Editor at hardshipposting@hotmail.com or fax 612-9499-5908. Justice will be done!

❖ 4 ❖

Dirty Laundry or What
Did Your Last Slave Die Of?

True tales of drivers and maids in Asia.

How many expats does it take to open a beer? None. It should be open by the time the maid brings it!

But, of course, when making a request of your domestic servants politeness is of utmost importance. So the magic word must always be employed to ensure the required attention and result. What's the magic word, you say? "NOW!!!"

If you're lucky, you'll find someone in this great lottery of household help who really fits in and makes your home seem a better place for their presence. Dave is still smarting from the fact that Barb hired the oldest and ugliest maid on the agency's books, and he reckons it just doesn't fit his image of what his dream home in the tropics should be all about … the gentle padding and sing-song of some comely dusky maiden delivering another round of gins and tonic as he reclines on the day-bed in his palm-filled garden. Sure she's a great cook, tidies up really well, and basically manages the household, but he's secretly hoping that she might do a runner via the bathroom window in the dark of night so he can wheel in a suitable replacement of his choosing. Not to say that she looks like she's straight down from the trees, but the local zoo did express interest in using her face for a promotional poster.

Here's a tale with a twist you might enjoy. In 1941, the military commander of Penang, Malaya, ordered a secret night evacuation of all European women and children. When their maids woke up in the morning they found their 'mems' had deserted them. Is this the first case of the boss running away from their maid?

Still, things could always be worse for old Dave. In the days of the East India Company, each house had a gent called an *aubdar* – a servant who specialised in cooling drinks and perishables inside cylindrical pottery vessels. Later, ice clubs – for which one signed up – were formed, and ice was delivered instead of each house trying to make its own pits and blocks (which was only possible in the far north of India anyway). But the practice of houseboys has continued.

"Why is it that when you find yourself posted to places like India, the company you're working for always provides you with a houseboy to do your cleaning, laundry, and cooking," bemoaned a good friend of mine, an expat bachelor in India, recently. "What the hell am I going to do with a houseboy?" His repeated requests for a house girl were treated with a dismissive "Nice try."

But, domestic engineers, it cuts both ways as this cautionary tale of one of Barry's mates illustrates: the husband comes home from work one evening, frowning. "The business is not going well," he explains to his wife, indicating some cost-cutting and belt tightening needs to be done. "Perhaps if you learn to cook we could fire the maid," he explains.

"Yes, and perhaps if you learn to fuck," she says, "we could fire the driver."

Well, that sounds like the car being brought round to the front. Better go.

Colonel Ken

The boy next door

Recently arrived for a few years' stint in Jakarta a friend of mine, plus wife and daughter, moved into their beautiful new home. A few weeks into the rainy season his wife noticed water dripping through the ceiling. Her maid indicated that the houseboy in a nearby house was quite capable of sorting this out so he was duly summoned, went up into the roof space and eventually declared the problem fixed.

A few weeks later the same thing happened and once more the capable houseboy sorted it out. When he presented himself for payment on the third occasion X's wife quizzed him on the cause of the recurring problem.

"Bucket full, ma'am," came the honest and innocent reply.

Soap kitchen or toilet bowl?

We had guests coming to stay in Manila so I briefed the maid to put soap and towels in the guest bathroom. I came home, and thought I'd check everything before the guests arrived. The towels were in place, but I was a little taken aback to see a bowl of *soup* next to the washbasin!

Sleep-in beauty

A young couple that I have known for a number of years would party hard and really enjoy themselves. They had a large house with several Indonesian servants and maids who did all the cooking and cleaning.

After arriving back one night at around 3am, rather pissed, they messed about a bit and the husband stripped the wife naked on the couch in the lounge room (as you do!). He then went upstairs to get something (a toy perhaps?) but fell asleep on their bed.

The following morning at around 7am, the wife was suddenly woken up with the noise of the maid vacuuming the carpet by the couch.

"Good Morning, Ma'am," was the maid's cheery greeting, without batting an eyelid.

Hose monster

After two to three months, the new maid seemed to be working out OK, with only the average number of stuff-ups. One day, as I was late leaving for a meeting, I asked her to clean the oven because it was dirty. She gave me a puzzled look (which should have been a warning) but I ran out the door without waiting for objections.

Arriving home later that afternoon, I noticed a large pool of water accumulating in the living room carpet, coming from the direction of the kitchen. My ingenious maid, in an effort to save work, had dragged the high-pressure fire hose through the kitchen window, and was happily spraying hundreds of gallons of water into the defenceless appliance.

A salutary lesson in giving specific instructions.

Overdrive

He was not averse to spending the odd hour or three down in Itaewon, Seoul. However, his driver was an older guy and, most surprisingly for a driver or Korean for that matter, wanted to go home rather than earn overtime. This hanging around the 'Won had hairs on it and finally got just too much for him and so the driver hightailed it back to the house and knocked up (as in rang the door bell) the wife.

"Your husband's down in Itaewon and has all these girlfriends and they are sitting on his knee and he is buying them drinks and …"

When our hero eventually walked up the hill to his house in a foul mood, he walked straight into a wife in a fouler mood and a 'please explain'. The driver was relieved of his duties the next day.

Good old black magic

Visiting Borobudur in Indonesia we ran into a class of schoolgirls from, I think, the countryside of Indonesia where they hardly see any foreigners. This I say because the girls kept following me and wanted to take a picture of me. My good old driver however kept chasing them away. When I asked why we should not let the girls take a picture of me – and let me feel a bit like a movie star – he said, "Sir, if they take your picture they will also try to get some of your belonging like a piece of hair … with that they will then go to a witchdoctor and put a bad spell on you so that you come under their control."

A little bit far-fetched I thought. But what do you expect in a country where they bring their cars to the 'ketok magic' to have them repaired by wizardry.

Morning in-all-his glory

We had just moved to Jakarta, Indonesia, and had our first live-in maids – something that I had been able to avoid in HK and Malaysia as I considered it a loss of my privacy. One morning my wife decided to go for an early round of golf, so she hit the shower before I could get in there. As I was in a hurry I decided to take the guest bathroom and have my shower over there. As usual I came stark naked out of the shower to walk to the drawers to get some underwear when, all of a sudden, I heard a big scream and saw the *amah* storming down the stairs.

Apparently she used to clean the upper floors early in the morning. Not any more though.

Job's not over till the paperwork's done

The seat on our western toilet was broken so I sent the driver to the market to fetch a new one. Up the stairs came the driver, houseboy, and the guard to fix the seat. They did their work and I took it for a 'test drive'… the seat wobbled as it was sitting on a nozzle through the back (an Indian version of a bidet and toilet paper all in one, as there is not really any paper used except in an expat's house).

That just would not do, so 'sir' actually touched the toilet to fix it once and for all. The three servants watched as I pulled the nozzle out and made it fit. Then the house boy, who had for months been dumping out our wastebaskets with wads of dirty loo paper in them, asked: "But, sir, how ... ?"

I lost it and then asked him what he thought he was throwing out everyday knowing full well they all scavenged the garbage for anything we threw out. All I could get was a giggle out of him.

No guts, no glory

Khumar was a good kid. He was our houseboy in Bombay, and took care of all the cleaning, laundry, groceries, etc. On my way out the door one morning Khumar asked, "Sir, what would you like for dinner tonight?" I asked him to get some chicken, vegetables, and rice.

Returning home after a busy day flying out to the offshore oil rigs, I looked in the refrigerator, and saw that Khumar had in fact 'done the needful'. There, in a dark green plastic bag, was a chicken. Picking the bag up revealed that there was some serious weight to this bird. Opening the bag I removed the chicken, and called Khumar through to the kitchen. I thanked Khumar for having 'done the needful' and for having bought me a very good chicken for my evening meal. However I did mention – as I held the bird up by its neck – that next time, "No head, no neck, no feet, and please no guts."

I then showed Khumar how to clean, cut and quarter a chicken. I don't know if he ever got it or not.

Pudding on a brave face

In Singapore in the 60s we had a brilliant Chinese *amah* who was born into being an *amah* through a few generations. She was just 18 and my wife and I loved her and, especially, her cooking. One evening she said she had a surprise for us and, after the main course, she delivered her surprise: bread and butter pudding. My wife and I, not being English, could never stand the stuff, but she had specially learnt how to make this and wanted to please us so much so we slowly nibbled our way through it, half gagging in the process. She was made for better things in life, so my wife taught her shorthand, and eventually she got a job with a private firm in Hong Kong. We've never had bread and butter pudding since.

Pocket python

In Singapore I'd just got a maid for the first time and, a few days after her arrival, she called me urgently: "Sir, sir, there's a snake in here!" I hurried downstairs to handle the menacing beast and asked her where it was as she stepped back out of the way. She pointed to the tiled steps but still I could see nothing.

"Where is it?" I asked, thinking maybe it had slithered under a chair.

"There," she pointed, approaching cautiously. I looked and saw what appeared to be a worm of less than an inch long.

"It's just a worm." I laughed.

"No, no it's a snake," she insisted. I looked carefully. She was right: it was indeed a very small baby snake. But where it's mother was I never discovered!

Driven to drink

A friend of mine in Kuala Lumpur had what must have been the only chauffer-driven Mini Minor in the whole of Malaysia. Regularly on a Saturday night (or actually any night of the week for that matter) he'd go out on the town and get completely plastered. At the end of the night, you'd see some of the club's Malay staff pouring this guy into the back seat of the Mini, whereupon one of the staff – complete with crisp starched white uniform – would drive him home and make sure he got inside and safely out of harm's way.

Mamma mia!

In Manila, I came home to an apartment reeking of garlic. I thought we must be having Italian for dinner, but nothing was cooking in the kitchen. I then noticed my maid had spread garlic all over the place.

"What the hell's going on here?" I asked.

"Bum fire vut, sir." Excuse me? "Bum fire vut," she repeated. Turns out a large vampire bat had got in through a window earlier and she was trying to ward the thing off.

All for chauffer

Growing up in the 'old days' in India, I remember my father had two drivers … one a 'real' driver, and his cousin who was the 'assistant' driver. They did nothing but polish the car from morning till night. My father used to drive, with them sitting in the back – I never quite understood that.

Rules maid to be broken

A British woman was banned from the Singapore Cricket Club for life after bringing her Sri Lankan maid in to the club to look after her children while they dined in the only child-friendly section of the club. Her husband, who wasn't even in the country at the time, was banned for six months.

Made in Singapore

In Singapore our maid had no days off. It was not a little suspicious then that she got pregnant. I mentioned this to my husband, who vehemently denied any such involvement. However, the maid confessed to their illicit dealings. Incensed, I beat my husband with a tennis racquet, smashing it into several pieces.

Not wanting to lose the expensive bond required by the government, we arranged for the maid (who was Indonesian) to go to the neighbouring Indonesian island of Batam to have the baby. From there, she flew to meet me in the Philippines (my home country) where the baby was adopted by me as my own child, and I then took it to Singapore to give it a home and a future.

My husband has subsequently moved on his own to Indonesia.

Here's one for you …

Looking forward to a RAAF posting to Jakarta with my darling Irish wife, and being a dab hand with the Indonesian language myself, I arranged some basic language training for her so she could communicate with the domestic staff and the like when we arrived in-country.

Naturally, during the settling-in period after we arrived, I helped her communicate and acted as an interpreter between her good self and the cook. After a couple of weeks, she came and told me we were running out of fruit and veggies and asked me to send the cook off to the market and restock.

"No!" I said. "It's time you had a go on your own – if you can't remember the words, draw pictures or show her the cook book … show her a carrot or a banana or whatever you want, you have to learn to communicate." I stood back and mirthfully watched a mini stage production as she held up a banana.

"*Ini*," she said, pointing to the banana.

"Yes, mem … *pisang*," said the cook. This went on for several fruits and vegetables and, when my wife couldn't show the cook a potato, she showed her a picture of one in a cookbook.

Armed with sufficient rupiah and her little message book, our confident cook headed off in a pedicab to the Blok M markets and returned about an hour later with our awaited logistics re-supply.

My wife went into the kitchen to check that she hadn't forgotten anything as the beaming cook unpacked the plastic bags. No, she hadn't forgotten one single thing as she produced *one* banana, *one* onion, *one* potato, *one* tomato and *one* of everything else my dear wife ordered.

    We ate out that night!

If you have a good story about drivers or maids in Asia, email The Editor at hardshipposting@hotmail.com or fax 612-9499-5908. We'll dust if off for you, check under the hood, and polish it to perfection.

❖ 5 ❖

Moving the Goalposts
or a Swing and a Miss

True tales of golf, soccer, and buzkashi in Asia.

It's been all go around my place as usual, what with my new-found lust object keeping me on my toes (and me, in turn, keeping her on her back). The cheeky little minx says I have the body of a God ... Buddha! That gets her a good spanking every time. But secretly, weight watchers, I've been doing laps of the spa and have also taken up meditation ... well, it beats sitting around doing nothing all day.

I know a few blokes at the local Hash club who often quote the Saunterers' prayer: 'Please, Lord, that this day I do not work up a sweat. Amen'. That'll do me. Or my other personal motto on fitness: 'No pain, er, no pain'.

But I don't mind the odd game of golf. In fact played quite a bit in the Philippines recently at – get this – the Whack Whack Golf Club in Manila. I kid you not. Which reminds me: what's the difference between golf and sky-diving? In golf, you go 'WHACK ... aah fuck!' and in skydiving you go 'Aah fuck ... WHACK!' I also played in the Park Hotel Classic tournament. I expected to see Tiger Woods there, but no, afraid of the competition appar-ently. And Foxy's tournament is a must-play on the professional circuit. Of course it's important to go and select your umbrella girl (or girls!) from Foxy's bar the night before. Suddenly Pro-Am takes on a whole new mean-ing. I also played in one of the most unique settings in the world ... Corregidor Island, Macarthur's headquarters in the Second Big One, which has had a golf course since 1920. You can't fail to get a hole-in-one there ... there's a bomb crater every 20 yards.

In anticipation of all this activity I went and checked out a new set of clubs, with a graphite shaft and the biggest bloody club heads you've ever seen in your life, NASA-approved, laser-guided and a money-back guarantee that you would be driving 500 metres with just half the swing. Hah! What do they think I am – gullible? So I bought them, and I'm pleased to report that I can now hit twice as deep into that grove of trees on the left than I've ever been able to achieve before. Of course, one of the other universal laws of this God-forsaken game is that the quality of the shot, and the distance travelled by the ball, is inversely related to the amount of people standing in the gallery behind you. I tell you what, I spent more time in the bunkers than Saddam and Osama combined.

But look at it this way – a bad day on the golf course beats a good day in the office. Some of the other interesting courses I can recommend (mainly because they've got less than 18 holes!) are the one at Napier Road in Singapore, which has only seven holes and was, I believe, built by the British occupants of the Ministry of Defence building behind it, and the six-hole course in Taichung, Taiwan, on top of the hill near the cemetery. I can understand why so many people keeled over there … that hill's a bugger. Still, as I've always said, you can't beat a good three-holer.

About the most remote course I've played on, and it must surely rank as the most far-flung championship course in the whole world, is at Kuala Kencanna, Papua. This damn thing was designed by Ben Crenshaw. Whether he actually went out to the site I don't actually know. But there's this great big course, fitted out to host the cream of the world's players. And who gets to use it? Only the executives of the nearby Freeport mine, and their hacking-wind-milling-slicing-cussing guests. Like me.

Actually, it's a good thing I'm a crap golfer. When Dave was in Japan I played a round with him (you will notice that 'a round' is not one word) and root-me-boot and polish-me-bumhole if one of the guys in our group didn't get a fabled hole-in-one. However, his joy was short-lived, as he hadn't taken out – wait for it – hole-in-one insurance. For a start it means a generous tip for the caddy to witness it and apply his much-valued signature to your card. Then it's gifts for the partners in your flight, and their families, to share the luck around. Then this club also insisted he buy a tree and a plaque to commemorate the great event. (Absolute fluke if you ask me, and that's not just sour grapes!) Then, of course, card behind the bar and drinks all round at the clubhouse, at which point my game really picked up. By the time we dragged our whiskey-pickled carcasses home that night, this poor bugger – I don't remember his name but can't forget the befuddled look on his face – was down about US$3,000 for his triumphant ordeal.

Oh, one of the things I learned that hot and steamy day was that Mizuno, one of Japan's big sportswear companies, have launched some undies specially designed to keep your undercarriage cool. It's called Icetouch, and apparently weighs in at a massive one degree cooler than your good old-fashioned cotton y-fronts (and about 45 degrees cooler than having some steaming *geisha* girl on your lap). I haven't tried them but they reckon they're the best thing since sliced golf shots.

On the subject of ice: ice, gin and tonics. Gin and tonics, Raj. Those chaps in India were actually responsible for inventing a whole bunch of sports, which goes to show what can happen when a) the TV's crap b) the local birds are not too shaggable unless c) you've got the beer goggles on.

Firstly bedminton, sorry, badminton. This was first played in Gloucestershire, England, in the mid 19th century, but it took the quinine-loaded British Army officers in India to give it rules, and they then re-introduced it to Britain in the 1870s. Since then, the Indonesians seem to have claimed it as their game and dominate world competitions.

The next game to come from the Raj was polo. By the way did you hear about the Irish water polo team? Their horses drowned. Polo was cradled in Persia and is, I reckon, an evolution of the Afghani national sport, *buzkashi*, which goes back to the days of Genghis Ken, er, Khan. For those who've never been to the Kabul Buzkashi 7s tournament, this is how it's played: it's a bit like rugby, except it's played on horseback. And the ball is a gutted and decapitated goat. In Genghis' day, prisoners were often substituted for goats. Anyway, the game of polo somehow evolved out of that and spread to India where it was revived and popularised by British officers once again, who in turn spread it and its plummy-mouthed supporters around the world.

Not content to leave well enough alone, two Brits dreamed up the idea of elephant polo, strangely enough while enjoying a couple of cold ones in St Moritz in 1982. James Manclark was there at the time representing Britain in the Olympic bobsled event, and his good pal Jim Edwards had come across from Nepal to support him. Manclark learned that Edwards had some elephants at his Tree Tops resort in the mountains of Nepal. "It's time your elephants learnt how to play polo," he joked. They giggled about this idea for a while, put it down to the beer talking, and no more was said about it. Until a telex arrived in Nepal saying: "Arriving April 1 with long sticks – have elephants ready." The date was a bit suspicious, a sure sign of a set-up but, sure enough, the perpetually-grinning Manclark turned up with the long sticks as promised, and a couple of soccer balls tucked under his arm. The first game was duly set in motion at Chitwan National Park, and the pacing pachyderms wasted no time in popping the soccer balls. Fortunately, some regulation polo balls were on hand, and the game continued. It was declared a success, and the World Elephant Polo Association came into being.

They now play three times a year: in Nepal, Sri Lanka (at Taprobane, which is home to my good friend Geoffrey Dobbs), and in Thailand. The game I witnessed at Hua Hin was quite a spectacle, the field dotted with village-style marquees, and gin and tonics aplenty. The rules are quite simple: four elephants per team, no elephant is allowed to lie down in the goalmouth, and others that are "often made up on the spot with a bit of spontaneous consultation". Two umpires on a suitably-caparisoned tusker presided over the affair. I recognised one as a high profile bar owner from Bangkok, so a bit of backroom payola was always going to be on the cards. But they tell me most of the glad-handing and politicking is aimed at getting the *mahouts* on side. The mahouts are the ones who actually steer the lumbering lumps of lard. However, they speak next to no English, so novices often resort to writing out the phonetic translation for instructions such as 'left', 'right', 'go', 'stop' and 'aah, shit' on their white *jodphur* trouser legs for quick reference in the heat of battle.

Not that the battle gets too heated, mind you. It's possible for an elephant to make a break mid-field, at which point you can retire to the bar, refresh your gin and tonic, and still make it back to your seat in time to see the resulting goal get scored.

Most of the entertainment comes from the peripheral action: 'ball girls' who rush out carrying a wicker basket to clear up the steaming piles of contempt left by the marauding mammoths. And the half-time hooter damn near gave me a heart attack … a giant Thai-style gong which was struck with some force right behind me. At half time the teams change elephants to ensure no side has an unfair advantage by virtue of their corpulent chariots.

Now, pool hustlers, take a seat: snooker was also invented by the

British Army in India. Sir Neville Chambermaid is said to have played it in India as far back as 1875, although it took our English friends back home over thirty years to latch onto it.

Another game invented by beer-fuelled bored expats was the Shanghai Paper Chase. Around 1865, when Britain controlled some parts of China, a pack of foreigners jumped on their horses, and chased after some bugger who had set a trail, much like the old public schoolboy game of Hare and Hounds. However, in the excitement, the bombastic Brits often went far beyond the borders of their settlement. The Chinese complained about this trespassing which, of course, the Brits duly ignored. Until the Chinese ordered them finally and officially to stop this madness. In 1929, the Shanghai Paper Chase was no more.

Asia has been a hotbed of sports invention by locals as well. Sumo wrestling, of course, started in Japan when traditional villages used to send their biggest and fattest out to wrestle in annual inter-village competitions. The site of these human blubber-whales dressed in Huggies diapers with all the grace and athleticism of a pregnant hippopotamus proved to be highly amusing for the locals who then demanded these contests become regular events. And promising career paths for Fat Bastards suddenly emerged. Although the expression 'Who ate all the tuna sushi?' doesn't quite have the same ring.

And here's a slap in the face for the Poms. Soccer football was invented by the Chinese – who called it *cuju* – in the Han Dynasty between 206 BC and 220 AD (with, presumably, a break for oranges at half time). It died out in the Qing Dynasty (early 1900s for the historically-challenged – truth be known, goal scorers, I had to look that one up myself) when the game it gave birth to, soccer as we know it today, took over as the predominant form. The great stadium-raising chant of 'Ole, ole, ole …' was also invented by the Chinese. They were trying to sing 'Hooray! Hooray! Hooray …'

Soccer was introduced to Burma way back in 1878 by George Scott. He got a team together from St Johns College and they lined up against a crew from Moulmein. The Burmese showed a natural ability for the game because they played the game *chinlon*, which uses the head and feet like *sepak thakraw* (which in turn is like volleyball using a hollow rattan ball).

Did any of you go out to the game, The World Crap I called it, organised by a Dutchman during the last soccer World Cup that pitted the two worst teams in the world together. Bhutan started as favourites as they were ranked 202nd in the world according to FIFA, and they were up against Montserrat, some lava-spewing Caribbean island, ranked last at 203rd in the world. Bhutan also had the home-ground advantage of playing in their hallowed Changlimithang Stadium, which brought the sea-level Montserattians to their knees with high-altitude exhaustion. Bhutan handed out a 4-0 hiding.

And, so, to Ping Pong. In an ironic twist, this game was conceived, invented and developed by the English in England. The Chinese call it Table Tennis.

Colonel Ken

Loo-ser!

At the Manila 10s one gent from Hong Kong was in full mufti, with team blazer, etc. After several beers he decided to go to the Port-a-loo. That was our cue to lift the whole damn thing – with him inside – into the middle of the field and set it down. With his wild thrashing and frantic attempts to escape, the Port-a-loo tipped over, and he emerged from the capsised cubicle in his smart blazer and absolutely swimming in blue-coloured swill to the biggest cheer of the weekend.

Ripping yarns

A golf day had been arranged by our cricket club, and I was a guest at the Sentosa Golf Club, Singapore. Not being a regular golfer I didn't have all the correct gear, but presumed a nice smart casual short-sleeved shirt would do. As we were about to tee off, a course official came across to me.

"No, no … you cannot play in that shirt," he barked.

"Why ever not, kind sir?" I enquired.

"Must be proper golfing shirt with three buttons."

I'd never heard such poppycock. "Only three buttons? But this is a very smart shirt…"

"No, sir, it must be a three-buttoned shirt."

One of the larrikins in our group could see this going nowhere, so came up to me and – RRRIIIIIPPPPPP!!! – tore the short open, leaving just three buttons in place. Amazingly, that satisfied the official and we commenced play.

In the drink

We had a dragon-boating team in Singapore, and used to train most Saturday afternoons. One of our team was leaving, so we decided we'd have a training with a difference: we rowed from the Kallang River out and back into the old harbour, past the Merlion and into the Singapore River to Boat Quay. Good spirits, wind behind us. Imagine people's surprise at this vision of 22 sweating Aussies in Speedos pulling up on the steps outside Harry's Bar, getting out of the boat, chugging as many jugs as we could in a very limited time, then back onto the river and out to sea again. A surrealistic vision!

The row back was dreadful – the booze hit our dehydrated bodies quick and hard. The tide was coming in and the wind was now against us. It took forever to get back to the launch point where our usual beer supplies awaited us, after which we felt no pain.

Liquid gold

In the expat division of the Singapore Invitational Dragon Boat championships, most countries managed to fill one boat and enter into the race … a motley crew along for a few laughs and a few beers, albeit with a little bit of international/patriotic competitiveness. One year, the Singapore Australia Business Council had three boats entered. The 'A' team was seriously after gold (a proud tradition by this point). Training was stepped up to twice a week and it was serious. Come race day, imagine their disgust at us (pot-bellied fellow countrymen that didn't give a shit) beating them by a whisker to get the gold medal. It took a lot of Foster's to get the glum looks off the 'A' team's faces afterwards!

Playing off the ladies tee

We made an annual pilgrimage from Korea to the Philippines to play golf (honestly!). Naturally in the evenings we went in search of sustenance and beer and, although there used to be about sixteen of us, inevitably the group fractured in stages during the evening. On this particular evening one of the party was invited to an on-on by some of the girls. Thinking all his Christmases had come at once he jumped at the idea and, after a torturous taxi drive, arrived at a seedy establishment positively bristling with nubile women. What he did find, however, was that they were all smoking some sort of sweet cigarettes and, more particularly – before he had time for any more in-depth research – was the arrival of a contingent of the Manila SWAT team.

Told to sit and be quiet, he watched as all the lovelies were bundled off into a paddy wagon and he wondered what would become of him. In the end it was his turn and he strongly protested his innocence. "Yes, I know," said the senior officer, "you can go home now," now being about 7am.

Only one problem: our hero had no idea where he was and, of more importance, tee-off was in half an hour. Thereupon he persuaded the police to drive him to the golf course and, as we were milling around wondering what the hell he had got up to the night before, he arrived at the first tee in a police car, complete with siren and flashing lights.

You couldn't beat that for an entrance, but his golf was pretty dreadful.

Off the rails

Covering the winter Olympics in Nakano, Japan, our TV broadcast was relying on a video feed from a Japanese station, supplied without commentary so we had to put our own commentary in. We covered some very obscure sports and contestants and had no idea who the various people were that the cameras kept zooming in to. Initially we tried our best, but it all fell apart when the producer starting feeding completely fictitious info about what/who we were watching to the commentator. "And that's Lars Sorenson, four-time luge champion," he'd say at the mere sight of a Swedish uniform. From there it just got worse. "And here come the remarkable German Hans Oppenheimer, who broke his leg in five places last year, and still has the steel pins in his knee, making an incredible comeback ..." our commentator would deadpan. We were howling with laughter in the control room, knowing that the audience watching would have no better idea anyway.

Running joke

Playing cricket for United World College in Singapore, I managed to score a career-best of 86 runs. Over the next few weeks, I started receiving postcards mailed from Malaysia, Thailand, Indonesia, etc, saying 'congratulations,' etc, and signed by international cricketing luminaries. I never found out from whom.

Burning sensation

In Calcutta, India was playing Australia at cricket. Nearing the end of the match, it got really scary as the crowd size swelled and they sensed a victory. Two-way slanging was going on but we were hopelessly outnumbered. We were even pelted with bags of curry (at least I hope it was curry!). Police moved in to separate us. At the final victory, the Indian fans lit up newspapers and whatever they could burn and wave around. Some of the Indian national team even gave us the one-fingered salute as they did their lap of honour. The smoke was overwhelming, and it took us literally hours to get out of the stadium afterwards through the crush of the crowd.

Action-packed day

Back in 1975 I lived in Jakarta and four of us (colleagues and fellow Scandihooligans) played golf at Senayan every Saturday morning. I was definitely a beginner. On the first hole I had an OK tee-off. It was a par four with a dog-leg to the left. I did not have a clear second shot to the green as there were some trees in front of me. I took out the five-iron and had a fantastic hit. The ball hit a tree and ricocheted back and hit my friend's caddie in the middle of his chest. We carried him off, got a taxi, gave the taxi driver some money and asked him to take him to the local hospital.

On the fifth hole I hit a very low, ugly shot. A hen and her five small chickens were crossing the fairway. The ball hit the hen, unfortunately killing it. On the 17th I shanked the ball and it hit a Japanese gentleman, who was on his last putt of the day, in the neck. I went down to apologise and he said to me: "This is not the way we play in my country!"

He wanted to fight me but my friend (a big Norwegian) stepped in, lifted the poor chap up, and said: "Fuck off you little Nip!"

I met a guy from the Norwegian embassy later in the day and asked him if he ever thought of playing golf. He said yes, and got my golf-set free of charge. I swore never to take up golf again.

Social circuit

Earlier this year, I found myself in Vientiane, Laos. Being a competitive long-distance runner I set off around Vientiane at a fast pace. I usually always run sans shirt, so you can imagine how noticeable a lily-white American man running fast through the streets of Vientiane would be. The great thing about Laos is that everyone just looks at me, smiles, waves, and says hello. After about an hour of running through the streets, I headed back towards my hotel, but first I wanted to stop off at the brand new Olympic-style rubberised track and finish off with a quick mile [Often do the same thing myself! – Col Ken]. I jump onto the first lane and notice what appears to be the Lao national track team hard at practice. So I hit the starting line and coast through lap one in a respectable 71 seconds [Nothing special, pal. I do the 100 metres in about that time as well – Col Ken]. Two of the male runners on the team notice this and, not to be outdone, they take off after me. One of the gents is toast after about 200 metres at this pace, so he waits for me to come around again.

Now the Lao national runners are feeling the heat: they have to 'save face'. So while I run the curve of the track, another runner cuts across the end of the football pitch and runs the straight, staying in front of me. He just has to stay in front somehow. By the 1200 metre mark, three runners on the Lao team are determined to stay with me for at least a lap, and they are sounding like a steam train going over a high mountain pass: HUFF!!! HUFF!!! HUFF!!! HUFF!!! I am feeling the heat, too, but laughing inside myself, then finish in a good time before I do my sit-ups and push-ups.

Afterwards, I spoke with the runners in my halting Thai/Lao-glish. The Lao runners are now my best friends in Laos, and I run with them and take them out to eat when I am in Laos.

Friend or faux pas?

After the HK Rugby 7s one year, we were helping the victorious Fiji rugby team with logistics on their departure. The guys were standing outside the Hilton Hotel as their bags were being loaded into the baggage truck. A Chinese guy was picking up suitcases and literally throwing them up into the back of the vehicle, which a player took exception to. So he leant across, grabbed the Chinese baggage guy, and tossed him on to the top of the pile in the back of the van! Much loss of face and protesting.

Then once we got to the airport, another of the players had bought a very expensive racing bike but was told he had to check it in. "That's not hand carry, sir."

"Yes it is!" he protested, lifting the racing bike off the ground with just his little finger.

Not taking it lying down

In Bali, we went to the Royal Bali Golf Club at Nusa Dua. Being keen golfers, I had even bought my own clubs. The green fees for a round? US$180. Picking my jaw back off the floor, I mentioned that my wife wouldn't be playing – I was the only player – but she would accompany me in the golf cart. A further US$20. Furthermore, the attendant told me – with clouds building in the distance as it was the shoulder monsoon season – all of this was non-refundable as soon as I hit my first ball off the first tee. Now I know why they call it the 'pro' shop.

Off the beaten track

We were at Phnom Penh Airport to welcome the participants in Cambodia's first Annual International Street Championship Go Kart Race. There were bound to be a few teething problems but, while the visitors were being given a heroes' welcome, the full enormity of these problems was only just being realised by the event's co-ordinator, a foreigner.

The go karts had been loaded in Bangkok and the plane was supposed to travel directly to Phnom Penh where the Cambodian customs officials had been fully briefed. However, as often happens in Asia, the plane made an unscheduled detour to Siem Reap where the customs officials had certainly not been briefed, and were rather taken aback by the sight of a hold full of rather large, suspicious looking packages. They promptly impounded them on the spot.

After an hour of intense pleading and bargaining failed to get the machines released, the plane took off for Phnom Penh: with the team, but minus the karts. Several frantic phone calls between the co-ordinator and the customs department in Siem Reap finally resulted in the release of the karts which arrived in Phnom Penh at six o'clock that night, and were immediately locked up in the customs store while the staff went off home.

A whole day had been lost which should have been spent assembling the vehicles and practising on the unfamiliar track. There was no option but to retire to their hotel and console ourselves with several glasses of strong drink.

Next day the karts were finally released by customs and delivered to the workshop where they were assembled in record time. However an entire day's valuable practice had been lost, then we were swamped by a torrential tropical downpour … just what we needed!

While race day dawned bright and shiny, it was a day of trial and tribulations as drivers came to grief on the unfamiliar track. The first official weigh-in of the day (which actually should have been happening at the end of each race all through the morning), revealed that some of the contestants who'd been performing well during the earlier part of the day had been taking liberties with the truth about their real weight.

The best entertainment was during the lunch break, when the track was taken over by a contingent of local *cyclo* drivers who actually did quite well for their efforts, the winning driver receiving fifty dollars.

After that day, watching Formula One will never compare for thrills and spills.

Who bares wins

In Manila our annual golf tournament has some special rules attached to it. For a start, any drive that doesn't go past the ladies tee results in the removal of one article of clothing. The second hole tee-off had to be taken with a running shot, ie, run up and hit the ball on the move. The 17th hole had to be played by your caddie, and so on. I have a great photo of one poor hacker lining up a shot with the historical Manila Hotel in the background. He is stark-bollock naked, apart from his golf spikes!

And the winner is ...

My son set up an invitational golf tournament in the Philippines to be held annually. Logos, caps, t-shirts were all designed and produced for the event, along with a beautiful trophy. As he had organised and sponsored the event, he thought it was only fair that he should win it, too ... so had his name engraved on the trophy as the winner for the first 10 years.

A day at the maul

The Manila Rugby 10s were on and it was decided to take some young Filipino guys to the game and see if we could get some interest in the sport at a local level. After watching the teams thrash each other about the field, with some spectacular moves and good solid tackles, at the end of the day we asked the guys if they were interested in playing.

"We enjoyed watching it," they said, "but if someone do like that to me on the field I follow them home after the game and shoot them."

Ugly behaviour

Playing in the Golden Oldies rugby once – which is a huge piss-up and the odd game of what is supposed to be almost non-contact rugby – we had a 77-year-old playing on the wing for our team. In one game against some Americans, they buried him, breaking his collarbone.

"You dumb American pricks," I remonstrated, this is supposed to be fun, non-competitive ... but if you wanna play hard we'll fucking tear you apart." I pointed to our very large and exceptionally ugly line-up of Australian forwards. They chose the 'friendly' course after that.

A big hole in his story

There were three holes-in-one I have witnessed in Asia, all in the Philippines as it happens. The first was an almighty shank that swerved off, hit a palm tree and bounced back into the centre and down the hole. The second: the guy over-hits it and it skidded along the ground, did a 'dam-busters' across the water and continued to roll till it went down the hole. The third: the guy hit his tee shot and it went straight into the lake.

"Fuck it, I'm having another go," he said, putting a new ball down and hitting it straight down the hole. "I got a hole in one, I GOT A HOLE IN ONE!" he screamed.

"No, you got a good par," we corrected him, as the course did not officially recognise the second shot. Pissed off, he made his own trophy and mounted his ball, and was carrying it around the bars that night, triumphantly.

"I got a hole in one!" he was telling anyone within earshot.

"No, you got a good par …" and so on till sunrise.

Losing face

I was getting on a plane in Bali when I saw this huge guy – big in every dimension – boarding. His face was black and blue and he had at least 15 stitches down the right side of his face. It looked like he'd been jumped by a gang of locals with an iron bar. Curiosity got the better of me.

"What the fuck happened to you?" I asked.

"Bali 10's," he replied through gritted teeth, referring to the not-so-serious rugby tournament. "Don't make me laugh," he said, explaining that he most feared his Chinese wife's reaction … she didn't fully understand this game that he played for fun.

Boot camp

Living in Aceh, Indonesia, in the period 1976-78 there was a lot of political trouble and gang/bandit activity. For our regular Hash runs in the countryside we had to be accompanied by military guards from the local refinery, and these poor buggers had to run with us in full army fatigues, boots and M-16s.

Levelling the playing field

My wife, a very sexy woman, looks Filipina but is actually Dutch. She entered this golf tournament at this really stuffy golf club in the Philippines. The regulars (old ladies, mainly westerners) gasped in horror as she emerged from the change room in the tight figure-hugging shorts she plays in. The organisers promptly told her she was in breach of dress regulations. She went and changed, and then they found another reason why she was in breach. Basically, the old bags didn't want her playing no matter what.

Just then this wrinkly old 80-year-old man called her across and took her into the men's change room. "Here, try these on," he said. His shorts, shirts, etc, fitted her fine. The organizers OK'd her dress as appropriate. Heading to the tee, she could see the old bugger cackling mischievously before flipping the bird at the outraged older members.

The final *coup de grace* that silenced them was her first tee shot, which she smacked a mile straight down the middle of the fairway.

Border dispute

In Papua New Guinea, the Australian Rugby League is well followed by locals and expats alike. When Queensland play New South Wales, in the State of Origin clash (which many locals think is the 'State of Oranges'), they develop fierce loyalty for one side or the other. Every year, five or 10 people will be killed depending on the outcome of the game. But it seems to be improving: this year only one person died … a local lady stabbed her husband for supporting Queensland.

Replacing the body fluids

The team had just been knocked out of the Manila 10s rugby tournament, after three or four gruelling games in sweltering 33-degree heat. As part of the post-game ritual, the captain took off his sweaty, sand-caked jockstrap and wrung it out into a large jug of Pimms, which the whole team then drunk heartily from.

Good clean fun

We had a soccer tour of Chiangmai, and one of our players was a hulking great guy from Sweden. All the local girls loved him, screaming each time he got the ball. It was pouring with rain and the field was a mud bath. Afterwards we all stunk to high heaven, being caked in mud, sweat and beers. Four of his instant cheer squad said: "We come to your loom." They took him back, and steamed and creamed and reamed and beamed him till he was shining in parts that hadn't shone for years. And not a cent changed hands.

Walking the plank

At United World College in Singapore, our cricket club was very social and matches would end up with a jolly good replenishment of fluids lost to the heat of the day. One of our favourite party tricks, with our own players as well as visitors, was to do the 'sightscreen walk' at night in which players – already slightly sozzled – were blindfolded in front of the sightscreen at one end of the field, spun around about ten times, then pointed at the field and had to walk till they made it to the sightscreen at the other end.

Hours of fun watching guys heading off into the bushes, into drainage ditches or simply going in circles and ellipses all over the field. In my time, only one gent ever made it successfully. He was obviously *really* drunk!

A real ear-bashing

A group of us from Hong Kong had gone on a 'golf trip to China' but – due to shoddy travel agency arrangements – ended up in Angeles City, Philippines, instead. Mt Pinatubo chose that exact time to explode and, with all flights cancelled, we were stranded indefinitely in the Philippines. One by one we had to call our wives and explain. I held the earpiece along way away from my ear!

Looking the part

In Singapore we used to field a pretty handy cricket team each Saturday. We once had a visiting team from the Australian navy who wanted to give us a game. Come the day, we all turned up in our cricket whites, warming up, and generally being the professional outfit we liked to think we were. Fashionably late, the navy team turned up … wearing shorts and t-shirts, rubber sandals, unshaven, with four of them lugging the biggest icebox of beer you've ever seen in your life. Those who weren't carrying it each had a can of VB already in their hands. They thrashed us soundly!

Gorilla tactics

Playing with the Hong Kong Police team in the Manila 10s tournament, we were so happy to have qualified in the main competition for the first time, we did something special to remember. Arriving early on the morning of the final day, the heat was already way over the 30-degree Celsius mark and we were badly hung over. However, that was the least of our problems because we had arranged to play the whole game in full gorilla suits!

By the end of the game, we were absolutely spent and damn near dead from perspiration and dehydration. It took more than a few San Miguels to bring us back to life.

If you have a good story about sports in Asia, email The Editor at hard-shipposting@hotmail.com or fax 612-9499-5908. The ball's in your court.

❖ 6 ❖

Are We There Yet?
or Wish You Weren't Here!

*True tales from holidaymakers, travellers
and backpackers in Asia.*

My good friend Noel Coward used to say: "Vacation time again. Two weeks devoted to discovering places you should stay away from next year." I suspect he said that because the travel expression from the 18th century "Well fucked and far from home" was already taken. I believe it was JRR Tolkien – you might remember him from Dallas, you know 'Who shot JRR?' – who said: "All who travel are not lost." Pig's trotters. Name me one person who hasn't at some time in a new place had to resort to looking at the map, looking up at the street names, looking back at the map, turning it around, holding it up the other way now, looking around for landmark buildings … and then asking a passer-by for help. My big travel tip to you young adventurers is to grab a trusty twatlas before hitting the road: that's a local interpreter who doubles as a tour guide, and happens to be, as luck would invariably have it, female and below twenty five.

In the good old days, you hardly needed a map as the hippie trail was so well worn. The Dope and Dysentery Trail we used to call it back then, which took you from Australia through Dili, Malaysia, Sri Lanka, India and Afghanistan. My, it's a different world today. You see, even Bali was only just getting on the map back then. An American surfie (and, some say, CIA agent) Robert Coke (yes, yes, knowing winks all round) set up some thatched huts on Kuta Beach in the 1930s, but it was a while before it became the quintessential pilgrimage destination for rock stars and end-of-season Australian football tours.

Holy smoke there were some industrial quantities of jazz tobacco inhaled back then in the great search for Nirvana (who, Pete tells me, were only finally discovered in Seattle in the 90s. Kurt Kerblam, I think he said the young gentleman's name was). Speaking of nirvana, one of the biggest con jobs of all time has got to be the whole concept of Shangri-la developed by James Hilton. He was the armchair traveller who wrote The Lost Horizon, a book about utopia. Hilton himself never went to China, where it was believed to be set. But he had read a National Pornographic, er, Geographic magazine about Zhongdian in Bhutan, which was then the verdant snow-capped playground of Austrian-American explorer Joseph Rock. This place, in reality these days, is not much more than a bunch of yaks, burning incense and lung-busting dust. However, the Chinese have laid claim to it as the place in question and have officially changed its name to Shangri-La (or *Xiang Ge Li La* in local parlance). They obviously believe the magic's all in the name.

And there can be a lot in a name. As many of the names of places around Asia attest, sex seems ready to rear its ugly purple head at a moment's notice. Take Bangkok. Bangalore. Battembang (pronounced 'bottom bang'). Lae (pronounced 'lay'). Johore. Mount Kumgang in North Korea. Bangi-dong near Seoul. Bai Bang in Vietnam. Fak Fak (pronounced with a flat 'a') in Irian Jaya. And my all time favourite in Luzon, Philippines: Sexmoan. Check the map, flat-earthers, there it is!

A funny thing happened when I was travelling in Laos recently. Just outside Luang Prabang, my local guide – the aforementioned twatlas – said: "Mount pussy?"

"Sure," I said, "I thought you'd never ask. It'd beat the hell out of climbing that damn hill." There was a moment's silence while she gathered her thoughts, explaining to me that actually the name of the hill we were looking at was Mount Phoussi.

Over in Vietnam I bumped into a lot of fellow Vets, coming back for an up-close refresher course on what used to be alternately our battlefield and playground. Often simultaneously on the same day. So there's a lot of mixed emotions tied up in that little jaunt back. "It's hell to be here, but it's the only way I can work this thing out," said one Vet, quoted in my good friend Christopher Hunt's book, Sparring With Charlie.

The locals are big travellers within Vietnam these days. Half a million per year visit the Perfume Pagoda, most of them seemingly at the same time as I was there; the lunar (actually 'loony' describes it better) New Year. If you haven't seen it, it's a series of Buddhist temples built dramatically into some limestone cliffs. Being Vietnam, or being in Asia for that matter, it wasn't long before the unmistakable pheromone of money was in the air and, bugger me, if no fewer than 40 fake temples had sprung up along the way to the real thing, hoping to dupe people into believing it's the real Perfume Pagoda. Of course, they had their buckets set up out front for 'religious donations' and coined a pretty penny before some spoilsport official closed them all down and ran them out of town.

If you want to see something more kitsch than a fake temple, Shenzen's where you want to be. This city in southern China must have been struggling for an attraction, so someone came up with the idea: "Aha! – (pause for light bulb to illuminate above head) – I've got it … Minsk World." Now, dear readers, Minsk World is a military theme park centred on an old Soviet aircraft carrier. Why didn't I think of that? Then there's Window on the World: spread out before you are the Sydney Opera House, Eiffel Tower, Bangkok's Grand Palace, and Buckingham Palace just to name a few. With some crafty camera angles, you could fool your friends into believing you've seen all these places in person.

On that subject, why is it that we don't have America Town or England Town in Chinese cities?

One place you won't find represented in Minsk World is Pyongyang, North Korea. Probably because no paper mache re-creation would do it justice – it would be hard to capture that exact shade of grey. So the Chinese have to go there to see it for themselves to remember exactly how bad communism was. Each year 100,000 Chinese hand over their hard-earned Renminbi to see Pyongyang. I wouldn't say it's poor and cheap and nasty but even the cockroaches have formed a picket line, and no more than 2,000 westerners form the elite corps of people they call 'tourists' in North Korea.

There are only about half a dozen hotels I'd let my dog sleep in, let alone myself. Only one of these has cable TV so make sure you book far in advance if your visit coincides with a major sports event. Sadly, their ambitious plan to build one of the world's largest hotels didn't get off the ground. I lie. Actually it did, but not very high, before they ran out of money in the early 90s. It was supposed to be 105 storeys tall, in the shape of a pyramid, housing 3,000 rooms. The empty triangle now stands as a forlorn reminder: don't be a dreamer! Or, if you want to be a dreamer, be a capitalist. A couple of little travel tips to finish up on North Korea with. Don't take your mobile phone in with you, that'll probably be taken along with your video camera at the airport. Fear not, you'll get a little tag identifying you as the rightful owner, and – if that counter's open on the day – you'll be able to claim it on your way out. Of course your Wheezer and Bastardcard aren't worth a pinch of proverbial poo.

Perhaps North Korea was the place Noel Coward had in mind. Memo to self: don't go back there this lifetime. Or the next. Or the next.

A better idea is to head on up to Nepal. Just make sure before you go that you don't suffer from vertigo or height sickness, because it's home to eight of the world's ten highest peaks. The Nepalese are delightful people, and you'll always find a comely Sherpa who's happy to lighten your load for you. Across the border in Tibet, I was given a sobering reminder of how the whole world hasn't been spoiled by the Americans yet. Soon after I arrived, I noticed people were sticking their tongues out at me. I thought it was a nervous tic, or they were clearing a constant nose-drip or some bloody thing. It's the oddest sight, and not a bit unnerving. Downright bloody rude, come to think of it. One guy just wouldn't stop, and I'd had a long flight and wasn't in the mood for it. I warned him three times, then gave him the benefit of the Colonel's knuckle sandwich in his moosh. It was only later that evening that someone explained to me the tongue thing is their way of welcoming you to their lovely peaceful land. Guess I owe him an apology.

My favourite travel show's just come on the telly. What do you know … they've got a special feature on India – the very reason Discovery channel was invented in the first place. I've had Bali Belly before, and Bangkok Belly and Just-about-everywhere Belly. But, hell, I'll tell you this, curry lovers, nothing comes close to Delhi Belly. I had to check the brochure to double-check I wasn't on the 'India on 10 kilograms a day' tour: the first three days I was seriously worried that I was going to die. They talk about the bottom falling out of your world … this was the world falling out of my bottom! I could see the headlines now – 'COLONEL KEN IMPLODES AND HANGS HIMSELF ON OWN RINGHOLE!' The next three days the storm did not abate and, by then, I was seriously worried that I *wasn't* going to die!

On that cheery note, let's close off with a little travel-related question from my good friend Steven Wright: if you take an Oriental person and spin him around several times, does he become disoriented?

Colonel Ken

Upping the anti

X and I were backpacking around Asia and had some curious situations in Cambodia. We did the usual touristy things in Phnom Penh and Siem Reap, which included a three-day tour of Angkor Wat. A driver/guide was found for US$20 a day, all smiles and slaps on the back stuff. So we sat down and plotted out the route of temple-hopping, and got stuck into some heavy sightseeing (and a lot more). Over the three days we knew we were getting ripped off for little bits and pieces, but the people were pretty friendly and the free dope was OK. On the last day it came to pony up the dosh for our eager driver and get on a plane back to Phnom Penh. We hand over the $60. "No, no, no! $80!!! I drive you looooong way on last day!" our driver screeches.

X and I had had it up to here with these over-priced deals and backhanders, and X put his foot down and launched into a tirade. Giving the rip-off merchant the final 'take it or leave it' spiel, X thrusts the $60 into the guy's hands and we storm off to find another form of transport to the airport.

We line up in the boarding line after checking-in our packs. The usual police (more like army in their camouflage gear and AK-47s) are walking up and down the line, and eye the two of us. "Passports!" the leader barks, and we have to try to explain to him that we have photocopies, but our originals are still in Phnom Penh getting Vietnam visas. We get taken out of the line and frog-marched out the back doors into some tiny little hut which is so hot they might as well stick forks up our arses and baste us on a rotisserie. We're pointed by the muzzles of their machine guns to the two available seats, as they stand over us with the orders: "No talk!" About five minutes go by and in walks the boss man, pistol on his hip, followed by our original driver.

"You owe this man $20. You are not leaving here until you pay," spouts the captain. In light of the situation, I'm pretty impressed I don't have a stream of warm liquid running down my leg. I peel out a ten dollar note and place it on the table, eyeing up X anxiously to do the same. X appears to hesitate, then slowly pulls out a $10 note, and slaps it down on the table with a ferocious thud.

"Thank you very fucking much!" he glowered at the captain.

I was waiting for the bullets to fly but, instead, was immensely relieved when they escorted us back to the line (now just boarding) and – with huge smiles all round – wished us a good stay in Cambodia.

Bark worse than his bite

On a five-week holiday in China: one morning after a rough night of karaoke I was taking a walk around thinking of how China is certainly opening up (quite literally for some of the ladies). It's a beautiful morning, clear and crisp, visibility unlimited. The locals are just heading out for their day of work. After a while I begin to feel almost human again and the little head begins to talk to the big head so my eyes start to wander. I was so busy looking at all the wonderful lovelies that I failed to notice a big old tree that was directly in front of me. Slam into it I go, knothead meets knothole. The locals got a good laugh and I got re-educated about a danger of being in the orient – too many beauties to distract a fellow. Glad I wasn't driving.

Raining on your parade

We had gone to Koh Samui at the height (depth?) of low season, knowing we might get 'a bit of rain' over the long weekend. But nothing quite prepared us for what we encountered: the power was out for 36 hours. Uprooted coconut trees lay across the road. Rain was coming into the villa *sideways*!

So we watched TV, drank much wine and read lots of books then flew home.

Two-wheeled tattoo

A group of us were on holiday in Thailand, and it was decided that we would hire some motor scooters to get around the island. The next morning we duly went to saddle up. Next thing there's a loud engine whine and we turn to see J appearing from a cloud of dust and leaves – he'd gone through a neighbouring villa's lush hedge, almost into their wall, and fallen off. A mixture of laughter and concern. One of the ladies also had a spill, so they and J then decided they'd take a rental Jeep instead.

We head off down the road and stop to fill up with petrol about 10 minutes later. Y is following us a bit slower and cautiously, so he arrives a bit later ... and, as he makes the turn into the petrol station, he accelerates instead of braking, and scoots ahead, narrowly missing a storm drain before hitting a brick wall and tumbling off. Blood spurts everywhere, and his whole kneecap looks like it's hanging off. We rush across with the Thai service station attendants, who point him across the road to a medical centre.

He received countless stitches to his knee, and went on to a cocktail of antibiotics, thereby putting him off alcohol and swimming for the whole week. Just what you need on a holiday on a tropical island.

Bali-Low

In Bali I headed for a very small town where a US shipwreck is just off-shore and you can go diving there. I found a room, and that night I stumbled across a very small bar on the beach. This very slick American dive instructor welcomed me. He told me to grab a couple of beers as they were celebrating the bar's opening night. I grabbed some beers and the first people I met were two girls from Western Australia.

"What are you girls doing in a small place like this?" I asked, cheesily. They responded that one of the girl's husbands had died in a diving accident in Western Australia. As the smile went away from my face I told them that I wasn't sure I understood. They had brought the husband's ashes over with them and the next day she was going to the cliff to throw the urn into the sea.

Well, I was thinking, these girls really know how to put a damper on a party. I also thought that some Balinese kid is going to find the urn and give it to his mum to use as a vase, or more likely sell it at the weekend market for $1.

Driving me crazy

I am the poor bastard in the car rental business in Vientiane, Laos, who has to put up with the bullshit from the other side of the counter: "Yes, we've been everywhere, done that, know it all, just hand over the keys," they say. One or two weeks later the remains of the car arrives on our desk neatly packaged in a few old plastic bags, with a comment like: "Gees, we didn't think it would be like that, you should have told us …" If we couldn't get pissed every night we might really go crazy.

If birds could fly

Before the airport was put in at Koh Samui I used to go there from Haadyai, when I was living there in the early Eighties. Great place: leave by bus 17:30, get to Surat Thani by 21:00 or so, on to an all-night boat to the island, then by an old pickup to Chaweng Beach in time to strip off and into the water by sunrise. In those days there were only a few bungalows on Chaweng, and it was even BYO birds.

J'ava good time?

A four-day weekend at Java Head, Indonesia, starts off promisingly with a tropical storm. We're in a 65-foot boat, the waves coming over almost past the wheelhouse, and back under the boat. So everyone takes seasickness pills, which knock us out, and we all go to sleep. When we finally get to the Head, we have a little BBQ on the beach. There's a park there and an island that sits right in the bay, where the ranger's station is.

After several hundred Bir Bintangs, FW says: "Let's go over to the disco." So we grab a bottle of whiskey, go out to the tender, go across and, of course, there's no disco over there. Instead we meet these guys who have this huge boat and they're out there shark fishing, and we have a few beers with them. Then FW comes up with a great idea: "The lighthouse ... there's a disco on at the lighthouse!" So off we go and, as we get further and further into the Indian Ocean, the waves are getting taller and taller so we cut inshore and go by this boat sitting there. We didn't think anything of it, till we ran into the set-net that they had out. Our engine's all gummed up with the net, and no-one has a knife, so we come up with another great idea ... we'll just take the petrol cap off and pour some gas on it. Of course the gas flames all over the place. We didn't quite get the net off, so we pour a bit more on, and finally get it off.

Then JM, similarly pissed, says: "Gee, I've never driven one of these things," so he starts driving it and starts swerving all over the place, and the thing flips right over ... there goes the whiskey, there goes the glasses, there goes every damn thing. Now we're upside down floating out to the Indian Ocean. We decide to sit on top of it and paddle it back to the boat, which is about four miles away. The crew help pull us in, and take the engine off and put it on the deck, and we go to sleep.

We get up the next morning, and the crew is surly as hell and we can't figure it out. So we go to the back of the boat where there's a big canvas awning covering the deck, and sit down to have breakfast, and there's this giant hole in the canvas. What happened is one of our guys got up at six o'clock in the morning and decided to clean the saltwater off the engine ... filled it up with gasoline, smoking a cigarette, and the engine and the barrel – and almost him – go up through the fuckin' awning. It also melted the top of the engine.

The captain was not impressed with our antics. They let us use the boat after that, but we had to paddle it around.

For richer or poorer

About two years ago I was on a break between jobs in the UK and decided that I could afford a month in the Land Of Smiles if I was frugal. I planned to go to Koh Phanghan and charm the countless young *farang satrees* (tight-arsed backpacking hippies) into bed. Due to financial hiccups I couldn't take a lot of spending money and an essential part of the plan was to avoid bargirls

Forget the jeep, Barry! This is the only way to see Phuket... the open road, wind in yer hair, and all the squid you can eat.

(more importantly bar-fines, lady-drinks and 'entertainment' fees).

I arrived in Bangkok and, as I was on a budget, checked into a guesthouse on Kao San Rd. After settling in I decided to go for a 'swift half' and soon got chatting to another British guy. After a while my new travelling chum suggested we go and get some action and proposed Pat Pong as the venue. I agreed but explained I was just along for the trip as I was skint, but that he shouldn't think I was being prudish by not dipping my 'toe' in the water. My mate soon paired off and disappeared. Putting a brave face on it I decided to stay in Pat Pong for 'one more beer' (euphemism) and warded off my female attackers with my extensive vocabulary: "You buy me drink?" *Mai Ow* … "You pay bar for me?" *Mai Ow* … "You want come my loom?" *Mai Ow* … "I think you nice man I come your hotel?" Mai Ow … The night wore on and my speech became increasingly slurred and distorted.

I woke at about 1pm the next day in my bed in the guesthouse. I had the hangover from hell, which indicated a doubling of price of shares in the Boon Rwad Brewery. But I consoled myself with the fact that, although I'd been very pissed, at least I hadn't blown all my cash on a bargirl. The next move was to check my wallet: I reached into my trousers on the floor and saw my wallet was empty. Shit! I'd managed to blow around a week's worth of cash in one night. I was still very groggy so went for a piss and, on return to the room, I saw a curled-up mound in my bed. At least that explained where most of the cash had gone. But I didn't even know how I'd got home or at what time [That'd be the famous beer scooter – Col Ken]. I decided to wake her gently and pulled back the sheets … I didn't even remember or recognise her face. I shook my head and did my best to explain the situation.

Once she understood my financial predicament she was extremely kind to me and looked after me in Bangkok, feeding me, introducing me to her friends, and plying me with Sang Thip for a couple of days. We became good friends and stayed in contact via email … well, until on one of my many subsequent trips I tried to bar-fine her best mate.

Done fare and square

I'd gone on holiday to Japan for a week and was on a tight budget. Unfortunately I hadn't done my homework very well, and arrived late at night, so caught a taxi to my hotel. My week's budget was blown by that one taxi ride.

Key information

I'd checked out of my hotel in Angeles, Philippines, in a very bleary state one morning, caught a cab to the Swagman Hotel and boarded the shuttle bus to Manila from there. Halfway through the journey, the conductor came straight to me and said: "You still have your hotel room key." Huh? I checked my back pocket and sure enough, it's there. The hotel had called the bus company, and got the cell phone number of the driver/conductor. But how she knew it was me, out of all those passengers, I still have no idea.

HARDSHIP POSTING

Bird's eye view

A few years ago I was walking along the streets of Hanoi, Vietnam. Being an 'obvious' American, my greying beard and my slight limp attracted the attention of a middle-aged local gentlemen who walked up to me and said, in English: "Welcome back to Viet Nam. Have you ever seen Hanoi before … from the ground?" But he was smiling!

Keep it simple, stupid

Wanting to escape the grind in Singapore, I travelled to Borocay, Philippines, for some much needed R&R and met a real country girl who was refreshingly simple. She had never read a newspaper in her life. Or watched the news on the telly. Had no clue what the stock market was. Didn't have a bank account. Had never worn a watch. I couldn't even make an appointment with her – she'd just show up whenever she wanted. I bought her a nice pair of shoes but she declined to wear them, preferring to go barefoot.

One week after getting back to Singapore I realised there was one more thing she had no knowledge of: basic hygiene. It took me weeks to get rid of the lice.

Spoilt for choice

In China in the late 60s, I decided to take a train from Shanghai to Beijing. It ended up being a five-and-a-half day escapade, sleeping on a wooden board with a one-inch foam mattress. But the food made up for it – we had a salivating choice between one-day old rice or five-day old rice.

Culture shock

Travelling in China in the Eighties we had some strange experiences. As we travelled a lot to the countryside, where they had not seen too many foreigners, they always thought that we were movie stars or something as the only foreigners they knew were the foreigners on TV.

So it quite often happened that, waiting for a train, a group of locals would gather around us and stare. By the time the group got bigger some of them even dared to come closer, others even tried to touch you. Whenever this happened my colleague would always shout very loudly: "BOOOOOOOOO!!!" and they would all run off, and slowly return. This process would repeat itself until our train came.

Sad case

One of my mates was off on holiday and I joined him for a goodbye drink. He called me the next day to advise me not to make the same mistake as him and pack the suitcase after 20 beers. He said when he arrived at his holiday hotel he was upset at the lack of suitable clothes he had managed to pack. However he had managed to remember half a bottle of red wine (leaking), an ashtray, and the TV remote from his home.

Trouser snake

We had sailed to Tanjung Pinang off Singapore and were having a great time with a couple of mates and about 10 Indonesian hookers in tow. We were lying in the shallow water, sipping our cocktails. Suddenly my buddy said: "Don't move now, but there's a snake between your legs." Sure enough, I looked down and could see this tail protruding from beneath my baggy shorts. Fearing a nasty bite or worse I held still, against my better instincts, for what seemed like hours. Eventually the thing just swam off, and inexplicably the water around me suddenly turned a lot warmer!

Room to move

Arriving at the airport in Ho Chi Minh City, we were supposed to be met by a guide who was to take us to our hotel. However, having finally battled through the chaos that calls itself customs, we emerged to find no guide. We found a taxi and made our own way to the hotel, only to find no booking there either (Kafkaesque!). However, since the hotel seemed very passable, had a room free and was, by western standards, very cheap we checked in anyway.

Having unpacked and settled in, we had a phone call from the lobby, where a very apologetic guide had arrived. He tried to persuade us to check out again, and move to another hotel that, he said, was the one we ought to have been taken to. We showed him our itinerary from the travel agent in the UK, which specified the hotel we were in, while he tried to explain that his (local) company no longer dealt with this hotel for some reason, and would we please move to the other hotel which, in any case, was much better.

Having settled in, we refused to budge, and when we came to leave three days later, the bill was all mysteriously settled for us.

Thai-tanic

In Pattaya, we rented a jet-ski to take out around the bay. The sea was pretty choppy and rough, which made for a more exciting ride. Half way through our time, as I pounded through the swell, the engine died. Nothing I could do would restart it, so I opened up the seat compartment, where the petrol tank and engine are housed. Just then, a wave crashed over me, filling the tank and engine with water and sending the jet-ski to the bottom. I swam back to shore –

not sure whether to laugh or cry – and we went back to the hire shop.

"Er, your jet-ski's at the bottom of the bay somewhere," I explained. The guys hit the roof. "You didn't tell me not to open the seat," I protested. The heated discussion reached a stalemate and we stormed off, after pointing them to where they could find it.

Last seen, they were in a boat in the surf trying to snare this thing with some ropes.

One way ticket

In the Philippines back in the early 80s, we borrowed a neighbour's car and drove from Angeles to Baguio, and from Baguio wanted to cut across to Bontoc, in the heart of the rugged Mountain Province. To say the road was rough was an understatement, but in some areas it was so narrow and treacherous it was only possible for one car to pass at a time. So when you got to a certain section, you had to get an attendant to call ahead to another station to see if the road was clear of cars first, then – and only then – could you proceed. It was absolutely one of the worst roads anywhere in the world. When the neighbour heard of our rugged exploits he was not exactly happy.

So-long-gapo

For a change of scenery, a friend of mine suggested Olongapo City in the Philippines. As usual we ended up in the bars and, towards midnight, I broke my own rules and went off on my own down an interesting-looking side street. The last thing I remember was sitting in this very seedy bar and when I woke up – approximately two hours later by my reckoning – I was out on the sidewalk. My wallet had been fleeced and I'd been unceremoniously dumped outside.

I went back to my hotel and recharged my wallet and went back to the main strip and took a girlie home. 'Security' assured me no one could leave the hotel without my saying so. I woke up in the hotel room the next day to find my shorts, shoes and wallet all missing. Rather annoyed, I stepped outside the hotel to cross the road, looked the wrong way (we drive on the left in my country) and was hit by a jeepney. Credit the driver … he hit the brakes and nudged me more or less side-on. Being my fault, I quickly peeled off two 500 peso notes and gave them to him.

Not going back to Olongapo anytime soon.

Doing the hard yards

I had been in Pattaya three weeks and, fair to say, I'd overdone it. I went for breakfast around eight in the morning and next thing I know I'm on the sidewalk covered in blood with my 'girlfriend' screaming. I had just collapsed from overdoing it and hit my head. Everyone was saying, "There's a hospital over the road – go there now."

I said: "Fuck it, I'm going to the travel agent instead." I went and booked my ticket out. Enough was enough.

Eel hauled

Sailing my old motorised junk up from Singapore to Pulau Au, Malaysia, one night, everyone was asleep and I was at the wheel. Next thing I heard the engine beginning to sound out of kilter. I checked the instrument panel – everything normal. I went to the back and looked – engine-cooling water flowing OK. Still the noise persisted. Maybe something on the propeller? I got my searchlight and angled it down the side to the water.

I couldn't believe my eyes … the sea in every direction was teeming with sea snakes. Millions and millions of them in a broiling mass as far as the eye could see. I thought I must've had too many G&Ts. I woke up the others, who freaked out.

The next day we ran into an old Malay fisherman who explained that for no reason this phenomenon occurs once every three to four years.

Like really cheap, man

In 1975, I did the whole hippy-surfing routine in Bali. I stayed with a Balinese family on the beach, who gave me room and board free in exchange for me teaching English to their kids. We just surfed all day, every day, surviving on bananas and coconuts free from the trees. My total expenses for that eight months' stay was AUD$140 [Approx US$80 now]!

Cola wars

In 1971 on a bus through Pakistan, there were signs alongside the road everywhere that simply read: 'CRUSH INDIA'. The bus stopped frequently for drink stops due to the heat, so I got out at the next one and thought I should try the local soft drink. So I asked for a 'Crush India'. Puzzled expressions ensued. No, they explained, 'Crush India' is not a soft drink: we are at war with India and that is what we want to do to them.

Dry throat

It was our first holiday in years without the kids, so my wife and I decided to do India in style. After a long, hot day of driving to and from the Taj Mahal, all I was thinking of back at the hotel was that first (of many) long cool beers. Oh, it was going to taste so good. In the lobby, I was delivered the shocking news. "Sorry, sir, it's a dry day, you can have orange or tomato juice."

Dry days are a hangover from the Raj, he explained, when there was no boozing on pay day so at least the wife got some money for housekeeping each month. So we went upstairs, had a beer from the mini-bar, then went downstairs to dinner, carrying a bottle of champagne which we'd bought to celebrate with.

In the restaurant, we were again told we couldn't drink the champagne.

"Sorry, sir, dry day."

Reserve bench

On a rugby tour through Cambodia, we had loaded the bus up with booze and broads, and brought big bags of dope from the market so were making excellent hemp pizzas, etc. The party was going off: songs were being sung, and people were getting laid left, right and centre.

However, I noticed a very young and innocent-looking girl at the back of the bus, crying her eyes out. I thought we'd obviously overstepped the mark and she was out of her depth. Going back to console her (honestly!), I put an arm around her and said, "What's wrong?"

"No-one wants to fuck me!" she bawled.

What a dive

A group of mainly European holidaymakers were enjoying a dive trip on Sipadan Island, Malaysia, when armed Abu Sayyaf guerrillas suddenly over-ran their resort. Twenty-one vacationers in all were herded at gunpoint onto a speedboat and ordered to sit down as the boat sped off: destination and fate unknown.

They were headed 300 kilometres away to Jolo Island, a Muslim rebel stronghold in the southern Philippines. One couple tried to sabotage the boat during the journey by puncturing the fuel tank unsuccessfully. Arriving at Jolo they were taken into the jungle to a camp, where they huddled together in the darkness, hearing what they thought were gunshots in the distance. It turned out to be the sounds of coconuts falling on the ground. The fear and boredom alternated for four months … as some contemplated killing their aggressive kidnappers with a smuggled penknife. The local villagers treated the camp like a zoo watching the 'animals' inside … TV crews came and went freely. Finally they were released after a military attack on their camp, and flown out of Jolo.

Pit stop

On Bohol Island, Philippines, we'd been travelling this windy mountain road for what seemed like hours and I was becoming desperate for a pee. (Of course, there are no public toilets in those parts.) I mentioned my need to the driver and, as we came to a suburban village, he pulled over in front of a house. He knocked on the door, told the owner my predicament, and they ushered me inside. Pit stop completed, they even offered me a Coke from their fridge. Apparently it's an old tradition to welcome all and any travellers.

Buying time

In the good old days on Lombok Island, Indonesia, we paid this local driver $10 for his four-wheel drive to take us to a deserted beach known as Treasure Beach. It was an idyllic and deserted spot that few knew about. To ensure we had it all to ourselves, we then paid him $15 not to bring anyone else there for a week.

Two days too long

The immigration officers at Dhaka airport, Bangladesh, must all think we come there on holiday and do not want to go back, as every time they ask me: "Sir, how many days you will stay?" Normally it's just two days as I am hopping in for some business and then get the hell out of there … but they always insist to give me a visa for at least 14 days so I can 'enjoy' staying in Bangladesh a little longer. Thanks, but no thanks: I will be out on the next flight to Bangkok.

The quick and the dead

A Danish tourist touched down in Bangkok for a holiday and within four-and-a-half hours was dead from a lethal combination of alcohol, pussy and bad drugs.

Cross fire

An American missionary and his wife, along with a tourist from California, were at a tourist resort in Palawan, southern Philippines, when they were abducted by rebels and taken to a jungle stronghold in southern Basilan. The Californian was beheaded soon after, whilst the couple were held for over a year, sparking a massive military manhunt. US Marines were even seconded to the area as 'advisers'. Eventually the husband and a Filipina hostage were shot dead in a botched rescue fire-fight, and the wife took a bullet in the leg. She was hospitalised before returning to their three children in the States.

Seeing red

A Briton, an Australian, and a French backpacker were travelling though south-eastern Cambodia on a train when they were ambushed. Whilst the Cambodians on board were killed, the westerners were abducted and held for two months before being killed. A former Khmer Rouge commander of that region was arrested for the 1994 murders but subsequently acquitted under an amnesty granted to defectors from the former regime.

Purgatory in paradise

This year I let myself get talked into taking the family to Borocay ("What, you've been here six years and haven't been to Borocay? You simply must go.").

Direct flights to adjacent Caticlan booked. So far so good. Next, a hotel. Well, I know of a guy who has a hotel in Borocay – a friend of a friend – so I call him. Mr X is an English guy, must have his act together, so we'll stay there. Hotel booked. This is too easy … something's bound to go wrong, I think.

The taxi to the airport arrived almost on time, but five minutes into the journey the air-con stops working. Proceeding along Roxas Boulevard, the driver has a brain fart and takes the wrong turning. Now we're in a traffic jam *behind* Roxas. The heat is stifling, the kids (aged 12, 11, five and two) are yelling. It's beginning to stink. Opening the window doesn't help because now we have the fumes as well as the heat.

Eventually we get out of the jam and unload at the airport at 2:35pm for our 3pm flight. We pay, and rush through – dripping, stinking and entirely pissed off. We arrive in the departure hall to be told, "Don't worry, no rush, the flight is delayed by one hour." Well, well, what a surprise.

One hour proved to be optimistic. We finally board at 5pm, then taxi out to the runway in this airplane that looks like it really oughtn't be allowed to fly. Then we sit. And sit. And sit. Naturally, no air-con, as if we didn't stink enough already. But eventually we take off. Its 5:25pm, and I manage to get one more phone call to Mr X on my mobile to let him know what time we will arrive. Then I promptly fall asleep. I wake up as the wheels touch down, look out the window at the most beautiful red sunset.

As we're walking towards the terminal I think to myself that this air-port is really well-developed for a provincial one, and was surprised at some of the tall buildings in the distance. I ask one of the passengers if they know what town that is. "No, but maybe Kalibo?" they wonder back at me. It turns out we're wrong by miles. Yep, you guessed – it's the buildings of Makati glittering in the distance. We've landed back in Manila: they just neglected to mention it to anybody.

Back in the arrivals area the airline rep tells me to "just go to the office, they will take care of everything." We finally got home at 9:30pm with replacement tickets on a different airline two days later, and the princely sum of 150 pesos (about US$3.50) as compensation.

I've naturally kept Mr X informed throughout, and he tells us not to worry, same plan for two days from now.

Two days later we make it to Caticlan with no more trouble than the usual traffic jam, delayed flight, and sitting on the runway for half hour with no air-con. But, nonetheless, here we are in Caticlan, and the amazing Mr X is there to meet us. He looks like an ageing hippy with his psychedelic t-shirt and ponytail. "Transport's waiting outside," he says, so outside we go. No transport. He starts running around like the proverbial headless chicken, comes back and tells us: "He was here just now … this has never happened before. Don't worry, let's sit and have a beer, I'm sure he'll be right back." First good idea I've heard, so I agree, and we're into the San Miguel. Meanwhile he dispatches somebody to go and find transport. Bear in mind that throughout the whole affair there's the wife, her sister, her friend, and four kids all wondering – in their own little way – 'What the fuck is going on here?'

Eventually along come two tricycles, the preferred mode of transport in Caticlan, and off we go to the harbour where the boat is waiting: me hanging off the back of one of the tricycles. We arrive at the harbour to discover, "The boat's not here … he was here just now, this has never happened before … let's sit and have a beer, I'm sure he'll be right back." So we're back into the piss, along comes the boat after a little while, and Mr X is happy again.

Ten minutes later we're wading ashore from the beach – kids, bags and all – but no problem, the transport will be waiting for us. Guess what? "The transport is not here … he was here just now, and I told him to wait. This has never happened before, let's sit and have a beer." We've only been off the plane an hour, and Mr X has had three good ideas already: I'm actually starting to like the bloke!

We eventually arrive at the 'hotel' and are guided to our rooms … at the top of about 200 steps on a hillside. The room is not air-conned, but of course we're getting used to that by now. The next three days are purgatory, with insects eating the ceiling and showering us with wood chippings all night. No menu ("Let's just see what's in the fridge … shrimps and rice OK for breakfast?"). Yes, breakfast and every other fucking meal we had in the place!

"Water … oh yes, we have that sometimes, just let us know when you want some and we'll see what we can do – what? – *hot* water – hmmmmm, now that's a new idea!"

Mr X, on the other hand, had a whale of a time … I didn't know he drank piss until I saw him sober once! And what's that funny smell every time he lights up a cigarette?

One day, he kindly booked us a sailboat ride around the island. We all jump on board and out to sea we go. We get about a mile out, the wind dies, and we're stuck. "That's never happened before … never mind, let's sit and have a beer." Then, "Oh fuck, no beer."

The whole time we're there the bed wasn't made, the towels weren't changed, the room wasn't cleaned. We put in some laundry on the day we arrived: the day we left they fished it out of a bucket of cold water, gave it back to us, and said, "Sorry, we forgot."

We got home after our four-day visit, and universally agreed the following:

We need a holiday.

Mr X is a cunt.

Borocay is very beautiful, but … if you want to go there, you've got to really want to go there.

If you have a good story about holidays or travel in Asia, please email The Editor at hardshipposting@hotmail.com or fax 612-9499-5908. He'll arrange for alternative tented accommodation for the night and tickets out on the next available donkey.

❖ 7 ❖

Castles in the Air
Or Don't Darken My Doorstep

*True tales of houses, apartments, and
flatmates from hell in Asia.*

Since my divorce from the dear old Dragon Lady, I have a new saying:
Home is where the tart is! I'm not sure if I told you this story last time, just
before our parting of ways. I'd come home nice and early one night, and as I
snuck in the door the cuckoo clock started up. I looked at the clock and it said
3am. Realising that the Dragon Lady would probably wake up and hear what
time I'd got home I hatched a quick plan and cuckooed another nine times in
my finest falsetto, before smugly heading through to the bedroom and feigning death.

Next morning she asked what time I got home. "Midnight," I told her,
remembering my cunning stunt.

"That's good, Ken, but we need to have the cuckoo clock fixed."

"Why's that, Hun?" (I used to call her Hun, as Attilla just seemed too formal around the house).

"Well last night the clock cuckooed three times, then said 'Ah Shit!'
cuckooed four more times, cleared its throat, cuckooed another three times,
giggled, cuckooed twice more, then farted." Fair cop.

Right, what are we going to talk about here? Oh, I know, as we've started on this note of romance and domestic bliss, let's continue it. I was always
amazed by the Mughal emperor in India, Shah Jahan, who had the Taj Mahal
built back in 1631. It was a symbol of love for his second wife. All I can say
is she must have given tremendous blowjobs … the sort that can make you
feel the bed sheets being sucked up through your arse. (A hummer in the nup-

tial bed – hmmm, that's about as rare as a domestic plane flight in Singapore, isn't it?)

Down in Sarawak, the Brooke family – the white Rajahs – created the Astana as their official residence in Kuching. To most people it was a palace with white walls and a thatched *atap* roof. However, one unkind observer described it as 'a fantastic medley of beauty and bad taste'. Something you might more often ascribe to a local landlord whose idea of taste runs to whorehouse nightmare décor. More inferior desecration than interior desecration.

In the nearby Philippines, the official residence came about in a very different manner. In the 19th century, Spaniard Don Luis Rocha built a country house. OK, so it was a large country house. But he soon fell on bad times, and sold this place for 1,000 pesos to another Spanish expat. The Spanish government themselves later bought it for the through-the-roof sum of 5,000 pesos, and the place was left neglected in its original state. It was only in 1847 that they decreed this place should be used as a governor's residence. Malacanang it was called, from an inscription found on site '*May lakan diyan*' – 'here lies a noble man'. Then in 1863 it became the seat of government after an earthquake wiped out the *Real Palacio* in the Walled City of Manila, and the Spanish government set up shop here. Malacanang has had its fair share of unwelcome houseguests since then including earthquakes, fires and typhoons. But its biggest natural disaster was undoubtedly Ferdinand Marcos.

Still in the Philippines, I've got to share this one with you: at Clarke Airbase, Angeles, in 1919 the 3rd Aero Squadron were a houseproud lot and decorated their street with white rocks in the shape of their emblem. They soon regretted this, given the amount of scrubbing and cleaning and general maintenance to keep their rocks, well, white. Not helped by the fact that each day – after they'd scrubbed their rocks – the cavalry officers from nearby Fort Stotsenburg would bring their horses along for their 'constitutional' right on their sacred emblem!

Back on to governor's residences. The Japanese PM's residence is now over 70 years old (younger than most of their prime ministers!). There were a lot of complaints over the years about rats, ghosts, cockroaches and mildew in the place. I don't know about you, but I think it's good for politicians to keep in touch with the common people that way. But, no, he gets a new place built, which has just been completed.

Official residences don't come any more grand and stately than that built by the Brits for their number one man in Hong Kong. However, the *fengshui* is apparently all up the creek and back. So much so that when the Chinese took over I believe the new guy refused to live in the colonial mansion. As May-May in Clavell's Taipan said: "This next time we build our house, first a *fengshui* gentlemens, please?" Just up the hill a bit from this is Genesis, a modest little 56,000 square footer on Hong Kong Peak, once the world's most expensive home. It was bought in 1996 for $70 million. That's not baht or ringgit or dong, slumlords – greenbacks! At that point I was desperately trying to find out if he had any eligible daughters: looks not important. Just a few months later the Chinese gent turned down an offer for $115 million, saying it was too little (mind you, what penis size has got to do with property value I've got no idea). Then the big crash came, the vultures moved in, and the receivers sold it for less than $30 million. A loss of $40 million. Now I don't care whether he has daughters or not, and don't go calling me for handouts, girls.

One thing you'll notice in Hong Kong, and places like Singapore as well, is if you invite local colleagues or staffers back to your house, they'll walk in, mouths agape at the size and space of your crash pad. "Waaaaaah! How much rent you pay one month?" Now I don't know about you, squatters, but that's personal bloody information – especially when my one-month's rent is more than their annual salary. So of course, I tell them double the figure.

The Chinese have an old proverb: 'A land title is the hoop that holds the barrel together'. Sir Victor Sassoon, one of the world's most successful hairdressers [Check facts –ed.], would certainly agree with this. He owned Shanghai's choicest properties in the 30s. Choice they might have been, but whether or not they had flushing toilets is not known. But what I do know is that by the 80s in Shanghai 10,000 tons of 'night soil' were collected from older houses which had no plumbing and used to fertilise vegetables.

Now, you are all aware that Englishman Thomas Crapper invented the toilet, the dunny, the thunderbox, the throne. He even patented it in the 19th century. Well his credibility has just been flushed down the drain with a discovery made by archaeologists in China: a 2,000-year-old toilet with a stone seat, fully-functional water system, and even an armrest (still checking to see whether it had a drinks holder fitted). It was found in the tomb of a king from round about the time Jesus graced the world with his short but impactful presence. Although I haven't personally given it a test run, archaeologists described it to Xinhua News Agency as being, "quite like we are using today."

How come then, the Chinese went backwards from here to those awful hole-in-the floor starter-block thingies? Absolutely no regard for ex-rugby players with bad knees.

Now, as anyone who's ever set foot in Asia will tell you, the biggest culture shock is not the hordes of uniformly dark-haired people, it's not the unintelligible alien language, it's not the spicy food reconstituted from extremities of endangered species. It's the state of the public toilets. I've seen things in multiple-body bag close-combat situations that were far more savoury than walking into your average public toilet. S-h-e-e-e-i-i-i-i-t!!!

Fortunately in Japan the folks seem to have a fixation with public toilets. They probably overdo it, if anything. I came across this device called the I-mode that is like a high-tech bidet that warms, sprays and blow-drys the nethers. Great fun – I went back twice just for the thrill of it. It also plays soothing music, and I've got a couple of suggestions that might help things along: Handel's Water Music, the 1812 Concerto or perhaps Springsteen's 'Baby we were bo-o-rn to run!' Other facilities I went to offered pleasant sounds to mask the unpleasant ones generated along the row of cubicles. The Japanese ladies apparently are very shy of the hiss generated by their peeing in public so these sound systems simulate the sound of flushing and flowing water. Maybe the odd bullfrog croak thrown randomly into the mix would cover all bases.

When I was over in Korea for the World Cup I noticed they also had an unhealthy fixation with public conveniences. But, believe me, this is not a complaint. The little town of Suwon seemed to take it more seriously than most. Its mayor, my good friend Sim Jae-Douk, started his Beautiful Toilet campaign back in '97. I got handed – I kid you not, arsewipes – a brochure proudly proclaiming Suwon to be 'A city with the most beautiful public toilet in the world'. The compelling text told me all about the *banditbuli* (firefly) toilet that I just had to see after that. Sure enough, I was on a tour bus that actually stopped at this place. It does, for all the world, look like a firefly with its big bulbous glass skylight 'eyes'. You are greeted first by a bougainvillea-clad courtyard, which would've been complete if it had an Italian restaurant set up inside it. Then you go through to the business centre itself, with floor-to-ceiling glass walls looking out over the lush gardens so you can stare lovingly at nature while you strain the spuds. The bus also stopped at a number of other contenders for 'most beautiful public toilet in the world': side-by-side models (I guess for mothers and trainee kids), and some with meeting areas so you could discuss business, er, on the run. Yes, that was an unusual bus ride where the toilet stops were actually the point of the journey!

And so to Cambodia, where the first-ever public toilets have just been installed in Phnom Penh to keep the sidewalks and bushes clean and green. Mention my name and you'll get a good seat!

Some unkind people say the Colonel talks a lot of shit. Now you know why.

Colonel Ken

White is right

In Manila I had a room above the bar that was used as accommodation for the girls. Just before heading off on a trip, I went up there with a contractor to see how things could be improved. "Paint everything white," were my instructions, before heading off. I came back several days later and, indeed, they had painted everything white ... windows, walls, carpets, taps, the whole bloody lot. How could I be angry? The painter did *exactly* what he was told – a first in the Philippines!

Money for old rope

A good friend of ours in Bangkok had an interesting marriage to a Thai in as much as it seemed to be fairly 'open'. He even maintained two homes – one with his wife, and another apartment across town for 'away games'. One night he got home uproariously drunk, came home, made love to his wife, and – still feeling rather tipsy – got up to go to work in the morning.

The next evening, he came home and his wife calmly asked him: "How was your evening last night?"

"Oh, not bad," he said, "A couple of drinks with the boys ... then straight to bed."

"Then why did you leave 500 baht on my pillow?" she asked, still a bit mystified.

Dog day afternoon

We had a big Indian rat in our house that had found our imported food cache, chewed through clothes and walked up the wall. This was no rat but rather a *bacuda*. We called the exterminator, whom we had gotten to know

quite well. After the *bacuda* walked out of a glue trap, we told the exterminator man to come and fix the problem. He laid out some poison.

A couple of days later, after the heat of a couple of summer Delhi days,
there was this obnoxious smell – so we searched for the *bacuda* but could not
find it anywhere. Madame called the exterminator and said it smelled funny
and asked if he could come and find it. The terminator man told her that we
should let the dogs upstairs and they would find it.

This did not go over well and madame said: "You are not sending my
dogs up there – I would rather send Indians."

"As you like, madam," he chuckled. The political correctness of this
could be debated, but to the exterminator he laughed as he was a self-pro-
claimed 'honest Pakistani'. The exterminator sent two young boys out and
they did indeed find the culprit.

Fangs for nothing

When the Japanese left Taiwan after the war, they bequeathed some of
the research that they had been carrying out; to wit, development of snake
venom. This bequeathal took the simple form of opening all the cages and letting the snakes escape.

Our company's house was up Yangminshan, the main mountain in Taipei
and home to some of the larger corporate homes in the city. A few weeks after
I arrived, there was a panic call from the maid. She had gone downstairs to
the laundry only to be hissed at by a snake lying in the middle of the floor.
Her initial reaction was to call the police, who were fairly quick off the mark
as they saw a good meal in the offing. They could find no trace and neither
could the snake-catcher. As a precaution he sprinkled lime around the garden,
on the basis that snakes would not cross the lime as it burned their skin. This
was all well and good, except that all it did was to keep the snake *inside* my
garden!

Snakes give me the creeps, even to see them behind glass in a zoo. So I
stuffed towels under every door from the basement to the bedroom, and took
all sorts of other precautions to avoid the inevitable confrontation.

Sure enough, the maid – who by this time was threatening to quit – came
across it again, each scattering in different directions. As it turned out the
solution was quite simple: the outlet to the dryer went through a hole in the
wall to the bush behind the house. When it rained the snake climbed up onto
a ledge and, when the dryer was on, it crept up the pipe following the warmth.

We managed to block the hole off, but the whole experience did nothing to enamour me to the reptiles.

Block head

In the early 80s some wanker with the only two-storey bungalow on the beachfront at Chaweng, Koh Samui, tried to con me into buying it for 300,000 baht. This place was sitting on a 100m x 300m waterfront block. He must have thought I was another *farang* sucker! I didn't fall for it. Today, that place probably goes for 10 million or more. Who wants to give up work anyway?

Steel yourself

In Hong Kong I shared a flat in a giant apartment block opposite the port gate at Western. I never needed to worry about sleeping in and being late for work … you see, every morning at 7am sharp the gates would be swung open with a resounding 'CLANG-G-G-ggg-g!' that would resonate round the whole harbour and shake our building.

Not sitting on the fence

I just finished the construction of my house in the Philippines and I can assure you I have faced all the problems a foreigner can face building a house. It started with the 'girlfriend' who suddenly and unexpectedly demanded a share because of the 'dummy' signature she provided. Now she is my number one enemy, because I didn't give in to her orders.

The list continues, with the mysterious 'walking' border marker-stones, the corrupt surveyors placing the markers wrongly in favour of a neighbour, the continuously lying and cheating contractor, refusal of an official 'right of way', and 'ghost' labourers being on the pay-roll but not present.

The architect told me that the building permit was no problem: he could handle that. But at the opening party of my house, there was still no building permit. The reason was the height of my fence (which is three metres), while the ordinance states the maximum height on the island may not exceed 1.80 metres. The fence was already built before I was told about the existence of that ordinance and I refused to tear down the structure, partly because my neighbour is a very noisy and nosey woman.

So I invited some municipality officials to attend my party in order to soften their hearts with the help of the native Tanduay rum. It worked!

"My friend, you make another drawing so that the committee can decide based on a drawing with a fence of 1.80 metres instead of three metres …" I'll drink to that!

Throwing good money after bad

When Singapore's property market was booming, I dived in and bought an investment apartment to rent out. As luck would have it the market levelled out soon after, and my 'fail-proof' business plan was in tatters. I tried to sell the new apartment but couldn't get an offer even below what I'd paid for it in the first place. It was supposed to be rentable at around SGD$6,000 per month but I couldn't get a tenant at $2,500. One of the agents proposed a solution: lease a car and throw it in as part of the deal.

York's brother

I've been going with this Filipina girl, X, who shares a house with another four Filipinas here in Hong Kong, but her Filipina landlady is a *tsismosa* (big mouth piece) who does not like me because of my reputation of having a good time with all the girls, never mind a few swear words.

I had to call X up on the home telephone line one night, but lo and behold, the *tsismosa* answered the telephone, so in my best Cantonese and her best English our telephone conversation went as follows:

Me:	"*Wai…*"
Tsismosa:	"*Wai…*"
M:	"*Wai, wai…*"
T:	"*Wai, wai*, who you looking for?"
M:	"Ah, a, a, Philip, a, a, Philip…"
T:	"No Philip here, no Philip here."
M:	"Ah, a, a, Michael, aaaa, Michael…"
T:	"No Michael here."
M:	"Aaaa … Mike Hunt, Mike Hunt."
T:	"No Chinese here, no Chinese here, only Filipinas, only Filipinas."
M:	"Aaaa, Mike Hunt, Mike Hunt."
T:	"No Mike Hunt here, no Mike Hunt here. No. No. No."

She is getting extremely angry with this bloody 'Chinese' man and beginning to raise her voice.

M:	"Philip, aaaaa, Philip…"
T:	"THIS IS MY BLOODY TELEPHONE, PLEASE GET

OFF THE LINE – THERE IS NO CHINESE HERE, NO PHILIP AND NO FUCKING MIKE HUNT! BYE, BYE."

At this stage I needed to get of the telephone before I blew my cover that I'm a *gweilo* looking to speak to X.

Talent pool

We were living in Jakarta in a nice compound with 12 houses. Half of them were occupied by some Lufthansa engineers who were stationed there, the others by a mix of Americans, Canadians, Dutch and another German with his wife and two kids. Now these engineers were not just checking the engines of the planes, they were also checking the engines of the local girls. This quite often resulted in a big party in the pool during the weekends. They often had more than one girl to each guy with them at the pool.

Apparently this was too much to understand for one of the kids who asked her father why these guys had two wives and daddy only had one. Being pissed off (and maybe a bit jealous) with these guys behaving like that in the common area in front of the kids he threatened them that they either start behaving like 'normal' people or move elsewhere. If they would not follow either suggestion he would contact Lufthansa personally and inform them about their 'improper' behaviour.

As they did not want to give up their newfound 'religion' – but were afraid of their Lufthansa bosses repatriating them – they decided to move elsewhere where there 'multiple wife' lifestyle would be appreciated.

Fine night for a drive

In Port Moresby, I was asleep one night when there was the dreaded proverbial knock on the door after midnight. I opened it to find a policeman on my doorstep, and my neighbour standing behind him. Turns out he was drunk and driving down a one-way street, so the policemen had levied a 50 kina 'fine' on him. As usual, he had no money on him, so they had driven his car home while he went in the back of theirs. I didn't usually carry much, or any, cash with me in PNG but luckily that day I had just been to the bank so was able to bail my neighbour out.

Big brother's watching

We were seconded from our office to cover some site personnel who were on leave. I was very upset that the 'site' accommodation was a two-hour drive from the site. As there was ten years' work, and the site was not going to get any closer to the flats, I queried the choice of location. I was told very sternly to leave it well alone. After a little research I found the local boss's brother owned the flats!

I see red

One of our Chinese neighbours in Chancery, Singapore, had redeveloped their house into a huge two-storey monstrosity. It was all finished apart from the exterior paint. One day the painters came along and painted the owners a choice of sample patches to choose from before proceeding to the final one. They were all pink: some quite light and rose-tinted, others increasingly pink, and one absolutely garish neon glow-in-the-dark pink. I laughed at the latter as obviously way out of contention. You guessed it – that's the one they went with. The whole damn house!

What's in a name?

My boss, D (an American) was staying at the Oakwood Corporate Housing in Bangkok and called room service to order a hamburger from the room service menu. They called back after about two minutes, advising him that the kitchen was out of ham and asking if a beef burger would be OK. He assured them that, as he was such a laid-back and reasonable guest, it would be just fine.

Kissed a few toads in my time

While at the Somerset in Bangkok, during the month of September and October, I was firmly convinced that after about 8pm, someone had parked a 1974 Thunderbird with a bad fan belt and pulley system outside my room. The grinding/squeaking sound continued throughout the night, audible above the TV, stereo and air conditioner. There was no car, so I thought perhaps it was a neighbour's air conditioning compressor, ready to give up the ghost. That was not the case either.

Calls to the front desk left both them and me baffled. My co-workers were certain I was delusional and had succumbed to the heat. Finally, one night I investigated: to my surprise the loud noise, which I could hear through closed doors, was a frog – smaller than a golf ball – which had taken up residence in one of the water lily pots in front of the residences, right outside my window. The security guard carried the little offender away. However, for the next three to four weeks, the creature – now nick-named Frogzilla – returned and when he started up, a call to the front desk resulted in front desk residence and security personnel chasing him around the water lily ponds and away.

Being good Buddhists, they didn't hurt the animal and, eventually, Frogzilla found the love of his life and moved on.

Love in a box

In the 80s, Hanoi was a hell of a duty station (you couldn't spend your money on anything at all), but also a devilish place to 'accommodate' a girlfriend as all hotels and residences were heavily guarded and local visitors forbidden from entering.

One day driving to the office I saw my sweet girlfriend from Saigon standing alongside the road, waving frantically with her arms. What to do? Ignore her, or send her off to far away Ho Chi Minh City with some compensation money? This wasn't my idea of a romantic reunion at all.

It took me a couple of seconds to hatch a plan: I stopped and picked up an aluminium trunk, stowed and locked her away, and off we went in my Land Cruiser to the heavily-guarded foreigner-only residence compound at Trung Tu.

Since the trunk was too heavy to carry alone, I asked one of the guards to help carry the "bloody heavy books" into my flat!

How sweet the following days and weeks were. Finally after two months – exhausted and slightly claustrophobic (she couldn't leave the flat at all) – she left me for her family in the South. But at least we had a device ready and tested to get her undetected out of the place. She came back north by train for two more episodes like that.

Phoney situation

We were working on a construction site in Bangkok. Mid-morning at work one of our guys, an electrical engineer, grabbed his hardhat, safety boots and a roll of drawings.

"If anybody asks, I'm on site. I need to get back to my flat and decant out the young lady who shared my bed last night." He was away for hours and when he returned I asked where the hell he had been. "Well, Noi looked so beautiful that I just had to give her another one."

He got his come-uppance at the end of the month when he found that the beautiful Noi had spent two hours on his telephone that morning talking to her sister in Los Angeles at a rate of US$6.00 per minute.

See right through you

Living in Solo, Java, for a few years one of the things I did was take up meditation. Over a period of time I got very friendly with my 'instructor' – this old Indonesian gent – and invited him home to our place one day. Sitting there sipping some tea, he looked around and said: "You have a young female ghost in the house." My ears pricked up (especially at the young, female part).

However, despite my best attempts, and my vivid imagination, no apparitions were sighted.

At the next opportune time we mentioned it to our local landlords. "Oh, she's still there is she?" they said, obviously familiar with the spirit. Turns out they'd paid someone handsomely to remove the ghost some considerable time earlier.

Run for your life

After the explosion of Mt Pinatubo, our town was literally buried in mud and lava. The sky was blacker than night, and I was clearing mud from my driveway, and out of the doors and windows, when a good friend dropped by and casually asked: "Coming on the run?" Response unprintable. We had no water for 15 days after that, and no electricity for two weeks.

Puppy love

I live in a cul-de-sac in Ubon Ratchatanee, Thailand, one of four families there. Although never antagonistic, the inter-family relationship between the neighbours was, at best, a little cool. Until the big event. The neighbour's male poodle, Buddy, decided to consummate his romance with my dog, Nancy, in the middle of the road. Contrary to western culture where cries of 'get a bucket of cold water' would be heard, all four wives from the neighbourhood were out shouting encouragement. After an excellent performance by Buddy, the ladies had all met each other and now they lunch regularly, shop together, and garden together, thanks to two dogs fucking. And we now have five beautiful puppies to remember that day by.

Monkey say monkey do

Driving a friend home one night in Manila after 'a few' he said, "Just here, through this gate." So I turned suddenly and went *through* the wrought-iron gate with a loud crash and bang, security guards yelling and screaming. The car was scratched and dented, pieces hanging off it. Gate unscathed. Hey, I was only following instructions.

Butter her up

A friend of mine had a very fancy pad in Jakarta, but was away. So we decided to use it one night for an impromptu late-night session. Being unprepared and being out of condoms, I needed some lubricant for a hand job. I couldn't find anything suitable in the bathroom or bedroom, so went to the fridge and grabbed the margarine. As we sat down to breakfast the next morning, the lads tucking heartily into their toast, little did they know where that margarine had been.

Nothing for the money

A new couple had arrived in Hong Kong, and the wife immediately set to finding a suitable residence to rent. After a while she said to me: "We just can't find anything in Hong Kong," and they ended up staying at the Mandarin Hotel for two months, in itself a pretty packet.

"What sort of budget are you looking at?" asked my friend, who considers herself a fairly high-rolling player. "Perhaps I can help."

"HK$130,000 per month," sighed the new expat. That's 11,000 Pounds *per month* for rent alone – makes you wonder what the total package was.

Got to be yolk-ing

One day going back by train from Xianfan to Wuhan, China, we met an Italian who was in our cabin and we started talking. The local management had made a special room for him in the factory – a two-hour drive out of Xianfan, which was itself in the middle of nowhere – so he could live on premises while they set up the joint venture. They had even arranged a private cook for him. The problem with his cook, however, was that he prepared only eggs for him – eggs for breakfast, eggs for lunch, and eggs for dinner.

Being tired of this after a week he made a lot of noise, and said he was going to strike if he did not get some more variety in his food. After some help from interpreters this was arranged and he had slightly more varied meals … the cook started combining some rice with his eggs!

Silent night

In Manila there were some really noisy road works going on in our street, which was still going when I came home late at night. I couldn't sleep, so I went outside and gave each worker 100 Pesos. "You boys go home instead." They downed tools and filed off.

Spiked drinks

I was coming home to my apartment in Makati, Manila, one night (OK, it was morning) and decided to take a shortcut over a 12-foot security fence. I slipped, impaling my hand on one of the paling spikes, hanging there till my bodyweight ripped through the rest of my hand, and I slid to the ground. I put my hand under my armpit to stem the blood-loss and went off to the hospital and got 25 stitches. There was also a gash in my elbow. I felt nothing for two days till the grog wore off.

Access all areas

We'd bought this beautiful plot of beachside land for a house in Koh Samui from an old family in the area who were subdividing their family's traditional lot. It was only after everything was agreed and signed that we found out that no provision for access to and from the road was made, ie, our lot was locked in on all sides.

The vendor then said an access way between the houses behind us could be made for, say, an extra million baht.

"No, too much, we'll just come in by boat then," we bluffed. The asking price was then lowered significantly and we now have a driveway to our house from the road.

In the hot seat

After repeated requests for engineering in our Bangkok apartment to check the under-sink hot water heater thermostat (the water in the shower could only be called 'warm' at best), I was advised that the engineer had checked the heater and the gauge was set to 'high' and it seemed to be in order.

Before leaving for work, I asked them to check the water temperature of the water coming from the shower, versus just looking at the gauge on the heater. When I returned home that night, I had a voicemail advising me that the heater was working fine and that they had left me a chair. Baffled, I looked in the room I used as an office and there was a comfy club chair that had not been there that morning.

I never made the connection between hot water and furniture, unless I was to use it for kindling to boil water, or perhaps it was for me to sit comfortably and meditate on hot water. The logic was never explained. I stopped asking.

Shock therapy

In Seoul, this expat had a feeling that his electricity bills came a bit regularly but, as he couldn't understand the writing and the company was paying these sorts of expenses on his behalf anyway, he just passed them on to the finance department who duly paid them. Until one day he caught a Korean guy outside his house trying to slip a piece of paper under his front door. It was another damn electricity bill. Turns out he had been paying half the neighbourhood's electricity bill for several months without realising it.

On the tiles

We had bought an apartment in Singapore, which was only about four years old and in good condition. I was a bit surprised then to find out a few months later that an area of floor tiles (over a metre squared) had popped up in the middle of the floor one day. Speaking to neighbours it seemed that all had experienced the mysterious popping tiles at some stage or another.

After we sold the apartment, my cousin moved to Singapore. Guess where they ended up living? That's right, the very next block in the same development. I emailed them and said, "Wow, what a coincidence. You'll love it there … just watch out for the exploding floor tiles."

They thought I'd spent too much time in the sun. But a few short weeks later, as they were watching TV, this rumble and crunching and cracking built up to a crescendo. Earthquake was his first reaction. No, just the floor tiles popping. Now they don't think I'm quite as mad.

Spinning a yarn

I had been in Hong Kong all of three days, temporarily living in my boss's house in Aberdeen, when there was a knock at the back door. I opened it, to be confronted by a tall, good-looking Chinese guy (I myself am a short female). "I have come to repair the washing machine," he said in good English. I let him in and he went straight to the bedroom. Bit odd I thought, so I called my boss, to check that she had arranged this service.

"What are you talking about, the washing machine's brand new," she said. "Get out of the house, run downstairs now!" I put the phone down and dashed for the door, not stopping till I got to Security. Having told them about this bogey repairman, they went up and confronted him. He was led away.

My boss told me that evening that the 14K triad gang was active in pillaging expensive homes in that area.

Corporate climber

In Hong Kong I was required to wear a uniform to work each day. I only had one at that stage, so used to wash it each night and hang it outside the window to dry. One morning I woke up, and noticed the hangar was there but the garment wasn't. Peering out the window I noticed it had been blown down on to the ledge.

Without thinking, I climbed out of the 13th floor window, and down onto the half-metre-wide ledge. It was only then I realised how high it was, and gingerly clambered along in my nightdress to retrieve the errant item.

By now, a few nosy neighbours and people in the street had noticed this crazy woman on the ledge. Most thought it was a suicide attempt. "Don't jump, don't jump." Others re-appeared with ladders. By now I was frozen with fear myself, hugging the plumbing pipes for dear life. But there was no way out other than to climb back up over the windowsill which now seemed impossibly high. I finally managed to scale my way back up and into my room, collapsing on a cushion and balling my eyes out.

Despite my heavily-bruised knees and forearms my boss gave me a serious scolding: "You bloody idiot ... that uniform's only worth ten dollars!"

Beauty sleep

I was sharing a flat with a mate in Causeway Bay and, after a heavy night in the bars of Wanchai, decided to head for home around 3am. At approx 5am I got up for a piss but went out the front door on the right instead of turning left for the toilet. So I was now locked out on the landing, completely naked. No matter how hard I banged on the door, I could not wake my flatmate who was by now deep into a drunken coma.

I finally summoned the courage to knock on our Chinese neighbour's door and ask for a pair of shorts and a t-shirt. You guessed it ... a lady opened it, screamed her head off and slammed the door before I could say a word. Within three minutes the 11th floor landing was swarming with police. Having explained my predicament, clothing was finally made available.

The police tried calling our phone and banging the door with no success. They in turn called the fire services who then smashed the door down (by which time there must have been about 20 people in attendance). After providing proof that I actually lived in the flat everybody left.

My flatmate, who slept through the entire episode, finally woke up at about 11am and – having surveyed the flat – came into my room and said: "What the fuck happened to the front door?!?"

Water feature

Some expats in Hong Kong prefer living in boats, mainly on big junks, which are literally huge floating apartments with old New Delhi bus engines in them. Our friend decided to buy one of them from a couple who lived on it uneventfully for around six years. The surveyor marked the boat as being in 'almost perfect condition' and the sale went through.

A few months later it was fully furnished, and our friend decided to take it into the shipyard for some minor repairs on the roof, and invited us for a ride. So off we go, us three sitting on the roof enjoying the sunny winter day, and the two guys hired to drive the darn thing.

About half way to the Aberdeen Marina, the two guys started running around in distress so our friend went to check what was going on down there. A minute later he comes back up: "Guys, there's about six inches of water in the lower cabin!" We thought he was having us on, but indeed there was lots of water down there.

Since we were pretty close, the guys gunned the poor bus engine, whilst trying to find – and temporarily plug – the leak. But the water was gushing inside faster and faster. Soon it became obvious that we were not going to make it, as the water level was getting dangerously high. But, as long as the engine was working, there was still some hope … it was still happily chugging away even though it was half way submerged. Oops, spoke too soon. We were stranded on a sinking junk in the middle of Hong Kong's very active shipping lanes.

The Marine Department rescue boats finally made it to us and whisked us down, with bits and pieces of our friends' salvaged things. We watched the junk slowly sink. Then a couch came floating by, followed by a carpet, some kitchen utensils. Our friend came back with just three trash bags of stuff and nothing else.

Maybe we should've called a plumber instead.

If you have a good story about houses, apartments, room-mates or contractors in Asia, share it with The Editor at hardshipposting@hotmail.com or fax 612-9499-5908. We prefer non-smokers, female, 18-25, with their own transport, who can cook.

❖ 8 ❖

A Dose of Your Own Medicine
Or Fly in the Ointment.

True tales of doctors, nurses, hospitals
and tiger penises in Asia.

Sitting at the regular boozer, tucking into several double Scotches as we talked about the various ailments of aging, I said to mein host: "I really shouldn't be drinking these with what I've got, Don."

"Why, what've you got now?"

"Only about 50 baht!" He gave me a timely reminder on the dangers of drinking on an empty wallet. Speaking of which, we've decided to nickname Barry 'Bazra' as he shows distinct 'pockets of resistance' when it comes to ponying up for a round of drinks.

My back has been playing up ever since 'Nam. Nothing to do with the war, mind you. Pete and I were in Ho Chi Minh City for a weekend recently, and I came away with a bad case of shagger's back. I've been bed-ridden for the past few weeks, but I'm responding well to the skilful manipulations of Khun Aei, which only makes it worse.

I've told her that I have been officially diagnosed with PFSB, an under-documented condition in these parts. In the interest of political correctness and tight health funding, the authorities don't want to know about it and this condition has been the subject of a massive cover-up at the highest levels. PFSB, as it is colloquially called, is known in medical circles by its longer full-style name: Potentially Fatal Sperm Build-Up. We're talking a bomb in an ice-cream factory, here. Jack-knifing the yoghurt truck, if you know what

I mean. This may onset when a man's tubes are not cleared often enough, causing nasty swelling and bad moods. Prescribed treatment, which I've shared with Khun Aei, must be followed rigorously if the treatment is to succeed long-term and the swelling reduced in the short-term. A strict regimen of, say, a blowjob in the morning, perhaps a nice post-lunch trip for Mr Porky to Tunatown, and repeated again just before bedtime, is about the minimum requirement. Ladies need to be sensitive to this condition in their man and take the initiative, as men typically don't like to talk about it. Much like a prostate.

The history of alternative therapies in Asia is a long and illustrious one. For instance, health nuts, did you know that the first recorded use of cannabis goes back to 2737 BC in China. It was used to cure – of all things – absent-mindedness. Maybe the physician had been on it a bit long himself and forgot whether it caused it or cured it. I, for one, don't know a single dope smoker who can recite the Shanghai phone book. Around the same time, betel nut chewing also made its debut. That's the juicy red nut that makes you look like you've just ripped the heart and liver from a live gibbon with your bare teeth, and drank its blood for strength. Betel nut was not so much chewed for medicinal purposes as much as just to get a buzz going. An early incarnation of Starbucks, if you like.

The Chinese were happy enough with all of this (and why wouldn't they be). But still it was not enough. Around 700 AD, the tradition of *Ko Ku* started. Now get this one, fellow brain surgeons: children had to donate bits of their thigh or arm to 'cure' a parent who was feeling a bit poorly. Before you dismiss this as hair-brained, try it yourself. A little nibble on the thigh of a young Chinese lass has long been recommended for its curative effects. Some children were known to protest this as hocus-pocus, which started a parallel tradition called *Fook Yu*.

The Chinese also started dabbling in other extracts, some herbal, and some animal. Open the average household medicine cabinet in China these days and you won't see Panadol, Band-aids, Berocca, Viagra and Vicks Vaporub. Instead it'll be leopard extract, tiger bones (not as good as Tiger beer), tiger penis, snake semen and chicken embryos. As they say in China: 'A bear's gall bladder a day keeps the doctor away!' No wonder there's 100 tonnes of bear bile consumed each year in China and Japan. Spare a thought for the 7,000 bears caged up and on-tap in China. They must be feeling a bit of bile towards their keepers.

Meanwhile, over the border in India around 500 BC – when Buddha was known to roam the earth – Jivaka Komarabhacca, doctor and slow left-arm bowler, founded the practice of massage. Over time, this caught on and moved with traders and religious types down into Thailand, where traditional practices were handed down, er, orally from generation to generation. With the destruction of Ayutthaya by the Burmese in 1776, many ancient medical texts were destroyed. King Rama 111 had the remaining texts carved in stone in 1832, and had the inscriptions set into the walls of the *Wat Poh* temple in Bangkok.

Thai massage is based on the principle of *sen* (major energy lines) that run through the body. There are said to be 72,000 energy lines in existence but, oddly enough, modern practitioners seem to concentrate all their feminine energies on just one from those I've, um, come across.

Another alternative therapy I discovered in India was a natural cure for bad coughs. Medical officials with furrowed brows take note ... it might even work against SARS. If you've got a really chronic deep-seated bronchial chest cough, order the strongest vindaloo curry on the menu and tell them you're not a bloody tourist so spice it up a bit. Then, down this together with about, oh, a dozen Kingfisher beers. After that you won't *dare* to cough. I love India ... a country where only the bravest men fart!

When the SARS outbreak first occurred, it was the holy weekend of the Hong Kong Sevens pilgrimage. Airline crew had been told not to board anyone who was showing symptoms of flu ... especially headaches or red and watery eyes. You've got to laugh – they just described three quarters of the bleeding stadium as they dragged their sorry carcasses to the airport for the flight home. At least we now know why that germ-laboratory otherwise known as Hong Kong has got the letters 'SAR' after its official name since the handover. Silly me. I thought it meant 'Special Administrative Region' or something.

Gandhi, of course, had his own theory on well-being: start the morning with a nice glass of your own steaming piss. Side effects might be shortsightedness and baldness if he's anything to go by, but Hindus in India have practiced this for thousands of years. In Jakarta, my good friend Dr Iwan Budiarso is a urine therapist who drinks a litre a day of his own by-product after several bypass operations and western style medications failed to restore him to full health. If there's any extra – which he stores in the fridge – he'll use it later for when he has a bath or a rub down. For those of you playing at home, this is what he recommends (I'll wait for you to get a pencil and paper ready): drink from the mid-stream, and drink it fresh. To get you started, the more squeamish amongst you girl scouts should mix it 50:50 with water. Alternatively, drink a can of any American beer.

As we're on the subject of inkahol (as in 'under the affluence of …') let me assure you that I take my role as imparter of important health information to you extremely seriously, and am always endeavouring to bring you the latest in positive health and lifestyle developments. Now silicon is an important element to keep your bones strong and healthy, and we need about 30mg of this per day, say the men in the white coats at King's College, London. Silicon comes from grains, and one of the most concentrated sources is – you've got to love it! – beer. The average glass of beer has around 6mg of silicon. So you now have a valid medical reason to drink five glasses of beer per day. "It's for me bones, dear." There's only one bad side effect: ever notice that guys who drink more than five glasses a day develop breasts? Must be the silicon.

A quick one for you: what's the definition of an alcoholic? Someone who drinks more than their doctor!

Don't forget your daily ration of red wine for the ticker. I tell you why. Lab warriors from Macquarie University in Sydney have found that of all men who have a heart attack while having sex, 85 per cent of those are having sex with someone not their wife. Draw your own conclusions there. Flicking through the Medical Journal of Australia, which I have flown to me specially at great expense each month, I happened across this little snippet: moderate drinkers outlive teetotallers and heavy drinkers by about eight months. At an estimated cost of around US$3,000 for a year's supply of piss, it is way cheaper than taking cholesterol-reducing drugs which can cost over double that amount for an extra year of life.

Japan's National Institute of Longevity found that drinking wine, specifically *sake*, may boost mental agility and IQ in older people. This they say is due to the presence of polyphenols, as you already no doubt knew. Kamato Hongo, was declared the oldest living person at 114. According to an AP report one of her favourite things is drinking rice wine. Unfortunately, you'll not find this ingredient mentioned on the back of beer, whiskey or gin bottles. So better add some *sake* into the daily intake.

If all of this sounds a bit much for some of you skim-milk drinking, muesli-munching, sensible-shoe-wearing, Volvo-driving, MBA-studying, off-shore-investing, floral tie-wearing, yuppie wankers, please note that cirrhosis of the liver is nature's way of saying 'Well done, you've conquered teetotalism!'

OK, enough about booze. My good friends at Roper Starch Worldwide conducted a survey (as researchers tend to do) and found out that for 63 per cent of people, the most stressful event in life was having serious dental work done. You might like to know that buying a swimming costume came in at 26 per cent. It must have been a survey of expat housewives!

Barry was telling me he was hoping for a little romantic liaison with his wife the other night, so hopped into bed full of expectation. She turned him down. "No, Barry," she explained, "I've got an appointment with the gynaecologist tomorrow." He persisted, knowing that a bad case of PFSB was not far off. "No, darling, I'm having a pap smear in the morning so we can't do it." So there he was, less than amused, with his little pup tent in the sheets wondering what to do with the one-eyed beast. Then he had a brainwave:

"But you're not going to see the dentist tomorrow, are you, darling?" He's such a sweet-talker that bloke.

By the way, why is that process called a 'pap smear'? Because if they called it a 'cunt scrape' no woman would go for one! Mind you, all of that sounds better than the invention by Mr Dodhi Pathak in India. He recently won an innovation award for low-cost dentures. No wonder they're cheap – they're made out of bloody bamboo. Still Mr Pathak, who has a gob full of bamboo chisels himself, reckons he can plough into a good steak with the best of them.

I remember, gee it must be in the late Sixties I guess, a sign outside this Chinese dentist shop in Singapore: 'All dental work undertaken. Artificial eyes also fixed'. Which reminds me of my very good friend Rajah Charles Brooke, who was part of the Brooke fiefdom in Sarawak. He lost an eye in a riding accident and was lucky enough to get a glass eye. It was actually supposed to have been for a stuffed albatross at the local museum, but it fitted him perfectly. Mind you, he'd give you a funny look every time there was fish served at the palace for dinner.

Next time, I'll tell you about a whole bunch of other stuff like *bomoh* medicine men and the epidemic of counterfeit medicine in Asia. But now I'm going to continue research into my ongoing hypothesis that Asian women do in fact have hydraulic hips. Starting with a thorough internal examination of my lovely research assistant, Khun Aei. Rubber gloves please, nurse.

Colonel Ken

Fuzzy logic

I was working as a medic with the US navy, and we were spending some quality time in Pattaya. One day two of my lads came to see me in dire straits. It seemed they were sharing a hotel room and had picked up some horizontal refreshment one evening after several Singhas. On returning to their room with the two birds they discovered to their dismay that they had but one condom between the two of them. The hour being late, and the beer taking full effect, neither one wanted to go out for more or knock on my door (that would have gotten them shot at that hour).

They decided to share. Being logical types, they flipped a coin and the winner proceeded to go at it with the dusky young maiden in his bed. When he was done he tossed the used prophylactic to his mate, who proceeded to turn it inside out and go at it with reckless abandon with his girl.

You guessed it: three days later gentleman #2 came down with a screaming dose of the clap, while his mate was fine.

Golden throat oil

I was posted for three months as the 'Guest Teaching Professional' at a private golf club on Lantau Island, Hong Kong. A few expat friends invited me to a three-day golf weekend to Bangkok and Hua Hin, Thailand. With all of the stories I'd heard about the beautiful Thai women, Patpong, and not to forget the great golf courses, my arm was easily twisted.

The day we were to fly out to Bangkok, I woke up with a nasty throat infection. Unfortunately I'm all out of the good US drugs I brought over to take care of such problems. So immediately I rang a doctor friend of mine who is a member of the golf club. Dr P gets on the phone and says, "What's the problem, B?"

I said, "Doc, I woke up this morning with a nasty sore throat and I'm off with the boys to Thailand this evening. You've gotta help me out!"

In his mumbling Aussie accent, Dr P says, "Well, first gargle some warm salt water and then take plenty of Ibuprofen or what you Americans call Advil

…" (At this point I'm thinking to myself this guy went to medical school for eight years to tell me this? I could've called my mom back in the States!) "… and when you're in Thailand drink plenty of Kloster Beer!"

"What the hell is that gonna do for me?" I ask.

"Nothing at all! It's just a good-tasting, cheap beer!" Both of us hung up laughing our arses off. Needless to say, plenty of Kloster Beer was consumed on doctor's orders, the gorgeous women were out in full force and, oh yeah, I think we played golf a few times.

Physician heal thyself

Living in Manila I started getting skin psoriasis about seven years ago. I went to the doc and he prescribed some prescription-only medication to clear up the blotches. To this day, when I need to fill a replacement I march up to the local pharmacy counter, assertively ask for the prescription book, and write out my own prescription putting my name down as Dr Rockhard, Melbourne, Australia, practitioner 2-4-69. I've never had to get an 'official' prescription again.

Dead head

An Australian backpacker fell into an amphetamine-induced coma in Thailand. He was stabilised and spent three months recovering in a nursing home. Following his initial evacuation and subsequent hospitalisation and rehabilitation, the bill was mounting steadily. By the time he was ready to check out, he owed half a million baht, but was uninsured and had nothing against his name. Instead the poor Thai staff who nursed him chipped in what they could and are slowly paying off his bill.

Wheels falling off

While teaching in Kunming, China, I contracted pneumonia. Taken to the major hospital I was examined by a doctor (I think) and sent for an x-ray. The person taking the x-ray was smoking at the time so that did not inspire confidence. I was then moved to a double room where my elderly Chinese roommate, on waking up every morning, would cough his lungs out and then light up a smoke. After a number of blood tests the head doctor informed me that I had typhoid – strange since I had been vaccinated against it. After a call from my insurance doctor in Beijing who informed me that the tests they used were totally unreliable I became, well, a little concerned.

Finally my insurance company decided to send me to Hong Kong. The nurse duly arrived from Hong Kong and assured me that everything was arranged for the next day. Having been woken at 2am by my drunken Moslem friend, H, who decided he would watch over me in the wee small hours, I was relieved to get into the ambulance. H, having a huge hangover, proceeded to lie down on the ambulance bunk until the nurse suggested he at least move over for me. We arrived at the airport and the nurse asked for Mr Li.

"Mr Li not here."

"I was told to ask for Mr Li and he would arrange for a wheelchair for my patient," explained the nurse.

"Which Mr Li?"

"He just said Mr Li."

"No Mr Li and we have no wheelchair."

After a frustrating twenty minutes, a wheel chair did arrive – minus Mr Li – but we were told that since this was a domestic wheelchair we could not take it next door to the international terminal. More arguments. So with me sitting in the wheelchair, the nurse pushing, and a very grumpy seventeen-stoner leading the way, we managed to get to the entrance to the international departure lounge when the back wheels fell off.

No, they couldn't get another wheelchair and, no, they didn't know what to do. Finally I got up and walked into the terminal shouting, "THIS PLACE IS A FUCKING JOKE!!!" A female attendant burst into tears because I had used 'bad words'.

Inside I was provided with the international wheelchair and, after much arguing, it was decided that since the wheelchair couldn't negotiate the escalator I could process immigration downstairs and head for the plane. Not so the nurse, who was informed that only the manager could give her permission to proceed with her patient.

"GET THE MANAGER!"

"He not here today."

Finally, with less than thirty minutes before the flight, she was allowed to accompany me. This after much screaming and some pushing and shoving from H. The nurse, carrying our luggage, wheeled me to the plane flanked by two security guards. Moral of the story? Don't get sick in China.

Speak no ill

As an athlete, I find it very helpful to my marathon training to visit an osteopath on a regular basis [I know exactly how you feel! – Col Ken]. This particular osteopath in the Osaka area was recommended to me by a friend. I found out where his tiny office was, but it took me two hours and a total of four different trains to get there. When I got to his office on the first visit, I found out that we had a bit of a communication problem: I speak little-to-no Japanese, which is a *serious* handicap in Nippon-land, and he speaks absolutely no English. This stern, 50-ish doctor reminded me of a gruff drill sergeant, built like a fire-plug, complete with flat-top haircut.

I tried to explain to him that I am a runner, then he laid down the law: "YOU COME JAPAN, YOU SPEAK JAPAN!!!" Only then did he allow me into his examination/treatment room, put me on the table and started chanting in Japanese, very loudly, while he cracked my neck, massaged my back, jerked out my head and feet, etc. Then he rolled me over on my back and I saw that his eyes were completely closed, and he was breaking a sweat, chanting in Japanese all the while. His breath indicated a five-pack-a-day puffer. I paid him the usual rate of 5,000 yen and I left feeling realigned and renewed.

It was a truly bizarre experience, but I go back to see him every time that I am in Japan nonetheless, since he is an extremely competent medical professional. If only I could remember his name ...

In cash we trust

I ended up in hospital in Shanghai after slipping a disc in the hotel gym, which proves it is safer to stick to the bar. I was on a drip and pumped full of narcotics for four whole days while they "waited for my pain to go to allow me to undergo an x-ray and back scan". After much waiting and more waiting I grew very impatient. I eventually found someone who spoke English and they confessed the scan machine was actually broken and they did not want to admit this to a foreigner to save face.

By the fourth day I was starving as the drugs wore off. I asked for some food and the nurse said OK. They fetched me some boiled eggs and demanded 15RMB in cash. I had no money as I was admitted in an ambulance. I explained I could pay – just add it to my bill. They said no way: "No cash, no food."

I checked out later that day and headed straight to KFC.

Gone, but not forgotten

A colleague of mine based in the Dutch office came twice a year to Hong Kong for a period of eight weeks in which he was responsible for preparing the new sales collection. One day he came to me and said: "I had this itchy feeling on my pecker the last few days. It was dripping a bit although that is less now … do you think I still need to see a doctor or will it just disappear like a cold?"

"Get into my car," I said, and drove him to the Adventist, where they confirmed what I already thought – he had gonorrhoea. Hearing exactly what the problem was and being told that he had to abstain from sexual intercourse for the time being, he became very nervous as he was about to return home at the end of the week to his girlfriend, who would be waiting for him. And what can you say as a guy after eight weeks away … sorry, dear, I have a headache?!?

Two days later he was very happy to hear that the management was not completely satisfied yet with the collection and wanted him to stay for a few more weeks to see it through. Saved by the bell.

Tropical medicine

We were going on a family holiday and I was to meet my wife and son in Bangkok for a night, before heading off to Koh Samui for a couple of weeks.

Meeting them at the airport, my son looked weak and pale, and had been nauseous for the whole flight. I put it down to airsickness. However the next day he was still a bit pale, and we flew off to Koh Samui. The second day there, he complained about severe stomach pains … doubled-over like an old man when he walked.

A dodgy-looking doctor's clinic in one of the small towns was the first we came across. The doctor diagnosed suspected appendicitis, gave us directions to the international hospital, and told us to drive there immediately.

We took our screaming son in, and tried to explain the situation to the all-Thai nurses and doctor. Glazed expressions all round. Fortunately, there was a Filipina nurse who spoke English so she helped translate. Immediately my son was put in a wheelchair and wheeled into a makeshift ward, running an extremely high fever. Dextrose drips were stuck into his arm along with an injection or two. Then he was wheeled off to the x-ray department.

Much paperwork and Visa card rubbing later, he was admitted 'for observation'. We stayed with him till night fell, then all fell asleep on the benches in his room. During the night, the drip came adrift, spilling blood all over the bed. Three days later, we hadn't so much as left the hospital yet. Fortunately fevers abated, various theories about dengue or acute something-or-another were bandied about inconclusively. But our son was now much better and discharged.

On the second last day of the holiday, I woke up feeling like I had been clubbed on the back of the head. Fair enough, we had drunk copious beers the previous night, I thought. I went to town to get some Panadol and anti-inflammatory pills. These didn't do much to ease the pain. The next day, same feeling. I asked for more Panadol at the check-in counter and crashed out on the flight home. About three days later I was admitted to hospital with dengue fever … my red blood cell count had plummeted from about 400 to just 49. I stayed in hospital nearly a week.

Beer Belly

A friend of mine lived in Aceh, Indonesia, for seven years in the mid-70s when it was real frontier territory. In that time, he never drank water, tea, coffee nor any fluid other than Bintang Bir. He swore by the fact that beer was pasteurised therefore all the germs had been nuked. Sure enough, he was the only one that never suffered Soekarno's Revenge (Bali Belly).

A wee dram of advice

I visited our company doctor, an old British chap in Malaysia, after feeling rather dizzy in the office. He decided to run a whole bunch of tests on me including a blood test. I had to come back a few days later for the results. He then informed that I had a Hepatitis E infection and that for the next six months I should stay at home, lay flat on my back in bed (no pillow, no reading, no TV), just rest.

I went home and lay down in bed and was already getting bored after 30 minutes. Besides, there was a lot of work to do as we just had opened our office here in Malaysia. I therefore decided to forget what the doc said and headed for the office. I informed my local right-hand-man and he told me to visit his doctor as he had made Hepatitis his main subject.

This doc explained, without even checking me, that he knew I did not have Hepatitis E as I would not be sitting there but would be in the last stages of my life on all kinds of tubes in a hospital. He then gave me a thorough check and suggested that I might have hit the whisky bottle a bit too hard lately, and should slow down on that. Otherwise I was as healthy as can be. I drank one to that.

You've got to be kidding

A British doctor was convicted of child sex offences in Cambodia. Several years later, he is now back in Phnom Penh, amazingly still practicing medicine.

Getting under their skin

My doctor in Malaysia had prescribed me some cream for a skin irritation that was still in the healing stage. As I was about to go off for a holiday, and the cream was nearly finished, I called my doctor to prescribe me more of the cream to take with me. No problem he assured me: I could either come and pick it up myself or send someone.

So I asked my Indian driver to go and pick it up. I explained to him where to go. After an hour or so he came back with a kind of cream I had never seen before. Studying it further I also noticed that the receipt he brought back was not from my doctor. Apparently he went to the wrong doctor (as there were several next to each other). Being a persistent bugger he kept saying to the assistant, who said she did not know any Mr K, that there indeed should be some cream waiting there for Mr K which he absolutely had to pick up, and that he would not leave before she gave it to him.

After much debate she had had enough of him, and just gave him any kind of cream so he would shut up and leave.

Eye for detail

One day in India I woke up to watery, scratchy eyes that were bloodshot [Isn't that normal? – Col Ken.]. I figured it was pink-eye but had not been in a pool for some time. So I went to the doctor that morning and he confirmed it was conjunctivitis. I then asked how in the hell I got that. The doctor just recited a few facts: "You see, *sahib*, at this time of year as you know, we have very bad dust storms. You also see the people are urinating and defecating everywhere. You see the bacteria from the faeces and urine go to the dirt and then the dirt is blown all around and then comes to your eye. That is how it is, *sahib*." Probably more than I really wanted to know.

Indian rope trick

In Penang, Malaysia, in the late-50s, five of us – plus one beautiful Indian hooker – repaired one night back to one of the guy's houses, and on his veranda he had all these nice long cane chairs. As we sat chatting to each other – reclining with an Anchor beer in each hand – she in turn unzipped each of us, hopped on top, and gave us the ride of our life whilst we swapped yarns.

As it turned out, one of the gang was newly arrived from England, the rest of us having been round the traps a fair while. A week later, one of the guys went to the doctor with a dose: yes, it was the new guy. "You old bastards have obviously built up an immunity to everything going round," he said. We couldn't agree more.

The tooth hurts sometimes

In a little village near Guilin, China, we stumbled on this dusty local marketplace. There was dirt and flies and crap everywhere. And in the middle of all of this was a dentist's chair with a little old lady in it. She was opened wide saying 'ahhh' and exposing her only tooth to the dentist. Because of really bad gum disease it was a really long tooth sticking out quite a bit, and the dentist was attempting to file it down. There was no anaesthetic in evidence, and when he started pedalling on this rusty old contraption on the ground to get his drill spinning, I had to leave. The thought of the pain was too much for me to bear.

Late check out

On holiday in Thailand years ago I had caught the train to the end of the line near Phuket and got out in this one-horse town. I checked into this very ordinary local hotel, and within a few days had come down with severe dysentery. I was whisked off to the local hospital where I stayed for ten days and went from 18 stone to just 11. In the course of this whole episode I lost my money, my passport, everything.

When I was discharged from hospital I went back to the hotel, and there they presented me with a bill for the last two weeks. Even though everything had been removed from my room, I hadn't checked out they said. All I was left with was my shirt, shorts and sandals. I got in touch with the Embassy and they eventually sorted the whole mess out for me.

The highwire act

In Bangkok I went for a check-up with my doctor, who works in a tiny cramped clinic. He needed to do the old 'wire down the dick' bit. As his door didn't lock properly, he asked me to stand up against it to keep it closed, which I did … my bare arse propping it closed. He then stuck this bloody wire down my dick and I prayed that the nurse didn't come barging in at that crucial moment and impale me on this deadly instrument.

Standard behaviour

I used to run a bar in Angeles and was pissed all the time, and very pissed some of the time. Back in Australia for a break, I went for a routine medical during which the doctor asked me how much I drank. "About four a day," I said.

"Four standard drinks *every* day?" he said in near horror, tut-tutting under his breath. Lucky I didn't tell him the truth – something probably closer to fourteen!

Cost-cutting

In Hong Kong, I interpreted my contract as entitling me to all things medical to be covered by the company. I had two nasty-looking lumps come up on my skin – one on the back of my neck and the other on my cheek. I went to a specialist who recommended they be removed, and went into great detail about how this would be a delicate piece of surgery but would leave no trace once done and healed over.

A date for the surgery was set, and on the day he spent what seemed like hours measuring the contours of my face and practicing the angle of the cuts to ensure there would be no scarring. The lumps were soon excised, analysed and declared benign. Meanwhile I was getting a lot of interest and attention from all the ladies in the office with these manly stitches in my face.

Shortly after, I left HK and moved to Singapore to a new company and a new job. Now a couple of months after the operation, my wound was still festering a bit and a very noticeable scar was in place. Then I received a bill for the surgery, forwarded from my previous company. I ignored it. Two months later, another bill and a stern reminder. Ignored. And so on each two months for a year, each with increasing urgency and desperation and threat in the plea to pay. I wasn't going to pay anyone for what was part of my package, but especially not as it left with me this lousy scar.

What a nerve

I had an uproarious night in Patpong, which featured a spectacular – if inexplicable in the light of day – dive off the bar counter. The next day I woke up sore, but had a flight to Guangzhou, China, to catch. By the time I arrived in China I could hardly move (guess the alcoholic anaesthetic was wearing off). I ended up in hospital there for a week, before I was able to regain full and comfortable mobility, because of a pinched nerve in the spine.

Word of mouth

In Ho Chi Minh City I had gone through a carpet store to reach the dentist shop behind, which had a huge tooth outside as its sign. I got an implant done for US$15, which would have cost me $750 back home. I suspect they probably mugged someone out the back alley to get the new tooth, but it's still working fine to this day.

Putting the bite on him

This expat gent in Hong Kong needed all his teeth replaced with implants. He was quoted US$30,000 in Hong Kong for the lower jaw alone. He flew to Australia where it was done for just US$8,000. Next year he plans to fly back and get his top jaw done.

Gutsy performance

In the Vietnam War, I was taken out by a mortar shell, which ripped into my guts and back. I ended up shortly after on a makeshift operating table, my intestines laid out on the table beside me. The doctor said there was no option to cut them out and replace them with a colostomy bag.

"Bullshit you will," I said. "I'm married with kids, but I still wanna look OK." With that I drew out my service pistol, held it to my head and said, "Shoot me instead." Given this incentive, the doctor managed to patch me up OK and, apart from a few scars and a funny hard lump in my stomach, everything's working fine till now.

Axe wound

My usual doctor (a male Caucasian from a European country) at the big fancy private hospital was out of the country on vacation, so when I needed medical assistance for a minor leg injury, I was assigned to a Chinese woman doctor. She examined my leg, gave me an injection, and wrote me a prescription. I found the woman doctor somewhat attractive and interesting and, when she did not bill me for her medical services, I took the opportunity to send her flowers with a card containing my email address. Now, every time that I find myself in this large South East Asian city, I give this female doctor an injection of a different sort.

Time limit

In the good old days of Hong Kong, you'd pretty much have to have an accident before you could be booked for drink-driving violations. If you were stopped, a blood test was required. The loophole was you could nominate the doctor as the police themselves were not allowed to carry out such a procedure. Always good to know a certain expat doctor: "What time can you do the test?"

"Tomorrow at twelve," was his standard answer. He'd duly troop down the next day, perform the test, and declare that the driver was well under the limit (all the alcohol having since been processed out of your system). With a night in the slammer considered due penance, you were then released without charge.

Doc of the bay

We sailed down from Hong Kong as guard ship to the China Sea Race, which ended at San Fernando in the Philippines. The ship was moored at San Fernando government naval dock. Naturally, the lads required some R&R, and the nearest place was a bar called the Stiletto Bar. As sailors do, we all arrived en masse at this bar, which was shaped like a big horse shoe: the lower rates at one end, senior rates in the middle, and officers at the other end, and got stuck in to the communion wine and general hymn singing.

About an hour later the coxswain approached me and informed me that there were no tarts available. I told him that there appeared to be plenty about, to which he informed me that they do not have their medical cards in order. Since the local pox doctor had gone down to Manila and not returned in time to check the girls they were therefore not able to play.

Since I was the 'Entertainment Officer' I had to contact the skipper, who was a very pious man seated only a few feet away from me chatting up a local nun. He informed me to contact that "useless bugger" who was on the ship to get it sorted out, because this was bad for the men's morale. The "useless bugger" was the ship's new second-lieutenant surgeon, who had spent all his time on ship lying in his cabin feigning seasickness. The coxswain was detailed off to get the young doc and I was detailed off to negotiate with the 'Mother Superior'.

We ended up getting two nights' free beer and the doctor was loaned out to the 'Nunnery' to check out the young novices for any 'spiritual problems' that they may well have had.

All went well until the Sunday morning, when we were about to sail: it was discovered that the doc was not on board, and nobody had seen him since the Friday night session. The skipper was out on the bridge wing and I had the job of informing him about the missing Doc. I was just about to enter the bridge when there was this screaming and general merriment coming from the pier adjacent to the ship – sitting on the pier was this Jeepney covered in tarts with the young doc strapped over the bonnet, pissed out of his mind, covered in lipstick, and not a care in the world.

Naturally he was very quiet on the journey back to Hong Kong.

If you have a good story about doctors, nurses or alternative quacks in Asia, take a couple of aspirin and email The Editor at hardshipposting@hotmail.com or fax 612-9499-5908 in the morning.

The Zero-to-One foundation is set up by the family and friends of Robert Thwaites, one of the innocent victims of the Bali bombings. Their mission is to support victims of terrorism by providing direct relief and assistance to them or their dependants.

For more info www.zero-to-one.org Please give generously.

The HARDSHIP POSTING team acknowledges the amazing work done with limited resources by the doctors, nurses, paramedics and volunteers in the aftermath of the Bali Bombings. We encourage you to help support the local and international victims by donating or supporting the RED CROSS BALI APPEAL. Details at www.redcross.org.au

❖ 9 ❖

Death by Mini-bar
Or Stay of Execution

True tales of hotels, motels and flophouses in Asia.

Is it just me or are hotel rooms becoming increasingly complicated? For a start, there's the confusing array of switches, buttons, controls, timers, dimmers, doo-dads and whatnots which seem to be running riot in hotel rooms across Asia these days. There's a bloody switch for everything and even – I'm most sure – switches for things which either don't exist, haven't been installed yet or, in any case, I couldn't bloody find.

The first thing you want do when you arrive is check out the room and the view. In the better hostelries someone from reception might accompany you up to the room … this is invariably a gay chap from front office. There'd be eight airbrushed beauties behind the counter and one fag, and who do you get? Always the pillow-biter! And he minces his way through the instructions: "And thith ith your TV thet, thir …" No shit, Sherlock, I was wondering what that big black box with the glass screen at the front was for. "Thith ith your bathroom, thir …" Really, here, where the tiled floor and the tub are? I thought I'd just go out on the balcony and hose myself down there! But then when he eventually buggers off, you're left to your own dear vices. And do you think you can actually find the button that draws the curtains – in the direction you want them to go? You can always find the other one. So you mess about with the bedside panel for a bit, and there are lights going on and off, toilets flushing, room service delivering bowls of soup, radio stations blaring out, housekeeping delivering towels, but do you think you can get the fucking curtains open? Not a chance. All right, sod the view. Let's just watch some telly and get over this jet lag before heading down for a massage or a night on the town. Let's see what the local news is.

And do you think you can find the 'ON' switch for the TV? Oh, it's there on the TV set all right but when you push it nothing happens. So you push every button on the set and … nothing. You check the wall to see that it's plugged in (don't laugh you arseholes, it's been known to happen to, er, friends of mine before). You then run through the dazzling array of buttons on the bedside panel. 'TV'. Aha. Push. Nothing. Push, push. Nothing. P-u-u-u-s-h. Nothing. Call housekeeping. Another mincer turns up. "Oh, thir, you thimply need to do thith …" (he opens a cupboard and pulls out a remote control from the third drawer) "… then thith …" (pushes a few buttons on it) "… then thith …" (pushes button on bedside panel) … "then thith …" (walks over and keys in a code into the room safe) … "then thith …" (swipes your room key card across the fruit bowl). Click, the TV crackles to life with the obligatory static charge. And guess what? It's fucking Who Wants To Be a Millionaire? The local version. The quizmaster looks exactly the same as the presenter wherever you come from, the background set's exactly the same, and the prize is exactly the same: a million. Unfortunately it's a million of whatever the local currency is … exceptionally bad news if you live in Vietnam or Indonesia.

By this time, techno-phobes, you're ready for a beer. Welcome to the living torture chamber that is the mini-bar. For your added convenience and service, they put you in a room with a cold box full of beer, spirits, and cashew nuts. And it's not like you have to walk all the way to the kitchen to get it: it's right there, staring at you seductively. Like Pavlov's dog, you're already drooling at the prospect of a refreshing brew, so you reach in and knock the top off an ice cold Heineken. (By the way, you tight-arsed Cloggies, I'm still waiting for my free case of your exceptionally fine product from the gratuitous mention in the last book.)

But, what's this? The price list: 'Beer – local US$68', 'Beer – imported US$150', 'Tiny bag of nuts in impossible-to-open-without-resorting-to-physical-violence foil containing mainly thin air and disappointingly few nuts when you do finally get it open – US$380'. Seriously, what's a man to do? Not having at least one beer from there is not a realistic option. Or – if it is – it's certainly not within the realms of humane treatment under the Geneva Convention (as opposed to the Ginivy's Convention in Singapore, which is something far more inhumane altogether unless you're a fan of *both* kinds of music – country and western!).

So now you're stuffed. You're staring down the barrel of US$150 for the beer you just opened recklessly and with abandon. That could buy you several short times with the pick of the crop in Cambodia! If not the whole crop. Time to wheel in the serious strategies: a) try and replace the lid and see if anyone notices it's slightly bent, a mouthful of beer is missing, and it's gone flat or b) finish your beer, enjoying it to the very last drop, then going down to Seven-Eleven and buying the self-same product for $1.50, sneaking it back to the hotel room, and replacing it in the mini-bar. The perfect ruse. Or, rather, it was. Now some hotels, in their ever-increasing wisdom (sometimes mistaken for greed by the more cynical), have started installing mini-bars with automatic scanners. As soon as a product is removed from the mini-bar it's automatically zapped like a supermarket checkout and your room bill charged.

I guess it makes more sense than the usual system upon checkout: "Anything from the mini-bar, Mr Colonel?" You try and act nonchalant, putting on your best honest angelic face (easy for me, you'd understand).

"Just one local beer." You have presented your evidence. Now they corroborate it.

"Housekeeping, room 1869 checking out." Then you wait, and wait, while housekeeping's key forensics personnel are dispatched to your room to gather all and any incriminating evidence of consumption. The reception phone rings.

"Sir, a sparkling mineral water, six local beers, nine imported beers, a small bottle of Johnny Walker, and a packet of Durex Comfort condoms for the larger man." All of this in earshot of the prim corporate lady executive checking out next to you, who shoots you a withering glance.

"I think you'll find a mistake, young lady … I believe the mineral water was free."

"You get one bottle of local still water free, sir. But sparkling Perrier is US$199 per bottle."

I was bending my good friend Heinz's ear about this recently. Heinz is an old Swiss mate of mine who has run some of the finest establishments across Asia, and a finer selection of sharp grey double-breasted suits I've never seen in my life. And the shoes … they are so polished, you can damn near look up ladies dresses in them. "Jah, jah, I understand, Ken," he said, not understanding at all. "But zis is vhere ve make ze rrrreal money," he confessed under my intensive interrogation. "You come back to your room, you haf a lady friend maybe and she vants to drink a vine. Or you haf some colleagues and they know it vill go on to your tab so of course they vill drink your mini-bar dry. Business is business."

"But, Heinz, don't you think a 10,000% mark-up is just a little too much?"

"Oh, excuse me, Ken, I must just go take care of this important guest arriving now."

With that he dashes off, all smarmy and smiley, to welcome the next suckers to the Mini-Bar California, where you can check out anytime you like but can never afford to pay the bill. A business built on the premise of resentment is an interesting notion.

Bring back the languid old days of hospitality, those envisaged by the Indian hotelier Mohan Oberoi. He started in a little run-down hostelry in India that he eventually got the opportunity to buy. His second-ever property was The Grand in Calcutta. This had closed in 1933 because of a cholera epidemic, and no one would go near the place. So he took it over and reputedly ran soda water through its plumbing system until rumours of its contaminated plumbing system died off and the business grew from there. Call me old fashioned but, apart from the Grand Hyatt, any hotel with 'grand' in its name invariably isn't.

On the subject of languor and charm, can we go past the Galle Face Hotel in Colombo, Sri Lanka? This beautiful three-storey Victorian building with its waving palms has been standing proud on the waterfront since 1864. Amazingly – and I can't figure this out – it's the only hotel on the waterfront in this tropical ocean-side city. So it's the pick of the spots to watch the sunsets that rival those in Manila Bay. No wonder it was the centre of British colonial life in Ceylon for nearly a century. All the Raj, you might say. And to this day, the smiling crew are still done out in the white duck suits of that era.

Recently I was also lucky enough to stay at The Strand Hotel in Rangoon, Burma, or Yangon, Myanmar, depending on your political persuasion. The Sarkies Brothers, the same gents who developed the Raffles in Singapore, built this in 1901. Similar to Gall Face, it's also a three-storey Victorian style place, with high ceilings and plenty of natural timber (although I did supply my own wood on one occasion there!). The ceilings were a lot higher back in the 40s when it took a direct hit from a bomb during the war turning it into what the Vietnamese would call a 'thousand star hotel', ie, you're sleeping under the skies. Mind you, I did find its rate of US$975 for the night for the top suite made Heinz's mini-bar look quite reasonable in comparison.

And it looks very reasonable when you compare it to the Idol Pet Hotel in Fukuoka, Japan, where pet hotels have become all the rage. Sometimes I wish I was making this crap up, but it's unfortunately true – people pay US$300 per night for their pooch or, um, pussy to be pampered with massages, mineral therapy and makeovers in their own little private apartment. Gourmet meals on tap, too. I'm sorry, but that's utterly pathetic! Actually I'm not sorry at all.

In fact, you don't have to spend big bucks to have a good night at a hotel. After all, it's only a place to rest your weary head (better make that *heads*) after another busy day at the orifice.

In Thailand, there've been some great hotels over the years. I remember from my Vietnam days the Trocadero, or 'The Troc' as we'd call it. It was close to Patpong and that's all you wanted in a place on R&R. These new-fangled West Point chaps talk of 'shock and awe' as a new military tactic to be deployed in Iraq, but way back in the Vietnam War I had more than my fairshare of shockin' whores at the Troc, I tell you. Went past it the other day on Surawong road and could hardly recognise it. The sign's the same and bits of the facade, but it's sadly been given over to progress.

Which is something that you could never accuse The Expat Hotel in Phuket of … it's been an absolute institution for oilies and itinerants for more years than I can remember. But that's not hard because I'm getting to the stage where last week's events have been transferred from short-term to long-term memory. Mind you, the short-*time* memories are still strong! And I was always intrigued by the On On Hotel in Phuket. I thought it had something to do with the Hash group headquarters or something, but Chiu Mai Kok (my resident Cantonese sleeping dictionary in Hong Kong who I treated to a little side trip in Phuket) assures me its name means 'comfort and happiness'. Well, I think they might just be done for false advertising there. But that place has been going since Pak Yok Tew, part of the Chinese immigrant invasion of the 20s, set it up in 1927.

A couple of years later, a new place called the Goodwood Park Hotel opened on Scotts Road in Singapore. Well, it wasn't exactly new – the Teutonia Club had built a new clubhouse in 1900 that was going along nicely, with performances of Mozart and Beethoven a regular attraction for the homesick. Then war broke out in 1914, and all the Germans were imprisoned and their assets auctioned off, including this ornate building with its distinctive spire. After serving a few years as an entertainment hall, it became the hotel as we know it today with all its old-worldly charm.

But the prize for 'original condition' must go to the Mitre Hotel in Singapore. The owner, my good friend Mr Cheam, was telling me over a can of Tiger beer the interesting story of how this ramshackle building came to be – and remains to this day – a hotel with spacious grounds and durian trees in the heart of the Singapore business district. This two-storey colonial mansion was built around 1860, probably by the Oxley family. The area, just off Somerset Road with its massive SingTel buildings and shopping centres, used to be plantations in those days. At some point, the Alsakoff merchant family took it over and turned it into the Windsor Hotel. By the time Cheam's old man took it over in 1948, it was – apart from the Raffles and Goodwood Park – about the most flash accommodation money could buy in Singapore. Mind you, that's not saying a lot. Only the biggest buildings had anything more than a bucket to deal with their sewerage. The Brits poured back into Singapore, and through the Fifties and Sixties the shortage of rooms meant the Mitre ran a full house. Its restaurant downstairs, leading out to the veranda, was always full with a lively crowd of professionals and their families.

Then, a funny thing happened. Around 1975, if I remember rightly, they opened the Mandarin hotel right on Orchard Road. This thing was like a glittering jewel on a rather dusty street. Everyone said: "Too flashy for Singapore, it'll never last …" There'd be a few people eating their words now. What does humble pie taste like anyway? Think I'll stick to fur pie. Less calories. Then came the Westin Singapore, the world's tallest hotel in a rather phallic 70-storey tower. And so on.

Anyway, where were we? Oh yes, back at Uncle Cheam's place, all this new competition was running him into the ground and I reckon the Mitre hotel last had a new coat of paint around the time the Mandarin opened. These days, there's a tired old hand-painted sign on Killiney Road, which is the only way you'd know that it existed behind the lush foliage. Upstairs, shutters hang off their hinges. You enter via the portico downstairs, and straight into an area with old armchairs with their fabric torn and springs poking out. I don't remember there being a light in the area, but if there was it was probably a naked light bulb hanging from the ceiling. But they do have a bar counter, and a fridge full of ice cold Tiger beer, drunk from the can of course. They can be proud of their mosquito to guest ratio, which consistently runs at about 25:1 or more. The rooms upstairs are accessed via a very creaky staircase. And these days you get a choice of rooms with a toilet or a bucket – sorry, fan or air-con – which runs you about US$20 a night. No exorbitant mini-bar bills to pay. No surcharge for visitors after midnight. And the cheapest beer on Orchard Road, never mind the fine crystal. No wonder it's still a hit with the oilies and divers.

My good friend, travel writer and author supreme Noel Barber, often used to say: "The natives were friendly, so we stayed the night." And I reckon that's spot on. Now, if I can just work out how to use this bleeding phone, I'm going to order some room service. But don't worry – I've already pushed my suitcase and a table across the front of the mini-bar so I won't be tempted to have a drink.

Colonel Ken

Behind the wheel

I was in Manila when Mt Pinatabu went off. Scheduled to fly out the following Saturday, Qantas cancelled due to the amount of ash in the air. They put me up in a hotel for free. Not wanting to waste any opportunities I went straight to Ermita (for the cultural events, of course).

Returning to my hotel much later that evening, the taxi died because the air filter was chocked. I opened the bonnet, cleaned the filter and jump-started the car myself. I told the driver to get in the passenger side and drove to the Intercontinental myself.

The hotel doorman got the shock of his life when he opened the passenger door and your standard t-shirted, shorts-and-sandals driver stepped out! Next evening I was down at the lobby asking for a taxi to take me to Ermita once again. The doorman said to me: "And will you be driving, sir?"

Not the marrying kind

Going into my Seoul hotel one night with a girl, I was stopped by the duty officer. "This is my, er, fiancé," I said, unconvincingly. He looks down his list.

"Well, sir, your fiancé's a prostitute!" I don't think he meant it to come out like that, but it was perfect, and she was turned away.

Low-giene

Staying at one of the best hotels in Colombo, Sri Lanka, I had to attend to a worsening leg infection. I asked for cotton wool, scissors, tape and surgical spirit. The attendant duly arrived carrying all the medical supplies within a few minutes.

Unfortunately, he had the cotton wool on top – unwrapped and out of its protective packet – and his grimy thumbnail stuck right into the cotton wool.

Doesn't hurt to ask

I travel a lot in Asia. When I fill up the hotel registration form at check-in, I always write down 'Yes' or 'Maybe' (or 'Hopefully' if the line is long enough) under the question 'Sex'. In ten years no one has ever made a comment about it.

Eat here or take away?

Four lads from the UK visit Bangkok for the first time. At their hotel a waiter takes them to one of Bangkok's famous restaurants. One of the guys – on seeing all the girls in the 'fish tank' – decides that he will have to take a photograph of the scene to show his mates back home in Belfast as they will not believe him. He pulls out a disposable pocket camera and proceeds to take a photograph. This results in the whole group being expelled from the premises.

Big J was not amused at this behaviour as he had already picked his number. He needn't have worried as the hotel waiter ended up being a lady-boy and took quite a shining to our Big J. Lo and behold when the boys phoned Big J's hotel room the next morning the phone was answered by the lady-boy in question.

Northern exposure

A decade ago, it was a real struggle to get a girl back to your hotel in China. Indeed, even if you were successful, the chances were that the Public Security Bureau would intervene in mid-performance. Still, getting every page of your passport stamped with a *Piu Ha* ('Whoremaster') was a good badge of honour to show to the chaps back home.

One time I was up in Beijing with my girlfriend of the moment (and my wife-to-be), M, a Hong Kong Chinese lass. We had trouble at the outset checking into the hotel (part of a five-star international chain) since the officious staff was convinced that my girlfriend was a southern floozy from Canton. Eventually, after lengthy negotiations and document filling, we were allowed in.

M was in a foul mood by this stage so we went out to find a good restaurant to calm her down. Back at the hotel, another half hour of arguments ensued before we were admitted again. We finally stepped into our hotel room to find a selection of condoms had been pushed under the door.

Very sensible I thought: as every good Chinese knows, it's only the *gweilos* who have AIDS and they didn't want me polluting the master race. For some reason, M was less amused …

Lucky number

One night during my first visit to Seoul, Korea, came a knock at my hotel room door. There stood one of the most beautiful girls I have ever seen. Unfortunately, it being my first trip, I spoke no Korean, so I was unable to determine what she wanted. Still, she was amenable to all invitations: "Would you like to come in? Would you like a cigarette? Would you like to take a shower?" Things went very well from there and soon I was ready to sleep.

Ms Park (the only personal detail I learned from her) had other plans. She had a grip on a part of me calculated to focus my attention, and kept squeezing until I rose to the occasion. By the time we finished, even she was worn out. I had to get up at 6am, and pantomimed that she was welcome to sleep in, but she followed me down to the lobby, where she fell into conversation with one of the *ajumas* sleeping there until day shift began.

That night I had business with Mr Lee, the hotel manager, and asked him if he knew anything about a girl named Ms Park. He looked up in surprise, then told me the story. It seems that the night before the guest in 315 had asked the bellman for a hooker, and paid 35,000 won in advance for an all-night service. My room number was 513.

Clearly unhealthy

While in Nepal in the early Nineties I sat in my room as the maids came in to clean. One of them noticed toothpaste lip marks on my glass in the bathroom. She picked up the glass, dunked it in the toilet bowl, and wiped it dry with her sari dress. I drink water straight from the bottle now.

Chinese water torture

During the early days in China whenever you came into the hotel they would always play the same piano music: Richard Clayderman (RC for short).

RC in the lift, RC in the lobby, RC on the sound system in the room and, worst of all, RC in the bar. This may not sound so disturbing, but if you are based for several months in the same hotel you might go a little bit crazy.

A German chap in the Yangtze Hotel in Wuhan very politely asked the girls to change the music: he had even brought some tapes, or was willing to listen to some Chinese music, but not again to the same old tape he had been hearing over the past three months. The girls insisted it was not possible, and the bar manager also told him 'no way' as the sound system was just one system for the whole hotel.

He then got so damned mad he tore the speakers off the wall: "Better no music at all than more of this Richard Clayderman shit!" he raved.

I also came to dislike this piano music during that period. But, nowadays, it is even worse because they have a karaoke set in the bar of the hotel and you have to listen to the local talent burping into the mike.

Time for the health club!

Room for error

It was my first visit to Macau, right in the middle of a series of car bombings and other triad-related violent crimes. Everyone was kind of edgy. There was a police car permanently parked in front of the New Century hotel where I was staying.

One afternoon I fell asleep in my room while reading the newspaper: I had forgotten to lock my door. I woke up with a start as two huge guys were menacingly advancing towards my bed. Oh shit!

"That's it, pick your things up, you're leaving now!" barked one of the two, as my eyes focus enough to realise that they are hotel security staff.

"What are you talking about, I just arrived a few hours ago!" I replied. The other security gorilla took his walkie-talkie and called his boss …

"Sorry, sir, wrong room."

Crawling with 'em

A few years ago I was travelling to the southern China city of Zhangjiang. A friend recommended the Peninsula Hotel to me. I was reluctant because I knew that, given the room rate, this would be your typical run-down Chinese hotel with smelly carpets and 25-watt light bulbs. But my friend was enthusiastic, insisting that the place was great.

Arriving there my worst fears were confirmed: the place looked terrible. However I was surprised to see a number of 'working' girls hanging around the lobby in the middle of the afternoon. As I was being shown to my room by the bellboy, some of them tagged along and offered me their service.

This was to set the tone for the rest of my stay. At any time of day or night the phone would ring, the doorbell would ring: it was impossible to sleep for more than 30 minutes without being waken up by a working girl. I had been to a lot of hotels which had cockroach infestations but this was my first with a hooker infestation! When I came back my friend innocently asked me how my trip went. Later on I learned that they hotel was nicknamed 'The *Penisula*'.

Learning curves

It is 9am, and I am unshowered, unshaved, unwashed, and not in my nicest mood or nicest clothes. I wander down to the breakfast buffet at the best hotel in Udon Thani, Thailand. The girls from the local vocational college are doing an internship that morning at the breakfast buffet. There are about two-dozen uniformed college girls and one *farang* man, me. Needless to say I was given many phone numbers. Unfortunately I was heading back home that day, otherwise …

High standards of service

After three-and-a-half years in South East Asia, curiosity finally kills the cat and I buy a round-trip ticket to Phnom Penh, Cambodia. I took a room at a quiet, secluded inn run by a jovial, continuously-stoned, usually-drunk, yet completely professional hotelier from a certain northern European nation. The hotel that he runs is mainly frequented by single male guests from this same nation.

On my third day of exploring the truly amazing, lively city of Phnom Penh I decide, on the spur of the moment, to go check out those Vietnamese brothels north of the city that everyone has told me about. I take a motorcycle taxi through the rain for the 30-minute ride. The ride ends at the line of brothels on a muddy road, with all the available young lovelies running out to greet me.

The driver parks at the far end of the lane, next to a small restaurant full of punters. I look up and whom do I see? It is my hotelier and three of his countrymen/guests! They are smoking joints as big as a Cuban cigar and have almost killed off three full 750s of Stoli vodka. The hotelier offers to give me a ride back to the hotel after I finish my business.

That was a hotel shuttle service with a difference.

Love is blind

A friend of mine was in Korea for the first time to visit a fair. After a hard day's work and some nice beers he thought about trying out one of the local girls and ordered an in-room massage (thinking they would also offer the 'special' services here). When the doorbell rang he quickly opened the door without really looking, and turned back to the bed to lie down.

All of a sudden – BANG!!! When he took a closer look it became clear what it was: the old blind masseuse had walked straight into his wardrobe that he had forgotten to close.

Not quite the special Korean experience he had in mind.

That time of the month

In the Eighties we had a reasonable amount of production in the area of Xianfan Hubei province, China, which was six hours by train from Wuhan. Wuhan in turn had at that time only one flight a week to Hong Kong. The hotels there were separated into hotels for locals and hotels for foreigners: but if they tried to make a good impression on us with the better hotel then I do not envy the locals staying in the other hotels.

We normally stayed at the No 1 Hotel. Breakfast was taken in a room in a small building where the door was always open, no matter how cold outside, and breakfast consisted of a fried egg on a saucer dripping in oil (fried above with a coal-stuffed oil barrel), one hard bun (with which you could kill someone if you threw it at his head), and something which was supposed to be coffee but tasted like melted tar of the roadside.

In the evening it was a bit better but very monotonous. If it was beansprout season they would serve you rice with beansprouts for the whole month, and if it was cabbage season you would get cabbage with rice. Besides that, dinner was served at a fixed time – one hour each night – and if you were too late, pity, no food for you. Luckily I was informed of this beforehand and was told to bring a suitcase full of two-minute noodles, cheese, etc, in order not to starve.

Captive audience

During my regular stays in Sri Lanka we had an evening curfew as rebels were terrorising some factories and calling for strikes. The managers/owners from those factories who did not go on strike were visited and either warned to close down their factory even longer or in case they had failed to close down despite repeated warnings, they were killed.

Sitting in the bar of the Meridien hotel in Colombo we had this nice waiting game with the local girls. The earlier in the evening, the more they asked to spend the night with you. The closer it came to curfew time they either had to strike a deal or go home … that was the time to go for it, and in the event that there were some extra girls left you could take two or three for the price of one.

Oh, oh, those lovely curfews.

Feeling no pane

It was 1996 or 1997 when I arrived in the Hilton in Colombo, Sri Lanka. The hotel had only 50 percent of its rooms available as a major bomb blast shattered the windows of the other half. The Meridien Hotel next door was completely closed and under major renovations as they were closer to the blast and had suffered far more damage.

One American customer apparently got so pissed the night before that he slept through the whole ordeal only to wake up to find out that his window was gone.

But I'm alright n-o-o-o-w

In Sri Lanka they were not allowed to sell any alcohol during certain days of the month, something that had to do with the moon or some such, and they were afraid that you would turn into a werewolf if you sold or bought alcohol during that period.

Sitting in a bar and drinking non-alcoholic beverages is not my scene so we started asking some questions whether this rule also applied to room service. It apparently did not, as they would not actually sell you the alcohol but only serve it to you and bill you the next day or so. So physically there was no selling going on.

It wasn't long till we decided that the bar was our room and we had room service ordered in there.

Bit close to the bone

I had been placed by my company into a very poor hotel in Kuala Lumpur. I had got to know the entire staff as I had complained to each member of staff at sometime during my first week. This particular evening I was feeling horny but lazy so a made a call to a 'visiting massage service'. The man on the other line said I would be supplied in 20 minutes.

After putting the phone down I thought to myself, I hope they come straight to my room and avoid my 'friends' at reception. Twenty minutes later

I had a call from reception.

"Mr X, did you order … a … um … a …?"

"Yes I did," I replied quickly trying to hide my embarrassment.

Two minutes later there was a knock on my door. I opened it to find *five* Thai girls. They were all wearing a uniform that consisted of a little black mini skirt, a small black top and a gold collar around their necks. They looked like a bondage team! I hurried them in my room and asked why there were five. They said I could pick. After making my selection the other four left, and I did what I had to do.

The next morning I felt every pair of eyes from reception watching me eat my breakfast. Later on I found out that our administrator at work was very good friends with the hotel manager. She has not stopped smiling at me since.

Wet dream

Surabaya was always the last city on our buying trips through Indonesia and we made sure we would be there on time by Friday late afternoon in order to take a good shower to refresh for the night to come.

We normally stayed at the Shangri La where you would get huge rooms at a very small price as the rupiah was not worth a shit anymore. After a meal at the Italian restaurant we would go down to Desperado's (the bar at the basement) where there was normally a good live band and a whole lot of lonely girls … although normally they would not stay lonely for long.

One evening I decided to go upstairs and do some (s)exercise. We were just showering when the girl's mobile went off: it was her girlfriend who did not have a 'boyfriend' and therefore nowhere to stay – did I mind if she spent the night with us? That is like asking Colonel Ken whether he would like to have another G&T!

Needless to say it was a great, though exhausting, night.

Wee Tarzan, you Jane

The Panda Hotel in Hong Kong has the following signs on its lobby toilets: 'Man' and 'Wee Man'. Doubly confusing for the Scottish!

Setting his sights high

After one hell of a night on the town with a group (including my wife), I returned to our hotel room. Too late I realised she had the key, so waited in the corridor for her to return. And waited. Until I eventually fell asleep waiting. I was found the next morning – one floor up from where I should have been!

World class balls-up

I was staying at a hotel in Bangkok during the World Cup. As I lost the game of cards with my new girlfriend I had to do a forfeit. I stripped myself naked and ran down the corridor to collect some more ice for the whiskey. On returning, the girl could not stop laughing. I told her it was no big deal and nobody had seen me. She reminded me that in the reception was the kitchen staff of the hotel watching the World Cup on the security guard's TV … the one that was next to the CCTV monitor!

On reflection …

My surname is 'Miller'. It never ceases to amuse me when hotel staff in Taiwan welcome me: "Greetings Mister Mirror."

Out in the cold

I arrived for my first night for a one-year assignment in northeastern China. The room was on the 24th (top) floor of a four-star hotel in which I will be staying for the year.

After travelling for two days from the US, my boss and colleague pick me up half an hour after my check-in to take me to a local bar for drinks. I had about four or so big Chinese mugs of beer before they dropped me back off at my hotel, so I immediately go to bed under the influence of alcohol and severe jet lag. Sometime in the wee hours of the morning I have some kind of dream that I don't remember, get up and race out of my room door. I don't fully come awake until I hear the door latch behind me. There I stand locked out of my room. Without any clothes.

So there I stand in my birthday suit wondering what the hell I am going to do now. Just before I could completely get into a panic mode, a Chinese man came out of his room a few doors down. He obviously looks at me in surprise and I'm looking at him and babbling trying to explain what happened. Lucky for me, he understood enough English that he gave me a robe and slippers from his room and called down to the reception to tell them what happened.

They came up, unlocked the door for me and let me back in … the whole time (and I can't imagine why!) laughing their arses off. The next day at work, I was stupid enough to tell the whole thing to my boss like it was just a bad dream (in a way it was). Of course, he never fails to bring that up every now and again to all the others that pass through on assignments.

All black, and blue

A group of Kiwis were staying in a hotel in Manila and decided it was a good idea to climb the fire escapes, which made an excellent diving platform into the pool. One silly bastard – there's always one – went up to the first-floor balcony of the rooms which is set back quite a way from the edge of the pool. Before he even had a chance to jump, he slipped, smacking his head on the concrete wall, then fell down – bouncing off the canvas awning below and landing flat and out cold on the pool deck.

A smear of blood all the way down showed his route of descent and he was whisked off to the local hospital for treatment. Fortunately, being a New Zealander, he'd only injured his head and nothing important or useful.

Nuts and guts, etc

Unfortunate wording on a short-time hotel sign in Makati, Manila: 'Rooms 800 Pesos – All in!'

Got your goat

Going on a rugby tour to Manila once, I had booked several teams into the Park Hotel. "Any special requests?" the owner had casually asked.

"Yes, actually, we do need a team mascot … a, er, blue goat," I half joked. I thought nothing more of it but, when we checked in, there it was in reception … a great big goat painted blue, with a ribbon around its neck. Our Tour Whore was promptly handcuffed to it and remained that way night and day for the next three days.

A tall story

A few of us were having a lads' weekend and were given rooms on the same floor but, due to the design of the hotel, the rooms were not exactly adjoining. Late one night I had come back with this local lass – a midget with glasses. After finishing with her, I took her to the balcony and said: "Go across and knock on my friend's window." I then half-threw her from my balcony to his, where she hung precariously by her fingernails before pulling herself up and over. The next morning, my friend said: "Thanks for the bird, but you're fucking mad … there's an eight-storey drop between our balconies." I couldn't disagree with his diagnosis.

Hospital-ity

My friend and I were sharing a very spartan twin room in Patong Beach, Phuket. Having just arrived after the horrendous overland journey from Penang, Malaysia, the day before we had gone out on an all all-night booze binge. Still disorientated from the bottle or more of Mekong whiskey in his system, he opened his eyes, sees the whirring ceiling fan, notices the bare whitewashed walls and fluorescent strip lighting and shouts: "WHAT THE FUCK AM I DOING IN HOSPITAL?!?"

Bloody guests

In Mumbai, India, I checked into my hotel, was given the key and showed myself into the room. Looking out towards the view I noticed a hole and crack in the window. Nice one, I thought. On closer inspection it was clearly a bullet hole. More eerily, was a trail of blood that had been poorly cleaned, leading from the middle of the room, across the carpet to the bed. I dared not lift back the covers. I instead asked for a change of room.

Who's on first?

In Langkawi, Malaysia, I was staying at a good hotel and wanted to order a light meal before hitting the sack, but the service wasn't quite up to the surroundings:

Dialed 0, no answer.

Dialed 2, no answer.

Dialed 5, housekeeping. "What number for room service?"

"0. What do you want I can arrange?"

"Remote control"

"Control?"

"Remote control for TV."

"Kettle and remote control."

"Whatever."

"OK, sir."

"What number for room service?"

"4." I dialled 4.

"Housekeeping." It was the same guy!

"What number for room service?"

"Dial 0 …"

Five minutes later, there's a knock on the door. A guy is standing there with a kettle only.

"What number for room service?" I ask him. He asks to use the phone and dials reception.

"Number 4, sir."

I made myself a cup of tea, with the kettle I didn't order, and went to bed to forget it all.

A short story

In Bali, Indonesia, I'd bought a whole bunch of those cheap shorts – colourful and loose, just how I like them. Back at the hotel, my wife wanted to do some laundry so packed them in the bag for the hotel to wash. She warned them that the colours might run so to be careful. Of course, they came back completely discoloured and dishevelled. The hotel management apologised profusely and gave us cash on the spot … more than enough to buy plenty more pairs of those cheap and nasty shorts. After all, they only cost 50 cents a pair!

So there

In Guangzhou, China, a sign at the entrance to my hotel read: 'No drugs or nuclear weapons allowed inside'. That'll put off any bad guys for sure.

Pisspots please

In Jakarta on business at the end of Soeharto's rule, I had been out to the bars of Blok M and was headed back to my hotel, in Mango Dua, around 2am in a taxi. A couple of kilometres short of the hotel, the taxi was stopped at a roadblock, and they asked to see my passport.

Naturally I couldn't produce it and they were after 20,000 rupiah (about US$2 at that time). In my pissed state, I stood on principle not to pay the dirty money. They didn't know what to do with me, so the top-ranking officer – who spoke good English – ordered me to pay off the taxi and get out. He then asked to use my mobile phone as he said his battery was flat. I said mine was, too, rather than risk losing it.

Another Turkish guy, who spoke no English or Indonesian, was ordered to sit with me in the back of their pick-up truck so they could take us down to the station. The truck's battery was flat so they had to push-start it. I remained seated: I wasn't going to help them arrest and charge me. When it finally started with a burst, the road signs fell back on the policeman pushing. They decided to put us in another vehicle, but the only one available was the top cop's jeep. As I got into the front seat, the driver gave me a funny smile. I soon realised why – that was his boss's seat! They laughed at their boss getting into the back seat for a change.

When we got to the police station they called my hotel and spoke to the duty manager. He decided to call the hotel manager, getting him and his driver out of bed. They all (including the duty manager's wife) trooped down to this police station on the other side of town, bringing my briefcase. I opened it and fortunately my passport was in it, so I was off the hook. However, they fined the hotel 100,000 rupiah (around US$11) for not telling me to take my passport with me.

Boys will be boys

I owned a hotel in Ermita, Manila, in its hey-day and a good friend, S, was staying there. He and some friends had come back with a load of girls one night and were having a few nightcaps. S's girl was beautiful, but we all thought he was a she. Beautiful nevertheless. We start kidding him about it, so he decides to offload the billy-boy: "Thanks for your time, here's the cab fare." With that the billy-boy gets indignant:

"I waste all my fucking time with you … I spend 100 pesos on my make-up … why you treat me like this?"

As the 'girl' storms off into the elevator, I chase her and say: "Sorry about that, but be in this room in two minutes," and throw her S's room key. I ordered two vodkas and tonic to be sent up to his room for them. S is kicking and struggling to be freed to intercept this now-unwelcome visitor to his room, but we held him back for a few minutes before he dashed off to his room. Half an hour went by, no sign of him. An hour, nothing. An hour and a half later, he turns up.

"Fucking maniac. He tried to take my wallet, my camera, threatened me with a knife … it took me that long to subdue him and throw him out." The others were apologetic for their bad prank, offering him a sympathetic ear. Not me.

"You're a lying bastard," I said. "I don't believe you … I think you bonked him." The other guys shot quizzical looks at me, S protesting his innocence and veracity.

"Bullshit, he damn near robbed me and stabbed me."

"Drop your trousers – put your dick out." He gingerly opens his fly.

"That's not lipstick on the end of your dick, is it?" Busted. Case closed.

Pit stop

After the Hong Kong Sevens one year, a group of us flew on to Manila to celebrate my 40th birthday. We were met at the airport by the hotel's own mini-bus, which we directed to drop us at the Firehouse Bar in Ermita. We got stuck into it and arrived at the hotel about six hours later – with tarts in tow – to check in.

Snail mail

In Manila, I had to call my local contact to arrange and confirm a meeting with him for that evening. I tried all known contact numbers for him, but no luck, I couldn't get through. Frustrated, I got on with the rest of my day then went out on the town, getting back after midnight.

Reception passed me a few messages on my way in. Once upstairs in my room, there was a knock on my door. I enquired who it was. "Bell boy. Letter for you, sir." Suspiciously I opened the door and the guy handed me a note marked 'URGENT'. It was from my contact: "Apologies I have to cancel tonight …". I looked at the time the message was taken: 10:20am. This message had taken 14 hours to travel, oh, 35 metres to my room. Lucky it was marked 'urgent'!

The Grand Teo Towers and Suites

Until I visited Cambodia I had never experienced such a high standard of service as the Teo Hotel in Battembang. I checked into my small, but extremely clean, room (I mean surgery-clean), paying for three nights in advance. The following morning, after a jog, I returned to find the maid cleaning my room. I was shocked to see some of my clothes on the floor in the corridor outside my room.

"WHAT THE HECK ARE YOU DOING WITH MY CLOTHES?" I said, suspecting she was planning to walk off with them.

"I crean for you," she said. Sure enough, that afternoon my sweaty, filthy clothes were returned, neatly folded, sans charge. She also scraped the mud off my black leather shoes, and sorted out the remaining clean clothes in my duffle bag and decided which ones needed washing, and folded the rest back into the bag.

The next afternoon I watched quietly as the maids toiled in the searing Cambodian sun, washing sheets, towels, and guests' clothing in large concrete vats. All for a princely room rate of US$11 per night.

Splashing the boots

It was a rugby tour to Manila. It was 5am. The team was celebrating their big win and big 'fines' were put in place for anyone going to bed before sunrise. One person was noticed to be missing, and his roommate had a spare key to his room. One minute this unsuspecting teammate was sleeping the sleep of his life, the next minute he had six brawny Black Watch soldiers carrying him by each limb down two flights of stairs accompanied by the woeful strains of 'Why was he born so beautiful ...'. With that he was deposited – cursing and swearing – into the deep end of the hotel's pool.

Cobwebs

I needed to use a photocopier so asked the receptionist at the hotel in the Philippines if I could use the photocopier I saw behind the counter.

"Sorry, sir, it's not working."

"Will it take long to fix, I can wait," I said.

"Already broken for six months, sir."

Lost his trolley

At a rather nice boutique hotel in Bangkok, a friend of mine – a great entertainer – invited 'a few' people back to his room. The gathering gradually got out of hand, with the music pumping and what seemed like hundreds of guests spilling out into the corridor. As I remember some people were in togas, and others were dialling room service, who came back and forth with trolleys of drinks and food as fast as they could. Trays of joints were also being passed through the crowd. The place was going off. Even some of the room service boys had been drawn into the fray by our host, who liked playing with the same team.

Then the lift doors opened and out strode a very flustered looking hotel GM who surveyed this bacchanalia. "Please return our trolleys and waiters!" he shouted above the crowd, then turned sharply and left.

Long weak end

In Jakarta, a buddy and myself checked into a hotel and took adjoining rooms. We went down to Blok M and brought back eight birds with us. From Friday night to Sunday night it was a lock-in – with the girls and us going backwards and forwards between the rooms, but nowhere else. Room service delivered meals and drinks, and the pile got higher and higher. By Sunday night we'd had as much fun as we could possibly handle, and let them go home.

Two's company

Walking into one of Manila's fanciest hotels (hey, the company was paying!) I arrived late at night with my consort. It was like something from Disney's Icecapades because they were fogging the lobby for mosquitos. The duty guy stood next to the elevators where a sign read: 'No visitors after 12'.

"But it's not after 12 ..." I said, pointing to my watch, "It's after two!" Protest successful, she was allowed upstairs.

One wrong turn deserves another

A friend of mine, who was staying at the Hyatt Hotel in Hong Kong, woke up cold and naked in the corridor. Grabbing a newspaper from his door, he went downstairs to reception to ask for a key. He now recalls how it happened … he'd woken up in the middle of the night, gone to the bathroom for a piss but had gone out the main door mistaking it for the bathroom door.

The mouse that roared

I was doing the longest of long walks through this hotel lobby with this little munchkin who seriously looked like Minnie Mouse. So I was quietly sneaking around the shaded edges of the corridor trying to make a clean get-away and get this bird out, when I walked smack into the glass doors at the entrance. The whole lobby turned to stare. Bugger!

Beer goggles

I was staying at a hotel in Bangkok that had a strict 'no visitors' policy in place. I called the manager aside one evening, complaining this was really a counter-productive practice. "Look," he explained, "I'm from South America … I fuck anything myself … but some of the things you guys bring back at night to my hotel … I'm doing you a favour!" Good point.

Eight is enough

A certain gentleman spent a quarter of a million baht (over US$6,000) locked in a hotel room in Bangkok with six girls and two *katoeys*. He apparently did not leave the room for a month.

Head case

Down in Pattaya a big party was held and I was misbehaving, just for a change. This big guy put me in a headlock and he beat the shit out of me. I decided to retire to my room. A couple of hours later I woke up, realised the night was yet young as I hadn't had a bird yet, and drove into the strip to find one. Back at the hotel, she looked at my battered and swollen head, and was gently caressing it, when the skin broke and all this blood poured out. She ran from the room screaming. I awoke the next day none the wiser as to how my bed came to be covered in blood.

Various people filled me in on the gory details later in the day.

Hot to trot

A few of the guys and I were on a business trip to Hong Kong. After a night of hitting the local bars, I went back to my hotel with a very attractive girl. No sooner had we got on the bed than her clothes were off, down to the bra and panties. A loud knock on the door, and there are all the boys, piling in and jumping on the bed to disrupt us: "Order some food for us, you bastard!"

No problem, I thought, and called room service: "I'd like a pizza please, and could you put as many hot peppers on it as will fit? Thank you." When the pizza got there I sat back and enjoyed the sight of my good friends and a girl in bra and panties crowded around the desk in the hotel room, stuffing their faces then yelling in pain from the searing peppers.

Tart with a heart

In Manila I'd taken this tart back my hotel room. We started with a little small talk as usual.

"Are you married?" she asked.

"Yes," I replied truthfully.

With that she started to gather her things together, we hustled over the cab fare home, and she left. Mr Wobbly not happy.

Less is more, more or less

Staying in Colombo, Sri Lanka, I noticed that if you upgraded to an executive floor – for a mere ten dollars more – you would then get free breakfast, free coffee/tea service during the day and free happy hour drinks with snacks for three hours till approximately 8pm. These drinks included major labels of liquor that would cost US$5 per glass at the bar downstairs.

Ever since then I always check what the price difference is between a normal room and one at the executive floor. Some hotels already charge anything between US$10 to US$30 for a breakfast. Being a lover of a good glass accompanied with a good snack you can save a fortune. Some hotels have such elaborate servings of snacks that you do not need to go for dinner afterwards.

Sibling revelry

In the late 70s, I spent a short stay at the York Hotel, Singapore. After lunch I found the hotel pub in the middle of the lobby. The barmaid was a pretty young Malay girl. As business was slow she spent quite a bit of time talking with me. Occasionally she would sit down and our conversation was bubbly, to say the least. I invited her to dinner but she explained she came from a strict Malay family and her father would pick her up from work each day. Sure enough, about 6pm her father arrived and off she went.

The next day, in hope of another pleasant afternoon with her, I arrived and there she was … but I got the coolest reception I ever got. I thought I'd developed the plague. It went on for as long as I could stand it, then I left. Mystified, the next morning I tried again, and there she was … all bubbly and friendly.

I finally asked what was wrong with her yesterday. When she finished laughing, she explained she only worked every second day – on the other days it was her twin sister!

Less enlightened times

In the 70s, shortly after the US normalised relations with China, a group of palaeontologists was allowed to enter to do some fieldwork in the Chinese countryside. At the end of their month in the field, they stopped off in Beijing for a few days before returning to the US. On their last evening, they decided it was time to get drunk.

Coming home from the bar at a reasonably late hour, they continued the party in one of their rooms with a bottle they had liberated earlier in the evening. It suddenly occurred to them that, since China was a communist country, the room was probably bugged and they decided to find the bugs. For the next hour they searched the bathroom, inside the bed, disassembled the telephone, looked behind pictures, and found no bugs at all. Finally, X thought to look underneath the carpeting (which must have seemed logical at their stage of inebriation).

They rolled up the carpet and, lo and behold, a round metal disk was found beneath the bed, held down by four bolts. "Here it is! We've found the bug!" they exclaimed.

"We'll show those communist bastards – let's take it out."

Being geologists they had all sorts of hand tools, so they set to work removing the nuts on the bolts holding the bug to the floor. As soon as the last nut was removed, however, the bolts whipped downward and they heard a crash from somewhere beneath them.

Sobering up suddenly, they remembered their hotel room was directly above the hotel's ballroom. This was followed by the realisation that they had just unbolted the chandelier, which was now shedding considerably less light than a moment before.

They were escorted to the airport the next morning by the Chinese police. None have had the courage to apply for permission to do research in China since.

If you have a good story about hotels in Asia, email The Editor at hard-shipposting@hotmail.com or fax 612-9499-5908. But please, no visitors after 12.

❖ 10 ❖

Chinese Whispers or
Easier Done Than Said.

*Scrambled messages of language
and miscommunication in Asia.*

Do the Chinese have alphabet soup? Just wondering. Now let's try and demystify speaking Chinese, or Mandarin, for you. To the novice, the outsider, it seems unintelligible and as if you would never be able to master it. But here's the easy way. Let's call this The Colonel's '5-seconds to Mastering Mandarin' course. Just say, quite quickly and quite nasally, in a monotone with emphasis on each syllable: "She. Sells. Sea. Shells. On. The. Sea. Shore." Go on try it. Break each word up with a gap, don't stretch it out. Now try again. That's better. See? Speaking like a native now. Not a native of China, mind you, but a native nonetheless. Go around saying this and people will actually believe you are speaking fluent Mandarin. For added effect and variety, you can try starting the sentence in the middle, or anywhere for that matter. There you go. Piece of piss, eh?

I'm not sure, but I think that's the technique used by Prof Victor Mair, who was appointed – not without some controversy I must say – as head of the Hong Kong University's Chinese department. Fancy that … there's over a billion Chinese in the world and they appoint a *gweilo!*

If anyone picks you up on your Chinese, of course you then just claim you are speaking a rare dialect. There must be several million in usage. The womenfolk of Jiangyong in southern China even invented their own secret language, *nushu*, so they could communicate secretively between themselves and exclude the menfolk. But mostly *nushu* is written down rather than spoken, and sometimes they even sing it for an added layer of mystery and discretion. As if women need that! *Nushu* was passed down from mothers to daughters: the rich ones even hired tutors to teach them. But now, with most Chinese lasses being able to get an education, and having a bit more say in matters, it's dying off. But my Chinese girlfriend, Ai Bang Yu, still uses it. She's forever saying, "New shoes, new shoes!"

The other most difficult Chinese dialect to understand is Singaporean. This language seems to be made up fully of three letter words: CPF, MRT, SIA, etc (see, there's another one!). The list goes on. The Central Business District is the CBD. The Urban Redevelopment Authority is the URA, the Ayer Rajah Expressway is the AYE, the Singapore General Hospital is the SGH, and the Singapore Tax Department is the IOU. Everything is an ACN, sorry, acronym. So invariably, if I ask someone for instructions they come out with these three-digit code words and I have ANF IWT ATA. I mean, Absolutely No Fucking Idea What They Are Talking About.

In Japan, it might be easier to actually understand what they are saying, but then you get caught up in the sticky web of meanings. As they joke in Japan: if a Japanese says 'yes' it means perhaps. If he says 'perhaps' it means no. And if he says 'no' he's no longer Japanese! Sounds like they've got a lot in common with the Filipinos then.

I think I promised you in the last outing (I don't know because I haven't actually read Hardship Posting) that I would give you a bit of a run-through on Tagalog. Stiff shit if I didn't because here we go anyway. I love that language, because it's always full of double and unintended meanings. Speaking of which, quick joke: this lady goes into a bar and asks the barman for a Double Entendre. So he gave her one! Anyhoo … in Tagalog, '*saput?*' means 'have you been circumcised?' Pronounced exactly the same way (with no variation in tone) it can also mean 'do you have any wrapping paper?' So if you're not holding a gift at the time, you're likely to have your lights punched out.

And they love a good pun. Take sexy versus *sik sik* which means 'fat'. Or teenager versus *tang*-ager, which means an old bastard trying hard to be a young buck. Or *passion* versus *passiona*, which is the difference between old and a very tired performance. There's also a fine line between *makatas* 'young and juicy' and *makata* 'nagging bitch' (yeah, just marry 'em to see that change kick in!). Funnily, *capon* means neutered, so suddenly Al Capone doesn't sound that scary. But some of the funniest moments come out of their use of

English. P becomes f, b becomes v, j becomes h, but a bj's always going to be trumps! A travel agent is suddenly a 'trouble agent'. And if they eat something dodgy, they get 'loose vowels'. The most commonly-used English phrase, though, is "I lub you, sir, no shit," which roughly translates to 'I'll put up with you until you've bought me a house and lot in the province'. "Unve-puckin-liebavle – youb gotta ve hoking!" I tell them. I remember kicking a soccer ball round with a few kids on the street in Manila many, many moons ago. It got a bit out of hand, what with the youthful exuberance and everything, and some old dear's drink stall got cart-wheeled over in a cacophony of broken glass. Eventually a Filipino policeman, one of the finest money can buy, came along and said to us: "Sir, it is frohivited to flay pootvall on de pootfath vecause dat's what de flaying pield is por."

You also find yourself in strife when you fly from one country to another, with a limited grasp of vocabulary of either language. It's like reaching into your golf bag and pulling out the wrong club. Easy to do, let me assure you.

In Tagalog, you could be telling someone they're a beast in bed: *hayok*. In Chinese, you'd be ordering beef! In Tagalog, *aso* is dog. In Cantonese *asu* is wife. Oh, the potential for disaster. In Tagalog, *baho* is smelly. I had to laugh when I visited the Ba Ho Falls near Na Thrang in Vietnam.

In Tagolog, *nana* is pus. Suddenly Soi Nana doesn't sound that attractive, as accurate as that description may be. In Tagalog, *lamok* is mosquito. I once got slapped on the face by a little Thai thing, who said: '*lamok!*' I thought she was kindly getting rid of a mosquito on my cheek. It turns out she was in a disbelieving frame of mind. In Thai it means 'bullshit!' you see. *Tanga* in Tagalog is 'stupid'. In Thai, *tenga* means to get married. Yeah, well, that's not too far off the truth. In the Philippines, you can tell someone to fuck off with a simple *potak* … then fly to Thailand and order a delicious bowl of seafood soup with exactly the same word! In the Philippines, *ohoh* is 'yes', in Thailand it's a young girl.

Now in Thailand, and I've been here almost twenty years now, it's all in the intonation. And, of course, whichever one you choose and no matter how carefully you mimic the sound, you're going to choose the wrong tone. I remember telling my Thai bank manager about my skiing trip to Canada, where there was plenty of cold snow, *hee-ma*. He was not in the least bit surprised that I enjoyed a place that had so much pussy (also *hee-ma*), but wondered why I was sharing this sort of personal detail with him!

One of the simpler things in Thai is how the words are constructed. For instance, ice doesn't have its own word. It is two descriptive words, meaning literally, 'hard water'. Cheese is 'hard butter'. And love is 'hard on'! And I've always loved pen ... *pak-aah*. How Parker pens came to dominate this category I'll never know. Ironically, though, it's very hard to insult a Thai by yelling, "Fuck you!" They're probably a bit baffled as to why all these *farangs* are jumping up and down, going red in the face, thrashing their fists about the air and calling them something as tame and inoffensive as yellow pumpkins! After all, *fak* is a pumpkin and phonetically *you* is yellow.

But one very confusing thing for Thai kids must be the name of animals. Your regulation garden-variety black-and-white cow goes 'moo'. But *moo* is the word given to describe a pig, or pork. It must take them years to figure that one out. Also, *kai* is chicken, it's also an egg. So which came first? Order one chicken dish and one egg dish at a restaurant and find out.

Now not a lot of people know this, cunning linguists, but the Colonel's sharing a rare snippet of declassified info from a chum of mine in the State Department with you here. Don MacLean, the songwriter, spoke (or probably even to this day if he's still alive, speaks) fluent Thai. He was an unpatriotic activist in the Vietnam War period. But the American government didn't want to be seen to be guilty of McCarthyism, so they didn't ban his song. Instead they requested its name to be changed to 'Bye, bye, Mr American Pie'. When he originally wrote it, it was as 'Bye, bye Mr American Pai', *pai* being the Thai word for go or go away, this telling the Yanks to get out of Vietnam and go home.

Actually, none of that's true. Or as the Thais say: '*Whatalotta khrap!*' The other song that was funny to hear the little Jungle Bunnies in the bars singing was the Live Aid theme song back in the mid-Eighties. "We are the wern, we are the peepin ..." Then of course, there are those little nodey things at the back of your throat, known to Thais as 'thompsons'. "Have you had your thompson out?" one well-meaning lass once asked, peering down my throat. Quite often, thank you. Which brings me to my two most favourite Thai words. One is *Ting Tong* (when pronounced with the right inflection), meaning crazy, goofy, off the planet. The other is *Bah bah bor bor* (most often used in the classics with the prefix *farang*) meaning mad white bastards.

An interesting area (to me at least, I frankly don't give a stuff about you lot!) is the amount of words borrowed from Asian languages and imported into English. The Raj in India had a lot to answer for here. Did you know or care for instance, that the word gymkhana, which usually means a horsey-type of event came from the Hindu word *gend-khana* meaning an athletic meeting? Or that the British Army, who always wore red coats, found supplies cut off during the 1857 mutiny in India. So they supplied their soldiers with a tan-coloured fabric requisitioned locally in India, without permission from HQ. This was known as *khaki*, from the same Hindu word meaning 'dusty'. By 1860 the British Army worldwide was wearing *khaki* uniforms. They didn't hide the blood as well as red did, but they made you a damn side harder to see in the first place.

The word swastika comes from the Sanksrit word *svastika*, which means good fortune and wellbeing. The symbol dates back well beyond 1939 … to around 3,000 BC in fact. The symbol was so innocent it was even given out on pendants by Coca Cola in its early days, and the Boy Scouts used to give these out till 1940 according to my good friend Steven Heller, who must have a hell of a lot of time on his hands because he wrote a whole book on it. In the First World War the US 45th Infantry even wore an orange shoulder patch with the swastika on it. So our friend Adolph didn't exactly have an original idea. Although I think he turned it backwards, didn't he?

Curry as we know it is taken from the Tamil word *kari*, meaning sauce. The sauce was flavoured by using the spicy-tasting leaves from the karippati tree.

The game of polo, popularised by the Raj in India, is however named from a Tibetan word, *pulu* (ball) just to confuse everybody. Chukka, the part of the game when the ball's in play, came from an Indian word, the Hindu *chakkar*. And, of course, they wear *jodhpurs* with the tight leggings and baggy thighs when playing, styled on the uniform worn by the people of that region in India. Naturally, they needed to slake their thirst after a few rounds of polo, so it might have been then that they discovered the joys of punch. Punch is essentially any beverage with wine or juice as the main ingredient to us, but in those days its ingredients were arrack, tea, sugar, lemon and water. The eagle-eyed Brits (you couldn't anything past them, no way) noted that there were five ingredients in this drink, so appropriated the Hindu word *panch* (five) or the sanksrit word *panchan* to name this rather agreeable beverage. So if you ever read a match-report of a polo game in the old days which says the game ended in an unholy punch-up, I don't think it refers to fisticuffs!

There are of course other languages we've begged, borrowed and stolen from. But would you look at the time already. I'm due down at the Polo Club at noon to meet Barry.

Anyway, let me tell you about the word amock, or amuck. When someone runs amuck it means they run around madly and randomly attacking people. This comes from the Malay word *amoq* meaning 'engaging furiously in battle'. You could take this a step further. If you made it *lamoq* in the Philippines, it could mean engaging furiously in battle with mosquitos. Or you could say that in Thailand's bars you are *lamoq* … engaging furiously in a battle with bullshit.

On that note, I'm off to the club to run amuck with the gin and tonics. If I'm late, I'll just tell him I was stuck in the queue for a phone box behind a Filipina. I'm sure he'll understand.

Colonel Ken

Canned laughter

In the mid 60s I'd been assigned to work in a refinery on an island off Singapore. At the end of work one day, I was more than ready for a beer so I asked the office boy to please get me a can of beer.

A little later he came back, with this beautiful Singlish utterance: "Boss. No can can … bottle can?"

Private parts

Coming from a relative small country with only 16 million people, where our mother tongue is not English, has some advantages. 'Private' conversations in public for instance.

One night a friend of mine in Hong Kong was a bit down and pissed so he decided to go to the Bottoms Up bar. He was looking at the topless Chinese lady behind the bar and commenting to another Dutch guy sitting next to him about the girl's body: Her tits are too small … she has no ass … her legs are a bit crooked, etc.

WHACK! He cops a smash in the face. In near-perfect Dutch the Chinese lass says: "I would like you to know that I have worked in an Amsterdam nightclub for ten years … go fuck yourself, you moron!" Flabbergasted, he orders another beer to console himself.

Two other Dutch colleagues in the lift of the Peninsula started commenting on a beautiful Chinese lady who entered the lift: nice body, nice legs, pretty face, etc. When the lift reached the ground floor she turned around and said, in fluent Dutch: "Thank you for the compliments, gentlemen, have a nice day."

One day in our Hong Kong office a Chinese girl enters with boobies like Dolly Parton. My colleague sees this girl and exclaims in Dutch: "Finally a Chinese with real tits!" at which she turns to him and introduces herself in Dutch as the new designer from the Amsterdam office.

No idea

I wanted to register a business, a creative venture in Singapore, under the name 'Gong Ideas'. 'Gong' is colloquial ad-speak for an award or plaudit, with the nice added overtone of the Asian instrument. The business name was registered fine, but when I went to open bank account the lady said: "Are you sure you want to call your business this?" *Gong*, in Hokkien dialect, means 'lousy' she explained!

Searching high and low

It's the habit of many male tourists coming to Thailand to 'keep' a girl they have taken out from a bar for the duration of their holiday. Having been with this particular girl for two or three days she told me she wanted to take me to her home. Fine, I said, where is it?

"Bangalore," she said.

"What? Isn't that in India? That's a hell of a way from Bangkok!"

"Don't worry," she said. "I know how to get there … but we have to take some food with us." So early the following morning she took me on a *tuk-tuk* and I was thinking we were perhaps going to the railway station. Ten minutes later we stopped.

"This one," she said. "We are here."

"Where's this then?" I asked. "Is this supposed to be Bangalore?"

"Yes," she replied, pointing proudly to the single-storey house: "My very own Bangalore."

"Oh, *bungalow*!"

Dog's body

I have been trying to learn Thai since I started working in Thailand. One has to be very careful when speaking as it is a 'tonal' language. I was speaking on the phone to a Thai friend when my Thai MD, Mr W, came into my office. I told my friend "Mr W *ma*" which can mean he has come into the room whilst I was talking. However I used the wrong tone, which translated as 'Mr W is a dog'.

Club specialty

One morning I went to my favourite golf course north of Bangkok. Being a member, the girls in the pro shop knew me quite well. I went to the driving range for some practice before teeing off and realised I had left one of my clubs at home. So I went back to the pro shop and asked whether they could give me a sand wedge, as I didn't have mine with me. "*Mai pen rai*, no problem, sir," was the answer. They would give it to me in a couple of minutes at the first tee when I would start to play.

I continued to practice a bit and then went to the first tee. And there she was, a young smiling Thai girl waiting for me with a white plastic box: in it a very nice-looking sandwich.

Sentenced to stay here

The brochure of the Nanjing Hotel, Shanghai, reads as follows: 'The hotel is infested with foreign adventurers stirring up charms and spangled with stars you can hear majestic tune of Huangpu River in morning and enjoy cheerful amorous feelings you can enjoy delicious dainties and tender feeling or you can drink to your hearts content family get together are satisfied fully it is galaxy of delicacy it has famous chefs and careful selection of stuffs in the colourful world of the multi function hall you can sing songs or dance trippingly in a simple, bright, silent and fragrant double room you can store up vigour for getaway or enjoy romantic fancy'. You can take a breath now!

What's in the box?

On the phone to my travel agent in the Philippines one morning, she asked me: "Are you interested in the fuckage deal, sir?" Fuckage deal??? Yes, it sounds rather interesting … sign me up. Oh, *package* deal! No wonder they can't stamp out sex tourism here.

Hold the Mei Jo

Travelling in the Eighties in China the first Chinese word that you had to learn was *mei jo* which means 'no have'. Everything you tried to order in a restaurant was *mei jo*, tickets at the train station, *mei jo*. Even in the coffee shop of the Hyatt in Tianjin everything I pointed out on the menu was *mei jo*. I then decided to order something that even in China they should have – noodles: but even this was *mei jo*. I then told the waiter to just make me anything he could find in the kitchen which was edible. Much to my surprise he came back with some fish and chips. At least that was what it was supposed to be.

What a dump

I used to stay at one of the finest hotels in Singapore. They had a executive floor where drinks and finger food was free every night till 7pm. Everyone used to sprint 'home' after work and make full use of the free grog before heading out on the town.

One night they would not let us out of the executive area into the corridor to the rooms. The hotel bartender kept saying in broken Singlish: "There is a big *shit* in the corridor."

All the guests kept saying, "No worries … we don't mind seeing the corridor full of sheets and towels. No big deal if house-keeping hasn't finished their rounds." So we pushed past him and out into the corridor. Which is when we realised our mistake: someone had crapped on the carpet in the hallway and they wanted to clean it up before anyone saw it!

Cool, dood

At the Royal Beauty Sauna House in Kashgar, China, the laughs I had reading their brochure were as therapeutic as the treatments:

'Dear Guests: Thanks gor your coming to Royal Beauty Sauna House. Our friendly and good quality services are ready to be sure for your comfort and satisfaction! THE DIRECTORY OF SERVICES: Deluxe room: computer-light wave room dreath oxyfen machine, rest room Standard room: all over doody bath needles prick dath, computer steam cold room, different dath, light mave dath surfing bath, dreath ocygen machine rest room'.

Red rag to a bull

After meeting the girl of my dreams, M, in a dentist office in Bangkok (she was a dental assistant), we began dating which quickly started to turn into a serious relationship. We were together every day and things were wonderful. Despite the fact she spoke only a little English, we had no trouble communicating ... at least not in person while we were together. Over the phone was a different story.

When it came time for me to return to the States, we agreed to continue our relationship and apply for a visitor's visa for her to come visit me. After I left Thailand, we talked – or tried to talk – daily. We had quite a few communication breakdowns, and many misunderstandings, but one I'll never forget: M had the chance to go for a weekend to Pattaya with all the girls (dental staff) in her office. I had been to Pattaya, and wasn't sure why a bunch of girls would go spend the weekend there, but I didn't let it worry me. At least not until I called her while she was there, and the first thing she told me about her trip was she had "big problems". I asked what the problems were and, in her broken English, she told me that all the girls were with "men". She sounded sad, and I had visions of all her friends running off with men they met at one of the bars, leaving poor M alone and leaving her out because she had a boyfriend (me). I consoled her, and asked her why that was a big problem for her. And she then told me: "Because I am with men too."

I couldn't believe what I was hearing! My girlfriend was "with men"! Not just a man, but with men, plural! I tried to get more out of her, but everything went downhill after that and she couldn't speak to me about it any longer.

After she returned to Bangkok, she still couldn't explain to me what had happened, but I had cooled down and decided to forget about it. A few weeks later, while waiting for the US visa, she was able to get a French visa and she met me on the Caribbean Island of St Barth's for a holiday. After our third day and night of blissful lovemaking, we woke up with some serious spotting of blood on our sheets, and she said, "Sorry, I'm with 'men' again!"

Oh, so that is what the problem was in Pattaya. We had a great laugh over that one … a classic misunderstanding.

Accent's the key

In my first year in Singapore our office moved to Clarke Quay. The first week after the move, I got into a cab and told the driver where to go. "Clarke Quay, please." With barely an acknowledgment we drove off. As usual, I buried my head in the Straits Times. When I looked up we were almost to Collier Quay. "What are we doing here?" I asked.

"Coll Quay, you wan Coll Quay!"

"No … Clarke Quay."

"Yes, Coll Quay!" he pointed frantically.

"No, CLARKE Quay!"

"Ohhh," it dawns on him. "Cluck-Kee. You want Cluck-Kee!"

And from that day, every morning I asked to go to 'Cluck-Kee' with no further problems.

Express check-in

This happened in a five-star hotel in Zhengzhou, China. I needed to stay one more night so I dialed '5' for reception:

"*Neehow*, good evening sir, how may I help you?"

"Hello, I need to stay one more night please."

"Excuse please?"

"I need to stay one more night."

"How may I help you?"

"I need to stay another night, that's all."

"Oh, I see … how may I help you?"

"Look, I want to stay another night here."

"But you already check out tomorrow."

"Yes, I know but now I stay one more night."

"So you leave and come back?"

"What?!? No, I just stay another night for God's sake."

"Please wait a moment." At which point I'm put on hold for a while.

"*Neehow*, good evening sir, how may I help you?"

"All I'm trying to do is extend my stay by one night."

"Oh, I see, you check out Thursday night?"

"No, of course not, I check out Friday morning."

"So you stay one more night?"

"At last, yes, I stay an extra night here."

"But you check out tomorrow?"

"Oh, God, please try and understand. Look, I only want to S-L-E-E-P in this hotel for one extra night, that's all."

"Please wait a moment …"

Dumping on the boss

Korean people used to laugh at the name of my boss, who was French. When I found out what his name meant in Korean I wasn't surprised. His name translated as 'Penis cow-pat'.

A word of caution

Early in my expat assignment I was assigned to teach the Malaysian Police in Penang the use and care of sophisticated electronic equipment my company had sold them. After a day-long training session, the local police chief invited me to dinner at one of the excellent beachfront restaurants in the city.

The beer flowed freely, as did drinks in coconuts, drinks in tall glasses with umbrellas, and wine (also in tall glasses). At the end of the evening I was well and truly sloshed.

The chief got up to leave and I, not knowing the geography or having the required physical skills to drive back to my hotel, insisted on a police driver. The chief acquiesced and assigned a relatively sober junior officer to drive me. He asked which hotel I was at and I fuzzily told him: "I don't know the name but it's across the street from AWAS, a sign I had seen across the street from my hotel. He laughed and we drove by many hotels until I recognised mine and hopped out.

The next morning, when I showed up to teach my students there was a huge 'AWAS' sign in the classroom. It was only then that I was told it meant 'caution'. It was as if I had told the driver I was staying at the corner of 'danger' and 'drive slow' in the States.

Golden opportunity

It was late at night and I decided to stop at one of the service stations on the Korean Expressway No 1. As I got back into my jeep a dodgy looking bloke appeared. "Do you like pissing?" he asked.

"No," I said and got into my jeep very quickly. I watched from the safety of my locked jeep as he walked up to the next car. This time a man got out of his car and followed the bloke to a van. I was pleased to see that when he opened the doors it was full of fishing equipment!

Bottom feeder

Having just arrived in South Korea I was given an interpreter to help me buy some furniture for my new flat. He was a strange-looking man in his forties and my first impressions of him were not good. As I stopped my car at a red light he said to me: "Mr R, do you like enema?"

I have never tried an enema and don't intend on trying one any time soon. Furthermore I did not want to discuss this kind of subject with a shifty looking bloke I have just met.

"No. I do not like enema," I said.

He looked upset and said, "You don't like enema?"

Again I said "No," and gave him a look that meant I did not want to discuss this anymore. After a short delay he said:

"I like enema … I have two dogs and three cats." I realised we had stopped alongside a pet shop.

Name your price

I walked down a Soi in Pattaya full of girlie bars. I spotted this really delicious young girl standing outside a bar, so I decided to stop and talk with her.

"Hi, beautiful girl, what's your name?"

"Five hundred baht," she said.

Obviously a newcomer from the province.

I for an I

A friend of mine was posted to Korea to start up an insurance subsidiary. Being a keen driver he wanted to be able to drive his own car from time to time and was told that, although he could use his own licence, he would need an eyesight test. Off he went for the test accompanied by a member of his staff. Arriving at the test centre he realised he'd left his glasses behind.

"Don't worry about it, sir," said his colleague.

After the test, administered by a female nurse, his colleague relayed the information that he'd passed. He mumbled that he'd got all the numbers all wrong. "I said not to worry, sir. She doesn't know any English."

Learn Cantonese, in a few easy steps

In Hong Kong in the 70s I was in the army. One night, after a very heavy session in the Wanchai bars, we decided to head for the Kismet or the Professional Club on Kowloon-side to continue the merriment.

The Star ferry had stopped running so we found a *walla walla* (motorised sampan). We wanted to cross the harbour to Kowloon Steps so O said, "Leave it to me." He spoke to the skipper in what sounded like surprisingly fluent Cantonese and, after we had paid the cash, off we went. A very long time later we hadn't reached Kowloon Steps: instead out of the darkness appeared a vertical steel wall and a huge anchor chain leading from it.

"God, we're in either the Quarantine or the Dangerous Cargo anchorage," someone said. "This must be Sham Shui Po."

O, awakened from his drunken nap for a 'please explain', admitted that the only words he knew in Cantonese were "Take me to Sham Shui Po, please." It cost a fortune to have the skipper take us back round to Kowloon Steps. And when we got there the bars were shut.

Captivating beauty

In Koh Samui, Thailand, Fuji Karaoke bar put up a big billboard on the side of the road to promote its services: 'TOP SERVICE BY ONE OF OUR BEAUTIFUL HOSTAGES' it claimed. Someone obviously pointed out the mistake and, a week or so later, the sign now read: 'TOP SERVICE BY OUR BEAUTIFUL HOST'. Either they'd turned it into a gay bar or the word 'hostesses' just didn't come to mind.

Mind your head

In Bahasa Indonesia, 'head' is *kalapa* and 'coconut' is *kapala*. Imagine the curious looks on the villagers' faces when I marched into a *kampong* one day wanting to meet village elders but asking to speak to the village coconuts!

Dick-shun-ary

In Jakarta, MacDonald's had an outlet opposite our office. The local girls were often there reading Indo/English dictionaries. They'd say: "Can I speak to you and practice my English?" 'Course you can. Then often they'd follow that up with: "We're from the south and don't have a hotel. Can we stay with you?" 'Course you can!

Waiting game

Living in Singapore, I was in love with this Filipino girl in Hong Kong and had promised I would come up and see her sometime soon. The anticipation grew with each letter (the days before email and mobile phones). About a couple of weeks before I was due to go, I got an angry call from her. "What do you mean you can't wait anymore? Is there another woman in Singapore? You have another one so you can't see me?" And so the inquisition went on. When I managed to get a word in edge-ways I realised the source of her anger. I had lovingly signed off the letter: 'I can't wait to see you again'.

Don't forget to remember me

At our hotel in Qing Dao, China, either the locals were not that good at English … or the hotel's German manager had helped them write the signboard for the restaurant: 'You will enjoy Korean Barbecue over hot rocks and have enjoyable time that give you forgetful experience'.

Stop, don't stop

A friend of mine, Geoff, came to Thailand to visit for the first time. Going with a local enterprising lass he was giving her the performance of his life, to her encouraging screams of, "Oh, Jep! Jep! Jep!" He thought he was a superstar and she a good audience, which only brought out the best in him. The next day, however, he felt bad for himself and for the girl, when I explained that she wasn't calling out his name at all. *Jep* in Thai means 'painful'!

Clock wise

In Thailand, I was talking to a stall-keeper who had a few small kids playing around her shop. She proudly pointed out her daughter.

"How old is she?" I asked.

"6:30."

"No, I mean how many years old … what age is she?"

"Er, half past six."

After more probing it turns out she was in fact six and a half years old!

Unpolished performance

During the time the Hong Kong Police force had *gweilos*, each had to undertake a three-month Cantonese proficiency course. One policeman was promoted to Brigadier. During his first parade, eager to impress and stamp his authority, he told one Chinese woman police constable that her shoes were dirty – she was to take one step back, clean them, then report to his office to show him. Or at least he thought that's what he said. Half the parade collapsed around him. What a shame the Cantonese words for 'shoes' and 'pussy' are so closely related!

Qw ert yuio paas dfghj klzxc vbnmqwer ty uiopassdfghjklzx cv bnmq email The Editor vb hardshipposting@hotmail.com or fax 612-9499-5908. Poi uytr ewqas dfg h jklzxccv!

❖ 11 ❖

The Bucks Stop Here
or Occupational Hazards

True tales from the workplace in Asia.

A funny thought occurred to me the other day, clock watchers: do *feng shui* experts ever go out of business?

Dave (who works at the airline) and Barry (who's in insurance, you might remember) are finding that the workplace is a whole different playing field these days. In the good old days, we'd slope off to Dux restaurant for a quick bite of lunch together (usually ending up in Patpong around two in the morning). But we were disciplined … we'd never do that more than once a day. The next morning you'd crawl into the office, fend off a few phone calls, scrawl out a few faxes to head office, and then well, whaddyaknow! it was time to go to Dux again, or maybe Napoleons or the Crown Royal just for a change of pace. The job was done, sales were made, and everyone was in clover.

But they regale me with horror stories these days of young management turks, wielding MBAs and throwing this week's buzzwords like 'user-friendly synergistic interface' and 'backward-compatible hardware up-sell' around as if they actually mean something. Bullshit Bingo, that's what I call it!

Of course, Pete the Portrait Photographer doesn't realise the 80s are over. Hell, we were afraid to mention that the 70s had ended until recently, but he gets by. Dave reckons you've got to put in 100 per cent these days … it's the ugly new reality. After a lot of thought, my solution was ready at hand: "Piece of proverbial piss, Dave. My suggestion is you put in 20% on Monday, 30% on Tuesday, 25% on Wednesday, 20% on Thursday, and that leaves you a manageable 5% to polish off before lunch on Friday. QED!" He mumbled something unkind about what would a walrus-moustached out-of-touch deadwood ex-civil servant know anyway.

He recently attended a management seminar by some chrome-domed chap called Steven Covey. Reckons he talked about sharpening the saw. See, even these gurus don't have a clue. It's called sharpening the pencil! Speaking of secretaries a colleague of mine worked in Kuala Lumpur where he had a beautiful young, if conservative, lass working for him. Noticing her boss's fly was open one day, she delicately broached the subject. "Er, your garage door is open," she said in that wonderfully obtuse Asian manner. The boss was a bit confused before she pointed to his offending zipper.

"Oops, I hope you didn't see my Mercedes 500 Sports!" he said, joining in the joke.

"No, sir, just an old pink Proton Saga with two flat tyres."

I also gave Dave and Barry my two cents' worth about dealing with head office. When I think of a 'head' office, that to me is Rosie's Bar upstairs at Patpong. But there are a few characters you've got to watch out for (at the office, not Rosie's). Every company has a Damaging Director. He's the highly overpaid one in the shiny suit, who spends half of his salary on hair gel, French colognes and ties … a quick inspection of his wardrobe might reveal close to 3,000 ties, organised by colour shade, pattern and designer. Of course, he's got the ones with Mickey Mouse on he pulls out for use on 'casual Friday' just to show his staff he is human and has a wacky sense of humour (which they wouldn't otherwise know). Don't fall for that old routine! He's also the guy who'll make you an offer you can't defuse with some sort of donkey-and-carrot incentive scheme … that's the one where they dangle the carrot in front of you, then lube up the donkey and put him behind you!

Dave recently had a meeting that went none to well with his Damaging Director. He marched into the guy's office which just happened to be in the corner, with floor-to-ceiling glass panels affording a 270-degree panorama of the skyline and said: "I'm not getting paid what I'm worth." His boss looked at him and said: "I know that. I'm prepared to pay you what you're worth, but ask yourself can you afford the pay cut?" I told Dave it was probably time to dust off that old resume … you know that work-of-fiction document that contains more lies than the average tales of conquest from your friend who just returned from Cambodia.

Dave was really hoping for a promotion from his current position which is, unofficially at least, Sexual Adviser: "When we want your fucking opinion we'll ask you!" is his job description apparently.

The other danger person to watch out for is the Seagull Manager ... he's the guy who flies in from regional HQ, makes a lot of noise, craps on everything you've done, then flies out again. We've all met him before!

If only we could wind back the clock to the good old days such as those when Captain Robert Forbes, an American, owned the first and only riverboat in the whole of China. He had the market sewn up and within about 10 years added 68 more boats to his fleet.

Before the Second World War Japan was the place to be, with its cheap exports (yes, you read that right). Huge resentment built up in the States against the Japs, so the crafty little buggers renamed one of their industrial centres 'USA' so their exports could rightfully be labelled 'Made in USA'. Maybe it was no coincidence that war broke out soon after, which introduced us to another larger-than-life character, General Douglas Macarthur, most famous for leaving a cake out in the rain [Check facts -ed.]. But did you know, corporate climbers, that his father Arthur Macarthur arrived in the Philippines in the late 1890s and had a whole bunch of businesses and investments there? So it was like a homecoming of sorts for young Doug when he was posted to Manila to head up the Allied forces in the Pacific. Hence his attachment to the people and the place. Now correct me if I'm wrong, but the San Miguel beer logo is a red shield. And does this, or does this not, closely resemble the Macarthur clan crest? What is doubly ironic is that Kirin, one of Japan's largest breweries, just bought up a sizeable chunk of the San Miguel brewery.

You wouldn't want to have worked for the Ford Motor Company in Singapore during the war, when their factory on Bukit Timah Road was used by General Tomoyuki to take Percival's allied surrender on February 15 1942. Not a lot of cars were produced that day according to company records. Percival pleaded for more time. "Sign or we continue the attack," barked Tomoyuki. With a shaking hand (and was that a tear in eye and a stain in his shorts?) Percival signed, giving us one of the best lessons in business you could ever learn: know your bargaining position. As it was 100,000 allies had just surrendered to less than 30,000 Japanese. Being a good poker player also helps. (It's often said the Japanese are inscrutable, but that's not true: I was in Tokyo recently for just a week and managed to screw three of them!).

After the war, of course, things got even trickier as the Raj handed back large swathes of the continent to its rightful owners. Or were they the rightful owners? Soon, *konfrontasi* was in full swing, with the Commies wanting a piece of everything. This led in short order to the Malayan Emergency. In *War of the Running Dogs* my good friend Noel Barber described those uncertain times when a day's work could be your last: "Like every planter's wife, Tommy faced one daily fear – the moment when Peter set off on his daily rounds before breakfast, for this was zero hour, this was the time when the wife could never be sure her husband would return."

And there was a similar situation in June 1965 when Indonesia seized rubber plantations belonging to American firms. The following month, they nationalised (that's a diplomatic term for saying 'we'll have that!') Goodyear and four American oil companies.

OK, so maybe the good old days were not perfect. But these days you've got all these pesky legislations creeping in to the game ... labour laws, equal opportunity employment, you name it. As a private business you should be able to hire exactly who the hell you want to hire, for the reasons you want to hire them. Hey, you're paying the wage, aren't you? So if you want to run a classified ad in the paper saying: 'Wanted. Single female, aged 18-25, 160 centimetres tall for light office duties' you should be able to do it. Why cast the net wider for hunch-backed males with a limp and a squint? And end up with reams and reams of applications from people you'd never hire if your grandma's dialysis depended on it. Barry was telling me about a classic in Australia just after they'd brought in the anti-discrimination code there: 'Wanted. Male or female cocktail server but must be prepared to wear see-through blouse and short skirt!' Mind you, they probably found a few male takers for that in Sydney!

They talk of the Glass Ceiling that restricts women from rising above a certain level. I say let women rise all the way to the top ... but keep the Glass Ceiling in place so we can sneak a peek up their kilts! Bit like that bar in Soi Cowboy with the Perspex dance floor.

The Thai PM is a clear-thinking man, obviously influenced by my sensible sartorial wear for the tropics, and has asked workers not to wear suits to the office in a bid to conserve energy. Not their personal energy, but the electricity needed to power the air-cons that cool these over-dressed workers. I think some nice lingerie would be a suitable energy-saver for the secretaries. Mind you, think of the extra energy you'd burn chasing them round the office!

Speaking of which, the first sexual harassment case in China in currently before the courts … Ms Tong vs Boss. He had allegedly touched her whilst promising her a good job. However, said good job didn't materialise, and bonuses and allowances were subsequently withheld. She filed a claim for these and was promptly fired. Her problem is that there are no laws specifically dealing with sexual harassment in China. The closest one is 'hooliganism' which covers indecent assault in pubic, er, public places, but an office is not considered a public place.

The likely winner? Lawyers, I'd say. Did you hear about Pete who was drinking in this well-heeled downtown bar after dealing with some burdensome litigation stuff? With a couple of drinks under his belt, he stood up and said: "ALL LAWYERS ARE ASSHOLES!" You could've heard a pin drop. A well-dressed gent in the crowd said:

"I resent that."

"Why, are you a lawyer?" said Pete.

"No, I'm an asshole!" said the gent.

Right-o, I seemed to have strayed off from China, which has its fair share of bad days at the office. My research has dug out the fact that 5,300 lives were lost to coalmining disasters in the last year alone. Just quietly, that sounds safer than being on their roads. How about the manager of the mine that had a nasty gas explosion (I know that feeling!) and admitted that, sadly, four of its employees had died. After the Communist Party newspaper investigated, it turns out that actually 42 had perished. He mumbled something about his abacus running out of batteries before he was, er, shafted for the cover-up. Which brings me to one of the Colonel's key pieces of advice for success in business: always remember, there's no problem too big or overwhelming that you can't run away from.

One the other end of the spectrum, a midget in Malaysia working for an optical equipment firm, is suing his now-former employer for unfair dismissal. He claims they fired him because they thought he was bad for their image, and made him hide in an office cupboard when the big bosses visited the company. Clearly they couldn't see eye-to-eye on this matter.

Hong Kong is also rather progressive in these matters, and they have started a compensation fund for workers in noisy occupations. One of the eligible parties is workers in *mah-jong* parlours. To give you an idea of how noisy these are the other eligible workers under this scheme are those who administer electrocution to pigs in slaughterhouses before slitting their throats. Take it from me, that's noisy! Where this money will come from, I'm not sure, because the South China Morning Pest reported that expats in Hong Kong had run up a HK$213 million unpaid tax bill.

But if they're lucky, the Hong Kong tax department might adopt the practice of debt forgiveness that Japanese banks seem to favour. Sogo recently asked for – take a seat, tax dodgers, there's a lot of zeros in this – 639 billion yen (about US$6 billion) in debts to be written off. And Hazama Corp asked for 400 billion yen to be wiped off just for the hell of it. If I tried that with my bank manager I reckon he'd repossess the house, sell the missus and auction the good crystal decanters before you could say 'interest rate rise'.

The Chinese have a wonderful expression that goes: '*mo cheng, mo meng*'. No money, no life. A bit more serious than the one I'm most familiar with: '*mo cheng, mo poontang*', no money no honey. In China, 150 billion yuan (about US$10 billion) has been written off since 1995 by the State banks on loans owed by State-owned enterprises. Sounds like they need to work a bit smarter over there. Mind you, as Confuse-Us used to say: "I am not wise by nature. I have become wise through hard work." Of course, no one believed the philosophical bastard, nor were they prepared to prove him right by trying it. In fact, China is right down the ladder when it comes to putting in the hard yards.

The good burghers at Roper Starch in 2001 found that workers in China and the US put in about the same amount of hours 42.4 per week at the salt mine, slightly below the world average of 44.6. This is way behind the South Koreans who registered a life-sapping, mind-boggling 55.1 hours on average, the most workaholic bunch in the world. "Korea is the one society in the world where the Chinese go broke and the Japanese look lazy," wrote my good friend Greg Sheridan. The Taiwanese were not too far behind at 53.4. Still, the hours put in per week don't tell you everything. I remember working at the embassy in Hong Kong: most of the locals would come in at the weekend 'to work overtime' simply because it was a nice big air-conditioned space which was nice and quiet, and they could get away from grandma's noisy *mah-jong* circle and the screaming kids. I also remember a tour of a sugar factory in Singapore where they had a little Malay girl whose sole job in life was to pick up sugar cubes, one by one, with a set of tweezer-like sugar tongs and put these in the pack. On a good day she must have produced, oh, five or six little packs of sugar I reckon. Same with the old Indian ladies at the mighty Boh tea plantation in the Cameron Highlands of Malaysia. These dear old ladies – I dare not call them 'tea bags' – would sit around gossiping like a knitting circle, and pick the ground tea leaves up, finger-full by slow finger-full, and pack them into the tea boxes ready for the supermarket shelf. The other thing you often come across in a third world economy is that four or five people are standing around, hired to do the work of one. Bit like a western road works gang – work fascinates them … they can stare at it for hours.

Point to note in the productivity survey: the French and Italians didn't even register on the hours-per-week radar … probably no-one could tell the difference between when they were working and when they weren't!

Mind you, the Koreans themselves are the past masters at that game. The unemployed in Seoul are too proud to let their families know, so they dress up in their suits in the morning, grab their briefcases and head for the train station as usual. But then they go off and spend their day walking around the lovely hills that surround the city. At knock-off time, it's back on the train and home again. Japan, of course, has its notorious 'window-watchers' who are not fired nor made redundant. Instead they are assigned window-seats and literally have nothing to do but stare at the view. Sounds perfect – when do I start? These are different from 'wet leaves' who are actually unemployed (ie, couldn't even get a job as a window watcher), retired or fired. They're called wet leaves because they are hard to get rid of or shake off. Much like a telephone salesman.

India seems to have the global market for call centres sewn up. Over there recently I heard that some of the biggest companies in the world have outsourced their service and technical hotline operations to India. And just so you are not confused by some heavily-accented hurdy-gurdy man on the other end of the line (and to no doubt cover their devious cost-cutting methods), these Indian operators are given crash courses in the cultures or countries they are dealing with. So they are force-fed videos of Coronation Street, the Bill and Neighbours, and watch the English football league. They are also given up-to-the minute weather forecasts and foreign-sounding names like Charles or Bruce to complete the ruse. So if you're calling your local bank from Birmingham, England, 'Charles' might say, "Gee, it's chilly tonight isn't it, Mr Smith? Nice night to stay in and watch the football." And he's got you on-side. Meanwhile, he's sweating his sub-continental bollocks off in blazing sunlight in New Delhi, being paid 25 cents an hour for his troubles.

There again there are those who say expats get paid unfairly and disproportionately high for the jobs they perform. There was a good explanation I came across for this in the Singapore Chronicles, so be ready to use it when next you get challenged: "Their salaries conformed to the general view at that time that Europeans ought to live a life of considerable luxury, lest they be looked down upon by the locals." So there.

But still, all the money in the world doesn't seem enough on some days when every bastard's out to get you, and the turkeys are really getting you down. Once again you might be interested in the fatherly advice I handed out – free of charge, no invoice issued, I might add – to Dave on the subject of stress management. I told him the only way to deal with stress is to look out of the window to the horizon (belching diesel smog permitting) and clear your mind of troubling thoughts. Then swing your arms from down at your sides to up above your head gracefully as you inhale and exhale deeply in rhythmic motion about ten times. Then make yourself a nice cup of boiling hot herbal tea – jasmine or camomile usually does the trick – then go and pour the scalding tea all over the computer of the person that pissed you off in the first place. You'll feel better in minutes believe me!

There's a good reason why no-one on their death bed ever said they wished they'd spent more time in the office.

Colonel Ken

Dead man sailing

Working with a trading company in Sabah, Malaysia, part of my job was to co-ordinate the shipping activities. We were expecting a ship in so I had arranged for the berthing, the harbour pilot, all the formalities. Our ship duly arrived, skippered by this 75-year-old Norwegian, and was due to depart the next day.

Next morning, everything's in order to sail, but the skipper is missing. I get back to my office to a phone call from the police: "We find your captain … he dead."

Turns out the dirty old bugger had gone with a young lady of the night, and she couldn't wake him in the morning. Not only that, but he left three wives behind – one in Europe, one in the Philippines and one in Indonesia.

Get forked

We were working in China and were installing a major piece of production line. The US$15 million piece of kit arrived at the plant in its shipping container to the bemusement of our local staff. When it came to unloading, they assumed that the usual adage of 'many hands making light work' would apply. Unfortunately with a production line weighing several tons this was going to be a major undertaking, requiring at least a couple of fork lift trucks. Imagine our engineer's surprise then when he came into work on the Monday morning to find his beloved and fragile kit being off-loaded with a couple of mechanical diggers!

Broad of directors

X was a director of our company, a very quiet, sober, refined character. He was travelling to visit our site in India, never having travelled to Asia before. In the departure lounge at Heathrow Airport, London, he ran into Y, one of our career-expat site engineers, who was on the same flight to New Delhi.

X was of course delighted to have someone to travel with. He was less delighted when Y informed him that, as the site was a very remote hell-hole, and a real hardship posting, there was a tradition that those travelling to the site would bring some porno magazines 'to brighten up the day for the lads at site'. (Completely untrue, of course.)

Y told X: "You get Razzle, Men Only, Parade and Hustler and I'll get Playboy, Mayfair, Asian Babes and Club." X was not very happy about this but proceeded to the top shelf in the nearby newsagents and picked up the porno magazines. He then queued up to pay the very pretty young girl manning the cash register. By the time it was X's turn to pay there was a queue of about eight men and women behind him. Y was right at the back of the queue.

As X put the porno magazines down in front of the young girl he heard a very loud exclamation of disgust from Y: "OOOOH! THAT DIRTY OLD MAN!"

Down the gurgler

In Jakarta twenty-odd years ago [Some of them very odd! - Col Ken.] the rupiah was at 425 to US$1.00. We heard through the grapevine, one Friday morning at around 10:30am, that the banks were going to close and there would be a substantial devaluation. I took all the company's cash from the rupiah account (you were not allowed US$ accounts in those days) and queued up to exchange it into US$ bills. This I did just before the banks closed, and kept the loot in a shoebox in my office for the duration. When they reopened, the rupiah was at 625 to the US$. But I realised that, in the rush, I had forgotten to do anything with my own personal money. Another poor company soldier!

Lock, stock and bottle

In China there is a silly tendency to lock things up for no reason. For instance they would lock the elevator after 6pm, which is very nice when you have to work in the evening on the 16th floor. You take the stairs up carrying an armful of heavy equipment and, when you finally arrive, you realise that you have forgotten some stuff downstairs. Or they would padlock for the night the door of the building where you work, which means no way out: doesn't matter if the place is on fire or if you have a heart attack and must go to the hospital.

But the best is locking up the water bottle. I was badly in need of hot water to make myself a cup of coffee. "Water ... hmmmmm ...," said the local guy, as if I was asking for something very rare and unusual. Away we went, trying to find the key to the water room, with me making lots of ironic comments about having to lock the door because the water bottle might decide to escape and roam wildly across town.

Finally we found the damn key and opened the door. I stand corrected: the water was gone after all! My colleague was astonished. Later it turned out that we had opened the wrong room.

Even Stevens

I get a lot of business phone calls from locals in China. This guy phones me:

"Hello?" I say.

"I want speak Steven," he says.

"Speaking," I reply.

"No, no, not Speaking, STEVEN!"

Fur flying

I had just spent a couple of hours with a highly-strung woman, charged with the responsibility of staging a major fashion parade and charity luncheon at our hotel in Port Moresby, PNG. Wishing to demonstrate how capable the hotel's personnel were, I rang the chief engineer's office, to reassure the dear lady that the staging logistics would pose no problem.

The chief engineer was unavailable, so I asked his assistant to confirm that they could construct a catwalk in the ballroom by the allotted date. After a brief hesitation, he replied that this would be possible but, for reasons of safety, they needed to ascertain the size, weight and number of cats intending to use it.

Training sucks

I was on the expat pre-opening team of a new international hotel in PNG. Housemaid training had commenced under primitive circumstances: the lesson on use and care of the vacuum cleaners was conducted without the benefit of electricity, and had to be pantomimed by the supervisors, with suitable translation into the local Pidgin English.

One day, shortly prior to the opening, I happened onto the executive housekeeper wiping tears of laughter from her eyes, having just gone to inspect progress on the team doing the post-builders cleaning. There were her maids, with their shiny new machines not plugged in (precisely as they had been shown), pushing the nozzles up and down the corridor carpets, humming the sound of a Nilfisk motor.

Fogged in

A secretary for a UK company working in Hong Kong decided that she would use her initiative to try and save the company 'a few bob' as to airfare costs for expats returning back to the UK. She obviously searched the market to find the bottom line and cheapest fare which resulted in X being issued a ticket to return back to the UK with the following route:

Hong Kong - Singapore - Dubai - Amsterdam - Manchester, with an overall flight and connection travelling time of 28 hours. This resulted in X being nicknamed by his work colleagues as Phileas Fogg.

Thankfully the MD back in the UK instructed the young secretary to wise up and get people a direct flight home.

Bottom line

An expat Brit having consumed too much alcohol one night falls asleep at a party in Hong Kong. So, boys being boys, they decide to shave off his eyebrows and redesign his hairstyle. He has to attend a high-powered commercial meeting for his company with clients on the Monday morning and decides that he is going to have to do something about his eyebrows.

He goes to the nearest Watson's store and purchases make-up to draw in new eyebrows.

The meeting takes place at construction site offices, with no air conditioning working. It's not long before the humidity takes its toll, and his eyebrows start to drip slowly down his eye, and down his face. All in attendance constantly staring at him, trying to work out what they're witnessing here … especially one little guy who was gay.

After the meeting his working colleague tells him that for the last couple of weeks the little gay guy had been giving him a very hard time. But somehow his attitude changed that day he noticed X wearing make-up. He must have fancied his chances.

Dive, dive

It was decided by the head office in the UK to send out their financial director, Y, to sort out all accounts and money concerning projects undertaken at the new Hong Kong airport. Before such wonderful roads and railways were constructed to the new airport the only mode of transport to Chek Lap Kok was by boat.

While disembarking from the boat at the Gold Coast on his first day returning from work, the poor sod – whose eyesight is not the greatest at the best of times – completely missed the gangplank and hit the water like a torpedo.

Posters went up in the office the very next day about poor Y being sent out to sink the company!

A load of junk

It had been a great party over at Lamma Island at the seafood restaurant. A stag night for one of the staff, we had started early, got the junk over to the island and now, several hours later, were pounding our way back to Central.

In the middle of the Lamma Channel, my boss R leaned down from the top deck to speak to someone on the lower deck, and quietly slid overboard. We all thought this very funny in our inebriated state, but at least the boat boy had the presence of mind to realise that with container ships hooning through the channel at umpteen knots it is therefore not advisable to go swimming at night.

Meanwhile R was totally oblivious to this and shouting from the darkness: "It's OK, I'm here and the water's warm." The boat boy was doing circles trying to find him. Fortunately we did, and continued on our way.

Upon arrival at Central we decided to keep the party going, and landed up at Joe Banana's. This establishment has always been a bit snotty about dress, but we were reasonably smart and so were allowed in. The problem only started when great puddles of water started appearing: every time R stopped moving, he started to empty the contents of the Lamma Channel from his clothes onto the floor. We were ejected shortly after!

The sequel came the next day when the boat boy fronted up to the office and, with the secretary to translate, gave the general manager a lecture on irresponsibility. He scored a new lifebelt with a light on it for the junk … and a handsome pay rise for himself.

Business on the slide

A few years ago whilst working in Bangkok I had to rush to give a presentation. Time being tight and the congestion bad as usual, I grabbed the slide set, put it in a plastic bag and jumped a motorbike taxi. Sod's Law of course dictated that the plastic bag give way en route, spilling my precious slides all over the road. Panic as I have to try and stop the 10am weekday traffic and collect up the slides, now scattered across the airport road. A swift look around: I could see no more so off we go again.

I eventually arrived and explained what happened, blaming the incident for my lateness. I am sure no-one believed the lame excuse but they were quite amused by it anyway. Until it came to about the 10th slide, that is, and there instead of the latest technical figures was the tyre print of a car!

Hurry up and slow down

I arrived in Kathmandu on Royal Nepal Airlines for a two-week buying trip and shot through the immigration line and customs with only a carry-on. Catching a cab at the airport I went straight to Patton village outside the city, and sought out a woman I buy an exclusive item from.

I purchased every thing she had and gave her money to buy materials for more inventory. Rushing along, I made it back to her village the morning of my return flight to pick up my inventory and pay the balance. She and her husband were sitting in front of their clay hut reading the paper. The kids were playing in the mud puddle from the previous night's rain. We exchanged hellos and I asked for my inventory.

"Not finished," was her reply. She gave me a puzzled look and exclaimed: "Because we still have rupees, sir, from when you came before." I walked away empty-handed in search of a cab to the airport, thinking I have rupees, too … why in the hell am I racing?

Agenda bender

We went down to a hotel resort in Sihanoukville, Cambodia. There was a UN conference being held … but for three days they never emerged from the karaoke lounge. Singing and laughter and squeals were heard coming from inside around the clock. We asked one of the delegates: "Any important agenda items?"

"Yes, we're all getting pissed and screwed!" Turns out they had been advanced the cash for this special meeting and put it to rather dubious less-productive use.

Not shore

During a visit to Japan in 1986 I went out drinking with a shipmate who, as I later found out, was an alcoholic. He decided to introduce me to hot *sake*. I was halfway through my first glass when he ordered a second round and, being sociable, I hurried up and gulped the rest of it down. Halfway through the second, he had ordered the third round, and by the tenth, I was feeling more than a bit tipsy. Some of our friends had arrived by then, and I calmly pushed back from the bar and announced: "If you'll excuse me for a moment, I'm going to go vomit." And I did.

Staggering out of the restroom, I decided to go outside for a few minutes to let the fresh air clear my head. Moments after sitting down outside the bar, I heard someone say: "This is Shore Patrol – we have an unconscious sailor in the street." I was curious to see who it was, so I opened my eyes, noticed the pavement was only an inch from my face, and sat up. That's when I noticed the Shore Patrol was apparently talking about me, so I reassured him: "I'm not drunk, my body just won't move." Just then, my shipmates came out of the bar and told the Shore Patrol they'd get me back to the submarine because we had to go to sea the next morning. With that, two grabbed my arms and helped me back to the base.

When we got there, the Marine guard checked our IDs and waved us through, at which point I told him how much I admired the pretty buttons on his uniform and asked where I could get some. This pissed him off and he started to call Shore Patrol, so my friends dragged me over to a cab, threw me in, and told the driver to take us all to the barracks. Once there, we had to collect up my belongings (since we all had to be on the boat at 3am for the reactor start-up) and checked out of the barracks. Finally, we headed down to the boat, about a 10-minute walk. On the way, we passed a few other Marines who appeared to be fighting. Seeing that one had blood all over his head, I asked him if he had cut himself shaving, and then my friends hustled me away before I caused more trouble.

I still have no idea how I managed to make it down the hatch: probably wafted down on alcohol fumes. Spending 16 hung-over hours on the surface in heavy seas was a killer. And I'm still not sure how I ended up with a hickey next to my belly button ...

In a flap

In Sri Lanka we were conducting a series of consumer research groups, held in the function room of a hotel. Because they haven't graduated yet to the level of using one-way glass so we could observe anonymously and silently from an adjoining room, we were ushered behind a flimsy makeshift rattan partition. All was going well, with the group in full opinionated flow when a gust of wind blew in to the room. The partition, almost in slow-motion, started to topple and then kept going, landing on the floor with a solid THUD!

The startled group swung round to see about six of us, sitting on chairs with sheepish grins on our faces. All we could do was smile, and say, "Don't mind us."

Pilot program

Our airline was starting a new service from the States to Tokyo to Singapore. Head office came to do the big sales presentation and road show to the travel industry in Singapore – imagine how embarrassed we were that they had put the dot for Singapore at the north end of Sumatra, Indonesia! Hopefully the pilots would be using different maps.

Why do you ask?

In Singapore each year, we have office celebrations for each of the major races ... Chinese New Year, Malay *Hari Raya* and Indian *Deepavali*. One *Deepavali*, our Indian staffer sent round the invitations and said that people were welcome to wear Indian costume if they wanted to get into the spirit of the occasion.

I thought I'd make a splash, so went to a costume hire place to find something perfect. I then spent quite a bit of time at home preparing my outfit and my whole look.

When I entered the party it was all worth it – everyone turned to see me dressed in full Red Indian Chief regalia ... a huge head-dress of feathers, war-paint, the works!

Inside job

I was a bank manager in Port Moresby for 12 years. In the whole of that time, I took only one day off for sick leave. That very same day, our bank was robbed. People often joke about how I came to be retired in the Philippines at the age of 39.

Long drop

One time in China my colleague had a sudden stomach attack and needed to go to the toilet urgently. The 'toilet' at this factory was a drain behind the main building where several guys were already squatting and doing their business. There were no partitions: everybody just sat more or less beside each other. As my colleague could not hold on anymore he decided to follow their example and do his business.

When he squatted down, however, several of the other guys stood up and stood in front of him to have a good look at what tackle this foreigner was packing! One of the reasons to always take care of business and not eat too much during the day in China.

Kicking up a stink

What about the Regional Creative Director for Asia of a major multinational advertising agency who was based in Bangkok but refused to travel to China on any assignments because of the state of their public toilets?

Blind faith

During one of the days of Ramadan (the period when Muslims fast during the day) I was travelling with one of my Muslim Indonesian staff through Indonesia. During the whole day he behaved like a true Muslim: no eating, no drinking, and even spitting out the saliva in his mouth instead of swallowing it to soothe his throat. However, when we arrived in the hotel that evening, we went to the bar and I asked him what he would like to drink: "A beer please."

Surprised I asked him: "F, you have been behaving like a true Muslim the whole day and now you are ordering alcohol?"

His simple answer was: "Allah is asleep right now, so he won't see." We had several beers that evening … and a few other things Allah was not supposed to see.

Keeping bad company

Having taken over the Indonesian office from my predecessor I noticed that the staff were always coming in late, ranging from 10 minutes up to an hour, and found difficulty in returning from lunch on time. They did, however, know how to read a clock, as they were very punctual in leaving for lunch and for home at the end of the day. Being sick and tired of this after two months in my new office, I decided to issue a memo reminding staff of the working hours. Anyone being late three times in a row would see their annual leave reduced by a day.

The day after I issued the memo, two filthy-looking persons visited me from the labour bureau. They told me that they had received complaints from my distressed staff about my memo. They were confused about what my task in the office was, as my work permit indicated that I was the 'commercial director' and the commercial director was not allowed to issue these kind of memos: he was only allowed to keep himself busy with the sales and other commercial activities. Besides, my staff informed them, I had frequently travelled outside of Jakarta to conduct business. This was not allowed unless I had permission from the police officer in my district were I was living.

As I was, therefore, abusing my work permit they would withdraw this permit and ask me to leave the country. Being really pissed off with my staff and, not knowing whether their story was correct or not, I decided to bluff.

In an angry and loud voice I told them that I would be rather happy if they kicked me out of the country as I did not like the country and, anyway, staff who behave like this are disgusting and needed to be fired. The firing of my staff they themselves could do immediately, I told them, as they should realise that this was a foreign company and I was the only expat around. So I asked them to leave my office, go to the work-floor and tell my 40-odd staff that they were without a job, and without any severance pay, with immediate effect.

"Sir, sir, please don't be so angry … we must be able to arrange something, please come to our office tomorrow and you can discuss this with our boss. Maybe he agrees to let you stay."

We set a time for the meeting and they left my office, after which I called the company lawyer. He advised me to have my title changed to 'President Director' and have my local personnel manager call the labour bureau the next they and tell them that I have to cancel the appointment due to a trip to Surabaya. Also, that if they have any further issues that they should contact the lawyer.

All of which I did, and never heard from them again. Their main reason for them to get me to their office was apparently to intimidate me by having more of their guys around so that I would pay them a bribe in order to stay in the country. Bad luck for them this time.

Looks all white to me

We had several garment-buying offices throughout Asia, all of them headed by an expat, and the bigger offices had several expats (one for each division). The Bangkok office at the time was a major office and the relevant expat manager always did 'major' decisions and approvals.

Much to everyone's surprise, then, the new expat technical manager allowed some low-ranking staff to do material and colour approvals. They soon found out why-what the human resource department had overlooked when they hired him was that he was colour-blind!

Local rules

I had a guy from head office out for a visit to our regional headquarters in Thailand. It is safe to say we didn't see eye to eye on most issues, and our meetings degenerated into point-scoring grudge matches. Being a very buttoned-down corporate type, he was slow to warm to the whole bar scene, but gradually got into it. "These girls could be models in New York," he enthused.

I disagreed. "No, they're guys."

"No way. How can you be so sure?"

"Because I fuck them," was my honest dead-panned reply. He went back to his drink for a little while, taking this information on board. Taking him to meet his plane, I instructed my driver in Thai to go as fast as possible so this guy wouldn't want to come back anytime soon. My parting words at the airport to him: "If you can't tell the difference between men and women, don't tell me how to run this country."

Brown-nosing

I was on a training course when I heard that a 'tart' in the office had just got a new Honda Accord company car. I was thinking of buying one myself and wanted to swap for a short time to check it out. As we were good friends I sent her a text message that read: "Can I borrow your car for a few days, I promise not to smell the seat." Just as I pressed the send key I realised I had selected the wrong number from the company phone's memory – it was sent to my boss by mistake.

Tea lady with a difference

Team briefs are good fun in Korea. We normally have a talk (one hour), a meal (two hours), a drink (three hours) and then a karaoke/sex show (several hours). On my first brief the Korean client got on stage where a young girl emptied his sacks into a kid's play tea-pot. She then emptied this over his head, which he seemed to enjoy! I'm not telling what happened to me on subsequent briefs, though.

Fishy behaviour

Our secretary told me that a girl in the next office had the hots for me.

Trying to be polite I told our secretary I thought she was a good-looking girl but it might not be a good idea to involve myself with company employees. Undeterred, she came into my office and gave me a very smelly dried fish. She then sat next to me and smiled. As she didn't speak any English I asked my secretary what the hell was going on. She told me it was a Korean custom, and she was showing me her affection. I would have to eat it to avoid her losing face!

I hate fresh fish, never mind one that has been dead for two years. I stuck it in my mouth and pretended to swallow. Luckily she left soon afterwards and I managed to get most of it out of my mouth and into the bin. I told my secretary to let her know whenever I smell fish I will think of little Ms B.

A speedy exit

I was coming to the end of my employment in Korea when I was caught by the police speeding (60kph over) and in a bus lane. I went to see the man in charge of vehicles/licenses at our office and pleaded for mercy. What would become of me? He said: "Don't worry about it. You leave the country in two weeks and they will never bother to chase it up. Anyway, since I found out you were leaving us, I have been putting all the parking offences and speeding tickets for the pool cars in your name."

Old wives' tales

It was the beginning of a new project in South Korea and everyone was new. The boss, who had just arrived from a long project in Malaysia, had a photo of a young Malaysian girl on his desk holding a baby. When I asked about the lady he proudly informed me it was his girlfriend and his new son. I was a little surprised as he was in his late fifties and she was about twenty. Later my girlfriend asked me what my boss was like. I told her he seemed OK and had a beautiful girlfriend and a baby.

Within the next month, the photo had disappeared from his desk and after a little research I found he had a wife of many years and she had just breezed into town. Unfortunately I failed to mention this to my girlfriend. The four of us eventually met at a company meal and my girlfriend asked his wife where the baby was! I have never seen someone age so fast as my boss that day. I hurriedly explained it was the client I had been working with and not my boss who was the new father.

Two weeks later I was relocated to the deep south and found myself with no laptop, no secretary, and the oldest jeep in the fleet.

Sleeping partners

In Singapore, a friendly competitor of ours was in an office that looked like a residential house close to Newton. I asked him how he got around the zoning laws to operate his business there. The secret, he said, was to have a fold-out sofa bed or two which could be wheeled out in the case of an inspection to create the impression it was indeed 'residential'.

Soon after, we rented a similar place, enjoying the low-key working environment. After a few years, the business grew and there was a steady stream of suppliers' cars, bikes and delivery boys in and out of our door. The fold-out bed saw active service on many a late night by various staffers.

Then came the knock on the door. The man from the ministry. "We have reports you are running a business here," he said. "Mind if we look around?" He asked to see utility bills to ascertain residency, and so on. By this time I'd got someone to go and fold out the bed and give it that mussed-up, just-slept-in-look. Nevermind all the computers and files lying around or the eight staff beavering away.

My spirited explanation was all in vain. A few weeks later we got our marching orders from the premises.

Lonely at the top

My boss was a director of the company, and based in Melbourne. I was the general manager, based in Hong Kong. He hated Melbourne and was after my job so he could be based in Asia. He called me to say he was en route to London, so could we meet during his stopover in Bangkok? I suspected something was afoot. Not wanting to take any chances, instead of the usual hotel, I booked us into the Montien (adjacent Patpong), which had a strict 'no tarts' policy. We met for dinner. After that he suggested we might go and check out some of the famed Bangkok bars … where could I suggest?

Me??? Oh, I'd heard of these places but hadn't actually been to them, I fibbed. We strolled down the great old Patpong strip, and kept walking and walking. Not wanting to make the first move, I waited for him to select a place. He never did and just as we got to the end of the strip, a bar door opened, with a raucous voice yelling out to me: "J, you bastard!"

"They seem to know you in there," he said, "Let's try it." My 'friend' inside welcomed us, and lined up the tarts, saying, "You remember this lovely lass, don't you?" Fortunately, my boss got into the swing of it, and had a couple of tarts on his knee before long. At the end of the night, we returned to the hotel with one girl between us. I still suspected my boss's motives, as it wasn't very clear whom the girl was for. On arrival at the hotel, the night manager stopped us:

"Sorry, sir, no ladies allowed after 10pm."

I just shrugged my shoulder to my boss. "I never knew that … sorry. Never bought a girl back." The tart was duly dismissed, and my reputation was saved. But the bastard never gave up. He subsequently had me tailed by private investigators in Bangkok hoping to get some dirt on me, which he never got. Well, until the episode with the twins in Sydney, but that's another story.

On the cards

As a design company wanting to break into lucrative government contracts in Singapore, I was delighted one afternoon to have a message to call back one of the largest bodies, the CPF Board. At first, the contact person couldn't place what it was I was calling about, then the coin dropped. "Oh, yes," she said. "We need someone to tender for a design of the staff Christmas party invitations … we looked through the phone book and, as we hadn't heard of you, thought you must be cheap." It was time for us to work on our own PR for a change!

It's a small whirlybird

I was landing my helicopter on an oil platform 50 miles off the coast of Bombay, India, and a rig worker came up to me and said: "Hey, weren't you at the Paradise Bar in Phuket last Monday afternoon?"

Flamin' hell

A recent management meeting in Pattaya found us in a flash Italian restaurant after the morning meeting and afternoon inhaling beers in an al fresco beach bar. Now we were onto the red wine and Irish coffees, me sitting next to my boss. I am talking shorthand and gazing at a flaming sambuca in front of me when I decide to extinguish it. I carefully placed the palm of my hand on top of the glass and, of course, it stuck and caused me to fling it desperately away. I now have a perfect circular scar on my right hand to prove how stupid I am.

By the way I am the Asia Pacific Health, Safety and Environment Manager for a major company!

Hit the ground yawning

I didn't get the welcome from my new boss that I expected when I first arrived in Korea. My new workplace was located about three hours south of Seoul, so my journey there consisted of flying from Perth to Sydney to get a visa, wandering around Sydney for hours waiting to see if I got the visa, then flying to Seoul via Brisbane before jumping on a bus for my final destination.

What with taking the Tuesday night redeye from Perth, I arrived on a Thursday afternoon, having not slept since Monday night.

Instead of taking me to my flat as I hoped, my boss took me straight to work. I wasn't happy as I was completely buggered. Imagine how happy I was when he then got on the phone to the guy in Seoul who had recruited me to complain that his new employee wasn't the happy or enthusiastic type.

The direct approach

In Hong Kong we had this company director who was tiny – probably about five-foot nothing. He was also a bit of a 'funny' bloke so we only introduced him to major clients if they really, really insisted on meeting the full board of directors. One time, we had a directors' meeting in Manila and he'd come along. Down the old Mabini strip, there was this tiny girl outside one of the bars, doing the old 'Come inside, sir' routine. At the end of the evening – 16 or so bars later – we went back to that first bar, and introduced our director to her. They stood back to back and were exactly the same height.

"What a perfect match!" we said. That was several years ago, and they are now married and have two children.

Sales target

I was in Guangzhou, China, at a customer site for a week. One day we were sitting, going about our business, when suddenly I see my host and the other employees in the room exchanging humorous remarks in Chinese, smiling, laughing. So I ask him what's going on, what is everyone smiling about? He told me that one of the female employees tried to commit suicide by jumping from the roof of the plant because her boyfriend left her. She was stopped by other employees.

It also was revealed to me that it was not the first time this sort of thing happened and that the last time the girl succeeded.

In the line of duty

The 'no-smile line' is a term given by American soldiers in Korea to the area north of Seoul just south of the DMZ. The reason for the phrase is because the Second Infantry Division soldiers tend to spend a lot more time deployed in the field than those on the rest of the peninsula, and live under more restrictions.

For example, most of the 20,000 odd soldiers there are not allowed to be accompanied on their year-long tour by their families, who typically remain in the States at the last duty assignment. Also, soldiers are not allowed to have personally-owned vehicles. Everyone lives in barracks, including the field-grade officers. The pass and leave policy is also pretty restrictive.

By and large, particularly compared to life in Seoul, life kind of sucks up there.

Snake in the grass

I run a company that arranges free and subsidised medical services for the disabled and handicapped throughout Asia. One patient was an old farmer in the southern Philippines and we restored his sight. He was so thankful he returned later. "Thank you, thank you," he said. "I have nothing in this world to pay you with, but please have this snake." He produced this tiny little snake. My colleague knew I was interested in snakes so accepted it on my behalf and the snake was duly crated and sent up by road to me in Manila.

Turns out to be a reticulated python, the largest breed of snake in the world. Currently it's a three metre 'hosepipe with attitude' and will continue to grow at one metre per year till it reaches ten metres. My wife tells me I will be releasing it before then.

For whom the bell toils

In Manila we had to fire our receptionist/ secretary and advertised for a replacement. We made the mistake of mentioning we were an *international* healthcare firm (read: dollars!) and received 190 applicants, including one doctor and two dentists. The person we eventually hired to man the phones had a Masters' Degree. Doesn't say much for the job market.

Untouchables

When the UN went into Cambodia, we scored a very secret contract to supply refrigerated containers to use as temporary morgues. These were all arranged in Singapore then shipped across. Fortunately, they were never needed, but we made our money anyway, so didn't really care one way or the other.

But on return, we faced an unexpected problem ... the Malay dock-workers refused to touch or unload these containers that they considered to be 'contaminated'. So we had to arrange a special work gang of Chinese dock-workers. Soon enough, the containers were unloaded and back in circulation, and got mixed up so no-one knew for sure anymore which ones were the black-banned containers.

Strong, silent type

One of the fellow crewmates on our ship was an insufferable bore with his 'been there, done that' bragging. Next time the ship called into Manila we thought we'd shut him up. Having got him completely plastered, we sent out to a well-known local establishment for a billy-boy with the biggest tackle around, and locked this guy in a cabin with our stupefied mate. The next day he was silent. Not a word. His photo appeared on the tour gazette and he left the ship shortly after.

Signing your life away

We have a staff of about 90 Filipinos working for us in Cambodia. We'd pay them a big salary in US dollars each month. Then I started getting calls from some of their families back home, whom I'd met when interviewing and recruiting: "How come you haven't paid Armando this month?"

I was mystified, and investigated. Of course, all these guys were taking their pay and spending it on piss and pussy and there was nothing left to send home.

So I started an automatic deduction, where they kept some and the rest was sent home automatically. Still the problems didn't finish there. One Friday night, after a couple of drinks in the office, one of the Filipino guys came up to me and said: "Treat me like a responsible man, for heaven's sake, and pay me … I need some money tonight." I explained our policy to him again, but he was insistent. So I paid him the full amount and made him sign for it. Next morning he came and asked for his pay again.

"But I gave it to you last night," I said. He didn't seem to have any recollection of that, so I pulled out my file. "Is this your signature?" He agreed it was, then started berating me for being irresponsible and paying him in full on a Friday night before going out on the piss. Damned if you do, damned if you don't.

Boner-fide credentials

Overheard in a Bangkok club, an expat was asking his friend how his search for a new secretary was coming along. "I had a bird come in today," the employer said, "she had a pretty face, but I asked her to walk up the stairs just to make sure she had good legs as well."

Stacks of dough

I had gone to Burma to meet with a general about a business deal involving their purchase of riot gear. I was collected by a driver in a Mercedes 500 from the airport, and driven to the general's house. As we approached his house, I spotted him sitting on what looked like a deck chair or day-bed on the roof.

"We pay cash," he insisted of the deal, and took me upstairs. What he'd been lying on, in fact, was a huge block of local currency, stacks and stacks and stacks of the stuff, all bundled up.

This was duly loaded into the car, leaving almost no room for the driver to see out the windscreen, and we drove to the central bank down town to deposit the cash and finalise the transaction.

Wad a wanker

A colleague from Bangkok had gone up to Ho Chi Minh City for a business trip. No doubt he was big noting himself and being somewhat conspicuous, and got mugged on the way back to the hotel; a wad of US dollars 'a mile thick' was taken. Fortunately they were only US$1 notes, disappointing for the mugger no doubt. He had the audacity to put it on his trip expense claim.

Victoria Cross? Viet Cong?

I was on a business trip to Cambodia and, as standard operating practice would have it, ended the day with several beers in some dives round the corner from the hotel, then took a bird back to the room.

When I got back to Bangkok, I submitted my expense claim, and the accounts clerk questioned one item on my hotel bill: 'VC'.

"What's this?" she asked.

"No idea … must be some kind of government tax," I said, and she seemed satisfied.

A colleague had overheard this conversation. "You dumb ass," he said. "VC is 'visitor charge'." Oops!

Repeat offender

I was lucky enough to have two jobs in Asia that were the ultimate in freedom away from the boss and the office. I used to inspect telecom repeater stations in Malaysia and Brunei, driving on average about 700 kilometres a day. The coast road in Brunei was excellent and beautiful, and I'd have to check the signal strength from the three or four towers en route, and check there was enough petrol for the generators and that the batteries hadn't been stolen (which used to happen about once every three weeks!). Of course you'd have to carry all these supplies with you and, if you ran out, that was a pain because the nearest petrol station would be probably fifty kilometres away and you'd have to go there and back just to top the drums up. In Malaysia, I used to cover the area north of KL to the Thai border.

Drinking to my health

On a new petro-chem assignment in Davao, Philippines, the management wanted to make sure we were well looked after and in good health. They asked the Japanese contingent what they drank, and they wanted Scotch. So cases and cases of the best Black Label were brought in. Anything to keep the management in good spirits. They asked me. "I'm happy to drink the local San Miguel," I said. Funnily enough, I was the only one to never get sick with a bad stomach or other mystery virus or ailment. Must've been the water they were mixing with the Scotch.

Strike me lucky!

In the good old days I was based in Australia but travelling to Manila a lot. On one trip, at the time of Marcos's collapse, there was a strike at the airport. I duly informed head office there was a strike and martial law so I couldn't get back to Australia. They panicked, concerned for my welfare. "Take care and let us know if there's anything we can do for you," they said.

The strike was only for one day, but I managed to stay an extra couple of weeks!

Three-sided affair

In Kuala Lumpur, a client of mine had a huge rectangular office with a few windows along it halfway down the corridor. On my next consultation to that company, I went down the corridor and the whole thing had been re-arranged and I couldn't find him. "Oh, John's in that corner now," an assistant said.

I found him in a tiny cramped triangular office right in the corner. "*Feng shui*," was his unsolicited explanation. It obviously wasn't good energy ... he was posted to Pakistan shortly after.

Model behaviour

In PNG, I hung a dirty calendar on my wall. My boss, a devil-dodging Pom, passed by, glanced at it and asked: "Is that appropriate?" I kept the calendar up, but fashioned some bra and panties for the pouting models out of post-it notes and stuck them onto the calendar. He was still not impressed.

The calendar now hangs in my toilet at home.

The odd coupling

Two Brits were working together in Jakarta, and one subsequently moved to Singapore. It was the days before email and probably even faxes, so A wrote to B saying he was coming up to Singapore; they should catch up. There was no reply, and several months went by. By now A was in Singapore and bumped into B at the Tanglin Club. B was rather cold to him and A asked him why he never replied to his letter.

"I've never forgiven you for bonking my secretary," explained B. Turns out A had knobbed B's secretary two days before her wedding, and then again a week afterwards. The secretary's husband had found out about this and came to the office to 'get' him. B managed to stall the guy whilst A slipped out the back out of harm's way. Over twenty years later, they are now firm friends again. A and B that is.

Blood brothers

I was based at Clarke Air Field when the Gulf War broke out and we had to load up the choppers. Knowing that the lads were going into dry conditions, we decided to cheer them up and loaded all the plasma bags with white spirits instead. These packages of plasma bags were questioned but cleared by Kuwaiti customs, and we heard later the guys appreciated it big time when they were plucked out of Baghdad on our specially-supplied choppers.

Clutching at straws

Starting a new job in Manila, I was introduced to the joys of the company's car pool. They presented me with my gleaming new chariot featuring one ripped tyre, a bald tyre, and brakes you had to pump. I told them it was a heap of junk: fix the brakes and tyres before I drive it. It was returned and I noticed it still had a slipped clutch.

"Why didn't you fix the bloody thing?" I asked them.

"You didn't ask us to change it, sir."

Ship happens

Our European client was arranging the major launch of a new ship – one of the world's largest in Korea. As we handled their dealings for the region, I thought I'd write myself a trip to Korea from Singapore as I'd never been before. I told the local office that Paris had suggested I attend. To Paris I said that the local office had suggested I attend. So I turned up in Seoul, and ran a disastrous press conference there as not a single journalist could understand

English let alone the haltering Franglais spoken by the French chairman. However, I understood enough to understand mid-way through that the ship itself was being launched in Pusan … nowhere near Seoul at all. I didn't get to see a single ship, but I did get to spend 12 lovely days in Korea on the client's tab.

Joint venture

On business in Bangkok I had a meeting with one of our suppliers, an expat whom I'd got to know really well over the years. Whilst waiting in reception one morning, I felt a craving for a cigarette, but I'd run out earlier. I asked the receptionist if she possibly had a cigarette.

Casually she reached beneath the counter and produced a tray with a h-u-g-e joint sitting proudly on it.

"Er, actually, I was thinking more like a Marlboro or something," I said, a little gob-smacked at that time of the day. She obviously thought any friend of her boss's must be into it, too!

Going for gold

The client's regional bigwigs had travelled to Singapore for our proposal presentation to pitch for their business. I was dazzling them (in my mind anyway) with a presentation of multi-media charts and graphs, building it up to fever pitch when suddenly this gold object shot like a bullet out of my mouth, skidding its way across the boardroom table before coming to rest in front of Mr Big at the top of the table. It was my golden tooth crown!

Embarrassed as hell, I carried on without blinking an eyelid. We won the business. The head Chinese client later said he was so impressed with my focus and dedication to the cause he just had to award the business to us.

A bum note

I was working for a major music store in Tokyo, and we had Eric Clapton come on a promo tour. So we arranged a big media event and a huge banner as a backdrop. On the day, there in huge red letters above him, the sign read: 'WELCOME ERIC CRAPTON!'

Crush the competition

As a financial adviser, I frequently visited my clients in Singapore where we have a representative office. Without realising it, I must have annoyed one of our competitors by stealing away too many of his clients, or some such. One night in Orchard Towers, having a drink and minding my own business I was set upon by this guy, who smashed me in the head with a glass. I was down and out, streaming with blood.

I was patched up at a nearby hospital, then flew back to the UK to get proper treatment. I was soon on the mend from the bashing and bruising, but lost sight in one eye. My assailant, who was known to me, jumped bail and shot through, probably to Indonesia. I had to wait to have confirmation from the police that he was not allowed back into Singapore as a free man before I had the guts to resume business in Singapore.

Double trouble

In PNG I was flying for survey companies. We were always on 'double time' even if the weather was too bad to shoot in, and we often landed at strips in darkness that were 'day-use only' destinations. The living was good – we had dope, beer, and occasional use of a couple of young Filipina wives of some of the old blokes living there.

One day this guy, J, said: "You look like you need a break," and gave me $1,000 to fly him to Manila. That was my first time to the Philippines and I loved it.

In all the six week job I had gone up to PNG for took nearly 11 months. Then my boss in Australia offered me another assignment: in the Philippines as luck would have it.

"No way," I said, playing poker with him, "if you think PNG is bad, the Philippines is worse … martial law, people with guns …" I squeezed every last cent out of him before agreeing. Yeehaa!

On-the-job training

I called a friend of mine in Australia and said: "Come to Jakarta, I've got a job for you."

"What is it?" he wanted to know, quite reasonably.

"I'm not telling just get here."

He arrived a few days later and I met him at the airport. "We're going to meet my boss at the pub," I said, heading for Blok M. He was duly introduced to my boss, a Scotsman nicknamed 'Helium Elbow' for his drinking propensity. By 8pm, he was smashed.

"Let's go next door for some entertainment." 'Next door' turned out to be full of birds, which outraged my friend who didn't drink or smoke.

"How does this work?" he asked. "Well, you just ask them if they'd like a drink, say you look nice tonight, and take them home," I briefed him on the complicated procedure of courtship, Jakarta-style. Overcoming his outrage quite successfully, he had a bird on his arm and was ready to go within 10 minutes.

The next day at the debriefing he confided his confusion: "I asked her if she wanted a drink and she said 'No thanks, I'm Muslim'. So I said 'Well, would you like to fuck?' and she said 'Yes please'."

He fitted in all right and my boss hired him on the spot.

The black book

Going into Bangkok airport, the expat gent was surprised to be hauled aside by the Immigration officers at the counter. He was 'arrested' and held for nearly a week on some spurious charge he didn't quite understand. Turns out his previous employer many, many years earlier had a vendetta against him and had 'fixed' the Immigration database to keep an eye out for this guy and teach him a lesson.

Trading punches

There was a company ownership dispute in Thailand so one of the expat managers of the company registered the name of the company as his so the parent company would have to buy it off him if they wanted to trade under that (their!) name. It turned very ugly, and resulted in the expat registering the name of the Regional CEO – who was due to fly in to resolve the situation – on the immigration shit-list. Imagine his indignation when, on arrival at Bangkok airport, he was turned away.

Separation society

We had a big VIP function while I was running a company branch in Manila. The big wig from America and his wife were in attendance, and showed up in glittering form for the evening. The smile was wiped off his wife's face, though, when she was ushered to one table and her husband to another.

"This is the Filipino way," was the explanation.

"Suits me fine," he was heard to say, out of earshot of his wife.

Sleeping on the job

We're having breakfast in the hotel restaurant, trying to crack the brief we'd been ignoring all week. All of us had been out the night before until the wee small hours, and were running on two hours' sleep, max. The design staff, a key part of our group, hadn't even made it down to breakfast yet when the head of the department comes stumbling in wearing the same clothes as the night before.

"What time is it?" he asks. When told, he says: "I just woke up in some girl's apartment and had no idea where I was, what time it was, or what day, even! It didn't help that she didn't speak English. Is my staff here?"

"Uh no, X, they're not down yet."

"Right, don't say anything about this, okay?" Off he went.

The staff came down minutes later, and X followed right after, cheerily greeting everyone and saying he slept very well, thank you.

Shift happens

I'm here in Shenzhen, China, working at Ling Ao Nuclear Power Station, and I'm starting a rotating shift as follows: seven 13-hour dayshifts, four days off, seven 13-hour nightshifts, four days off, then dayshifts again, etc.

Old dogs, same tricks

In the original Gulf War period, I was fresh out of flight school and was assigned to a US Air Force reservist unit to train in the Philippines. Some of the guys were Vietnam vets and now flying commercial airliners, but still hard-living fellas. Most ignored the regulations of the air force, such as the 'bottle-to-throttle' ratio, which stipulated that you couldn't drink a bottle of beer within twelve hours of flying. That was easy to get around – they just switched to cans!

They were often so hung-over and on the verge of vomiting and greying-out on practice flights that they used to go out over the sea, drop their fuel (worth about US$2,000 per tank) and come back and sleep in the hangar. The fuel consumption would indicate that they had done their requisite hours of airtime.

Whilst I fully expected Angeles to be 'Sodom and Gomorrah', the reality only struck me when I stepped off base into the first bar and saw the base chaplain bouncing a bar girl on his knee.

Road rage

My secretary in Port Moresby was a rather quiet and shy girl when she started working for our company. As it happened she lives on the way from my home to the office, so I used to collect her from the Port Moresby Yacht Club each morning and drive her to work. This has been going on for some time, and now when some idiot does something crazy on the road, I hear this booming voice from the passenger seat: "Aah, shit for brains!" or "Where'd you get your fuckin' license!" Don't know where she got that sort of language!

Going loco

When based in Malaysia with the Australian Army, there was a guy who'd served for 20 years in the forces, and he was going – or had already gone – a little native. He asked for a discharge from our base. Although this was against protocol and standard practice, it was granted to him. Upon his discharge, he promptly changed into a sarong and walked off into the fields. He was last seen living with two wives in a nipa hut near Sungei Petani.

Safe and sound asleep

When Clarke Air base was reverted to the Philippines, we were supposed to hand over x million dollars worth of equipment and leave all the safes empty and open. We had other ideas and handed over jeeps with only one wheel, typewriters with no keys, and so on. This wasn't government policy, just ours.

Then with the surprise eruption of Mt Pinatubo, our withdrawal plans were thrown into disarray – because of the smoke, lava, and so on we were evacuated to Subic Bay in a hurry. The final day was like leaving Saigon in '75 … we had spun the combination locks and slammed the doors shut. So there I was, hopefully unknown to anyone else, with US$2 million in wages and cash under my mattress in Subic. The temptation to do a 'runner' was immense, I can tell you.

If you have a good story about work, bosses, colleagues or suppliers in Asia, email The Editor at hardshipposting@hotmail.com or fax 612-9499-5908. Office hours are 10am -3pm Mondays to Fridays, with a couple of hours or so for lunch.

❖ 12 ❖

The More the Messier
or Despots and Demigods

*True tales of red-tape, officialdom
and embassy life in Asia.*

There's nothing better than a great moment in bureaucracy to bring tears of bellicose laughter to my eyes. Especially when someone gets consummately 'done' in the process. As learned history scholars, you will know that Japan was referred to as 'the Hermit Kingdom' up until the late 1800s for its refusal to trade with the western world. The US was looking for a way in to the Japanese market and sent Commodore Matthew Perry as their chief negotiator (mainly because a couple of warships have been known to be a useful bargaining tool). The Japanese *shogun* got a minor provincial official, dressed him up, and placed him on a mock throne. This gave Perry the illusion he was dealing with the real leader of Japan, the top dog. So he handed over a letter from the US President, which said something like 'you sell us rice and we'll sell you big automobiles … or else'. When nothing came of it, Perry realised he had been stiffed and the ruse was discovered.

Ever since then, working out who is actually running Japan has been an international mystery. They seem to go through prime ministers quicker than a Balinese masseuse goes through a bottle of baby oil. When PM Obuchi recently keeled over with a stroke, Chief Cabinet Secretary Aoki even convinced everyone that he had personal instructions from the PM that he was now in charge. Obuchi slipped into a coma a couple of hours later, leaving the supposed verbal instruction officially undocumented. Rather be lucky than good any day, eh?

Little wonder then that 60 per cent of schoolboys in Japan aspire to join government ministries. Or perhaps the reason is they dream of setting up their own fiefdom and enjoying the trappings of leadership like King Mongkut, the King of Siam in the 1860s. He had something in the order of 23 wives and 42 porcupines, er, concubines. Not as many as the emperor of China had in his day, but still a worthy effort. You'd need a sophisticated roster-planning software program like they use for airline crews to schedule bouts with each one, wouldn't you? And to think he did it all in the days of the abacus.

The cat is now officially out of the bag (or should that be 'the pussy is now out of the sack') with the expiration of various statutes and declassification of information from that period, so you may as well hear it from me first. Yes, I was indeed Defence Attaché and First Secretary at a number of postings throughout South East Asia. There was nothing like embassy life in my day: all care and no responsibility taken. Cocktail parties at sundown each evening. And lots of subversive behaviour, which may or may not have been part of an official agenda at any given time.

One of my all-time favourite stories of embassy-types in Asia is undoubtedly General (later Sir) Gerald Templar. You probably remember him from the hit TV show, The Saint [Check facts -ed.]. Back when the Poms ran the Malayan peninsula he came to power in a rather unfortunate way, as the replacement of Sir Henry Gurney, the British High Commissioner who was ambushed and killed driving up to Fraser's Hill. Anyway, Templar brought in the Ghurkhas and mopped the floor with the Commies so that showed them. One day, according to my good friend Noel Barber, he was doing the rounds of one of the more sleepy outposts, and in one town was a two-man British police outfit with just a single cell. In that cell was a gaunt old Chinese man, looking very sad and sorry for himself.

"How old is the prisoner?" enquired Templar in his gruff British military manner.

"Seventy years old, sir," replied an officer.

"And what's he in for?" he barked.

"Rape, sir."

"Oh, good … there's hope for me yet," he reportedly replied. That's my boy!

There were a lot of colourful episodes around that time, some of which completely ruined the gin-and-tonic *fest de jour*. In June 1965, 500 Indonesian students invaded the home of the US ambassador. He had a big place, but it was never going to sleep 500 in their wildest dreams. In 1967, the Chinese downed a couple of US Navy planes, and there's nothing like military involvement to get the telex machine clacking away at an embassy. Soon after, the Red Guards sacked the British consulate and attacked the staff.

But one of the most amazing things I'm still trying to work out from the late 60s was Charles Fenn. An American officer in the US Marine Corps during World War 11, he went on to work with the Office of Strategic Services (OSS) and subsequently the Air Ground Aid Services (AGAS), engaged in the rescue of downed pilots and liaison with prisoners of war in Vietnam. Going back to 1945, one of his military intelligence (there's an oxymoron for you, peace lovers) students was a gent called Ho Chi Minh. Because of this existing relationship, Ho Chi Minh gave Fenn invaluable help on the ground in carrying out the work of AGAS. One of Ho's greatest ever speeches was apparently written by Fenn, who based it on the words of Jefferson's Federation speech. The similarities were remarkable, and Ho Chi Minh never knew it, but neither did anyone else in North Vietnam for that matter. In 1973, after Ho's death but before the end of the war, Fenn published a biography on Uncle Ho. No conflict of interest there.

One of the prisoners of war who Fenn might've counselled in that time was a downed airman, Douglas Peterson – 'Pete' to his friends (I'm still trying to work that one out myself). He spent six years as a POW before entering the diplomatic corps and was recently appointed as the US ambassador to Vietnam. He's got a slightly more comfortable bed this time around.

Speaking of books about leaders, Chairman Mao produced a little book with the catchy title Quotations From the Works of Mao Zedong. It sold 800,000,000 copies in just five years in the early Seventies. Of course, it's always easier to sell books at gunpoint (note to editor: let's try this with Hardship Posting next time).

Not selling in quite the same numbers is my good friend General Wiranto's romantic CD, For You My Indonesia. The former Indonesian military chief put out this platter of his silken crooning to promote his kinder, gentler, soft-guy image. This was slightly tarnished by him being found guilty of crimes against humanity. Apparently playing this CD loudly in confined rooms was his troops' main weapon of brutal torture in East Timor.

OK, enough about ruthless bastards. Asia, for all its 'it's a man's world' posturing, leads the way in putting women up where they belong. On top. Sri

Lanka's Sirima Bandaranaike (or Mrs B to her friends) was the world's first premier with XX chromosomes back in 1960, when my voice was on the verge of breaking and I probably only had a whisker or two to shave. But let's talk about my favourite, Aung Suu Kyi from Burma. How good does she look for a woman in her late fifties? Mind you, I shouldn't be too astounded: she's only my age and my youthful looks have not diminished either over the years. Her NLD party won the 1990 elections, but the junta refused to let her take the reins of the country, and she was placed under house arrest for the second time. On a scale of one to ten, I'd certainly give her one! She looks like the type of lady who'd look you in the eye, as you dragged on that hard-earned post-coital cigarette, and say 'thank you'.

Down in Papua New Guinea is another interesting lady, and this one's a real Lady ... Lady Carol Kidu, widow of Sir Buri Kidu. Covered in tribal tattoos, she's the first white woman ever to be elected to PNG parliament and lives in a humble fishing village on the bay in Port Moresby. There's not a lot of her type up there, so it would be difficult to accuse her of *wontok*, the PNG version of cronyism.

Another Australian in the echelons is Kirsty Sword, the first lady of East Timor (although it doesn't say anywhere what she was the first lady to achieve). She used to work for the East Timorese Resistance in the bad old days and was known as Ruby Blade – sounds more like some firm-titted double-agent from a Bond thriller. While working on a documentary she witnessed Indonesian intimidation first hand, and decided to move to Jakarta and teach English. She had access to email and translated documents and sent faxes from Xanana Gusmao to western leaders, alerting them to the plight of his country after he was jailed in 1993. She met him by pretending to visit an Australian uncle in jail, then bribed a warden to smuggle a cell phone (geddit?) in for him. They were married five years later when he was released and – apart from her being stabbed a few years ago – they are living happily ever after. Everybody: "Aaaah."

Mind you, the political arena is no place for most women. Question time in some Asian parliaments is better than watching WWF (that's the World Wrestling Federation, not the World Wildlife Fund). The way they go at it in Korea, Taiwan, and Japan ... fists flying, cups and saucers scattered, chairs smashed in anger. It's an all-in brawl in double-breasted navy blue suits. Apparently news footage of these explosive bouts is used as training films for

US ice hockey teams.

But don't expect Japan to have a woman leader anytime soon ... in May 1947 a law was passed preventing women from reigning on the men's parade. The last woman on the throne in Japan was back in 1771. But Japanese women have their own little ways of getting their point across. Exhibit A: Misuko Nakani, a *geisha*, was the mistress of Japanese PM Sosuke Uno (sounds more like a small two-door hatchback, doesn't it?). Feeling played out, she came on national TV and said he'd treated her like a common whore, gave her nothing at the end of their relationship, and worst of all he had ... no leadership capabilities. He was out of office very shortly after, fortunately with his tackle still in tact. Exhibit B: the Thai princess, Luk Pla (which means 'Baby Fish' to the best of my Thai-speaking ability!) was jailed for six years recently after killing her husband – a sixty-year-old prince who'd been her lover since she was 14 – by poisoning his coffee with insecticide. She had tried running away and escaping before, but to no avail ... he ran large ads in the papers offering a reward for her safe return. But she apparently didn't want his fancy sports cars, aeroplanes, jewellery and land dotted all over the country. Instead, the 30-year-old adopted princess wanted to be with her toy boy, a 19-year-old chestnut vendor. The whole thing sounds nuts to me!

In Malaysia, the king and eight sultans were previously totally immune to prosecution. But in 1993 they decided that no-one should be above the law so a special court for 'rulers' was set up to deal with any offending royalty. A plausible move but, strangely enough, the court has never convened.

And how about Dipendra the Crown Prince of Nepal who allegedly massacred his whole family, including the king and queen? Investigators say he was drunk and had also smoked hash before putting on his army gear, grabbing an arsenal of four of the finest assault weapons, then going downstairs to where the family was sitting down to dinner. "Not yak meat again!" he bellowed [Check facts -ed.] before blazing away at all and sundry, including himself. To protect Nepal from further ill fortune, a Brahman priest offered himself as a sacrificial lamb in a *katto* ceremony. For those who don't follow Tibetan customs closely, this means the vegetarian ate a meal with meat. He then dressed in royal gear, including a crown and a pair of the prince's shoes, hopped on an elephant and rode off into exile in the Himalayas. By way of thanks, the Nepalese people gave him a TV set, fan, sofa, desk, bed and some clothes. Better than winning Wheel of Fortune!

Talking of making an arsenal of yourself, how about the rebel troops in PNG who had taken over the main armoury of the army there. They had all the guns and the bullets. But somehow the prime minister managed to talk them into putting down their weapons. That's what I call a good negotiator. Or a lousy rebel.

But one bloke who doesn't know when to quit is (this week's) Japanese PM, Yoshiro Mori. He was apparently playing golf when he was told of the sinking of the 'fishing trawler' by the American sub off Hawaii. A compassionate humanitarian, he allegedly muttered something along the lines of "fuck 'em" in Japanese, and continued his round.

In the same vindictive spirit, the Singapore tax department has come up with a masterstroke in trying to reel in some of the island's tax cheats. It is appealing to disgruntled spouses and lovers to dob in their partners and ex-spouses who are not playing ball, in exchange for a reward. They claimed to be receiving something in the order of 15 letters a day from jilted squealers, adding US$30 million to the government's coffers in the first year.

Still in Singapore, the Working Committee (there's another oxymoron!) on Marriage and Procreation is devising ways to reverse the nation's declining birth rate. It's urging the four million population to multiply as fast as it can but, as I understand it, nine months is not negotiable with Mother Nature! My two cents is this: if most married couples weren't sharing a small apartment with their mothers-in-law, they might have a better chance of attaining a rampant rager and scoring a direct hit with those dog-paddling tadpoles. But if this doesn't work, they might need some outside expertise to add to the gene pool. I'm available at short notice. Just send recent photos (in a bathing suit please) of the Singaporean lovelies in question. I'm prepared to do anything to save the nation, and Pete says he's happy to help out, too. See, this program's working already.

Colonel Ken

Making waves

I met C in Pattaya bay where my yacht chartered in 1972. He was the black sheep of the family, whose father was head of British Intelligence MI6 and lived in a castle in Scotland. C used to be a CBS cameraman in Vietnam and lost an eye from a mortar round. He had long blond hair and looked like a pirate – indeed he had a big blue macaw on board, acquired while gun-running in Paraguay. His brother built hi-tech multi-hulls in Negros, Philippines. The boatyard was owned by an influential sugar and molasses family and C could sell any amount of weapons he could acquire when he sailed to Thailand. Unfortunately he was caught off Samut Prakan and jailed.

C was eventually freed by an irate female British consul with the quote: "I don't know who you are or who you know, but I am the unfortunate one to bail you out. Now get out and get the fuck out of here and don't come back!"

He was later caught shagging the American immigration officer's wife who had invited him home, having been impressed by our noisy table celebrating my success at winning the Cup at the Varuna Yacht Club in Pattaya.

Sadly C and his brother were lost at sea off Cape Conception in a hurricane in 1987 while delivering a new trimaran from the Philippines.

Taking my ball and going home

At the Australian embassy in HK, an immigration official was caught having solicited bribes totalling US$500,000 for favourable treatment of visa applications. His superiors confronted him, told him the game was up, and that when he got back to Australia he was going to be pilloried. As he was half English he had a Pommy passport and promptly shot through to England, where he set himself up as an immigration consultant. The Australian authorities were happy to have him out of the system and never pursued the matter further.

Driving blind

When based in Indochina, these expats were driving home slightly intoxicated (OK, really, really drunk!) one night, swerved to miss someone or something, and ended up in a storm drain, upside down.

The police were soon on the spot and their passports confiscated. They had allegedly killed someone in the process. New passports were issued at the embassy the next day, and they were spirited out of the country.

Sticks and stones …

The Australian consul-general in Indonesia got kicked and punched by a mob of Indonesians in Sulawesi chanting "FUCK YOU! FUCK YOU!" when he went to open a new western insurance company office in that province. This took place amidst the East Timor tensions. Fortunately he was unhurt. Police took over an hour to arrive and put up barricades so he could leave afterwards.

High tea

A mate was in India and went to visit another friend who was a high-ranking expat embassy official. Later than night, when offered a drink, he asked his host for some tea. The long-serving embassy gent said: "Oh, dear, my servants have already gone to bed…" The visitor volunteered to make the tea and the official was amazed that he could actually make his own tea!

Documentary evidence

An Australian who worked for the Australian Defence Intelligence Organisation allegedly stole nearly 1,000 documents, including many US satellite photos of Malaysia and Pakistan. Thinking he could turn this loot to his advantage, he reportedly contacted members of the Singapore embassy in Thailand to see if they were interested. They feigned interest, whilst reporting him to the FBI. The FBI then lured him to the States on the pretence of a sale, where he was arrested on arrival in Washington.

Let's hear it for the boys

In Hanoi, Vietnam, the ambassador of a major western country was recalled because he was allegedly indulging in the young local boys. His replacement was soon on the plane home too for the same offence. And *his* replacement and *his* replacement. Unbelievably, four ambassadors in a few short years. Back home, a recreational area was built in the Foreign Affairs ministry. It was promptly nicknamed 'Paedophile Penthouse'.

Hook, line and stinker

A wealthy fisherman from Darwin, Australia, owned a fishing boat fleet. He married a girl from the Philippines and applied for a visa for her to come live in Australia. After submitting the application, he got a call from the embassy. Suspicious of the short betrothal period, the Australian embassy in Manila had apparently sent a private investigator out to her village where they had a snoop around.

They called the husband in Darwin with the news: sorry your 'wife's' visa is declined – she's already married.

Judge and jury

In Malaysia, M, a Canadian journalist, was jailed for a month for contempt of court over an article that allegedly amounted to an attack on the Malaysian judiciary. The authorities kept his passport for two years whilst legal proceedings went on, so he couldn't leave the country and had to face the music.

Stamp-ede

I arrived at 12:45 for the 1pm opening of the China visa office in Hong Kong. There was already a pretty good crowd of people in front of the closed and curtained glass doors. Around 1pm people became more agitated and at 1:15pm the doors to the visa office finally opened.

In a rush of excitement the crowd began the 20-foot dash to the teller. One lady tried to get ahead by hurdle-jumping the ropes that mark out the line inside the office. Her back foot caught on the line and she went smack down on her face, pulling the entire rope system down with her. The remainder of the crowd, myself included, stampeded over her as if nothing had happened.

Overstaying her welcome

X's girlfriend got deported back to the Philippines from Hong Kong for overstaying her visa. X went down to Manila and toured the back streets of Pasay City and got his girlfriend a forged passport.

They then went to the Chinese Embassy in Manila and, because Beijing had just taken over visa control and immigration for Hong Kong, they were unaware that they should only stamp the Filipino girls' passports for maximum of a two-week visitor stay in Hong Kong. X, being an expat Brit, politely asks the embassy officials for a two-month visa for his girlfriend. This they kindly grant.

The fun starts at Hong Kong airport when going through Immigration. At the counter a lady immigration officer looks at the Filipino passport and her visitor visa stamped for two months by the Chinese embassy.

"How can this be?" she queries. Confused, she calls over a senior officer and X and the girl are brought over to an end counter and interrogated. The Hong Kong immigration officers begin to get stroppy and uptight with the pair. X patiently sits back smiling at the officers, knowing that they will have to stamp them into Hong Kong and let them proceed. Finally, after a soul-searching hour by immigration officers, the pair are stamped and allowed to proceed.

To add salt into the wounds of Hong Kong Immigration, the girl extends her stay in Hong Kong for another six weeks by travelling with X to and back from Macau and Shenzhen.

The show must go on

We were organising an expat national day celebration in Ho Chi Minh City, Vietnam, with most of the entertainers coming up from Australia to perform at a big outdoor concert and fair. There were local permits to secure and authorities to appease.

Because securing a work visa is difficult, we told the bands (including one of Australia's most successful bands) to come in as 'tourists'. They duly arrived at the airport with a few roadies in tow and a bunch of guitar cases, drum kits and amplifiers. Nothing to declare there!

The owner of the park (a large field on the outskirts of town) was adamant that by 11pm everything must be finished: lights out, everyone gone. In addition, there were to be a few consular guests from both Australia and their Vietnamese government counterparts to officiate proceedings.

For one reason or another, the show was running late and running over-time. "Don't forget … 11 o'clock finish," reprimanded the park owner, who had been invited and was enjoying copious quantities of free Foster's beer. The various performers and acts did their bit: he continued quaffing the Foster's. Despite trying to speed things up, the night was running way over time. Then a funny thing happened – the park owner passed out and fell off his chair! He was bundled off into the corner, whilst the enthusiastic Vietnamese officials clapped and said, "Carry on." The show ended well after midnight, everyone having had an elegant sufficiency of beer and fun.

A stack of reasons

I have an Indian passport, and they only give a few extra pages (like a mini-passport) every time you need more. My regional role for a major soft-ware company means I am a prodigious traveller, so I ended up having six passports in a pile stapled together (with my original visas, etc, in the main one on front).

Going into Malaysia on holiday once, the immigration official leafed through every single page, very sceptical, questioning my motives for enter-ing Malaysia. My friends were impatiently waiting. Still, he kept flicking through with a furrowed brow. Eventually I snapped.

"Look here, asshole. I'm a PR in Singapore … do you know how much bloody money I'm earning there ? Why would I want to come and overstay in your damn country?" On and on I went. Eventually, my passport was stamped and I was allowed through.

Thankfully, I've just got my Singapore citizenship. Now I can say good-bye to that fucking passport forever!

Emission control

In Hong Kong I owned a classic Alfa Romeo 2000 GTV Bertone. A beautiful car. As I was moving to Singapore, I enquired about shipping it there. The Singapore authorities told me that it needed an emission certificate to be allowed in. Where could I get that? The nearest authorised testing centre was Japan. Or Germany if I preferred. Running through the logic and mathematics of that little lot, I decided against it, and off-loaded the car for a song as I was about to leave.

Imagine my disappointment to get to Singapore and find there are dozens of exactly the same car on the roads. One friend advised I should've just shipped it there with my personal effects, because once it's on the dock you have a better chance of arguing your case.

Behind bars girl

A friend of mine in Hong Kong had his father and a friend of his over for a visit. His father and friend went over to Wanchai one evening and the friend gets the full attention of one of the Filipino girls, treatment he was not used to in his home country, the Netherlands. That evening he falls head over heels for the girl and they meet each other the next several days, until he finally proposes to marry her. He would like to meet her parents and they decide to go to the Philippines.

A problem arises however at Chek Lap Kok immigration as it appeared she was overstaying after she had been fired from her job as an *amah* two months before. She ended up in jail for a few months for this offence but he told her he would come back once she is out. Fortunately for him he came back to his senses when he was back in Holland and decided to forget about it. He might as well, as he ran out of money and would not be able to afford the ticket anyway.

Getting the green light

I needed a Korean driving license, so my boss arranged an interpreter to accompany me to the test. The dreaded eyesight test came up with the red/green colour flip cards, which apparently have different numbers on them. Being colour-blind I always have a big problem with this test. I guessed my way through the cards and was very surprised to hear I had passed. Upon leaving the test centre, my interpreter said: "I didn't know you were colour blind." Yes, I said and thanked her for her informed 'interpretation' – she had been able to see the cards and had corrected my mistakes.

Friendship up in smoke

We had flown from Australia to Bali for a holiday, just two of us girls, looking for a relaxing time. As we landed, and waited to clear customs, my girlfriend – who looked a bit restless and out of sorts – suddenly said, "Please mind my bags, I've got to go to the toilet." As the queue was moving quickly and she was nowhere to be seen, I went through customs with all her bags as well, and waited for her on the other side. She eventually came out, we hopped into a taxi, and it was only then she told me why she was so nervous.

She had brought some marijuana with her, and had got cold feet at the last minute, leaving me to carry her bags. That was the end of a very close and long-standing friendship right there. Needless to say, the rest of our time in tropical Bali was rather icy.

Hot and sticky

I had not been long in Indonesia before being exposed to their wonderful hospitality, and subtlety. Together with a handful of government officials, I was doing a tour of inspection of projects in Java. After a long sweaty day, we reached a small beach resort, where we intended to spend the night. Over a few drinks, my hosts casually remarked that the night would be cold. I paid this no attention, thinking it was just small talk. As the sun set (with the temperature and humidity still off the scale), the comment was made again: "Your room will be really cold tonight."

I failed to react. My host, eventually losing patience, was forced to come out with the much less subtle offer: "Look, do you want a bloody girl to warm your bed tonight or don't you??!!"

Nicely does it

Mothers are all the same – rhinos, lions, elephants and humans: when our young are threatened we charge. My two sons were leaving for Britain from Jakarta for a school term and naturally we were all sad and wound-up. The eldest had been living with us for a few months, so he had a Residence visa and the youngest, who was only twelve, had a Tourist visa.

I kissed them goodbye and went up to the waving gallery for one last look. I waited and waited for what seemed like ages, and all the other passengers had gone through into the lounge. Blood pressure up, heart racing. Five desperate minutes after departure time, I heard running footsteps and panting behind me, and there was the youngest, sweating and asthmatic: "They want to know why we have different visas!" he panted.

I saw red! I marched downstairs and demanded to be allowed into the airport. Little skinny guard with big gun refuses entrance, because I have no ticket. Sizing him up I estimate that I probably outweigh him by a few kilos, so I push past him and storm into the official's office. There is your typical impassive uniform loaded with gold braid. Slow down, I tell myself, it's not *halus* (refined) to shout and swear, especially for a lady.

I explained slowly and gently the situation, smiling all the time in best Central Javanese fashion. As I spoke I saw him relaxing, then adjusting the date on his stamp and, with a flourish, he stamped both passports. The other passengers must have been fretting all this while, but at least my boys got to school on time at the other end, and Mom had another grey hair to add to her growing collection.

Thai-tanic struggle

So there I am on my boat, a 40-footer, at the Boat Lagoon Resort on Phuket. It's a picture-perfect Sunday afternoon near the end of the month. I'm getting the boat ready for a run the next morning down to Langkawi, Malaysia, 125 miles to the south. The boat had been in Thailand for the previous five months undergoing a refit and yachts are only allowed to stay in Thailand for six months, otherwise the owners face a 128% tax and duty. Great incentive to go sailing, I'd say.

I am in the cockpit cleaning things up when I hear: "Excuse me, Captain." I look around and there, walking down the dock, are six Thai customs and immigration officers all dressed to kill in their pearly white uniforms. The officers ask to see the ship's papers. Knowing that everything was in order, I really didn't think I had anything to worry about. Wrong! After looking over my paperwork, I was advised that my paperwork "was not in order", and that I had to pay a 10,000 baht fine … right then and there. When I inquired why, I was told that I had not paid a visit to the harbour master at the deep-sea port when I first arrived in Thailand. That's right, I hadn't – I went to the harbour master at the Boat Lagoon where I was keeping my boat who advised me of what then had to be done re customs, immigration etc, and I did it.

After some haggling back and forth with these guys, who were by now on my boat, I advised them that I didn't have that much money onboard (I lied of course), and that we should visit the harbour master's office at the Boat Lagoon the next morning, (Monday) to talk about it. The fine all of a sudden dropped down to 5,000 baht. I paid the 5,000 baht, got them off my boat, and went and had a few much-needed beers. About a week later I found out that the maximum fine that they're able to impose for such an offence is … 5,000 baht.

I have also heard of other boats that were actually boarded by Thai customs/immigration while at sea underway, and told to hand over 'fines' on the spot.

Cover me, I'm going in

I was part of an entourage that went on an official visit to the Philippines and had an audience with then-President Ramos. As we were ushered in to see him, an official photographer took our happy snap. Meeting finished, we filed out, to be given a souvenir of our visit – faked-up covers of Time magazine with our photo emblazoned across them, headline wording to the effect of 'Joe Bloggs meets President Ramos'.

How time flies

One evening I had landed back at Chiang Kai Shek airport in Taiwan. Changes of plan meant that I had to extend my stay longer than I had originally planned. Arriving at Immigration, I showed my landing card and passport. Asked how long I intended to stay, I answered two weeks. (This was both how long I expected to be staying there, and how long UK citizens may stay in Taiwan without a visa.)

"Entry not allowed!" the officious young lady told me. I asked why – she told me that I could not stay because my flight out left before the two weeks were up. So there I was with most of my possessions already at my hotel, my luggage (including all my colleagues' telephone numbers) already in the airport, and little prospect of ever seeing any of them again. I asked if I could be escorted through to change my flight but was told, "Not allowed." I asked if I could buy a visa, hoping to bribe my way in somehow, and was told, "Of course, but you still need the airline ticket out." I was by now the only passenger left on the wrong side of immigration, and the staff looked as if they wanted to go home.

After a lengthy conversation I found the answer … I had to go up to a desk I hadn't tried so far and say I wanted to stay 36 hours, and I would then be duly stamped in for two weeks.

Stormy waters

I had travelled to Phuket and from there was to sail on a yacht to Langkawi, Malaysia. The skipper just told me to be at the dock at 8am on the day, which I was. We duly set sail, and half way to Malaysia I realised that I hadn't cleared Thai immigration. The skipper had apparently collected all the others' passports, entered their names on his manifest, and got clearance. But not for me. Oh, well.

We then ran into some problem with the yacht, a broken propeller shaft or something, which had us drifting aimlessly out to sea at night, precariously close at times to many of the thousands of little islets in the Andaman Sea. We had some mining engineers on board so fortunately they repaired it and off we went again, only to bugger up a couple more times in the next day. The skipper now was in the rubber dinghy with its little outboard motor buzzing away, holding onto the railing of the yacht and inching us ever so marginally toward a Malaysian island for shelter. We finally picked up some wind and limped into a marina for the night. Next morning I said, sod it, I'll find my own way from here, as the repairs would take a while and Langkawi was still some way off. I got a bus into town and onto Langkawi from there. A couple of days later I realised that I hadn't made myself known to the Malaysian immigration authorities either yet. I duly did so, and no problem. But I was due to go back to Thailand, flying to Koh Samui next.

"That'll be a big problem," everyone said. "Thailand's computers are all linked and they'll want to know how and where you exited." The boat skipper was nervous – after all he had omitted me on his manifest. "Tell them you came over the border by bus and you don't know why your passport wasn't stamped," he advised. I thought I'd just get into more trouble by lying. I decided to take my chances and just front-up and see.

As I boarded the plane to Singapore (to get my flight to Samui), I loaded up on beer so I was in fine form by the time we arrived at Changi. Thinking I had loads of time before my flight to Samui, I found the bar and had a few more. Then I went to the check in.

"The gate's closed, sir." Expletive deleted. Not taking no for an answer, a five-way radio conversation with various parties ensued. No. More expletives. Finally: "OK, sir, but your bags may be on a different flight." No problem. Crackle of radio. "OK, sir, they're loading your bags now." Crackle of radio. "But there'll be no dessert for you, sir."

"Do you have cold beer?"

"Yes, sir."

"Then I think I'll survive." Boarding pass issued, I ran with the assistant to the gate to find a terminal bus waiting for me. Feeling conspicuous – ie, the arsehole that delayed the plane – I thought I'd quietly enter the back and find my seat. As I got on board, the assistant chased me up the aisle. "And remember, Mr Smith, no dessert!" Everyone turned to stare. They had plenty of beer, and after dinner the hostie came across and whispered conspiratorially: "There is some dessert left over if you want." No, just more beer please, as I was now nervous about my imminent discussion with the Thai authorities.

Plane landed. We queued for clearance. My turn came. Handed over my passport. Much typing into computer, flicking of passport pages, then stamp, stamp, stamp, "Welcome to Thailand, sir."

As you were ...

In Beijing I was in the private room of a karaoke bar with some girl practicing her microphone technique on my dick. The door of the private room suddenly burst open and two official-looking gents with badges appeared. They read me the riot act about decadent western behaviour not being acceptable in their country, then threatened me with deportation and the dreaded red stamp which bars you from re-entering China ever again.

However, for a consideration of US$1,000 they were prepared to reconsider this. I asked if I could make a phone call. "No, no US Embassy," they said. I said I was just calling a friend, a Mr Wong (he was a freight forwarder and spoke pretty good English).

"Put them on the phone," Mr Wong said. Suddenly the officers go ram-rod straight: "Yes sir, yes sir, yes, yes, yes ..."

"We are sorry, sir, a big mistake. There is no bill for your drinks tonight. We will get you more drinks for free," and words to the effect that I could screw all the women in the whole place at the same time if I wanted.

Good old Mr Wong just happened to be very highly contacted in the PSB, China's much-feared security arm.

On again, off again

On the last day of a Vietnam trip, I checked into the 60s-style 'luxury' hotel (as described by Lonely Planet) right by the gates of Ho Chi Minh airport so I could stroll up the driveway for my early flight back to Taipei, thereby avoiding rip-off taxis.

Next morning, the terminal seemed awfully quiet as I entered, two hours before take-off. Yes, despite reconfirming the flight two days previously, Pacific Airlines (not Cathay Pacific) – who operate banged-up old 737s with pissed-up old French pilots out of Vietnam – had brought the flight time *forward* by two hours. However the good news was that there was an extra flight that evening. OK, no problem, put me on that.

So I rickshawed back to town for some extra beers. Back in good time, through customs and immigration, waiting by the gate when a Pacific official came across and informed me the plane was too full – apparently there was no room for me and this other American girl, who promptly burst into tears. Instead they promised me a seat on their flight to Kaohsiung the next day plus a free lift up to Taipei and a free night at the Saigon airport hotel. However, as I had gone through immigration and been stamped, I had to leave my passport with some official. Strange feeling to be wondering around in a communist country that evening, sans passport, sans visa.

Baby blues

We were having a child with a surrogate mother. Around seven months into the pregnancy she inexplicably decided to fly from the States to Japan for a holiday. With the long-haul flight, the baby decided to pop out prematurely and so this lady was rushed to hospital and the baby was delivered … very tiny and very fragile. A couple of months of intensive care ensued, and we flew to Japan to be there. The medical bills were stratospheric but that wasn't our concern just yet. The real problems started once our newborn son was ready to leave and we were going to take the baby home … the Japanese authorities don't recognise surrogacy so the biological mother's name was to be put on the birth certificate instead of my wife's.

"No, we see the baby come out of the other woman," the authorities argued. It took months more wrangling before we had the paperwork in order to bring the child back home.

A quick buck

As a permanent resident of the Philippines I have to secure a re-entry visa in order to regain admission to the country. On my last exit I approached the Immigration cashier's desk, staffed by two lovely-looking Filipinas.

After giving my papers to one girl she stamped the visa and handed it to the cashier alongside her, who duly made out the receipt for 500 Pesos for 'Express Lane' service. I asked why I was required to pay the premium as I was the only person at the counter. She coyly answered that I might miss my plane otherwise. I replied (truthfully) that my flight was three hours late. The other girl then replied that three hours might not be long enough time to get my papers processed through Immigration headquarters in Manila. The three of us smiled, all knowing the game that was at play here.

HARDSHIP POSTING

Taxidermist

I live in Hong Kong, but spent 180 days last year in Thailand … every weekend, long weekend, holiday, etc. I tried to get the company to set up office in Thailand but they didn't go for the proposal. Such was my love affair with the place [Yes, the temples are great, aren't they? – Col Ken] that I once took a flight via Manila to get there because I couldn't get a direct flight. On one of my last trips, the Thai authorities stopped me as I exited and requested a tax payment before I could leave.

"No," I said, "I'm only a visitor." They repeated their claim and worked out I owed 80,000 baht tax. "I don't have that sort of money," I said.

"Then you must leave our country," they said.

"OK, I'm going now."

"But you can't, you haven't paid your tax."

This circular argument went on for about twenty rounds before I got firm. A deal was negotiated and my company paid the revised amount of 20,000 baht.

Pay now, fly later

On leaving Hong Kong, this guy decided to do a runner on his tax bill figuring it wasn't his favourite city in the world and, if he had anything to do with it, he wouldn't ever be back anyway. It wasn't long before he was moved up into a regional position that included Hong Kong as part of his territory. He declined a few trips to Hong Kong, making the management a little suspicious, and he explained the situation to them. He then wrote to the Tax Department in Hong Kong and came clean. They allowed him to pay it off in instalments.

Another gent was not so lucky, having done a similar thing. He went into Hong Kong seven years after he left and no-one blinked an eyelid, but on the way out he was stopped for 'unpaid tax'. They made him telegraphic transfer the funds in before he was allowed to leave.

You wouldn't read about it

A friend of mine was going to live in Vietnam for a couple of years so packed a lot of good wines, wrapped well in cartons, and labelled the boxes in large letters, 'BOOKS'. So all these boxes are there with BOOKS, BOOKS, BOOKS written all over them. Turns out to be the worst thing he could've done as the Vietnamese are very suspicious about any foreign printed matter.

Off with their heads

In an ad we were doing we wanted to use a wad of 500 baht notes, with a rubber band around it, as the main photograph. The ad duly appeared and we were hauled up before the authorities to explain ourselves. "We know the rules," we cockily said, "and use of banknotes in ads is permitted."

"Not with a rubber band around the king's throat," they frowned. I looked at the ad … sure enough. Oops! In fact, the king's image is not allowed to appear at all, the opposite side should always be used.

Caught in the crossfire

The Home Affairs Minister blocked thirteen foreigners – working in Brunei to oversee and liquidate the Amedeo Development Corp which was controlled by Prince Jefri – seemingly after they started enquiring the prince to explain his receipt of funds from the company. Some were stopped at the airport about to board flights, and their passports tried to be taken from them. The scenario goes a little deeper. It seems that there are factions within the government, and the royal family plus the Education Minister who is endorsing the liquidators' work is an old adversary of the Home Minister.

All that glitters is out in the cold

Gary Glitter, English glam rock star in the Seventies, was permanently barred from Cambodia by the authorities. At first, they confiscated his passport and asked him to request permission if he wanted to travel outside the capital. He stayed in a guesthouse, and had a motorcycle rider go out and buy his meals for several days, before he was finally deported. The authorities said he hadn't broken any laws but his previous convictions in England gave them concern about their country's image as a haven for paedophiles.

The things we do for love

Working in Indonesia, the paperwork for leaving Indonesia at that time was very complicated and expensive, with departure taxes, assurances that you would be coming back to clear tax, etc. I was pulled over at Immigration without the requisite forms and assurances, and it was proving sticky. "But I must go to Malaysia immediately," I protested, "er, to convert to Islam so I can marry my beautiful Muslim Indonesian girlfriend." With that, a nod of approval, and bang, bang, stamp, stamp I was waved through. All lies of course!

Unofficial photographer

There is a certain photographer who has made the Philippines his base since 1979 and has never actually had an employment pass from the officials.

HARDSHIP POSTING

Front page news

I had a case to answer in Thailand, and went off on a scheduled business trip to Amsterdam. It was splashed across the front page of the Bangkok Post that I had fled the country. I called my lawyer for his advice. On re-entering Bangkok, I immediately asked to speak to the colonel in charge.

"No, no, don't come down today," he said. "I'm busy." The misunderstanding was cleared up without much further ado.

A problem, by any other name

Typhoon Herb proved one of the more devastating storms of the 90s, kind of ironic given my nickname at school was Herb. At Hong Kong airport I went to the Thai Airways counter: "Are you flying today?"

"Yes, typhoon will only come later." I inexplicably checked in my small bag, which I usually just carry on. Landing in Taipei was no problem (although my boss's Singapore Airlines flight later took three attempts I heard). Going though Taipei customs I realised my stupidity ... my new Resident visa was in my small bag, which I had checked in, on the other side of the barrier somewhere. I explained this to immigration who were understanding and just asked me to call Thai Airways ground staff and get them to bring it up. Twenty minutes later I called again. Nothing. And another twenty minutes later, as the wind and rain lashed the terminal.

I called again. "Ah, slight problem ... our man will come and explain," said the Thai personnel.

Turns out that on landing, it was unsafe to open the baggage doors of this type of aircraft so all the bags had been flown back to Hong Kong. An enterprising and opportunistic customs lady tried to flog me a one-month landing visa, despite my protestations that I had just invested in a whole years' worth of new visa.

Eventually an official agreed to let me in as long as I deposited my passport, to be collected when my bag arrived.

Identity crisis

Whilst shopping in Surin, Thailand, I lost my British passport. I was issued a new one, which was stolen within six weeks (by a Dutch person known to me I later found out). "You can't lose *two* passports," said the Thai at the UK embassy in Bangkok, incredulously. Eventually, a new one was issued, which I didn't check, then headed off to Malaysia.

"But you just arrived two days before," said the Malaysian customs official, puzzled. Indeed, whoever was using my stolen passport had just entered the country ahead of me. Back in Thailand, I spent a whole day at Immigration sorting out the numbers, plus I needed a three-day visa extension before leaving for the UK. Leaving Bangkok I was pulled over by immigration, as the computer obviously flashed all sorts of warnings. "*Bad farang* ... read this story in the paper," I explained to him about the case of the perpetrator who'd just been arrested. "Oh, OK." Stamp, stamp, stamp. Done.

Missing the big picture

We needed to import a final fill-level meter into China for this big installation project we were working on. This was a laser device that checks for under-filling. Unfortunately for us, it is illegal to import any laser device into China as they are deemed as radioactive devices and therefore could have military purposes. The shipping company refused to carry the device. Being the fool I was I agreed that I would hand-carry the kit from the UK on my next visit (thinking it would be a small box that I could discretely conceal amongst my other luggage).

Imagine my horror then when a crate measuring about a metre square arrived at my UK home. Size was the least of my problems. On every surface of the crate was a large, bright yellow, radioactive danger warning. With little options (we needed to start production pretty quickly to keep the HQ happy), I proceeded to apply copious amounts of brown paper and tape over the warning signs.

On arrival at Beijing my hopes of discretion faded as most of my handiwork with the tape had been undone during the baggage handling and the bright yellow warning signs were on full view for everyone. I lugged the crate onto the baggage cart with my own luggage and sped for the 'nothing to declare' exit. Having never been stopped before – and being only feet from the safety of the crowds in the arrival hall – I thought I was home and dry when I had the dreaded tap on the shoulder.

"What's in the box?" the customs officer asked.

"Just some spare parts," I replied.

"Please put on the x-ray machine." At this point I was wishing I still had the embassy's number, and proceeded to load the crate and my luggage onto the x-ray machine. "Please come with me," he ordered. I pushed the offending items into the customs office and began wondering how I could possibly deny that this most international of warning signs did not relate to the contents.

"Please open," I was instructed. At this point I began fumbling with the seals on the crate. "Not that one, this one," he said, pointing to my own suitcase. Somewhat confused, I opened my case to reveal a video copy of 'Murray Walker's Motorsports Mayhem'.

"We have to check the video," he said as he removed the 'offending' article and sent me on my way. As Murray himself would say: 'Remarkable!'

If you have a good story about officialdom in Asia, don't bother to email The Editor at hardshipposting@hotmail.com or fax 612-9499-5908. We've already heard it ... next time, don't talk so loud next to that flower vase! The walls have ears, you know.

❖ 13 ❖

Getting Away With Murder
or Trial and Error

*True confessions about police,
traffic police and jails in Asia.*

Here's something I can talk about with authority, for a change. I've had a wardrobe full of lawsuits over the years ... you could say I've been up to my arse in allegations. All of them trumped-up charges, of course, which amounted to nothing other than a withering disrespect for the oldest profession in the world – prosecution!

Let's start off with a hearty laugh before we get into some serious stuff. Flipping through the Star newspaper in Malaysia, I came across this report on a recent murder and rape verdict: 'The high court ordered him to be hanged for the murder and to receive the maximum jail terms and whipping for the rape. The two punishments are to run concurrently with priority given to the death sentence'. Talk about flogging a dead horse. I get these images of this guy swinging from the gallows, all the while being administered the rotan as the officer sees a good angle to get a shot in at this lifeless corpse. I had some guy collar me in the Tanglin Club in Singapore once and argue me till he was blue in the face that suicide was an offence punishable by flogging in Singapore. He was saying the corpse was retrieved, taken to the station and flogged. It seems to work ... there are few repeat offenders! I will flag the fact that this conversation took place at a rather late stage of the evening.

Pakistan is also in the hit-them-where-it-hurts club: it recently sentenced four rapists to death and fined them 40,000 rupees each.

Some, who love to quote the existence of the Internal Security Act (ISA) in Malaysia and Singapore as evidence, see those countries as draconian. But who do you think introduced the ISA to the peninsula in the first place? The blasted British, of course! A damn useful thing it is, too … detention without trial for two years, renewable indefinitely.

Still, there is a lighter side to the Malaysian judiciary. As Malaysians love a good bargain, Ipoh City Council used an interesting technique to get all the delinquent buggers to pay their outstanding parking fines, which had reached a whopping US$350,000: a 50 per cent discount was offered to anyone who paid their fines before the year-end deadline. But why stop there? Why not have a lucky draw, a holiday for two, or a cheese wheel.

Speaking of innovation, did anyone see the 'net gun' that Japanese police developed to fight soccer hooligans at the World Cup with? This device, like a hand-held harpoon, fires a nylon net that traps up to three unsuspecting thugs in a Spiderman-like web. And did you hear recently that the Japanese have started putting sumo wrestlers out on the beat in local precincts, just by way of a bit of intimidation?

The Thai police force has not been left behind in innovation either. This was to help their poor border patrol police out in the remote areas where the communists lurk, where the work is often lonely, and there is a distinct lack of womenfolk around (well, they're all working good jobs in Bangkok, according to their mums). The solution to boost morale was Japanese blow-up dolls. Each is five foot two inches tall, costs US$100, and is called Irma, after the movie prostitute Irma la Douce. Equally innovative, but perhaps not quite as titillating, are the motorised paragliders deployed by the Thai police to monitor townships, reporting any incidents below via two-way radio. I guess they needed some fun after the newly-appointed police commissioner in Bangkok banned his senior officers from playing golf, because he thought they should spend more time on the streets and less on the fairways. Mind you, this seems at odds with the declared intention of reducing Thailand's prison population by 40 per cent. One report in the Bangkok Post said there were currently 88,000 people in prison awaiting trial. So they're looking at ways of not putting people away for things like unpaid fines by offering instalment plans: there's a get-out-of-jail-free pass for about 20,000 lucky winners. The problem is that the country's jails are designed to hold 102,627 prisoners, and at the moment there are … hold still, you buggers, I'm trying to count you … 253,370 behind bars (or behind bras even, keep reading). This ratio of 0.83sqm per prisoner is just a shade under the mandated international standards of

7.5sqm per prisoner. Maybe if they got everyone to breathe in, that would help. These cramped conditions apparently lead to more rapes and murders inside (well, what are they going to do … jail you?).

Now here's the rub. In Thailand you are detained in jail according to your sex at birth, so even *katoys* with their pert silicone knockers and the full nip and tuck get sent to men's prisons. As they give the best blowjobs (go on, try and deny that one, fellas) and have a fully-furnished parking space, this would make conditions, er, inside rather more bearable I would imagine. Because of this same law, *katoys* can also bare their breasts in public, because a man is allowed to show his chest … even if it is adorned by a magnificent pair of 36DD jugs.

However, just before you get carried away and think this is some sort of Club Med, you might want to read my good friend Warren Fellows' book, The Damage Done. In it he talks about his twelve-year stay in the notorious Bang Kwang 'Bangkok Hilton' jail. 'Think of the most wretched day of your life … maybe it's when somebody you loved died, or when you were badly hurt in an accident, or a day when you were so terrified you could scarcely bear it. Imagine 4,000 of those days, together in one big chunk, and you're getting close.' OK, everybody happy?

The Dutch established a penal colony at Nusakambangan in 1923, which was considered the harshest prison in the Dutch East Indies. And that's saying something because Batavia (Jakarta) was considered the dirtiest and sickliest city in the East back then, too. Criminals and political activists are still held there for a bit of special treatment today. The POW camps over in Palembang, Sumatra, in the Second World War were equally notorious. But at least one person found some inspiration there: the Captive's Hymn, a song featured in the movie Paradise Road, was written by Margaret Dryburgh, a missionary who was interned there after the fall of Singapore.

In the book Glory Denied, my good friend Tom Philpott describes in searing detail the punishment handed out to US Army officer Jim Thompson (no, not the silk guy) at the hands of the North Vietnamese. Of all the American POWs, he was held longest – nearly nine years: 'I was put into a horizontal cage maybe two feet wide, two feet high, and five feet long. There I was kept for four months, chained hand and feet'. On top of that, he sometimes copped a beating in order to force a statement condemning the American effort: 'I sat there with a pen in hand as they shouted at me to write.

Periodically they hit me with bamboo. Just enough to hurt. They kept at it for eight, ten, twelve hours a day'. He eventually signed it. If that was me, freedom lovers, I'd have been asking for the pen up front and let's get this paperwork over with. Sod that for a game of soldiers! Sadly his life back in the States didn't improve a whole lot … his wife took up with another man, his family fell apart, and his son was convicted of murder. So he reportedly did the only honourable thing – got stuck into the grog.

Of course, there were many other poor fellas who got to enjoy the sterling service at the Hoa Low 'Hanoi Hilton' prison in that period, as well as other salubrious cesspits in Vietnam and Cambodia. And no doubt they won't be the last, as I just read somewhere that about 70 percent of trials in Vietnam today have no defence lawyers due to the heavy load of court cases going on, and a shortage of lawyers. Sounds like the perfect country to be in … just don't screw up, though.

The other place you don't want to screw up in is China: dear forgiving, compassionate China in case the cadres are listening in. At the turn of the millennium 1.4 million comrades were scratching their nuts (if male) behind bars. There would be a lot more if not for those pesky executions they keep on carrying out. Almost 2,500 a year, which is 80 per cent of all executions carried out worldwide. And they send your relatives the bill for the bullets used if you want to retrieve the body. I am deadly serious.

Now, did you know this, lawbreakers: the Chinese invented sunglasses in the 12th century. In those days they were ornate frames to hold smoked glass lenses in place. But it wasn't for the sake of fashion or protection from ultraviolet light. Instead, they were created for judges to wear so that defendants couldn't see their reactions or emotions as they handed down a sentence. The original Po-faced Chinese!

Law Kwok-hing (I think Kwok-hing means 'breaker') from China probably wouldn't get much sympathy from a Chinese judge. He's languishing in a Hong Kong jail for stealing, but has appealed his sentence beautifully, if unsuccessfully: "I am a native of Hunan and I like spicy food, but there is no spicy food here," he told the South China Mourning Post. Court attendant, smoked glass lenses please!

He's lucky he's not being held in the old dungeon cells of Fort Santiago in Manila. These were situated below sea level and, when the high tides came in, the prisoners would have a bath and their cell cleaned simultaneously. Is that what you'd call a crime wave? Mind you, not all Philippine prisons seem so bad. How about that nutter, Norberto Marero, who murdered the Italian priest Father Tulio Favali in 1985? Marero escaped from jail a couple of years ago after a conjugal (a polite word for 'bonking') visit from his wife. She simply loaded him in the boot of the car at 3am and drove out the main gate. A couple of extra facts I wish to put forward to the jury here, your honour … his victims were not just murdered, but cannibalised, too. And President Estrada, the worst B-grade actor the world has seen since Ronald Reagan, had seen fit to pardon this monster a few years earlier, before revoking it after public outrage. Just to prove that I'm not making this up, the Philippines Daily Enquirer said – so you know it must be true! – he was given special treatment inside and was allowed to carry firearms and even a grenade for self-defence. Question: what sort of woman want to have nookie with Hannibal Lector? Mind you, I guess that does rather lend itself to some obvious lines about flesh-eating.

And the laughs keep coming in the Philippines. I love the irony of the anti-crime volunteer in the Philippines who shot dead a policeman, then went on the run with two Armalites, an M-60 and a grenade launcher. Lucky he was a good guy! And what about the ex-police chief, and current head of the Traffic Management Group, who was busted with three allegedly stolen cars? And what about Rogelio Aparacio who, in 1994, pulled out a gun at the front stairs of his house. He put the weapon to his head and pulled the trigger twice, missing with both shots but denting the police car that had come to investigate. He was arrested for damaging the police car!

Now if this were a TV show, the floor manager would be giving me the frantic 'wind-up' signals. But how can I help it, surrounded as we are by this bumbling cast of Keystone Cops.

In a case in India, the police made a mentally-ill prisoner stand in for the accused in a murder case. As he was mentally ill, of course, no-one believed him when he pleaded that he wasn't the murderer. Heard it all before, smoked lenses please! The court process dragged on for eight years with this poor sap paraded in front of the judge. The truth only emerged when he finally regained his sanity (the accused, not the judge) and he spilt the beans on this whole ruse. It seems the police had actually 'killed him off' by faking his death in the first place, now the police are charged with holding back treatment such that his mental condition wouldn't improve.

Well, none of this is doing my mental condition any good. So I'll leave you with some special advice – always remember the 11th and most important Commandment of them all: thou shalt not get caught.

Colonel Ken

Turban-charged motorbikes

In Hong Kong, this Brit was pulled over for not wearing a helmet.

"I'm a Sikh," was his improvised defence.

"So where's your turban?" asked the incredulous officer.

"At the dry cleaners."

In a separate incident, three guys were riding from Central to Wanchai on a motorbike … naturally, the bike only had two helmets, so the third guy improvised by wrapping a towel around his head. Fortunately they escaped the notice of the police.

But another gent had a prang and wasn't wearing a helmet.

"I'm a Muslim," was his desperate excuse. When asked for his turban licence (ie, license to ride without a helmet) he actually produced it, but it had expired. He was thus fined for 'expired turban license'.

Membership drive

One fine night in Singapore, this gent had a few drinks at the Tanglin Club, and proceeded to drive home. Nothing unusual there, you might say. However, he had an accident, the police turning up and enquiring as to his state.

"I've had a couple of drinks," he confessed. Exactly how many they wanted to know.

"Two, maybe three." The officers weren't convinced, and went to the club (which was nearby) and demanded to see his bill. Let's say his estimate was a slight understatement!

Private-see policy

In Jakarta, I was at the police station (for administrative not punitive reasons) and was watching the officer tapping away at his computer. One driver's file photo came up, of a really attractive Indonesian lass. I jokingly leant across and said: "Very pretty! Where does she live?"

With that he smiled, turned the screen to face me, and brought up the window of her personal details … name, age, address, etc. Tempted as I was, I never followed up on it.

POLICE & TRAFFIC POLICE

Let sleeping logs die

While visiting the pleasures of one of Portland Street's brothels in Hong Kong, X was diligently being satisfied by a mainland girl who kept complaining in Mandarin that his cock was too big for her mouth, while giving him the usual start-up blow job.

All of a sudden the door bursts open, shouting and panic ensues, and the girl runs out screaming.

X quickly realises that it is a raid by the police and immediately jumps into his shorts. Using his instinctive survival techniques he decides to play drunk and pretends to sleep and snore. The police fall for the old story and, after their departure, X got entertained by another girl, compliments of the management.

Cup runneth over

Korean police had (before the days of breathalysers) an interesting way of testing for drunk drivers – you were given a paper cup which you had to breathe into and the cop then sniffed it to decide if you were drunk or not! I guess there were not a lot of volunteers for this particular patrol.

One particularly merry band of expats were pulled over for one such test, and one of the guys in the back seat leant forward and said: "Give that to me." He thereupon proceeded to be violently ill and handed the cup back to the cop with great aplomb. They were quickly waved through.

Vicious cycle

Police disappear very quickly in a number of Asian countries, especially if a foreigner is involved. Apart from the communication difficulty, there is also a heap more paperwork. On one occasion in Beijing, China, an expat carelessly parked his car on top of a roundabout, oblivious of the fact that the road actually went around it. To make matters worse, there was a bicycle and a human sitting on, or under, his bonnet.

The whole population of Beijing (about 10 million at the time) came to watch, as did Mr Plod. Once he saw the protagonists, he was last seen doing the 400-metre sprint in the other direction, which left a rather messy situation to sort out.

Golden Wing, or White Feather (or whatever they were) bicycles came at about US$12.50, admittedly a fair sum for a Chinese worker. I recall seeing several notes with zeros on them handed over before the car left the middle of the roundabout.

Of course, there was the alternative ploy of one of our employees who was driving to the Beijing airport (in the old days before the motorway when the road went through the forest) and who in the gloom never saw the bike. Apparently, if you hit them exactly square on they will cartwheel over the car, at least, so he tells me. Last seen in the rear view mirror was one very pissed-off cyclist sitting in the middle of the road alongside a broken bike shaking his fist at the receding car and rubbing his head.

Hair of the dog

I was passing through Hong Kong when there was still a lot of tension over the border, and staying with an old flatmate of mine, a surveyor building the new MTR. He lived up in the New Territories and we were driving back almost at dawn having 'done' most of Wanchai which you could in those days without breaking the national budget of the US. On a particularly deserted piece of road a dog ran across and we skittled it well and good. Being in a loving and compassionate frame of mind at the time we did a quick U-turn to go and see if the poor thing was in some kind of misery.

Unbeknown to us, there was a police roadblock just ahead looking for illegal immigrants. Once they saw us do the about-face they thought they were on to a certain thing and their Land Rover came hurtling after us with sirens and lights flashing. When we pulled over, guns came pushing through the car windows into our faces. Fortunately, being round-eyes the tension of the moment diminished rapidly, but we still had to explain our actions.

Rummaging around in dawn by the side of a deserted road also sobers one up quite quickly, but fortunately we found the poor deceased mutt and so were allowed to continue on our way. The reception at home upon arrival was only a little less dangerous!

Leashed we could do

Two of my crazy friends were driving back home after a night's drinking when they ran over a stray dog. It was dead but was not bleeding. They decided this was too good to miss. They scooped it up and put it in the boot of the car. After a little thinking they pulled up outside another friend's house. Using a towrope they tied the dog to the back of the friend's car. My friend was woken by the police the next day, only to see a group of crying children around his car. That took some explaining.

Winged him

I must be the only person who has knocked a policeman off his bike, nearly killed him and was given an apology.

It was in Hong Kong and we were driving home after a party from Central up to the Mid Levels on Cotton Tree Drive. I was roaring up the inside, which in fact was a bus lane that disappeared. At the bus stop was a group of Hong Kong's finest, some on their little 150cc scooters, and one on a great big Yamaha. These are big bikes – this poor copper could not sit astride it and touch the ground on both sides. As a result he got a sway on and just as we passed he fell over and hit the car with a resounding crash.

We screeched to a halt, the kids in the back burst out into tears: "Daddy, you've killed a policeman!" My wife (at the time) who was a well-qualified nurse did the practical thing and rushed back to the hapless cop. He was at least sitting up, but his crash helmet had been knocked to the back of his head and the chinstrap was over his throat and quietly throttling him. His mates looked on as my wife took his helmet off and he showed signs of life. English-speaking police in Hong Kong have red flashes on their shoulders: none of these did. But one was a sergeant and I faced him and said very indignantly (and surprisingly soberly):

"It was his fault … he fell in front of the car."

"I know, I'm sorry," came the reply. Whew! In the clear. We piled into the car to carry on home when I realised that he had in fact hit the wing mirror, which was completely wrecked. Wing mirrors on Volvos in Hong Kong are not cheap (I had destroyed the odd one or two before) so I retraced my steps to lodge a claim. At this stage it got messy, as after discussion it became clear that firstly, the poor guy was going to have to fork out from his own pocket and, secondly, that it was going to be the best part of his month's salary.

At this stage the family persuaded me that discretion was the better part of valour, and we went our separate ways.

Pole position

I am a large man. While sitting at a traffic light near a busy traffic circle in Indonesia, I watched a cop in the centre with a long bamboo pole. One or two out of a hundred riders (including myself) were without a helmet and, as the unfortunate rider passed, the cop would reach out and swat him on the head with the pole. I watched him do this to a man and, as my light was turning green, I gave the cop a big smile and shook my head 'no' to convey to him that he and I did not want to go there. He shook his head in agreement, smiled, and I rode on.

Head-to-head

I love to ride motorcycles without a helmet. Regrettably most counties not only have laws requiring the use of a helmet but they enforce them. Indonesia enforces these laws sometimes. I had driven past the same traffic cop five times within an hour without a helmet on. I knew he saw me, and he had passively tried to whistle me over. I kept going. On my sixth pass he was waiting in the street blocking my path. He was clearly agitated.

"You set bad example," he said. While I was still seated on the bike I gave him a polite line of bullshit, which normally results in a handshake and 10,000 rupiah exchanging hands. Not this time.

He puffed out his chest and suggested: "Maybe you need a lesson." I put down the kick-stand and got off the bike. I carried my 270-pound butt over to his four-foot-nine frame and got close enough for him to stare straight ahead into my shirt pocket.

"What lesson is that?" I asked. He quickly regained composure and walked me off the road – purely for my safety of course! – where we shook hands and exchanged the 10,000 rupiah.

We wished each other well under sighs of relief from both of us.

Photographic evidence

In 1988 I was in South Korea for a few weeks while our submarine had some repairs done. Taking a day to visit Pusan, I was walking along with a friend, my Canon camera on my shoulder. At one intersection, a policeman came up to me.

"Nice camera," he said.

"Thanks, I like it, too."

"Can I see?" he asked. I let him take a look at it, but made sure to hang on to the strap. "Very nice camera. You give to me?"

"No, I don't think so."

"Very nice camera you give to me!"

Afraid I'd be given a choice of parting with my camera or spending some time in a Korean jail, I grabbed my camera away from the cop and sprinted across the busy street and down an alley. Apparently, the idea of playing Frogger didn't appeal to the cop – I never saw him again.

Totally 'armless

I was on assignment in Hong Kong instructing the Royal Hong Kong Police. This led to an invitation to accompany a police unit in the raid of a shop that was selling counterfeit and cloned electronic devices. Intelligence had revealed that there were guns in the shop (very unusual at that time).

Such a raid in my home country would involve SWAT teams, guns, vests, and all the stuff you see on the cop TV shows: this raid included two uni-formed junior officers, a woman constable and me, the unarmed *gweilo*.

The WPC and myself took up a position at the back entrance and await-ed the radioed signal from the two officers at the front. I looked down and noticed my partner had no side-arm (all WPCs at that time were unarmed). I asked what do we do if they pull weapons? She replied that in the whole his-tory of the RHKPD, no woman constable had ever been shot: this was, after all, Hong Kong.

I told her I wasn't worried … about *her!*

Motor mouth

When I lived in KL I had to go to the south of Malaysia once a week. Driving on the toll road in the early days meant that there was hardly any traffic after the Port Dickson exit and you could go full blast until you reach KM sign 70 then had to slow down, because at KM sign 72 there was a police-man sitting with a radar gun and you would be stopped at KM sign 73.

This was the same for a few years. Driving down one day at the obliga-tory 200kmh I said to my colleague: "These guys are really stupid by always being at the same point. If they ever change their policy I will be in big shit." Not even five minutes later, as if someone had overheard me, we were pulled over. They had indeed changed their checkpoint. So it was off to the shop to buy a radar detector.

Getting the green light

As in many Asian countries in Malaysia you can also 'buy' your drivers license. Apparently the cop who stopped me after making a u-turn did, as he was not sure about the traffic rules.

He wanted to give me a fine as I made this u-turn that, according to him, was not allowed at any traffic light. I started arguing with him that if that was so then why there were signs at other traffic lights that you were *not* allowed to make u-turns and not at this one. If it was forbidden at every traffic light it would be a waste of taxpayers' money to place those signs at all these other traffic lights, wouldn't it?

He could not cope with so much logic and, after checking with his col-league, they decided to let me go.

No can do

Occasionally I would drive from Singapore to Kuala Lumpur as a change from the shuttle plane and, on one occasion, arrived in KL by an unfamiliar road. Realising I'd taken a wrong turn and needed to backtrack, I followed another car and made a u-turn. Immediately I was pounced upon by a large, turbaned, Sikh policeman on a powerful motorbike who pointed out that I'd just committed a traffic offence.

"But the car in front of me did the same and there's no sign to say I can't u-turn here," I complained.

"There's no sign to say you can!" came the instant retort. 'Nuff said. Fifty ringgit 'instant fine'.

Blew that one

Driving home from work late at night I was stopped by the police at the toll-gate to the expressway. The officer looked surprised to see a westerner driving a locally-registered jeep in the deep south of Korea. As he clearly spoke no English he politely smiled and held up what looked like a mobile phone. I have seen this in taxi-cabs where an interpreter is on the other end. I took it off him and said "Hello" into the perforated plastic where I presumed there to be a mike and speaker. The policeman quickly grabbed back and demonstrated blowing into it – it was a breathalyser, and if he had any doubts before as to whether I was drunk or not, he was certain now!

More than a mouthful

It is Christmas 1961. CM and I are down to our last HK$10 and work out that it's enough for two more pints of San Mig each and a session on 'the rooftops'. Having polished off the San Migs we ascended to the shacks on the rooftops to find some accommodating and very cheap ladies who could use their toothless mouths to great advantage.

As the heads were bobbing we heard a loud voice: "Don't move! Stay where you are!"

Thinking it was an American sailor I yelled out that he should go away, only to find myself looking down the barrel of a pistol. It was an Inspector of the Royal HK Police, accompanied by six constables – they were raiding the place. CM and I were arrested and detained in Eastern Police Station until 4am when we were handed over to the provost marshall and taken back to the ship.

Our divisional officer said: "My God, you two, do you know how many previous convictions those two ladies had? Thirty-seven between them! I've a mind to send you down to the sick bay for shots now before you start squeezing up little bubbles and peeing razor blades."

Cat and mouse game

In the mid-70s I was with the Hong Kong police on a nightshift on Kowloon side. We got a call-out and, approaching this old apartment, the stench of death was very apparent. This did not bode well. Once inside we saw this old guy on his bed, dead all right, but with these huge chunks taken out of his neck. Vampires was my first thought, but decided to call out our regular pathologist to analyse it. He arrived, took a quick look at the old body and declared: "Natural causes."

I shot him a quizzical glance. "Rats," he explained.

Spitting image

Driving on his way home in Port Moresby, PNG, a mate of mine was pulled over at a police roadblock one night. The police demanded to see his license. I can't remember whether he didn't have one or just wasn't carrying it with him, but he produced his wife's license (complete with photo ID) to the officer.

The officer looked at it, looked at him, then waved him on: "OK, sir."

She's a pale-skinned redhead; he's got dark hair and a moustache!

Watered down charges

In Singapore in the mid-60s a group of us were driving home one night, absolutely plastered. The driver was perhaps in the worst state. Along River Valley Road we were pulled over at a police roadblock. The driver is now hiccuping so often and so loudly it's almost reverberating off the nearby buildings. Shit, we're done for. Not a bit of it – the policeman takes pity on this poor soul.

"Lucky, we have some water in the car," says the officer, and trots off to fetch it. Our driver takes a few swigs, assures the officer he's now much better thank you. The police then held up the traffic on the road and waved us on to ensure we got away without further hitch.

Bag of laughs

A few years ago I was working/living in Ban Chang, Rayong, Thailand. One (very) late evening, after a huge amount of Heineken and vodka chasers, I decided to drive back to the main town to continue the merriment. I gave my friend a lift, and we zig-zagged back to the main road, did a u-turn, and proceeded back to town.

A police roadblock was in place and, as I approached, it was withdrawn to let the car in front of me proceed. In my pissed state of mind, I thought the cops were letting me go, too, so I carried on without slowing down. Immediately, the gate was flung back into position, and I accidentally rammed it!

There was immediate pandemonium all around. My friend D became extremely agitated and screamed: "He's going for his gun, go, go, go!!!" I panicked, floored the pedal, and off we sped … straight to the nearest boozer.

Inevitably, the cops arrived five minutes later and impounded my car but not me, strangely enough. I had to report the next morning to the police chief, at eight sharp.

I *wai-d* everybody in the station, even the office cat, and we got down to business. Luckily my Thai is quite good, so there weren't too many misunderstandings.

"If you did something like this in England," the chief said, looking at my passport, "what would happen to you?" I mumbled something about driving bans, huge fines, prison, etc.

"Well, you're lucky here, because you're only going to pay for the damage you caused to my gate. Incidentally, one of my officers had his motorcycle parked behind the gate, and you damaged it, too!"

The upshot was that I paid 5,000 baht for the damage, and another 5,000 for the loss of face involved to the duty officers manning the gate, who wanted (still probably do!) to shoot me like a dog. Anyway, the police chief peeled off one of the notes and sent one of his minions off to buy a carrier bag full of beer cans.

We spent the next couple of hours drinking and having a pleasant chat, *and* he let me have the car back. What a bloke. I'm still living here.

Barf fine

One memorable run-in with the police in Singapore was courtesy of JS who was making his way home slowly and not so surely from an evening of revelry. So close to the kerb was he, he didn't notice the police car parked on the side of the road. The shunting of the car, even at this low speed, seemingly upset his bloated stomach and he generously shared his bellyful of lukewarm Tiger beer and curry with the helpful sergeant who was trying to assist him out of the car.

Three's a crowd, anyway

In Puerto Gallera, my friend had gone out, got blind drunk, and taken two girls from the bar home with him. Having a very small pick-up utility type van, he sat one girl next to him, the other in the back tray. Halfway home, he braked suddenly, swerving to miss some obstacle in the road: a close shave, but he continued on.

Getting home, he grabs his girl from the front, and goes to get girl number two from the back – alas, she's nowhere to be seen. He presumes he must've only taken one girl home from the bar after all. A night of passion ensues.

The next day, back at work at his dive shop, the police arrive and say: "Come with us." Girl number two is in hospital. Turns out she was flung from the vehicle when he swerved. She is bruised and scraped, and her whole family is gathered around her bedside. Negotiation ensues, and 6,000 pesos is finally deemed fair compensation.

Swerves him right

Driving through Manila with my wife and kids one night, I got hopelessly lost. It was dark, and the traffic was going a million miles an hour, not helping my plight. As we came off a freeway exit, there was a motorbike cop so I happily pulled over off the road to ask directions. This craggy old bastard in an ill-fitting brown uniform struts across.

"Good evening, officer, we' re lost …" I start politely.

"Swerving!" is his one-word summation, accusing me of reckless driving. I explain that we're lost and needed his advice, and he goes on about the dangers of bad driving. Meanwhile cars, trucks and buses are whirling and screeching and darting manically all around us.

"I'm the only prick driving properly in this country," I said. He asks to see my license. My Filipino wife then jumps in and says I've lost my license, my passport, everything so we're going to the embassy to report it. Besides, she says, we've driven a long way and I've only just taken over from her for this leg and we're nearly home (largely, OK completely, untrue!). With that he turns on her.

"Your license please, madam." She hands him her Australian license, which is a Provisional License as she's only a new driver there. "Ah, *Professional* driver," he says. "Are you sure this is real?" She gives him a bollocking about the Philippines being the home of fakes and counterfeits. He then steps up his case, and the volume escalates.

"We must take the plates," he says. This is the big move, because then you have to go down the station to retrieve them and it costs a bomb. My wife jumps out of the car and goes toe-to-toe with him for what seems like half an hour. The body language is not good. He reminds her he's a police officer and can handcuff her.

"Yes please, that's my favourite, go ahead!" She invokes names of influential relatives, like the Defence Minister. He questions her that if she's really the minister's niece, then where does he live and what are the names of his kids. She answers this easily and screams him down (like she's done so often with me in the past).

"I can't win – you remind me of my daughter! Just go, just go," he says. He throws his hands in the air.

Eventually, the officer walks towards my window all meek and mild. "Hello, sir, your wife and me are friends. Now if you turn left here, stay in the middle lane …"

All for 100 Pesos.

Abusing the friendship

It's Manila, it's 2am, and a few of us drunkards are looking for the LA Café. My friend is in the front and his wife is driving. We turn left into a street, when someone says: "Hey, it's a one way street."

"Whatever," she says, continuing the wrong way up it. Just near the top, a cop car turns the corner and nearly runs straight into us. On go the flashing lights; out jump the cops. Being half Filipino, she fires off some choice Tagalog in their direction.

My friend, a long-term denizen, says, "I'll handle this," and jumps out of the car.

"B …" say the cops, recognising him.

"Mate …" he says to the officer.

"Is that your wife?" they ask. "She's very aggressive!"

"Well, do you wanna deal with her or do you wanna do business with me?" he says. They agree that he's probably the softer option.

They agree on 500 pesos split between the coppers, plus the coppers will show us the way to LA Café. We then make a u-turn to follow them, nearly causing an accident in the process. Soon enough, we come to LA Café but it's busy and there are no parking spaces. There is a traffic barrier on one side – the police honk their horn and abuse the attendant to move the barrier aside for their special guests. We park. We pay the cops. Smiles and handshakes all round, and best wishes for a pleasant evening.

Forced off the team

The police, who had been cruising around for three consecutive nights, cased my wife – a nightclub manager in Manila – as she left work. My daughter was also with her at that time and I suspected a possible kidnap job. So a plan was hatched and I hid flat on the floor in the back of the car, having programmed the number of my security chief into my mobile.

My wife set off after work as usual and, sure enough, it wasn't long before she was pulled over by the police who give her the macho bullshit intimidation treatment. With that I got up from behind the seat and shone a torch in their faces.

"What the fuck do you guys think you're doing? Fucking nobody dickheads … I will bury you!" I got their names. "I'm calling the General now."

"No, sir, don't ruin our careers, sir…" I spoke to my security chief. After some string-pulling behind the scenes with some high level contacts of mine, all were dismissed from the force.

Straight behind bars

This guy was a police captain in Bangkok and came down to Singapore for a while and we used to play on the same rugby team for a season. He's now in Bangkok and at least twice he's picked me up from the airport with motorbike outriders, straight through the traffic – no delays for this important cavalcade – into town and into the bars in record time.

Run it up the flagpole

I was in bed with a couple of enterprising young birds in Singapore when the phone rang. My son had been arrested for stealing a Singapore flag and was being held by the authorities. Our lawyer in Australia said,"Don't panic," so of course my ex-wife (who was now living there) had panicked. My son was eventually released without a charge after 14 hours, but it did spoil my evening's fun.

Crappy birthday

In Angeles, Philippines, I was arrested for pissing in the street late one night. A bunch of policemen came up to me. The leader said it was a serious offence, but US$1,000 between them should settle it. "Don't be fucking ridiculous," I told them, "a thousand *pesos*, more like it." They agreed to that. I opened the wallet, which had been severely dented by a night on the town, to find only 74 miserable pesos left.

"Right, I need 40 pesos for the trike home," I said, handing over the balance of 34 pesos to the none-too-pleased officer.

"Why were you drunk?" he questioned.

"It was my birthday," I explained. With that all the policemen shook my hand and off I went into the night feeling goodwill to all mankind.

Leave now, pay later

Driving home in Manila one night, a group of us were smashed, singing ABBA songs and having a whale of a time. Stuck in the city traffic, I thought it would be a good idea to get out into to the traffic and do a little jig, culminating in dropping my trousers for a finale. Unfortunately, this was all seen by a police patrol, who promptly moved in with the tough questions.

They requested US$1,000 each, which I didn't have nor was I prepared to pay it. I was then held overnight. I needed to get released the next day, Friday, or else I'd be held over the weekend till Monday. The transfer between jails was filmed and screened on the news, where unfortunately my boss got to see it. I was eventually released after brokering a deal in which I was given an 'instalment' program, with a month to pay the fine. Boss none too pleased.

Beer money

I'd been on the piss at the Cat House in Makati. I came out with a half-full beer and was walking (staggering?) home, only 75 metres away. Just past the Burghos intersection, outside the gate of my place, the police – sitting in their car all this while – got out and accosted me.

"You are drinking beer in public, sir. You must come to jail with us."

"Jail???" I said, suddenly sober. "Can't we settle this here?" The security guards and even my Filipina wife were by this time watching this whole episode unfold. They took me down the station into the 'interview' room. The officer sat behind the table and produced exhibit A – a half-finished bottle of San Miguel. "Officer, I think we can come to some sort of arrangement here."

"Two thousand pesos," he barked. I would've gladly paid 10,000. I gave it to him and he put it straight into his own pocket with all the other officers watching.

"Now drink your beer," he said passing exhibit A across the table, "because it is the most expensive beer you have bought in the Philippines."

Make a grown man cry

There was a fight in one of the many pubs in Burghos St, Manila, with about 50 or 60 large expat footballers piling in to each other. The police were called and duly arrived. As they were about half the size of the footballers, they decided they didn't stand a chance so, next thing, tear gas was brought in and fired. The crowd slowly dispersed. Fortunately the police didn't use their M-16s, which were also on hand.

Old money

A Dutchman lived on Koh Samui, Thailand, and married into a Thai family with a little house and restaurant on the beach. He would ingratiate himself with new people on the scene, and soon put the squeeze on them for favours or money. He subsequently leased his restaurant to an Englishman, but then allegedly threatened the Brit's wife with gang rape, etc, while her husband was away. They sold the restaurant and moved.

He came undone when he met a 65-year-old Dutch lady and got her to sign over many of her things to him. He allegedly strangled her with a dog leash, whilst trying to get his hands on the few million baht he knew she had left. He was arrested and held in prison at Surat Thani amid fears he might try to buy his way out.

Go with the flow

In the 1980s I took up an assignment in central Java and, being a naturally law-abiding person (it was my first Asian posting you see), I went along to the police station to get a local driver's licence. Because I already had national and international driving licences, the practical test was waived, but I had to undertake a written exam. This consisted of multiple-answer questions of stunning complexity. For example: 'If, while driving at night, you are approached by a vehicle with its lights on full beam, do you a) continue driving as normal, b) put your own lights onto main beam and continue, or, c) drive straight at the oncoming vehicle and force him off the road?'

Despite my upbringing in Africa, I scored 100% on the written test, and was duly awarded a local driver's licence. The policeman in charge gave me some very useful advice: "Congratulations! You have passed the test and know the rules of the road very well. But remember that nobody in this country follows the rules of the road, so if you obey the traffic laws you will cause accidents. If this happens, you are automatically the guilty party, because you are a foreigner, and therefore a millionaire. So forget the rules of the road … just do what everybody else does!"

HARDSHIP POSTING

If you have a good story about police or traffic police in Asia email The Editor at hardshipposting@hotmail.com or fax 612-9499-5908. Failure to deal with this matter promptly could lead to cancellation of your license and the initiation of court proceedings against you.

❖ 14 ❖

Genuine Imitations
or Service with a Snarl

True tales about markets,
bazaars, and shopping in Asia.

Let me take you back to the good old days of shopping in Asia. The buzzing old *hutong* (alleyway) districts around Tiananmen in Beijing, where prices and products were yelled out across the labyrinth of single-storey shops and courtyard houses, and everything could be had for a song. But you still haggled and bargained, of course. Or pre-revolution Shanghai which was in full swing as the eastern capital of debauchery: opium dens, gambling halls and interesting little alleyways with promising names such as 'Galaxy of Beauties' and 'Happiness Concentrated'. Who could resist looking down there to see what was on offer?

Nothing was more charming than the Shanghai advertising posters from the 30s and 40s – Dupont, Ewo Beer, cigarettes and insurance companies all put out their version of the Pirelli calendar … all with winsome-looking *cheongsam*-clad Chinese blossoms dominating the poster with their tiny little product buried almost incidentally down the bottom (of the poster that is!).

Up until the early Eighties I remember you could find a little shop or stall which was happy to sell you just one sock if you didn't feel like lashing out on a whole pair. Under the commies, of course, everything had a number rather than a name. Witness Department Store Number 1. Then of course you had the Friendship Stores, the only place you could spend your Yuan, while the locals who were restricted to Renminbi had to shop elsewhere, but presumably weren't too interested in Mao caps and panda bear souvenirs anyway.

But now it's just become The Great Mall of China. Gaudy neon signs, especially for modern icons such as Amex and Visa and those fast-food-types, have replaced the seat-of-the-pants charm of yesteryear. The old shop-houses have been bulldozed to make way for the marble and glass edifices of the Wangfujing strip with their fancy fixed-price brand names.

I read the other day that a shopping centre in Shanghai plans to build a full-sized replica (all 269 metres) of the Titanic as a centrepiece of the themed

Look on the bright side. With customers like me and the Colonel, you don't have to worry about no 'low season' slump in business.

centre. Interestingly, it is planned to be housed in the New York zone of the centre, the small fact of the Titanic not actually completing its journey and reaching that destination a mere trifling detail.

Still, why wouldn't they be thinking grand plans? The nearby Nextage department stores had over 1,000,000 shoppers pass through its doors on a single day in December. And most Chinese don't even believe in Christmas! To give you an idea of how many people that is, that's almost how many queue up to see Mickey and friends at Disneyland in California each *year*.

No wonder China's retail sales are more than $450 billion per year (just slightly more than I earn from Hardship Posting royalties). And what do they spend it on? Well, US$5 billion goes on moon cakes, or *yue bing* as we say in English. And 1.3 billion ducks are bought each year. And in Beijing, where the average wage only just passed US$1,000 per year, the young and pretty things are spending US$8 per month – that's nearly ten per cent, facelifters, on cosmetics alone.

OK, it didn't take long to get onto the subject of the young lovelies, so let's stay with it for a while. Shopping is of course foreplay in Asia. But there are a few caveats that I must pass on to you young players. When the pretty young thing is trying on dresses and turns to you and says: "Does my bum look fat in this?" … duck for cover. This is a trick question. There is no correct answer. Whatever you say will be misconstrued, and nuances so subtle as to be invisible, nay, non-existent, will be dug out and held to your face for full accountability. You are doomed.

Also, make sure you've gone through the necessary preparations before taking a Chinese girl out shopping: this typically involves phoning the bank manager to mortgage the house. Make sure your credit card is well-oiled, and your optimistically-named savings account nicely topped up. Then cross your fingers as you help her lift all the items onto the checkout counter. One of the longest measurements of time known to modern man is the duration it takes for your card details to be punched into that little online thingy and the wait … the wait … the cold clammy hands … the wait, the wait … the perspiring forehead … until whiiiiiiiirrrrrrrrrrrrrrrrrrrr, the transaction is approved. It's the sweetest sound in the world. Because the down side is that you've got to explain to little missy that, well, actually, all those carefully chosen garments and trinkets – which in her mind she's already wearing out to dinner that very evening and has probably called at least three of her best friends to brag about already – well, um, they've got to go back on the racks. The only sweeter sound than that reassuring electronic whir is the sound of your balls slapping up against her arse later that day by way of a little 'thank you' for mortgaging the house (see Chapter 16).

You've got to laugh otherwise you'd cry. A sex shop opened recently in Cambodia, and closed again just as suddenly. A judge ruled that the dildos and vibrators on display were way too big and thus dangerous. Apparently the prosecuting police officer held up Exhibit A – a giant dildo, possibly modelled on the Colonel's tackle – and reportedly said words to the effect of: "Your honour, where the hell is this going to fit?" The judge agreed and the store-owner now faces up to 15 years in jail for selling dangerous goods. After 15 years in jail, I know exactly where it will fit!

Speaking of unusual merchandise, a shop in Central Plaza, Bangkok, opened and introduced healthy country fare on its menu. Nothing wrong with that, except when 'country fare' in Thailand is basically fried crickets. A cupful costs you 30 baht, with your choice of tomato sauce or chilli. Coming soon to the menu: grasshopper salad and cricket tempura. And down the road at the Siam centre, an Oxygen Bar has opened … along the lines of the ones they used to have in Tokyo for a breath of fresh air and respite from pollution. It's not a bad idea, but it won't catch on like beer and pussy bars. After all, those are necessities!

And Indonesia has its priorities right, too. In a country with an average income of around, oh, US$4.50 per year, where traffic rarely gets out of first gear, Ferrari opened a showroom in 2001. Cost of the cars? For you, sir, special deal: $280,000. Mind you, they might find a customer in the gent who owns the MacDonald's franchise. When it first launched in Jakarta, there were queues around the block for miles. That said, doesn't it happen everyday in Jakarta anyway?

At least the Ferrari showroom has price tags, though. In Burma, with its powerhouse currency the Kyat doing a double swan dive with pike and twist of late, some prices of consumer goods have risen by as much as 100 per cent in a few months. So most stores don't even bother to put tags on anymore.

In shopping, nothing draws a crowd like a sale. I've always wanted to open a pet shop in China just so I could put up a sign: 'Buy one dog, get one flea!' But tell me this, bargain hunters, has any one of you ever seen a Persian rug store *not* having a 70% off clearance sale? Are they ever for sale at full price? One place in Hong Kong used to advertise in the South China Morning Toast back in the mid-Eighties: 'Everything must go!' Nigh on twenty years later they're still running the same ad. But I guess it suckers the jet-fresh tourists and newly-arrived expats in. "Oh look, Harry, our lucky day – they're having a sale. We can't miss this opportunity!"

Closer than they think … they couldn't possibly walk out without buying something, because these smarmy gents could sell a ham sandwich to a Muslim fundamentalist. Or dental floss to a toothless grandmother, even.

There is no way out of there. Except if you go into a store where that beautiful young lass called 'Trainee' is on duty. Have you noticed what a common name in Asia that is? More often than not, she'll make you run out of the store empty-handed because of her dire lack of product knowledge.

Which is where specialist centres are such a great idea – if one lot dicks you around, you just move along to the next fellow. You must've noticed in places like Singapore that entire areas or centres are devoted to one theme: gold, computers, electronics, and so on. And walking down the old quarter of Hanoi you'll come across 36 narrow streets each named after the goods sold there. So there's Basket Street, Paper Street, Silk Street. I looked everywhere for Poontang Street, but couldn't find it. Although Pete, the little deviant, assures me it exists.

And that's where I wouldn't mind running into a lass wearing a badge that says 'Trainee.'

Colonel Ken

Stuck record

I spent a week in the southern China city of Zhongshan. While eating at McDonald's I realised that the 'background' music (always very, very loud) was looping the same ten seconds or so of music over and over. The CD must have been defective, as is sometimes the case with copy CDs. After a while it was driving me nuts, so I asked one of the staff to fix it and they did.

A couple of days later I returned to McDonald's, and yes, it was the same defective CD playing the same annoying little segment of music over and over again. At this point I just chose to take my meal out.

It must have been at least a year later when I ended up in Zhongshan again. I had of course forgotten that music thing when I showed up at McDonald's for my grease fix. Well, the same ten seconds of music was still playing, and I have no doubt that it had been so for a whole year without any staff or customer noticing that something was wrong.

Getting a shot off

In Del Pilar, Manila, the lads had just finished another successful tour of the strip, and were getting their photos developed at an instant processing shop there, for good reason. It seems that most of their shots, which came off the machine in full view of all other customers, were of nubile young things who'd carelessly misplaced their bathing suits. Just then, a *gweipo* lady walked in with a roll of film, and joined the queue. Glancing at the developed photos spitting out of the machine, she hissed, "I'm not getting my photos developed here!" and beat a hasty retreat shooting horrified looks back at the customers to the collective mirth of the lads.

Small deal

On a tour of Bangkok, my wife and I had been doing the rounds of all the shops and markets and noticed that the locals often used a little bargaining trick to squeeze a bit more out of you. If they were noticeably pregnant, they'd rub their tummies and say, "Little bit more for baby?" Racked with guilt, you'd hand over their asking amount.

On our last day, buying some souvenirs in Patpong Market, I was haggling with this lady and, just when I knew we had reached 'last price', I rubbed my not-inconsiderable beer belly and said, "Little bit more for baby?"

She was momentarily confused, then got the joke, bursting out laughing: "OK, for you very special price."

Doctor Feelgood

A pharmacy round the corner from us in Manila is proudly called DRUGS 'R US.

Less is more

In the markets in Bangkok, I had haggled with this vendor till we eventually reached an agreement: I'd take eight items for 1800 baht. In packing it, he tried to include just six of them.

"There must be a misunderstanding," I said, and set about re-negotiating in the heat, my patience shrinking by the minute. The compromise was these eight items would now cost 2,000 baht.

In packing it up, he tried to slip just seven items in, the other mysteriously disappearing down the side somewhere. Where are the Tourist Police when you actually need them?

Sari state of affairs

I was talked by my Filipina girlfriend into setting up a 'sari sari' convenience store business. I duly shelled over the money before I returned to Australia and she proudly sent me photos of the 'shop' stall, all nicely stocked and displayed. Next, she asked me for more money.

"But what about the shop?" I asked.

"We've sold out," she complained.

"So buy more stock," I suggested, rather logically I thought. There was no money left – all the proceeds had long been spent.

Truck me dead

Between China and Nepal the Khasa/Kodari border was a no-man's land of shanties sagging over muddy cliff-sides. We hitched a ride in the back of a huge truck, painted with psychedelic designs and loaded with other Nepali and Tibetans.

The streets of Kodari had tin shanties selling beans, bread and Tupac Shakur 'Thug Life' t-shirts. A young woman picked one of these shirts off the shelf. As she did so, a man rushed up and socked her solidly in the back of the head. He struck her repeatedly and kicked her in the groin. A Chinese cop? We all ran up to stop it – I bravely grabbed the little man's shoulder – then sensed that he had no qualms about killing me. He turned on me, I cringed, and the girl crawled safely beneath a truck with me following right behind her.

Confusing label

I saw this pack of fortune cookies on the shelf in my local supermarket: Kong Foo Sing Fortune Cookies.

Real concern

In China almost all girls wear padded bras to enhance their modest attributes. The added volume ranges from conservative to exuberant. This has, of course, led to major disappointments for many guys when the time came for the girl to get undressed. Those promising bumps had simply vanished into thin air.

One day I was buying copy CDs and fake clothes with S, and he remarked to me: "In China everything is fake, even the girls."

Top kwality

In China some fake goods are of excellent quality. So much that it is sometimes difficult to distinguish the copy from the genuine. I was debating whether a bag was the real thing or not when I spotted the label: 'Made in Ytaly'.

Private banking

I recently transferred some money with a well-known bank from Bangkok to a girlfriend up-country. Unfortunately, although the account number was correct, her name had not actually been registered on the account. Being convinced that the account number was definitely correct I said to send it anyway.

The bank, cautious as ever, and no doubt wanting to protect me from error, then accessed every single detail of her account for the past year, printed it out in full, handed it to me, and asked: "Does this look like hers, do you think?"

I hope my wife doesn't ever try to transfer money into *my* private account!

Honour amongst thieves

It was in the Seventies in Saigon. The GIs had left, but the black market on the sidewalks in the Nguyen Hue area remained. That's where I spent many an hour browsing and watching the action. That place was also the spot for various sorts of people, pickpockets in particular, to loiter.

That's why I immediately checked my belongings when some guy bumped into me, murmuring some excuse and walking off. Sure enough, the Parker ballpoint pen I carried in my breast pocket was gone. Looking around me, I saw a younger fellow inspecting some stuff displayed. I noted that he tried to watch me with the corner of his eye but turned his back when I approached. The amateurish acting making him the suspect, I put a smile on my face, tapped him slightly on the shoulder and extended my arm, palm open-handed.

He turned around, returned the smile, reached grudgingly into his pocket and handed my pen back with the words: "You very good ..."

Permanent wave goodbye

Anyone who has been living in China knows that hair salons can offer much more than haircuts. For years I had been going once a month but had never indulged in anything else than a shampoo and cut. As I was now finally leaving China, this would be my last visit to the hair salon, so I was firmly resolved to get a nice body rub from the shampoo girl and whatever else was on the menu.

I was smiling with anticipation, as the shampoo girls are invariably all young and very attractive. In I go ... only to be confronted, for the first time ever in more than 50 visits, with a smiling shampoo boy.

Stamped it out

In the early 70s in KL, it was my job to put 100 newsletters in the mail each week telling others of a club sports event. One week, nobody turned up to the event. It turned out no-one had received their newsletters.

After a bit of detective work, we discovered that the guy in the local post office was steaming off the stamps and re-selling them. So we started driving around to more remote post boxes and dropping off around 25 in each one so at least some people would get their newsletters each week. Attendances up dramatically.

Swap shop

Walking down Magsaysay in Olongapo, Philippines, we were beset by guys trying to sell us sunglasses, t-shirts, necklaces, and everything else. One persistent guy was on one side of us selling sunglasses, and a t-shirt vendor was on the other side. My friend, who'd been to the PI once before, took a shirt from the one guy and handed it to the sunglass salesman, then handed a pair of sunglasses to the t-shirt man. We all walked on happily as they started fighting each other to recover their merchandise.

No cheap imitations

Coming off a boat cruise in Bangkok, a tout approached and made me an offer I couldn't understand: "Genuine imitation Rolex, sir!"

Part of the furniture

In Queen St East, Hong Kong, is a furniture store called the Fook Hing Rattan Company. Obviously named by disgruntled customers or employees.

Dumb question

In a bank in a province north east of Beijing, was a sign meant to indicate the 'Information/Queries' desk. The unfortunately-worded sign ironically read: 'Question Authority'.

Battle of the bulge

In Changi Village, Singapore, I had found some really garish flowery shirts [Pray tell where? – Col Ken.] and was interested in one design in particular. The shirt on the rack was a small size so I asked the assistant stall-keeper if they had bigger sizes.

"No, this one only small size," she said, and hung onto the shirt as I implied 'no deal'. I wandered about a bit and then, just as I was about to leave, she came racing across with a shirt.

"Have big size," she said, showing me a shirt with exactly the same pattern as I wanted earlier. I looked at the label to check the size, but there was none. Being in a hurry to catch a flight, I paid the money and left.

When I got to try on the shirt, it was way too tight for me ... the sleeves were like a strait-jacket and the buttons bulged to the point of exploding around my belly. The bitch had just snipped off the label.

No such thing, etc

During the Vietnam War, there was a little place in Bangkok called

Johnny's Gems and all the visiting brass and celebrities would go there to shop. It was only a tiny little place but Johnny was a good bloke and would take care of you. Thirty years later I moved to Bangkok and this friend said: "I must introduce you to some of my friends in the jewellery business."

He drove us out into the wilds of Bangkok and we turn up at this little place, Johnny's Gems. Sure enough, it's the same Johnny and we struck up the friendship again. I used to call it the world's most expensive lunch ... he'd order in some food from nearby stalls and then the ladies would settle in at his counters and end up buying all this stuff.

No skin off my nose

I was walking around the market area in Baguio, Philippines, and saw this hand-painted sign:

'Haircut & massage $2.50

Circumcision $2.00'

Must be the massage that costs the extra four bits: take a little off the top but leave it long on the sides and back, eh?

Wish you weren't here

Three people staffed the bookstore at the departure lounge in Taipei airport: a girl at the cash register, a guy stacking magazines, and another guy just walking around. I noticed a high-design writing pen behind a locked glass door, selling for US$150, and I wanted to see it. I asked the stacking guy to open the display for me. "Ask the register girl," he said, and went back to stacking magazines.

She was in the middle of a transaction, and had four additional people in queue. I walked around to the other guy (who was doing nothing) and asked him to open the glass door so I could have a look. "Ask the register girl," he said. I looked at the girl, who now had six people in queue. I noticed that virtually everyone in queue had postcards to buy.

"Look," I told him, "the girl's busy, and I'm just trying to look at your $150 pen. What the heck's wrong with you, can't you see she's busy? I'm trying to buy your most expensive item, and she's busy with postcards. Why can't you just open the door and make it easy for me?"

By now, everyone in line (all English-speaking) is looking at me, and they're cracking up, laughing, because the scene is so absurd. The guy looks at the pen through the glass, now sees the price, and mumbles something about maybe lowering his in-store status and opening it up.

"No thanks," I said, turning the tables. "I wouldn't want to bother you with a high-end item, when the three of you are so busy with your postcard business."

My buddy was at the head of the cashier line now, where they were trying to charge him $20 for a magazine that was clearly marked $12.50. Even though he clearly pointed out the price to her, she insisted on $20. We suspected a bad case of congenital ignorance had afflicted the staff, and left the bookstore without making purchases, advising the remaining people in line to carefully watch what they were being charged for postcards.

Cracked me up

A sign in Tokyo, Japan, outside an ice-cream shop proudly read: 'SOFT BUM ICE CREAM COMPANY.' Don't ask me where they keep the cones!

Home ground disadvantage

In any Chinese market there are at least three prices for everything: local price, other Chinese price, and foreigner price. When I was in Hangzhou with two Chinese colleagues one thing we didn't get much of was fruit, so one day I went to the local market and bought us all some. One colleague asked me how much I paid, and was appalled at the enormous amount I had been skinned for (even though it had seemed cheap to me).

Imagine my joy and his embarrassment when two days later he went to the same market, and for the same order of fruit had actually ended up paying more!

Bagging a bargain

Having spent years living in Indonesia and becoming quite fluent in Bahasa, I befriended some shop-keepers and learnt a real trick of the trade. Depending on how well you bargained, your goods will be given to you in a colour-coded plastic bag in order to alert other shopkeepers.

If you drive them into the ground and leave them little or no profit you get a black bag. A moderately pleasant transaction with a bit of give-and-take will earn you a striped bag. And for the 'suckers' – white. That way other shopkeepers can see you coming a mile off. Literally.

Cop shop

A sex/fashion/toys shop in Central, Hong Kong, is owned by a female expat. They held a 'mixed play party' on their premises, which involved three young female performers, and guests were invited to wear leather, uniforms or any kind of fetish gear. Audience participation involving planks and ropes and lashings of leather belts was also in full swing when police raided the store, netting an audience of elite expat socialites and legal fraternity. Those arrested were released on bail.

Short-time, back and sides

In need of a quick haircut, I head for one of the numerous salons in Soi Post Office, Pattaya, before going to collect my mail from Post Restante. Explaining that I would like a 'Number 1' (near total head-shave) the dusky maiden proceeds to methodically and painstakingly begin the operation. This takes longer than I was planning, and – worried about whether I would make the post office before closing – I lean back in my chair and politely enquire, "Do you have the time?"

The dusky maiden leans forward and replies, in a voice considerably deeper than my own: "Why, what would you like to do?" Haircut finished, I gratefully pay up and rush to the post office just in time.

Local lingo

In a Patong Beach shop in Phuket, the Thai shopkeeper *wai'*d us and asked us where we were from. Australia, we said. Without missing a beat, he then broke into a broad Aussie accent: "G'day, how's it hangin'?"

Pope-on-a-rope

In the Philippines several years back, the Pope came to visit. In a catholic country this was akin to the second coming. So we hatched a plan and created these pendant necklaces of the pope. We even gave one to Cardinal Sin, who wore it with pride thus giving us tremendous free publicity. They were only $1 each. Population of 65 million. You do the math!

Water bed

It was a hot day outside Hanoi, so I was looking for a drink. I went across to these food stalls, of the makeshift undercover marquee type. At the first one a big Vietnamese lady with very white skin greeted me. "Water? US$5," she said. Too much. I went next door, and the same lady scurried in from behind the tent. "Water? US$4." And so it went on till I got to the last tent. "Water? US$1," she said. I paid up and, as I sat down at the table to drink it, she started massaging my shoulders and pulled out a paper fan to cool me down.

"Massage?" she asked. As my kids were playing outside, I declined. "I give you good massage," she promised. I relented, and at the back of this stall tent she gave me a brilliant Thai-style massage, bending me over her knee and generally kneading, stretching and manhandling me into shape. Every now and again she'd grab my willy and say "Massage this one?" I simply wasn't interested – I was sober and she was ugly. This didn't stop her from trying again and again till my resolve weakened.

A successful sales technique … after that, I needed another bottle of water!

What price integrity?

I had a cheque drawn on an American bank for US$3m from a property sale, which I wanted to cash in Singapore. I had banked there for years, and always came and went, no questions asked.

I was informed by the bank that their fee for cashing the cheque was S$12,000 (approx US$6,000 then). "And we need to give you an integrity interview," they added.

"I've been banking with you bastards since 1979," I said, "and I've never heard of this nonsense." I was informed it was a new anti-money laundering requirement.

"Look, for US$6,000 I can fly my wife and I business class to New York to cash this thing … it would be easier, quicker and cheaper." They agreed to reduce their fees to S$6,000 and waived the integrity interview.

A bit off the top

I've always had an aversion to getting a haircut. That is not because I like long hair but because I hate sitting in the barber's chair. That is still true except for one place – Barrio Barito, Philippines. I needed a haircut badly and found the Pretty Lady Beauty Salon and Barber Shop. Upon entering I was seated on a stool and the barber came out. She was a very voluptuous young lady who managed to massage my back, shoulders and face while cutting my hair. How so? She used a couple of her other endowments whilst her hands were busy. At the same time, an equally-endowed lass massaged my feet and legs. For an additional fee she would massage your third leg, 'no hands'. During my stay in the barrio I was the best groomed man in town; I needed a trim every day!

One size fits all

I don't know what business they were in – debt collection, gay escorts or vehicle rentals – but the big sign outside a shop in Koh Samui loudly proclaimed: 'BIG BIKERS FOR RENT!'

As seen on television

In Lucky Plaza, Singapore, I was having a good old haggle with a guy and was beating him down on the price for a video. "I can get this exact same model for $750 down the road," I said.

"Good, if you can get for $750, please buy me three," he said, putting me in my place.

Created a storm

It was pissing with rain in Hong Kong, real swirling typhoon-type rain, so I had no option but to duck into a shop and buy an umbrella. Seizing the sellers-market moment, the lady charged me five times the usual going rate for a crappy umbrella. I cursed her business in Chinese and walked out, and she chased me for miles down the road.

Chain of shops

I discovered several hours later that I had left my valuable gold chain at the knocking shop I had frequented earlier that day. I raced back across town at about 300 kmh … and got there just in time to see the maid, having finished cleaning up the rooms, walking out with it. Thank you, I'll have that back.

Not worth a pinch

On my first trip to Phnom Penh (in the early 80s) it was the first time I saw a hotel (the Samaki) heavily guarded, with barbed wires, and all. This was shortly after the Vietnamese liberation of the capital.

During my first stroll around – more or less right outside the hotel and in full view of the guards standing on the curb – and observing the few rickshaws going by I noticed a bundle of new-looking banknotes, right there among some rubbish along the footpath.

I shifted nervously around, carefully observing the scene whether anybody else had noticed the bundle or, even worse, seen me. My foot was swiftly placed on the money and, faking some adjustment to my shoe, I palmed the bundle of banknotes, got up, rushing back to my hotel room. On closer inspection, the money was in high denominations, all Riels, the local currency. I stashed my windfall away.

Next morning, I went with my counterparts to the market to buy some fruits. To my utter surprise (and embarrassment) I saw the market women gluing old, obviously worthless, banknotes together, which was then used as wrapping paper!

Off I went with a red face … my mangos wrapped in shiny money. Until now I haven't told anyone about my 'good fortune'.

If you have a good story about shopping in Asia email The Editor at hardshipposting@hotmail.com or fax 612-9499-5908. In return you'll get absolutely nothing, and that's our best offer. Oh, alright, we'll give you a free book. That's our last price.

❖ 15 ❖

Road Rage
or Life in the Slow Lane

*Tales of transport and transportation
from the highways and byways of Asia.*

My good friend Chin, the emperor of China in the 3rd century BC, has a lot to answer for. He developed the first roads in Asia, you see, connecting all the kingdoms of China, plus its river ways and waterways. (He was actually a bit of an overachiever … he was the same bastard who built the Great Wall to keep tourists off his roads.)

Little would he know that now there are over three million cars on the roads of China, and that figure is growing by 30 per cent a year thanks to local car manufacturers offering cheaper wheels. Mind you, even considering that if the average Johnny Ricebucket puts his entire take-home wage towards car repayments, it would still take him half a century to pay it off by which time I suspect said vehicle would be a rusting hulk, sheltering a family of pigs in the province somewhere.

It wasn't that long ago that China was hell on two wheels. Bicycles everywhere, and sentry posts with loud-speaker systems that would do the Rolling Stones proud barking out at major intersections: "Hey you in the blue polyester suit and the black hair … no, not you, the guy next to you …". Mind you, the two-wheeled circus of terror still exists, in the scarier form of 500,000,000 motorbikes buzzing along Emperor Chin's roads. That is a lot of zeroes, comrades. And 11,000,000 more are added to the roads each year, despite the fact that nearly 60 cities in China have banned the noisy monsters.

Singapore didn't ban motorbikes, but they did ban full-face helmets for many a year, the reason being you might wear your helmet as a disguise and pop into the local bank to make an unauthorised withdrawal. It worked. They haven't had a bank robbery in something like 20 years now, which is good news for shareholders and insurance companies, and bad news for security officers (who thought they were getting into an exciting job) and all those who've lost their head on the roads in the meantime. They recently allowed full-face helmets again.

Speaking of high-speed thrills and spills, Emperor Chin might like to know that 81,000 of his lane-switching brothers died on his roads in 2001. Police say that driving in the wrong lane is the biggest cause of accidents, but I can't understand that – surely *one* of the lanes they're in must be the right one? Mind you, it probably explains a lot when you learn that the first driving school in Beijing started only in 1986. And even now, learner drivers muck around on a practice track before being let loose on the real thing with their probationary license, at which time they're dubbed a 'New Road Killer' (more poetic in its original Chinese form, *Yu Doh Pee Kun*).

India, the second most populous country in the world, loses 36,500 potential software programmers, spin-bowlers and tailors each year on their roads. Let's call it one hundred per day. In Thailand 12,000 die on the roads each year, officially, but many feel that figure is closer to 20,000 once you add up all the body parts correctly. A further million (again, a lot of zeros which are so nonchalantly tossed around) are added to the injured list. And Vietnam is doing it's best to catch up, with over 10,000 meeting their maker (no, not Honda!) on their roads each year. Hardly surprising given that the number of motorbikes has grown from just half a million to around eight million in just over a decade.

And here's a gem to wow them with at your next cocktail party: 70% of the Vietnam government's entire health budget goes to traffic accident victims. Now I'm no Einstein (and he's no Colonel Ken for that matter) but as 8,000 of these deaths are from head injuries and they're not required to wear helmets, I reckon dishing out a free helmet to each rider might – and I stress might – just be in the national interest.

But to me the classic accidents are those that happen on the shoulder of the road … you know, the bit which you're not supposed to drive on, and only stop there in an emergency. But not in Asia, oh no, it's a valuable bit of tarmac going begging! Which is why in Singapore the Department of Roads has big concertina-like buffers fitted to the back of its trucks – imagine a gigantic inflatable accordion being dragged along by a bright green 40-foot truck and you get the idea. Drivers actually hit these vehicles, with their orange flashing lights and pulsating arrows, on the side of the road on bright sunny days with amazing regularity. Now at least they get a soft, or softer, landing.

But Sri Lanka can't afford to laugh. A bus driver once ran into an elephant on the side of the road. I'm not sure who got the bigger surprise! But according to the Daily News there, the driver claimed the mammoth beast was too small, he couldn't see it. Sorry, pal, elephants only come in one size and one colour … I'd be asking big questions of your driving capability before pointing that grimy finger elsewhere.

Only South Korea it seems is winning the battle, with accident-related deaths down by 30 per cent due to a crackdown on seatbelts and other violations. And in Zamboanga, Philippines, a mandatory drug test for license applicants was imposed – yes, I know what you're thinking … anyone found to have not consumed drugs doesn't qualify! Applications immediately dropped by 50 per cent, but it's not that they're a bunch of hardened junkies. Oh no, it was the cost of going for the drug test – at 300 pesos it was more expensive than the license itself which cost just 200.

But we can't hide from the fact that the Asia Pacific region owns less than 16 percent of the world's motor vehicles but accounts for half of the world's road deaths.

So I've got a suggestion, lane-switchers. It's time to stop all these half-cocked pussyfoot measures: it's time to introduce a standardised traffic offence code across the region, with serious charges imposed for DWA – Driving Whilst Asian. That ought to make the roads safer.

Or else find alternative means of transport. Japan's got it figured out. It's shiny new Maglev train system (don't ask me but it levitates above the tracks or some darned thing) is capable of over 550 kilometres an hour, making the *Shikansen* (bullet train) at a downright tardy 443kmh seem like an overloaded logging truck climbing a windy Cameron Highlands road in comparison.

Mind you, that logging truck would probably fairly whiz by the train that operates in the Khyber Pass, Pakistan. It runs from Peshawat and was built by the Brits in the good old days of the Raj to shift its troops and vital supplies (gin, tonic, lemons, that sort of thing). It's one of only two railway tracks in the world that cross an airport runway (the other being in Gibraltar but, sorry, no prizes being offered by our sponsor this week). So it waits for a plane to land before making a mercy dash across to the other side. When it first opened back in 1925, an expat housewife drove it. 'How so, Colonel?' you might well ask. Well, it seems that the local tribes were vehemently against this great big steam-blowing metallic thing and all the imperialistic white trash it brought with it. But they figured the tribes would not show disrespect to a foreign white woman. So the wife of Victor Belay, an engineer on the project, was given the task. The fact that she didn't stack it on debut is also something of a minor transportation miracle.

Mind you, the trains in Manila don't travel much faster than that. They crawl through the city because the tracks are full of squatters who live in little shanties on either side of the line (a real estate agents' dream – I can see the advert now: 'close to transport and facilities'), and often use the train tracks for trolleys to transport their goods, and as a playground for kids. Then, with the train continuously blasting its horn, children and chickens scatter, whilst other bystanders throw their garbage and plastic bags on its roof. It's like the world's first mobile tip!

The opposite occurs on the train line from Malaysia to Thailand. The guards meticulously collect all the rubbish on board, pack it into plastic bags, tying them tightly so as not to spill any contents. And just when you are full of admiration for their hygiene, diligence, and environmental consideration they throw the whole fucking lot out the door! Hence this train line is dubbed 'the Polyurethane Highway'.

Some pluses and minuses of rail travel. In Osaka, Japan, such is the speed and efficiency of their system that if the train is late or very delayed, you are given an apology note to show your boss. India would run out of paper in three days if it adopted that system. But the problems there are of a slightly different nature. In Calcutta, some porters trained monkeys to sit in the unoccupied seats. Obviously when a fare-paying passenger came along, he'd rightfully expect the monkey to give up its seat, and call the porter for assistance. The porter would be only too happy to oblige, sir, for a small fee. The transit authorities eventually got wind of this – like most things in India – and 25 porters and 28 monkeys were arrested. So maybe trains aren't the ideal answer.

Let's consider ferries then. The Philippines seems to be a leader in this field with 72,000,000 trips undertaken by the brave and stupid each year. Why do I say that? For no other reason than there have been 14,000 deaths from capsized and sinking ferries in the Philippines since 1980. One particular ferry incident claimed nearly 5,000 lives. And it was only licensed to carry around 140 people!

Which leads me to a natural conclusion: the only safe and reliable form of transport available is the Beer Scooter. God knows how it works, but it never fails to get you home safe and sound, no matter what.

Colonel Ken

Feeling horny

I was taking a cab to my hotel in Chinhae, South Korea. At one point the driver abruptly pulled out into the left-hand lane (on a two-lane road, going up a mountain) to pass a long line of cars. When on-coming traffic appeared, he started honking and waving at them to get out of his way. After a few minutes of this, steadily losing my equanimity, I leaned over and asked: "Does this cab have brakes?"

His response? "No, no, no. Brakes for stopping – horn for driving!"

The scenic route

In good weather on a normal day, it takes me about 20 minutes to get from Makati to Ermita, Manila. But it once took me eight and a half hours for the same trip when rain starting pelting down around midnight and flooded the city within minutes. Fortunately my girlfriend gave me directions to a series of back streets and we made a huge ring around the outskirts of the city. Otherwise we'd probably still be there! Driving from Manila to Angeles once took me about six hours – it's usually a two-hour drive – because of a series of accidents.

Thais that bind

My friend X is married to a Thai woman. In the days when taxis did not have meters he once took a taxi and was asked an exorbitant price. His wife told the driver that she knew her way around and bargained the price down.

"Why bargain?" said the taxi driver, "the *farang* (foreigner) will pay."

"This foreigner is my *husband*," replied the wife.

"Who cares?" said the driver. "*We* are Thais."

Van go

In the early 80s in Thailand, the general advice if you'd had an accident was 'don't stop for anything'. Coming home one night in this big heavy van,

I whacked into a car, and remember seeing it disappear up an embankment in the rear-vision mirror. As advised, I just kept going (mainly because I was not in a very fit state to drive). The next day, curiosity got the better of me so I went back to the scene and saw this car banged into a telegraph post. Fate of the occupants unknown.

Bar-gain fare

Going by taxi from downtown to the airport in Northern China city, the driver – a brave man – decided to make me save the 10 yuan (less than US$2) toll-fee and take small country roads instead of the usual highway. The said country 'roads' were more suitable to horses than cars, and the journey took more than three times longer.

I ended up missing my flight. The 10 yuan 'saving' was consumed several times at the airport bar waiting for another flight.

Road raj

Working in Kuala Lumpur with a boss in Singapore required lots of travel to and fro. One trip back to KL, I boarded a taxi after a bloody hard day in Singapore (boss ranting, raving, etc). The taxi driver was all over the place: changing lanes, swerving in and out to my total exasperation. Eventually I said to him, "What do you think these white lines down the road are for???"

"I am not sure, sir. It's something the British left behind." I am a Pom. To this day I cannot work if he was telling the truth or taking the piss!

Batter up!

I was on a trip in Taipei about ten years ago and, as usual, the traffic was going nowhere fast. The taxi driver decided he'd had enough of one particular jam and spun off left the wrong way down a one-way street driving head-first into an oncoming motorcyclist. Understandably the biker was not at all happy and, after picking himself up, proceeded to offer to get close to the more fragrant parts of the taxi driver's mother.

The taxi driver calmly walked to the back of his cab, opened the boot, took out a baseball bat, and started to smash up the already-battered motorbike. The cyclist obviously decided that he was next, apologised profusely and rode his damaged vehicle away as fast as possible.

Deflated ego

Back in the Seventies in Saigon, I introduced my younger colleague B (fresh from affluent Switzerland) into the thriving nightlife. We used my car to drive from bar to bar. At one spot the street urchins were especially pestering, trying to make some money by offering to 'watch the car'. Wanting to teach my colleague an important first lesson, the one of not spoiling the market, I explained that there was no need to fear them. To underline my point, I chased the kids away with some tough words to get lost.

Out of the bar, into the car, engine on and driving off to the next bar … the annoying sound of a flat tire was heard. You guessed it; the rejected 'watchers' had taken their revenge. From then on, B didn't follow my recommendations anymore. Can't blame him.

Traveller's tip

My first time in the Philippines, I ended up with a bargirl my first night [Fancy that! – Col Ken]. The next morning, I realised I had no idea where in the city I was, and she helped me flag down a cab to take me back to the base. A few hundred metres down the road, the cabbie slowed and another guy jumped in. "My friend," he said, "he need ride to work."

After another ten minutes of driving, I realised that I still had no idea where we were, the cab had stopped, and the cabbie was telling me a tragic story about a US sailor who just the previous week was stabbed to death by his cabbie for not giving a good tip. Just as the story was over, the friend jumped over the back of the seat, stuck his hand in my pocket, pulled out a $10 bill, and jumped back into the front all within about ten seconds.

He showed it to the cabbie, who nodded: "Very nice tip. Thank you!" and started the cab again. Who was I to argue? I was just glad he'd not reached into the other pocket, where I had my twenties.

Whoresmen of the Apocalypse

Coming out of Apocalypse Now bar in Ho Chi Minh City one night, we split into two groups to go and get some noodles. Arriving at the noodle shop in our car, X did not turn up and we presumed he'd gone home. Wrong! He had apparently taken a *cyclo* (which he had hijacked) and raced down the street, only to be hit by a car at the intersection, sending him and the *cyclo* sprawling. Result: gashed head, injured arm, no noodles.

Personal space

In Japan, I sit down on the train on my way to the river to go for a run. I sit in the only available seat. The gent next to me gets up and stands the rest of the trip. At a transfer station where many people get on and off, the two spaces to sit down next to me on either side stay empty, even though many people are standing and there is room to sit down … next to a *gaijin*. I feel like a white nigger.

Know go

My friend X had an evening appointment and was short of time. Thus, he rushed down to the Soi (Sukhumvit area) and waved a taxi. As customary, X asked the Thai taxi driver if he could drive him to the Prince Palace hotel in downtown Bangkok. The driver answered, "I know," and X jumped aboard. The taxi driver repeated, "I know."

X just told him, "Well, that's fine. Go, go, I'm in a hurry." Then off they went. While stuck in the usual late afternoon congestion on Sukhumvit Road, X dozed off. When he woke up and looked out of the window he realised that it was dark outside with no lights and no high-rise buildings in sight – the cab had travelled outside Bangkok. X asked the driver where he was going to, and the driver answered once more, "I know."

Then X got the puzzle: the driver hadn't said "I know" but rather "I no," which should have indicated that actually the driver neither knew the way to the hotel, nor could speak English. X had to navigate them back to town. No need to mention that he missed his appointment.

Piece of old hat

On holiday in the Philippines, I was taking a taxi from Manila to meet a tour bus in Makati. I hopped off in a hurry, late onto the tour bus, which then took off. Fifteen minutes later, there's a frantic honking of horns next to us. The bus door opens and the guide reaches down and holds up … my sun hat. I'd left it in the back of the cab, and this guy had gone back to the hotel, ascertained our route and tracked us down. He'd be a little disappointed if he knew I'd bought it in Bangkok markets for only about $2.50.

Four? We'll drive

I picked up a mate of mine from London at the Swagman Hotel in Angeles, Philippines. He had a few bags with him, plus one huge suitcase. I took him out the front for his 'lift' home … my 50cc bike! We fell over two or three times in the first ten yards, as there was no weight on the front wheel, but eventually sussed it out and got home.

Another time, four of us largish expats were on the bike going down Macarthur Highway towards Santos St (Blow Row for those in the know), legs hanging out all over the place. Inevitably, I lost control, hit a pile of dirt and we wiped out, pissing ourselves with laughter. How we didn't kill ourselves, I don't exactly know, and how come there were no police to be seen that night also remains a mystery.

Sobered slightly by the experience, I rode home and my three friends caught a tricycle.

Lost in time

When I was working in Jakarta, I spent a long weekend in Yogyakarta. Saturday evening I went to the centre, about 25 minutes by *becak* (three-wheeler). Around midnight, after some visits to bars, attraction parks, etc, I decided to walk back to my hotel. After some time I realised that nothing in the street seemed familiar. After another five minutes' walking, I was pretty sure I had never been to that place before. Looking around, a couple of *becaks* stopped and, after the usual discussions – "Your hotel is very far" and "It's late, so we want to go to bed" – they decided to help me for a fee, more or less equal to the ride from the hotel to the town centre. I agreed and stepped into the *becak*. The man turned into the direction I came from, drove 30 metres, turned left, drove ten metres and with an immense smile on his face he pointed to my hotel. Yes, I was all of 40 metres lost!

Keep heading south

In Manila for a long weekend, I was 'pissed as' coming out of the joss house in Manila. I came out and hopped into a cab. The driver asked, "Where do you stay?"

"Wamberal," I slurred, before passing out. Wamberal is a sleepy little town about 7,000 km south in New South Wales, Australia. My hometown. We eventually worked out which city we were in, which hotel it was, and he drove me there.

Dead right

Having spent quite some miles as a car passenger in China I have seen many near-misses and many head-ons. What keeps amazing me, however, is the kamikaze-style driving of bicyclists. Without looking they just turn in order to cross the street. This means that the cars coming from behind have to step fully on their brakes in order not to kill them. When I asked my local Chinese secretary about this she explained to me why they don't look: "If you look behind you whether there is a car coming, and you see a car, then you have to give him way as you know he is there. If you do not look behind you, you do not know whether there is a car coming, so if there is a car coming, the driver must have noticed that you did not look behind you so he must give way when you make a sudden turn."

I then told her that sometimes it will be impossible for a driver to stop in time which may result in them being killed. In that case the driver would be wrong so he should pay for the damage, she explained. I tried to explain to her that getting paid after you died was not much use. She however kept insisting that this was a proper traffic arrangement and she seemed to be more interested in being right then being dead.

How come there are still over a billion Chinese if they all think this way?

Thick-skinned

Whilst travelling on a Philippine Rabbit bus between La Union and Angeles City, I could not help but notice the speed at which the numerous hawkers, with all their goods, embark and disembark ... sometimes with the bus only slowing due to traffic or whatever, these hawkers just jump off the bus then run several yards to keep their balance.

Well, this hawker got it wrong. He was selling *chicharon* (crispy pig skin) and had a huge bag on his back and a large bottle of vinegar and chilli mix swinging from his shoulder. He jumped off the bus, still going quite fast, and started his balancing sprint. Underestimating his speed and the fact that we were on a bridge with a very low guardrail, straight over the side he went and down about 30 feet into the filthy water below. The Filipinos screamed and our bus stopped.

He surfaced, the screams turning to laughter as only Filipinos at times of potential disaster can do. The bloke splashes his way to the muddy riverbank, scrambles up the muddy bank, shakes himself, checks he still has his wallet and he, too, bursts into laughter. Luckily for him this river had plenty of water in it.

Ear muff

After a night in Bangkok I got a taxi to Pattaya. Five minutes into the journey, the driver put a CD on. The first song was the old classic 'She wore an itsy bitsy teeny weeny yellow polka-dot bikini'. The driver seemed to enjoy this song and asked me: "You like?"

Being a gentleman I said, "Yes, very, very good." This I would soon learn to regret as the driver took it upon himself to select the 'repeat' function and, for the next 50 minutes, all I heard was 'She wore an itsy bitsy teeny weeny yellow polka-dot bikini'.

Having heard that song played around 20 times repeatedly, I arrived in Pattaya a different man!

Ride of his life

His girlfriend had just dumped a friend of mine. As we were sitting in the bar of the Dutch club in Dhaka, Bangladesh, he was getting more and more sad about his broken heart with each successive beer. When we finally left, he said to the rickshaw driver that he needed a fuck. Before he knew it, there was a girl sitting next to him. The driver moved the rickshaw to a darker side of the area and left the 'lovebirds' alone and came over to my driver to have a talk with him. When all was apparently settled, we left for the hotel. I was amazed that the rickety rickshaw survived the ordeal.

Corporate heavyweight

I had taken one of the pool cars to inspect some civil engineering. To access the site I had to drive through some very long newly-built tunnels. These tunnels were not open to the public yet but I could get past security due to my ID, and the tunnels were a great shortcut.

Unfortunately, I found that the floor of one of these tunnels had not been completed and it took a lot of effort to retrieve the car from two feet of wet concrete. After getting out of the mess, I quickly cleaned the bodywork and returned it to the office saying nothing. I believe since that day this pool car has not managed to get past 80kmh and the miles per gallon are not quite what it was. Probably because it weighs twice as much as it should!

Planes, trains and ought-not-to-be-on-wheels

If travelling by train in India, make sure you get the best class possible and allow for delays. In terms of time planning, just figure half as much as you could cover anywhere else … the trains are slow, planes are delayed inevitably, and the roads are slow; maximum average speed of 50kmh on the best of roads. The best time for the roads is early in the morning, just to see the flipped-over trucks and the road-kill from the night before. It's best to not travel the roads at night.

It's Mao or never

The most frightening journey I have ever had was one weekend while working in Hangzhou, China. Two Chinese colleagues and I took a taxi out to what had been Mao's summerhouse, a journey of about 45 minutes out of town, mainly on a freeway. In China the rule of the road is advisory at best, and this taxi driver spent the journey dodging this way and that, round lorries on either side, and dodging potholes in the road, often by switching to the opposite carriageway at high speed. Once or twice I crossed myself thinking that my hour had come. The final straw was the flock of geese we had to avoid that were being driven along the hard shoulder and inside lane.

As a footnote, when we finally got to Mao's house we found that we were just about the only people there. Apparently Mao is not well thought of any more.

Miles and miles of smiles

I had hired a car from Budget on Koh Samui. It was being driven by one of my staff when another Thai lady hit her from behind, pushed her into the lorry in front, and so damaged both the front and rear of my car. The Budget staff was quickly on the scene and sorted things out and, within half an hour, had brought me a new car to the scene of the accident. We completed the paperwork to transfer to the new car and – as she took back the old car somewhat damaged at both ends – she *wai*-ed and said, "*Khop khun khaa* – thank you for looking after our car." As they say, this is the land of smiles and I could not help but add a huge one to my face!

Price hike

The place is Hong Kong in the mid-70s. Three of us were out on the town and finished up very late being decanted out of the Bottoms Up in Canton Road, Kowloon. A rickshaw operator outside said to us: "You want Jig-a-Jig? I take you only 100 dollah each."

We duly paid out HK$100 each and piled into the rickshaw. Up and down back alleys we went and eventually finished up at a non-descript door. A large Chinese guy opened it and said: "300 dollar each, please." Not a bad price – we paid, expecting to be taken in to the house. No – the door was slammed shut. We thought we had been conned but the rickshaw driver said: "Now we go to see the young ladies."

Up and down more back alleys and we came to another house. The door opened and the mamasan opened the door. "300 dollah each, please." It was getting more expensive. We were ushered in and mamasan said: "You stink, first you have showah." A shower applied by a delightful nubile creature was worth waiting for. We then did the business and left.

Our rickshaw man was still there but, knowing we would never find our way out of this catacomb, the business acumen took over. "You want ride to Kowloon Steps, only $200 each … or I do you special deal, all three for $500 total." We had to pay up.

In the land of the blind …

We were living in India and a friend of ours was going to get laser surgery for his eyes in Bangkok [Used the same excuse myself before! – Col

Ken]. We mentioned to him that someone should go with him to help as he would be blind, with covers over his eyes, for a couple of days. Our main concern for him was the taxi rides – while the Thai people in general are nice and helpful, the cabbies are often another story. I ended up travelling with him.

The procedure was in the morning, and I waited for X, who duly came out with patches on both eyes, groping for the door. A cab pulled up and we got in, telling him the hotel we were going to. As chaotic as Bangkok traffic is, it's hard to tell where you are going. But after 30 minutes I knew the cab driver was taking us on his own scenic tour at our cost. I started to get a bit vocal about his choice of route and threatened to get a policeman, a tactic that works well in India.

The driver got very angry and I told him to stop: we were getting out without paying. Then he threatened us with a policeman! So I got angry and pulled out my friend's black diplomatic passport and told him this was going to be a diplomatic incident. Soon, with all the squabbling, a policeman arrived. A large crowd started to form. All the while my blind friend was in the back of the car, silent, while I waved the passport and demanded to call the embassy.

In the end the policeman arranged for another taxi and appeared to pay the original cab driver what was due. Lucky I was there to keep an eye on the driver.

Hell on two wheels

The last time I had been on a motorbike, I was eighteen years old and thrown off the damn thing when a police car hit me. It was his fault: three detectives heading back to the office after a liquid lunch.

So there I am in Phuket, 20 years later, looking for transport. The old Honda Dream was mine for 200 baht a day. Day one, I get a ticket for not wearing a helmet. OK, no sweat. I pay my fine. Day two, I'm driving said bike between A and B when I have a very strong premonition to put my helmet on (I'm a slow learner). I pull over, put the helmet on, tighten up the chinstrap, and off I go again. A couple of miles later a 60-foot tour bus full of Japanese tourists, travelling in the opposite direction, pulls over into my lane. The bike goes down and underneath the bus, with yours truly going down on my left side, dislocating my shoulder and smashing my head against the pavement.

I'd like to thank my Dad who I'm sure was up there with 'Big Buddha

Bob' looking down on me that day, trying to figure out how to get me put to my helmet on before that bus driver tried to kill me. I don't ride bikes anymore.

Blood money

The Bali bombs went off in the main street of Kuta on a Saturday night … it was a war-zone, with people dead or dying all over the place. But most were running anywhere, in any direction, to get away. We eventually found a taxi further out of town. "Let's get the hell outta here!" I said. But he would-n't take us. One of our friends had blood on his clothing. Oh, and he wanted US$50 for the trip anyway. We just kept running.

That's telling them

On this really bad road in the Himalayas, where you could barely get out of second gear because the road was so bad and bumpy, I saw a road sign: 'Accidents are prohibited on this road'. Optimistic, yet confusing.

Cliff hanger

In Kota Kinabalu we were going to get a train upcountry for a white-water rafting expedition. We saw hundreds of kids from various international schools loading on rafts, life-jackets, helmets and oars as well. It was so crowded we thought fuck it; we'll just hop onto one of the flatbed carriages where the rafts were stored and that'll stop them from flying off as well. The canopy of trees and vines completely overhung the track, so occasionally we needed to duck our heads at short notice. Worst, though, was the part where the train (noticeably wider than its wheelbase) overhung the side of a cliff and we could see straight down the side of the mountain for hundreds of feet to the churning white-water below. Rafting that section of the river later, I could-n't help looking up at the precarious train track and thinking it was absolute madness.

Jeep at half the price

I was due to drive into Beijing to run a few errands one day. As my Jeep Cherokee was filthy from top-to-bottom I decided to drive first to a carwash. I never tried one out here in China: usually when you park your car someone comes and washes it for 5 RMB. I thought I'd try one of the city's new-fangled modern carwashes.

With a little bit of Chinglish, I was told how to proceed, and we went through the big scrubbers. At the other end, I was directed to a large building full of parking spaces and Chinese attendants. One Chinese threw me out of my car, placed me on a bench and – voila! – I had a cup of tea in my hand.

Then three Chinese marched in and took to my car with a vacuum cleaner, a bucket of water, maybe ten towels and, within three minutes, it was in show-room condition, inside and out.

While I was sitting there watching them I realised something was missing on my roof: one of my roof racks had come off in the rough and tumble. They offered to fix it, which I declined so I knew it would be done right.

Twenty RMB (US$2 including the tea) paid, I continued my trip into the city on the 4th Ring Road. The sky was blue, I was singing to the music, and I had just got onto the highway when suddenly the little red taxi in front of me hit the brakes, clouds of blue smoke everywhere. I similarly applied my brakes and stopped just behind him, but a quick look in the mirror told me the car behind was heading my way. Fortunately, the driver behind me was so kind as to place his right into the crash barrier instead. The following car pushed him a little bit closer to me but he didn't touch my freshly cleaned nice-smelling car.

I found myself standing right in the middle of five-car pile-up, sitting on the crash barrier waiting for the police. The guy who crashed behind me was yelling at me in Chinese. I preferred not to say anything ... I know enough Chinese to get myself in trouble, not enough to get myself out again. So I thought I'd better shut up and finish my cold coffee latte. The other three Chinese in front of me were yelling and close to hitting each other, as were the two behind me. All I could think was I wished I'd brought my video camera.

After a little while the *Jing Cha* (police) arrived and tried to calm all the drivers down, but soon they'd entered the yelling match as well. Finally one *Jing Cha* asked me what I was doing there. I tried to explain in Chinese that my car was the shining Jeep, untouched, but I was trapped in the middle of the carnage and couldn't go anywhere.

With a little pushing here on a wreck and there on another wreck, I was finally dismissed from the scene. Apart from one loose roof rack it had been my lucky day.

Carry-on

A group of us were in India, and late to arrive for a train from Mumbai to Goa. Our fearless leader, "who knows how trains work in India," tells us to run down the platform and dive into the very first carriage. Which we do only to find ourselves spending the next 11 hours locked in an empty baggage compartment!

Highway to hell

The intercity transportation system in Cambodia makes the Thai bus system seem like riding the Concorde in comparison. I crossed the border into Cambodia at Poipet a couple of years back and needed a ride to Battembang. A young entrepreneurial fellow approached me and arranged a lift in the back of a small Japanese truck. I had to wait until the truck was full – that is jam-packed, chockers, like sardines – before it left. The little Isuzu had 28 souls on board before we left, including the driver and some small children but not counting some very dead fish, a set of truck tires, a rusty spare transmission, and other sundry cargo. Being the rainy season, the dirt road was pure mud, with potholes the size of houses. Half way through, the little children started throwing up, and my clothes were covered in mud. The ride of 120km took four hours due to the condition of the optimistically named 'National Highway 5'.

Heap of trouble

I had been living in Manila for years when I decided to get a car. As I didn't really need it (cabs are cheap and plentiful) I set a budget of 50,000 pesos. A few days later I was the proud owner of a bright green heap of shit with bald tyres, a flat battery and god knows what else. Oh, yes, it was also an ex-carnap car, written off by the insurance company and resold. My local partner then informed me that it was still officially a wanted vehicle on the police database! Lots of paperwork was required to make it legal again, which he kindly offered to take care of.

Driving over the Pasig River Bridge one day, the thing ran out of petrol. People were honking and carrying on, when a police car came by. "Don't worry, we'll help you, sir." They went back to the police station and came back with a rope and towed me to the petrol station. After asking for the obligatory 'donation' they were on their way. The fact that it had no plates and was a wanted vehicle didn't seem to register with them.

Almost a year later I was pulled over for expired registration. Anticipating this nonsense at some stage, I told them the longwinded story about the carnapping history and feigned surprise that it was out of registration already. I produced the paperwork, transfers, etc, as if to prove what a burdensome and confusing process this all was, and was relieved to be sent on my way with a warning.

Pub crawl

Coming out of the Merville Subdivision in Manila one day, the traffic onto the highway was crawling. So slow in fact that one of the guys was able to walk to a provision store, grab some beers and have a cigarette until we caught up with him, and he hopped back in and off we went.

In Bangkok, the traffic was similarly bad and a friend of mine used to leave the office each evening, instructing his driver to meet him at Soi Cowboy. He'd walk around the corner to the pub and by the time he'd had a couple of drinks, he'd go outside and his car would be there or just approaching still.

Nip it in the bud

In a taxi in Singapore once, the driver – a fairly pleasant old Chinese chap – was driving us down through Orchard Rd. Suddenly he spotted a couple of young Japanese women out on a shopping expedition. He went purple with rage, pointing, swearing, shouting and carrying on at them. Afterwards he let on that he'd witnessed some atrocities during the war that he cannot forget and was not ever going to forgive the Japanese for. I didn't probe too much further, quietly paid my fare and stepped down. I then noticed, ironically, he was driving a Nissan!

Hell dent on revenge

I was riding to work on my motorbike through the Tsim Tsa Tsui tunnel in Hong Kong after heavy rain. Near the tunnel entrance there was a huge pool of water and people were slowing down and skirting around it. Because of this bottleneck jam, I was stopped in the traffic when this guy in a gleaming Mercedes just sped through it, sending up a shower of spray and soaking me through completely. I managed to catch up with him, as he was now stopped in a jam ahead. I drew level and took aim with my serious hard-toed riding boot to his passenger door, and then sped off. His dent was going to last a lot longer than my dampness.

Don't bank on it

On holiday in Samui, we'd rented a jeep and were going to the Thai kick-boxing arena behind the main street. With the monsoon in full swing, the roads were flooded. Turning into the back street, the river had broken its banks and what was a little stream was now a rushing body of water more than 100 yards wide. People were slowly making their way across in cars and vans, indicating that the road went fairly straight across to the opposite bank, the water half way up their doors.

I decided to follow a taxi van in front, closely, as he would surely know this road back to front. Following behind him, I saw him suddenly veer off to the right, and into deeper and deeper water till his van was half floating, half sinking. Panicking passengers leapt and swum in all directions out the back, grabbing their kids and bags. I kept straight on and made it. What was he thinking?

Death wish

A friend of ours was killed in a motorbike accident in Rayong, Thailand. His parents flew over from the UK to take him home. However, we told them that their son as a convert to Buddhism would have had other ideas. So we had him cremated and he now rests in a brick wall at a Chinese temple in Thailand. They were initially horrified, but came to accept it.

Hairpins and needles

One night at Sangatta, Indonesia, we decided a visit to the local 'entertainment area' was on the cards. I was in the back of our Suzuki Jimny, and said, "Slow down, C, I think there's a bend ahead." Indeed there was ... a notorious 45-degree hairpin bend. The Jimny failed to take it, rolled twice, and we spent a couple of weeks in Bontang Hospital.

Our mate, R (in another vehicle), was unaware of our fate and he continued on down to the entertainment area near the river. However, he didn't get off lightly either – he contracted a dose of clap that he had to go to Singapore to sort out.

Crossing the line

Next to my office building in downtown Taipei is this small one-man valet-parking service. I drop off my car in the morning and the guy worries about finding a spot for my car, which is not easy in Taipei. Just outside his little office the curb is painted red: no parking (if it's painted yellow it means five-minute parking). A few weeks ago I took my chances since the parking guy was not to be seen. I left my car outside his office, thinking that he would soon be back to take care of my car. Of course, when I came to pick up my car in the evening the cops had managed to give me a ticket.

Last week I arrived at the parking service as usual. The guy comes up to me and tells me to park my car outside his office. I kindly inform him that I just got a ticket from parking there. "Oh, nooo ploblem," he says. "Yesterday I go buy black paint! I pain' myself very good, look, no red line. Parking no ploblem!"

HARDSHIP POSTING

If you have a good story about cars, taxis, trucks, buses, pack-mules, or anything vaguely involving a road in Asia email The Editor at hardship-posting@hotmail.com or fax 612-9499-5908.

❖ 16 ❖

I Luv Chew
or The Ex-Files

True tales of spouses, mistresses, sugar daddies and casual flings in Asia.

Dave was out to dinner with Barb, his long-suffering wife, to celebrate her 40th birthday recently. They've been having a bit of a rough patch of late, but he's keen to make amends. "So what gift would you like, my darling? A BMW? A fur coat? A diamond necklace? Perhaps a cruise in the Caribbean …"

"I want a divorce," she told him plainly.

"Shit, I wasn't planning on spending that much," said our beleaguered Dave. I'm the resident expert on these matters having been through a starter marriage (you know, that's the one where there's no kids, no property and no regrets) and my recent parting of ways with The Dragon Lady. Not that I'm bitter, though. Give the old trout full marks … she was a great housekeeper – kept the fucking house all right! Why are cyclones like marriages? They both start off with a lot of blowing and sucking and in the end you lose your house. Bitter? Nah!

Anyway, I told Dave there were plenty more bearded clams in the sea and cheered him up over a beer or three hundred. Told him my philosophy on this whole love thing: it's a little bit of heart and a whole lot of head. Or, as Confucius may have said: 'Man in dog house soon find himself in cat house'. Which got us thinking: how much was this divorce going to cost him, and … which is cheaper: sex for money, or sex within the hallowed institution of a loving marriage as endorsed by the pope?

Let me paint the parameters of this painstaking research first; and there has been a lot of pain involved, believe you me. All statistics are based on American figures for consistency. Well that plus they've got more divorce lawyers than you could point a pit bull terrier at, so statistics from the US Census Bureau are plentiful.

The median duration of a marriage is 7.2 years, and the median age of divorce is 35.6 for men. During that time, sex – more commonly known as Giving the Ferret a Run, Hiding the Salami, Putting the Tool in the Shed, the Matrimonial Polka, or the Magic Disappearing Cane Trick – is likely to rear its ugly head 6.9 times per month (according to Edward O Laumann, Americanbabies.com). But let's go with some more generous statistics from the Illinois State University, who say that married couples make the Beast With Two Backs two to three times a week in their twenties.

Assuming the average man therefore marries at 28 years of age, let's allow for three Horizontal Cha-Chas per week for three years, two per week for the next three years, and then – as kids and boredom from eating from the same menu and dissatisfaction creep into the game – let's say once a week for the remaining 1.2 years. That, ladies and genitals, gives you a grand total of 842.4 rounds with the Chubby Conquistador (well, you remember that time you fell asleep on the job, don't you?).

Now, my good friend Dr Sam Vaknin – financial consultant and economic advisor to the stars – calculates that the average couple in the west accumulates assets of US$100,000 over seven years of marriage. We could argue maybe a little more for expats, but let's stay with the conservative figures.

If divorce now takes place, kiss goodbye to half your assets. It just cost you $50,000 for 842.4 grease and oil changes. Or $59.35 per time with the Chief of Staff.

But, and this is a big but (perhaps I should spell that 'butt'!): the cost of legal fees, etc, for the divorce itself is $15,000 and takes a year to complete. During that time, let's presume the Purple-Helmeted Warrior of Love is enjoying no attention from your ex-partner (although, if the mood seems right, you might want to ask if you could finish off that missing 0.6 from the better days).

Plus, you've had two kids in the meantime, and the cost of child maintenance for two kids is 27% of net wages. This could be more for expats, but let's just call it a nice even $1,000 per month. For a period of, oh, 13 years just till the older one turns 18. So we're on the low side again. That's a total of $156,000 in child support.

So you actually spent $221,000 for those 842.4 Air-flown Kobe Beef Injections at $262.34 a piece. But hold on, we haven't even factored in those fancy dinners, cocktails, bunches of flowers on Valentines Day (or the day after, when she reminded you), fur coats, and trinkets. Oh, the trinkets!

Now let's look at the alternative. You swan down to Soi Nana in Bangkok. Let's call it the epicentre of the universe, just for illustrative purposes you understand. You browse the 3-D living blackboard menu on stage, with the soup of the day changing everyday, with Chef invariably offering a specialty of the house.

Let's say you're between 35-45, slightly overweight and balding (ie, you possess all the best attributes of the male species!). According to the website www.bangkokbargirls.info someone of that description would averagely be paying 1,195.12 baht for a Bounce With Mr Wobbly at Soi Nana with a medianly attractive girl who can joke and have some fun with you. (Face it, fellow stud bulls, we're paying more than Mel Gibson would have to.) Now let's throw in 250 baht for ladies drinks, 300 baht for a short-time hotel room, and 500 baht as bar-fine. That's a grand total of $2,245.12 baht for the satisfaction of the One-eyed Wonder Worm. At 43 baht to the dollar that's – dadaaaaaah!!!! – just $52.21 per go to put a smile on the face of the Bald-headed Butler. All in. And you don't have to discuss her feelings afterwards. Even if you did a personal best of 0 to 100 in 7.8 seconds so you could get back to watch the second half of the game!

So ladies and genitals, irrefutable proof of what you always thought: it's cheaper to buy a litre of milk as required rather than the whole cow. Paying for sex is cheaper. And the golden rule I'm dispensing for free here is this: if it flies, floats or fucks, you're better off renting it.

Anyway, back to young Dave. He said Barb was apparently dissatisfied with their love life, which came as a bit of a surprise to him as he couldn't remember the last time they'd had sex. (A bit of definition required here: 'making love is something a woman does while a bloke is fucking her!') Anyway, this is the same reason quoted by a third of the 1.2 million people who get divorced in China each year. So I therefore conclude that Dave must have a small dick.

Reading Newsweek the other day (must be slow readers if it takes people a whole week to read that thin magazine) a recent survey showed only 5% of Hong Kongers are happy with their sex lives. It could have something to do with the fact that they only 'do it' 57 times a year, and then only for 13 minutes at a time (does this include the cigarette?). By comparison Americans apparently have 138 mattress thrashes a year, with 38 minutes spent each time. So I can't see myself moving to Hong Kong anytime soon, although my girlfriend up there, Chu Mai Kok, spends more time on her back than a tortoise climbing stairs.

I also came across (not literally, you'll understand) a Durex sex survey that showed that Americans and French have the largest amount of sexual partners in a lifetime. Aussies came in third with 11. China came last on the list with an average of 2.1. How can you have 0.1 of a partner? Is that an 'Oops, never mind I'll try again a little later … tissue please' sort of occasion?

And in the Nation newspaper here in Thailand, a survey on the sexual techniques of 18-39 year olds caught my eye (well, there's a surprise, eh?). I swear in my next life I want to be a market researcher specialist, female 18-25 division. Anyway, the good folk from Asia Market Intelligence came up with all sorts of fun findings: contrary to popular belief, sexual practices are not handed down in 'birds and bees' discussions between mother and daughter over generations, preserving traditional practices and ancient Oriental techniques of lovemaking. In Thailand more than half of them learn from the movies. Mind you 61 per cent of Koreans learnt how to jig-a-jig from the movies. Here's my favourite: on average around the region, 16 per cent enjoyed a good spanking, but the Thais came in at a windmilling 36 per cent. Sixteen per cent of Singaporeans had sex in a park (compared with 100 per cent of Koreans who'd had sex with someone named Park).

And anyone who thinks Asians are drastically more conservative in their approach to sex had better think again – 67 per cent across the region said pre-marital sex was acceptable … 88 per cent of Thais said 'yes'. After all, LBFM is not a radio station! Only 29 per cent throughout Asia felt that marrying a virgin was important (and to think I had saved myself for that special night!). The big question I've got here is who or what or where are the missing four per cent? Sixty seven plus 29 gives you 96. I think someone's telling porkies.

Now, as I said to Dave, somewhere over our 175th single malt by this stage, is that if he does get divorced and get back into this single man's game, he must watch out for one of the real risks of living in Asia, STDs. That's right, Sexually Transmitted Debts. Because, as you all know, there is no aphrodisiac with quite the potency of poverty. And to most Asian honeys, a sex toy is not a vibrator, it's your wallet. I further advised him that the days of local girls marrying foreigners just for their visas are well over ... these days they want someone with MasterCard and Amex as well!

Luckily in many countries of Asia, alimony amounts to nothing more than the telly set (the one from the bedroom with the slightly fuzzy picture, not the beaut 68cm set in the lounge room hooked up to the cable service), the fridge, and all those dresses and matching shoes she just had to have. Oh, and possibly a one-way bus ticket back from whence she came.

I asked the ever-romantic Pete if he'd like to add his two cents worth on dealings with women: "If they didn't have cunts you'd chuck rocks at 'em!" he eloquently mumbled into his beer.

To those dear female readers who may feel aggrieved at my opinions, let me say this: there is absolutely no truth in the allegations that I treat objects like women. Let me give you one (as it were) back on the guys. What's the difference between a boyfriend and a husband? About 15 minutes! And one for the fellas: What's the difference between a wife and a mistress? About 20 kilograms. Boom-tish, thank you and good night.

Colonel Ken

Smooth talking bastard

My good buddy and his Filipina missus live in the apartment facing us. He's well over six feet tall and a big guy. I opened the door one morning to see him backing out of his apartment with a stool raised in self-defence. His wife had two knives and was going ballistic. He eventually managed to pin her against the wall with the legs of the stool, and I will never forget his soothing words: "C'mon, put the knives down ... put the knives down ... and we'll go shopping!" A winning psychological strategy as it turned out.

Sailing off into the sunset

My tenure in Singapore was coming to an end and I had met this Filipino tart who I wanted to take back to Australia with me. The only way to get the visa was if we had cohabited for more than a year, so I decided to take a job in Mindanao, Philippines, for a year so we could qualify for the de facto visa. I set up house in Mindanao, and gradually more and more people got involved with us, as happens with 'extended family' situations. After nearly a year, I thought, 'Hold on, there's 26 adults and three screaming kids living off me' but never mind because we'll be moving to Australia soon.

Every evening at sunset I used to go down to the beach and talk with this old Filipino guy, who had interesting stories about the Japanese occupation, etc. One evening he said, "I've got something to tell you, but I'm afraid you'll punch me." He told me the 'cousin' living next door was actually my partner's husband. It also turns out she had three kids (she had admitted to only one before) and had worked previously as a courier with the NPA (rebel army) so had connections in very low places.

The next morning I told her I was going to Manila to finalise our Australian visas, hopped on the next bus and never went back.

Sister act

I was approached one night in the Hilton disco in Kuala Lumpur by a very pretty Chinese girl that I had a nodding acquaintance with, and she wanted to introduce her sister to me. The sister was 26 years old and had a '9.5' figure. One thing led to another and they both came home with me. The next time I took her out she confessed that she had only had one boyfriend before who 'only lasted one second' and that she wanted to be taught everything and wanted to try *everything* that I could teach her.

A truly memorable 12 months of 'what can we do next?'

Repeat performance

In the days when the age limit in Thailand was well below 18 I took out a 17-year old girl from a bar intending to have a bite to eat together (Col Ken, don't get that wrong) and then proceed to my hotel. However I was first taken by her to a dark, wet, slum to meet her mother, who quizzed me on my earnings and prospects back in my home country. I obviously passed muster as I was then allowed, and indeed encouraged, to take her daughter back to the hotel.

At about 1am she told me she had to go and said something in Thai, which I did not understand. I gave her my dictionary and she immediately pointed to the word 'homesick' (her home was about 400 metres away!).

I paid her off and thought that was that. Blow me down if she did not return a few hours later knocking on my door at 7:30am for more, on the assumption that two short times are more profitable than one all-night.

A new meaning to the term 'double date'.

Making money hand over fist

I was with a British Army regiment based in Fanling in Hong Kong in 1957. We could get a fuck for $5 in Temple St back then, but we used to have these Hakka hookers come down the river to our camp each night. For fifty cents they'd give you a quick hand job on the riverbanks. Wednesdays was happy hour ... they'd do two of us simultaneously for twenty-five cents a pop!

More than a mouthful

An Irish expat Y touches for a Thai girl down in one of the girlie clubs in Wanchai. After a few candle lit dinners with this girl he informs all his mates at work that his girl just serves drinks in the club and does not get involved with other men.

His mates find out which club the girl works in and decide to call in and see if she is as good a little girl as Y says. The four jolly-go-lucky boys throw photographs out the next day to Y, each showing them getting a blowjob from the Thai girl.

Needless to say this broke the poor Irishman's heart.

Roses are red, my love

X and Y are with two Filipino girls having a drink in the Sky Lounge, Hong Kong, when the topic of female dressing and colours arose. Y says that he likes girls dressed in red as he thinks this colour is sexy and a real turn on for him. At this point one of the girls decides to go to the ladies room. Within a few minutes a girl sits down beside the group dressed in a bright red mini skirt and blouse. Both X and Y have to really focus their eyes on the girl to find out that it's the same Filipino girl who went to the toilet. Now that's what I call pleasing a man.

Easy rider

A German friend and myself went to Hanoi, Vietnam, in 1988 when you could go only on business visas, and had to go to Hanoi before we could go to Saigon. There wasn't much to do except for a dance night at a different hotel each night. Our *cyclo* (rickshaw), hired for a princely $1per day, knew where to go. As we were on the piss until late we told him to go home, not wait for us as they did normally.

After a few beers I decided I had to try a Vietnamese girl, like the lovelies offering themselves for $5 on the street. It should be easy at this dance but with their little English and our zero Vietnamese it proved a little difficult. But

I did find a girl, after my friend had gone back to the hotel with the last available *cyclo*. No need to worry, she gave me her pushbike and got me to follow her on another bike which she sat at the back of.

So there I was at 1am, pissed as, trying to ride a bike (which I haven't done for 15 years), and following a pretty whore on the bike in front of me in the dark. I have no idea where I am, then we go around a corner and they're gone. I see a house with lights on and go in the wrong place, apologising. Then I see my hotel and think, OK, I'll take the bike home.

Just near my hotel, I hear this 'pssst' sound: there she was in the small watchman's room. She operated the lights using two bare wires in the wall

Like I told ya Floyd-you and me may be gettin 'older but when it comes to attractin' girls, we still got what it takes.

(standard switch there) and we got down to the deed. Job done, I only needed to walk next door to my hotel.

All in the family

In Cambodia I met this pretty local girl who was 21. She introduced me to her mum, who had started early, and was still only 32 and damned attractive with it. I tried my best, but failed to engineer a threesome.

Batteries not included

In a bar in Ho Chi Minh City, I'd only met these local ladies a couple of times before (they used to be bargirls and were now working in the family business, or whatever). They heard I was travelling back to Australia, and requested that I bring a vibrator each for them, because they missed 'it'.

"Make it a big one!" they said. I obliged, feeling very nervous and uncomfortable walking through customs.

Big reputation

My 'thing' is on the large side, if you know what I mean [Oh, I know the problem! – Col Ken]. This is usually greeted with eulogies in the west, but in Asia it sometimes causes something closer to panic. X and I had been working 18 hours straight and it was time for some R&R. We picked a bird apiece and headed back to our hotel room. But as soon as my 'girlfriend' got a glimpse of my thing, she ran away in panic next door. Over breakfast the next morning X – who knows about my 'problem' – explained with a huge smile that my girl came crashing in and excitedly described the size of the problem to her friend. He ended up having to spend the night with both of them, poor guy. I had to physically shut him up as he was describing the delightful night experienced.

Months later, another town over a thousand kilometres away, still with X: it had been a slow day so we decided to go for some afternoon entertainment. We were greeted by mamasan and the girls lined up for inspection and selection. I pick one but, to my surprise, she backs away in fear uttering, "No-no-no." I turned to mamasan to enquire about this most unprofessional behaviour. Animated discussion between mamasan and the girl. "Sorry," says mamasan, "your thing too big." X turned to me, half serious, and said: "They know ..."

A rush of blood to the head

I got a call from a friend one day, saying please come over she needed us. Two of us girls raced over to find she had a huge gash on her forehead, which required 14 stitches. Her boyfriend (at least twice her weight and age) who she had been living with for years, was there looking sheepish.

What transpired is that they had had a drunken argument, he accused her of something, picked up an expensive ornamental tiger or dragon and smashed it over her head, breaking it into pieces at the same time. He said: "You bitch, I'm gonna charge you $3,000 to replace that, too." Seeing all the blood, etc, he then drove her to the hospital.

Afterwards, he couldn't believe what he had done ... in fact, had no recollection of the incident at all.

Nineteenth hole

They were a high-powered couple in Manila ... he was a lawyer, and she was a Filipina financier. They had been married several years when, one day, he picked up his golf clubs, said, "I'm just going for a game of golf," drove to the airport and flew back to his home country. End of marriage. Simple.

All's well that ends swell

When I first went to Bali, I had been counselled by a friend as to where to stay, eat, party, etc. So I told the cabbie at Denpasar airport to take me to the Three Brothers bungalows. The cabbie told me that he knew of a better place and explained that its location and price were much better than Three Brothers. None of this turned out to be true: he was simply (unbeknownst to me) a paid tout for the other hotel where I stayed that fateful first night.

I woke up because of time change at 4am and went looking for a place to eat. Right across Legian Street was an all-night restaurant/bar called Mama's. I went inside and sat down and, across the bar from me, was this young, attractive Indonesian girl. She looked at me and motioned me to come sit with her and her friends. I turned around to make sure it was indeed me she was motioning to and then joined her.

"Hi, my name is A, welcome to Indonesia!" She looked to be around 16 (she was 19). We talked some more and I asked her what she was doing later. She said she had no plans so I asked if she would like to be my guide, to which she agreed. To make what turned out to be a very long story shorter, I'll just say we ended up spending the entire week together. I went back to Bali five more times to see her before finally bringing her to America and, three years later, we got married!

Now if the cabbie *had* taken me where I asked him to ...

The family that plays together ...

In Malaysia we had this Dutch quality control manager who spent a lot of time on the road and, in the evenings, a lot of time in the clubs in whichever place he'd be staying overnight. Often he'd take a girl back for the night. One time when his wife's sister and her husband came over for a holiday, he took his brother-in-law with him on one of his trips, and they both got laid several times. The following week the in-laws flew back to Holland, and the brother-in-law decided he had to confess to his wife about what he had done. His wife was very shortly after that on the phone with her sister who confronted her husband with the story and gave him a good scolding (it wasn't his first offence).

Arsehole brother-in-law: at least his father-in-law knew how to keep his mouth shut.

Too hot to handle

Mustard seemed to be a well-educated wench who came from a prosperous family in Manila but just loved to be a slut, and a delightful slut to be sure. We sort of adopted her.

She got her fame from licking mustard from MO's asshole: no small feat considering M was a retired Sergeant Major from the Australian army and approaching 300 pounds. Anyhow if you had mustard she would lick it. No ketchup please.

When she was off the mustard she kept us amused, whether it was running around Foxy's naked until they caught her, or posing as a respectable lady. I liked her best the time she pissed in the street … walked out of a bar on Del Pilar, past the ladies room, pulled down her Levis and managed to piss into the gutter without a drop wasted. How can you not love a lady like that? Later she demonstrated the technique of the toe fuck for our entire staff on her unfortunate girlfriend who was taking a nap … until she woke up, but did not mind a bit.

Last I heard Mustard was assistant manager in one of her mother's paint shops.

Not a hair out of place

A couple of bartender buddies used to entertain a local lady on their day off, Sunday. She liked her rum and cokes a bit too much and would often pass out on the couch at midday. Bored, the guys decided to give her a bit of a shave while she was napping. None were unfamiliar with her ample *bulbul* (pubic hair). So they pulled her panties down, clipped off all her *bulbul* and inserted it neatly into the crotch of her panties and put everything back in place.

The reaction when she woke up and went to the toilet was memorable … half of her pussy hair fell into the toilet, and the rest on the floor. She thought she had the bubonic plague, and the rest of us couldn't get off the floor laughing.

She decided she liked a bald pussy better and still shaves now, last time I saw it.

Wives, knives and endangered lives

The stress of working and living in Singapore used to get to me. I once threw a plate of chicken rice against the wall one night, and lectured my wife on how my mother used to bake roasts, potatoes, vegies, etc, not just a simple chunk of chicken on top of some steamed rice. I then proceeded to get a meat cleaver and hack one of our dining chairs into matchwood. I regretted it after the first blow, but had to keep going to prove the point (plus it was bloody satisfying!). I ended up buying a nice expensive dining suite to replace that one, and she now cooks wonderfully.

Another time we were in bed when we erupted into an argument. We wrestled, and I then ran downstairs to escape the madness (she's only small, but when she gets started …). Downstairs, she accosted me with a big kitchen knife. I told her to put it down. The maid by now came into the kitchen to see what the fuss was about: I told her to talk some sense into to my wife, but she came at me with the knife, swinging. The blade embedded itself in the door and I wrestled her to the ground. "Call the police!" I instructed the maid.

"Call the police and I'll kill you," countermanded my wife.

"Call the police!" I ordered again, and held my wife on the ground with all my force.

By the time the police had arrived, I was sweaty and covered in scratch marks. I told them that it was much ado about nothing, but now my wife was asserting that I had tried to strangle her. I saw her one strangulation and raised her one knife attack. The blade was still stuck in the door. However, neither of us really wanted it to go any further so assured them it was just a silly outburst and let's leave it at that. They took our statements and left.

My wife and I returned to bed. No sooner had we fallen asleep than the doorbell rang. Detectives this time. They came armed with a print-out of our records of any and all police dealings and who knows what else. "It says here you are in process of divorcing?" detective one said.

"No, no … all patched up and rosy."

"Where is your wife now?" Upstairs asleep. They didn't believe me, and wanted to see her.

"If you wake her up you'll really see the bad side of her," I said. They insisted I went down to the station for questioning.

"That's bloody ridiculous. I'm asleep already. It's fucking 2am and I've got work in the morning."

With conferred looks all round, they seemed to sense that they were on a losing wicket here, but promised to follow it up in the morning. That was the last of the matter, and since we left Singapore we've now got more kids and been married 15 years.

Doesn't know his arse from his, um, elbow

I was with a rather young and naïve-looking Thai girl in bed. I asked her if she would roll over as I wanted a little doggy-style. She was adamant that there was no chance of that. I asked why, as I thought it was no big deal. She told me the last time a *farang* gave her it doggy-style she had to spend the next hour on the toilet. I said, "That's not doggy-style, that's something else." It turns out he was a German.

Paid for it dearly

One of my friends had only been in Thailand for a short time but found himself married to a local and the proud owner of a girlie bar. I took him out for a beer a few days later to celebrate. After far too much Singha we found ourselves back at my place with a girl we picked up from a bar, deliberately a very long way away from his area.

It wasn't long before we were both getting stuck into the same business. He finished and explained he had to get back to his bar before closing or his wife would suspect he had not just been out drinking. After I'd finished, I sent the girl on her way but she wanted 3,000 baht! When I said this was too much she explained my friend had agreed to pay this amount; the extra expense was because she didn't like getting 'spit-roasted'. I knew my friend was a soft touch with the ladies so believed her story. Reluctantly I paid the 3,000.

The next day I asked my friend why he had agreed on such a high fee and, also, why he didn't leave any money before going. He informed me he didn't agree to 3,000 and had paid in full before leaving the bar. I had been done! He said my problems were nothing compared to his: the bar next door to his bar where his wife's friends work share the same name, the same owner and the same girls as the bar we were in the night before. What was worse is that by the time his wife had been out to pick up something for breakfast the next day, the story was out. His new wife had gone with the company credit card to console herself. Fortunately for him she returned and forgave him after a lot of money spent.

Unfortunately for me, whenever I go to his bar with a girl in tow she insists on telling my new squeeze what a bastard I am.

I now pronounce you … screwed

Like so many customers, this gent paid his regular bargirl enough money to stop working in the bars. As the relationship deepened, she managed to get money from him to buy farmland up north, built a nice house, even got a car. They planned to marry. So arrangements were made for hundreds of people to attend the grand occasion. He was going to be lord of the manor.

Halfway through the celebration, a Thai man approached him, saying: "Thank you, you can go now."

"Go where? This is my wedding … "

"No, you don't understand. My house. My land. My car. My wife. Everything mine. You go." All true. Everything, of course, had been bought in the Thai guy's name and the *farang* had no leg to stand on.

Keeping bad company

An English guy living in northern Thailand was married to a local lass. It wasn't long before the half-arsed business proposal was made to him: she wanted to start a business, so he had to lease an office, and get all the furniture, computers, etc. Not long after, he did one of his regular visa runs to Malaysia. Coming back a week later, there was no sign of her, no sign of the office, the equipment, nothing. All vaporised mysteriously.

Body language

I stayed on Soi Post Office, Pattaya, at a joint called Fun Bar. It's a girlie bar on street level with rooms on the floors above. Perfect for a lazy dude. One evening this really unbelievably tasty young girl shows up at the bar. Perfect body, tanned, and a great set of boobs bouncing to the music as she was dancing around. I quickly made up my mind – gotta have her! And so I did. The next three nights (which is very unusual for me). I wanted to spend more nights with her but one afternoon she told me: "My boyfriend Finland come Thailand tomollow. He love me too much. I cannot see you more. I go Bangkok see him."

Then I got this nasty idea. A guy from Finland, hmmm. Finland is the neighbouring country to my ex-home country Sweden. There is always this love-hate relationship thing going on, so here is my big opportunity to pull off a practical joke.

So I went to the bookstore and bought a big blue marker pen. After that night's lovemaking session, I pretended to fall asleep and waited for the girl to fall asleep as well. Once I was sure she was sleeping, I executed my plan. I carefully pulled the sheet off her and exposed her back, took the blue marker pen and started to write on her lower back a message for my Finnish 'friend': "*Hej du, Finn javel*" in Swedish (which Finnish people understand as well), which translates to something like 'Hello there, Finnish bastard'.

In the morning the girl got up and had a shower. But of course not all the blue text came off in the shower. She got dressed and prepared to go to Bangkok to greet her friend. My Finnish friend, if you read this, I hope you appreciated a good joke.

Boys will be girls

An Italian guy married a Thai and they lived in Thailand. About a year later he was going to go to Italy and show off his beautiful bride, so went to apply for a passport and Italian visa for his wife. He got a call from the embassy: "Sorry, sir, your wife's not actually a 'she' according to her birth certificate." He boarded the plane alone and never went back.

Withering on the vine

This guy who lived in Manila and was married to a Filipina was coming back from an overseas trip. But before going home he wanted to have a couple of days of 're-acclimatisation' in the fleshpots of Angeles. Clearing Immigration, he then headed off to get transport to Angeles. Having just arrived in Angeles, he checked in and was gearing himself up for a big night out. Imagine his surprise when there was a knock on the door. His wife! Hot water doesn't quite describe the temperature or depth of his problems. Turns out someone on the Immigration counter at the airport had recognised him coming through and put in a call to his wife. With the might of the Philippines' 'intelligence' network, she had arrived at his hotel in Angeles just an hour after he did!

Big cover up

I run a hotel and used my very attractive Filipino wife in her bikini on the cover of our hotel brochure (given that the swimming pool and bar area is the most appealing part of our hotel). Some years after, we split on less than friendly terms. She took up with another westerner who thought she was purity and innocence personified. I wasn't having any of that. So I dug out the old artwork and reprinted 20,000 brochures, with her splashed all over the cover, and sent him 200 copies.

Crack paratrooper

Many years ago, a British soldier was assigned to the Indonesian back-country. He went out and found there wasn't a great selection of ladies in the town, plus they'd all gone 'round-the-block' more than once. Anyhow, he took the best he could find, took her home and gave her one up the arse – thinking it was the performance of his life – and heard these sort of half-squeak, half-grunt sounds coming from her. He looked at her face and she'd fallen sound asleep, snoring! We can safely assume it wasn't her first time.

Gone bananas

I created a monster. After my Filipina wife caught me shagging a Swedish backpacker things have not been quite the same. OK, I sleep with one eye open. We're building a house at the moment in the hills of Puerto Gallera. At Christmas she said: "Don't worry about jewellery this year, maybe just a gun." Noticing my quizzical and nervous look, she quickly explained: "For security as our house is alone on this hill."

"If you have a gun, then I get a gun," I said, figuring we could at least have a stand-off if it came to that. Shortly after, I came home pissed one night and she beat the shit out of me with a cane stick, and I chased her around and she locked herself in the bathroom. I grabbed a mat and a pillow and went up the hill to our construction-in-progress and slept under the stars there.

The next morning I returned home and the blue ensued. She locked herself in the bathroom again. There happened to be a big bunch of bananas in the kitchen so I threw these at the bathroom door, smeared them on the walls, and created an unholy goo all over the place. I came back later in the day and found all the bananas and mess still untouched, with a note: 'Please clean up your miss!' I thought fuck it; we need a break so headed to Manila the next day, but not before leaving a note. 'I'm gonna mess you!'

Dozen get better than this

In Bangkok one weekend a friend of mine, a long-time resident, told his wife he was just stepping out to get some eggs. He reappeared exactly 24 hours later, with a carton of eggs under his arm, as if it were the most natural thing in the world. His wife threw everything that wasn't bolted down at him.

An honest mistake

This English guy lived in Indonesia for a while and was dating a local lass for quite some time, before he was posted to Kuala Lumpur. So he said his farewells to his friends and sweetheart, packed his bags and disappeared.

A few months later, there's a knock on his door in KL … he opens the door to find his Indonesian girlfriend, heavily pregnant. She had tracked him down. He decided to make an honest women of her, so they both flew back to England to break the news to the family. They turn up unannounced in his parents' little Yorkshire village, and announce they're getting married.

A ceremony was hastily arranged, the bride looking gorgeous in white with her huge round tummy. She gave birth a couple of days later. The little town still talks about that.

Time lapse photography

S was having his buck's night in Pattaya and we were having a whale of a time. We then decided to take it up a notch. So we got the buck and strapped him to the chrome pole on centre stage. He decides to put on a show for the whole place, pulling out his tool and having a good play with himself while all the girls scatter down to the area in front of him. I decide some photos are in order. A few days later I presented the photos to his wife: "What do you want to do with these?" I innocently enquired. She laughed, but said rip them up.

"But the world deserves to see these," I said.

"If these get out I'll fucking kill you," she replied.

"OK, what about for one year?" I negotiated, to which she agreed. A year later, to the day, they had all forgotten about the episode and, good to my word, I produced those photos for all to see.

Drive, he said

I arrived in Manila for the first time, and called an old friend of mine. He said they were in the middle of a dinner party, but come on over. This I did and it was good to catch up. Towards the end of dinner, I casually mentioned to him that I was keen to check out some of the local action, being my first night in Manila and all.

With that, he calls across to his wife (who's European) and says that I need to be driven to a whorehouse, pronto. She drove both of us there and collected us four hours later. "I can't tell anyone about this," I said. "Nobody would believe me!"

Stormtroopers in a tea cup

After the Second World War, I was posted to Indonesia with the Royal Army after the Japs pulled out. We used to pay the local birds we shagged with Tetley tea bags. "Collect 10 and get a free shirt," we told them.

Friggin' in the rigging

There was an oil-rigger based in Singapore married to a beautiful Vietnamese lass. As he was always away, I used to, er, fill in for him on the home front. He got wind of this and drove by my place and let off a few rounds. Not long after, he was on board the rig going out through Sentosa channel when it struck the overhead cable car wire, causing several deaths. The crew, including himself, were all detained. He died of an overdose two days later.

Jacking it in

He'd had the big talk with his Thai girlfriend and, before setting off to work, said: "Don't be here when I come home." She was upset at this turn of events and tried for the sympathy vote … she grabbed a bottle of Jack Daniels and popped 25 sleeping pills and locked herself in the bedroom. Fearing the worst [What, that she'd polish off his Jack Daniels? – Col Ken] he had to climb out through his twelfth floor apartment window and into the bedroom window. She scratched him to pieces and, to this day – many girlfriends and a few wives later – he still bears the scars as a souvenir of that lovely day.

Lifestyles of the rich and aimless

In Bangkok in the early 70s there was an Aussie guy who worked in advertising, a real snappy dresser. His wife discovered he was playing around on the side and confronted him one day by going straight to the drawer where she knew he kept a pistol. She picked the thing up and emptied the eight-shot magazine at him at point blank range. One shot hit his huge TV set, another his latest state-of-the-art music system, and one went through the closet wall, drilling a neat hole through all of his finest suits hanging in the wardrobe. He was happy to be alive, but not best thrilled that he was now under interrogation for possession of an unlicensed pistol. However, things were less formal in those days and things were sorted out on an 'unofficial' basis.

Shot himself in the foot

A Brit, married and living in Thailand, used to do regular visa runs to Phnom Penh, Cambodia. Until one day his wife found a video lying around and popped it in the player. There he was on his 'visa run' with a couple of barely legals. His next 'visa run' was a very expensive shopping trip to Hong Kong with his wife.

Whorex

In Singapore I picked up a regular Thai tart and went back to my house. In the morning I noticed something sticking out of her bag … a 10,000 Kenya Shilling note, which I had kept as a memento of my time there. Not many of those in Singapore. I challenged her, at which she replied her customer had given it to her. With that, I grabbed my key ring and took her through to the locked cupboard and, sure enough, it was empty. She confessed and apologised.

"It says 10,000," I said. "That sounds like big money to you, but do you know how much it's worth?" No, she did not. "Less than a fucking dollar!" I told her she was lucky I didn't call the police, didn't pay her for the previous night, and told her to fuck off. That was the end of our friendship.

Burnt bridges

I was living in Surin, Thailand, with my girlfriend when I got wind that she had started seeing (or had always been seeing) a Thai guy. I got all her stuff and threw it out on to the street, emptied my bladder over it (I'd had two bottles of whiskey by now), then torched the lot. A little later she came home, pushing her motorbike. "Where's all my things?" she asked.

"Out there," I pointed to the pile of burnt offerings.

"I want 20 baht for petrol!" she said. Too easy, I thought: gave her money for petrol and she rode out of my life.

However, she was back soon with her boyfriend, and a big blue ensued. "Bring it on, I'll have you." I was so enraged and hell bent on ripping his head off and sticking it on the fence post for all to see. They threatened to bring back a whole bunch of bad characters to sort me out. "Fine, I'll take some of you down with me." Eventually, they disappeared, and I feared that indeed I would be facing a mongrel mob. I slept with one eye open that night, and heard the next day that she and her boyfriend had taken a bus to Bangkok.

Old habits die hard

Having been a free-wheeling bachelor in South East Asia for many, many years I guess it took a lot of getting used to when I first got married. I got extraordinarily pissed one night shortly afterwards, and took a tart home. I got home to find the gate locked. Then it dawned on me what I had done. Shiiiiiit! I got stony silence for a week, which was then broken by a lecture from hell.

Revenge, a dish best served cold

A private detective had broken the bad news to a friend of mine that, while he was away in Europe, his Thai girlfriend was in fact living with her husband in the northerly provinces of Thailand. He was shocked. Stunned. And mad at himself for falling for this bargirl, something he swore he'd never do. So he hatched a sweet plan for revenge. Next time they spoke on the phone he pretended everything was going fine, and he'd come back to Thailand for her birthday. As a present, he would throw a big party and buy her family a pick-up truck, something she had been hinting at for a while.

She was excited, saying she'd bring the whole family down to Bangkok for the party and would decide what the best pick-up truck would be. He told her to make all the arrangements and he would pay for it all when he arrived in a few weeks.

He spoke to her again the day before the party … said he was going to the airport to fly to Thailand now. She and her sister were going to meet him at the airport in Bangkok, and the whole clan was making the long trip down to Bangkok.

Of course, he had no intention of coming back to Thailand, least of all to see the girl who was deceiving him so badly. The day of the supposed party, another friend had the job of calling her and telling her that his flight had been delayed so they should start without him. He never showed up, leaving her with the bill for the day's festivities, embarrassing explanations to the family, and no new pick-up.

If you've got a good story about a relationship, spouse, partner or any strange bed-mate you've encountered, email the Editor at hardshipposting@hotmail.com or fax 612-9499-5908. He'll grab the video camera and be right over.

❖ 17 ❖

Arrai Gor Dai, Bahala Na, Tid'apa or Bits'n Pieces

True tales of anything else under the sun in Asia.

Which is the odd one out? a) Lobster. b) Crab. c) Chinese man run over by a bus. d) Eel. Answer: d) Eel. All the rest are crushed Asians!

Have you noticed how whenever there's an accident in Asia, people scurry about looking for a pen and paper. First thing they do, like a reflex. Some unlucky bastard's stuck under a bus; they'll write the number of the bus down. Not to report the incident, mind you, but to use the numbers for the next four-digit draw, Mark Six, or whatever lottery game they play in their country. In the week of the Russian sub Kursk sinking, millions of Thais took numbers ending in '118' (the stricken vessel's number).

Eight itself is a lucky number almost universally throughout Asia. Which is why everything from set menu prices to car license plates to phone numbers have lots of eights in them. The Bank of China building in Hong Kong was opened on the 8-8-88. In New Zealand, a guy offered his number plate, NZ8, for sale and allegedly didn't accept the offer of a Chinese person who came to inspect it. He was later shot dead. And all this because the Cantonese word for eight, *fat*, sounds like the Cantonese word for 'prosperous'.

Same for the word four, *say*. *Say* sounds dangerously close to 'death' so this is the devil's number. Notice how Hong Kong hotels, apartment blocks and offices will happily have a 13th floor but you'll often find the fourth floor missing. Japan and Korea even have alternative words and pronunciations for the word 'four' to avoid any nasty negative connotation: *yon* instead of *shi* in Japan, *net* instead of *sa* in Korea.

And aren't Asians the world's biggest gamblers? Every time they go out on the roads they take their lives in their hands. But apart from that, they love a flutter or a punt on anything. As long as there's half a chance or even less of getting one extra dollar they'll be in it with both feet. The Japanese bet around US$450,000,000,000 each year at casinos, on the horses, etc. To give you an idea, this is just more than those in the United States spend, and it has over double the population of Japan. Even the Hong Kong Jockey Club earns US$10,000,000,000 per year. Some countries have wanted to keep their citizens pure from this vice but it's a vain struggle. For years, casinos in South Korea catered only to foreigners. Now they have one that caters to the locals, but they made it way out in the sticks, a four-hour drive away from Seoul. Not that it's going to deter a hard-core gambler. I mean some high-rollers are happy to fly to Las Vegas for gambling weekends.

Barry told me that the casino in Genting Highlands, Malaysia, came to be in a very round about way. Of course the prevailing sentiment there was that gambling and all related vice was out of the question. But one day, over a golf game, an entrepreneur put it to someone high in the ranks that it would be perfect to construct a casino on top of that remote hill. The official or Sultan or whoever the hell he was, said: "If you can build anything on that steep, mountainous, inaccessible place, you are welcome to do whatever you want to do." Dadaaah! Jackpot.

Singapore still outlaws any kind of gambling apart from horse-racing. Instead, the cruise business has curiously picked up. The ships go out into international waters, where all bets are off (or on in this case), cruise to nowhere for a weekend with card games, poker machines, roulette, etc, in full swing, then return to the cloistered halls of Singapore. I've been on these things and there are people who don't even look out of a porthole the whole trip. On board, it's straight to the buffet, hoover a small boatload of noodles down, then straight down to the tables. "Picture, picture!" they yell out, willing the blackjack croupier to deal them a royal card. Where's the romance of the sea voyage with Kate Winslet standing on the focsle with arms outstretched saying, "I'm flying …"? Or better still, Gong Li or Lucy Liu. Down boy!

Maybe this fixation is easier to understand if you know that the Chinese invented playing cards, back in the ninth century. They also invented paper, money, the wheelbarrow, the crossbow, the canal lock gate, porcelain. Even spaghetti: this was on the emperor's menu at the time Christ was born over 2,000 year ago, and presumably taken back to Italy by Marco Polo. In three

AD they also invented the compass, after a fashion … this was the 'south-pointing Buddha'. This Buddha figure was mounted on a complicated cog system and mounted onto bullock carts to tell them where south was (pre-dating the magnetic north compass by centuries). Quite useful. As I've always said, as long as my arse is pointing south everything should be fine. Speaking of explosive substances, gunpowder was invented around 900 years later.

Tea drinking also comes to us courtesy of the industrious Chinese. Well, actually, that's not quite accurate … emperor Shen Nong was having a little nap under a shady tree during a lull in battle in 2737 BC. He was drinking his usual lip-smacking beverage – a cup of boiling water – when a leaf fluttered down and landed in it. He declared it tastier than his usual drop, thus tea brewing became the thing to do. So if someone calls you a 'complete Nong' it's actually a compliment. What I want to know, is how come over the next 4,000 years the Chinese were not able to invent a simple teapot that doesn't leak everywhere when you pour it? They've always got to have those little rubber thingies at the end of the spout.

It was only in the 17th century that the English had their first cuppa. And in the 19th century the Brits were importing ice into India and China from America. What they obviously didn't know is that 'ice-houses' dated back to the seventh century BC in Yong Cheng, Shaanxi. Chou rulers in the fourth century BC had a 'royal ice service' who chilled, refrigerated and stored everything, including the dead bodies of kings.

One thing they didn't invent, but have cornered 70 per cent of the world market in, is cigarette lighters. Wenzhou in China is what Detroit is to motorcars in America. Around 300,000 people depend on cigarette lighters for their livelihood (ironic as that may be to the more astute readers). Four hundred cigarette lighter factories churn out 1.3 million lighters daily (you'll need to take both shoes off to add that up, so I'll do it for you … that's 500,000,000 a year, arsonists).

From Zippos to zippers. Look at your zipper. On your fly. On the tart's dress. There's a 90 per cent chance it says 'YKK' on it somewhere, only because they can't fit the full name of the company – Yoshida Kogyou Kabushikikaisha – on it. This Japanese company kicked off in 1934 and today makes 7,000,000 zippers a day. That's roughly, give or take a couple, 1.82 billion per year. Now you know why they call Japanese 'zipperheads'. It's not derogatory as some might think; simply a compliment to their industrial prowess.

But the Japanese are not just about hard work. They hold some of the wildest festivals going. Like the Naked Festival held each year in Inazawa. Just in case you've already booked your ticket, I should tell you that not everyone's naked ... just the main guy Shin-Otokoa (Naked Man to his mother). He runs down the street while all the guys try to touch him to rid themselves of bad spirits and their sinful deeds. Meanwhile his bodyguards ride shotgun, splashing everyone with water. The women can watch, but can't touch. I think there's room for an alternate event there ... all the women run naked and we splash them with water as they run past. How about it, Inazawa? You know it's a good idea!

Which brings us to *Songkran*, the Buddhist New Year water festival in Thailand. Suffice to say it's a nationwide wet t-shirt contest each April, and everyone's fair game ... bosses, teachers, monks, etc. But *farangs* count for double points. The Phuket Vegetarian festival is not as much fun. Held at the start of Asian 'lent' these sirloin-avoiding masochists stick knives and swords through their cheeks, run over hot coals, and climb ladders with rungs made of sharp blades. If that's what you do when you're a vegetarian, I think I'd rather have Mad Cow disease!

You get the same human skin kebabs at the Hindu *Thaipusam* festivals. Last year I happened to be in Malaysia at that time ... I thought word had got out that I was in town for a book-signing as there were 800,000 people thronging the streets. Then I noticed these gents with hooks and skewers through their skin, carrying giant ornate floral frames. My good Malaysian friend Ahmed Khaz explained to me that devotees often fast for a month and a half to get into a trance. Never mind a month or so – if I don't eat lunch on an average day I go into a trance. Then they pull these bloody great wire frames three kilometres up the road to the Batu Caves, where they bite on a lemon to wake them up. For the soft cocks there is apparently a Plan B: they are allowed to carry a coconut and then smash it against the cave wall.

All quite spectacular, but not a patch on the Khumble Festival in India, that attracts 30 million seething bodies in a single day. To give you an idea, this can be seen from outer space, which, just quietly, is the best place to view it from as there were no Port-A-Loos in evidence. To give you some idea of how big the crowd is, I'm not even sure why they were there or what the attraction was. We were miles away from whatever action was taking place. They were just there, jostling, pushing and shoving like another day down at the markets in Old Delhi. I had to retire to the hotel for a bit of spiritual cleansing, Raj style, with several thousand gin and tonics.

My favourite festival in Asia, though is the Naadam Festival held in Ulaan Baatar, Mongolia, each July. This is like WWF Mongolia style ... millions of nomads on horseback descend on the town to show their skills in the Mongolian triathlon – horse racing, archery and wrestling. The pomp and pageantry is on a scale hard to emulate anywhere in the world. The opening ceremony is a display of marching, marching and more fucking marching. If you can't count to four you'd be out of place there. But the colourful warrior outfits make it all worthwhile, with striking red tunics, and some teams holding aloft what look like large jellyfish on spears, but are apparently some kind of parasol device. And it's all very picturesque ... with the green hills as a backdrop to the tree-lined streets and stately Parliament House buildings. Then you have the little side events, all of which serve as a curtain raiser for the big deal of the weekend ... a ten-kilometre horse race featuring more than a thousand horses. That, dear race-fixers, is a sight to behold. Questions will come to you faster than a bargirl getting dressed after a 'short-time': Who should I bet on? How do I know who's winning? And what the hell am I doing in Mongolia anyway?!? Fair to say, if there was a beauty pageant as part of the weekend, horses might have taken the top three places, and maybe even the Miss Congeniality title.

Speaking of beauty pageants, the Miss China contest is officially a 'no-no' and has to be held underground, so to speak. Officially no beauty contest has been staged in China since 1949. Officials recently raided the auditorium where it was being staged as the organisers had no permit for such a 'cultural' event. Later, once the guards had cleared off, the judges and contestants reconvened, and a winner was declared. When the delightful Zhuo Ling (tall, with black hair, would you believe?) got a podium placing at the Puerto Rico final, it was a little hard to keep it under wraps any longer.

Thailand, far from banning pageants, make it virtually compulsory for all ... well, I was going to say able-bodied people but in fact any-bodied ... people over the age of 15 to compete in at least one pageant of some description each year. There's a pageant for any shape, size, gender or mutant category you can think of. Like Miss Jumbo Queen. The criteria? The woman who best exhibits the characteristics of an elephant – grace, elegance, size – to help promote the cause of elephant conservation. The delicate little flower of the east, Lalita Songrat was a recent winner, weighing in at 191 kilograms. More chins than a Chinese phonebook, as my good friend Joan Rivers once said. You'd have to roll her in flour just to find the wet spot.

Organisers of another recent beauty pageant in Bangkok took back their 5,000 baht prize purse from the 22-year-old winner after other contestants complained 'she' was in fact seen tucking her testicles into her g-string back stage. Details, details!

And Vietnam recently gave this decadent western imperialistic practice of beauty pageants the green light for the first time in 15 years. Competitors compete in bathing suits and glamorous *ao-dais*, and big prize money is at stake, not to mention the sugar daddies who wait in the wings. The Communist League Newspaper has organised the contest all these years, just there was no official recognition of the contest. According to the cadres, women are supposed to be workers, soldiers and mothers, not air-headed objects of frivolous beauty. The Ministry of Culture and Information apparently instructed the organisers to prepare the questions for the interview round in advance so contestants could go away and study it over a cup of coffee and prepare a suitable answer.

The Vietnamese certainly picked the brains of their Gallic governors on this when they had the chance – their coffee is the best this side of the River Seine. Funny thing is there was never any coffee grown in Vietnam to speak of until 1990. And now, little old Vietnam is the world's second biggest coffee producer after Brazil. But the absolute best, the wide-eyed experts tell me, comes from Indonesia. Now we're not just talking any old Java blend here, no sir. The rarest and most expensive coffee in the world comes from the *kopi luwak* bean. This stuff costs over US$600 per kilo. How come, Colonel, you so rightly ask? Because the beans are collected from the droppings of the Sumatran civet cat. No, seriously. That explains the much-desired earthy aroma. The civet cat eats the beans off the tree, and its digestive system strips off the pulp, leaving just the beans. One question, as always: who first discovered the joys of civet-filtered coffee, and how and why? OK, I know that's three questions, but it does make you marvel at your fellow human beans, er, beings sometimes.

All this talk has made me thirsty. I've got Rattana, my French-polishing maid, to brew up something I've been dying to try for a while here … some Maxwell House 43-bean coffee which the gardener fed to the neighbour's chicken. I can see the marketing slogan now: 'Colonel Ken's Super Rooster Blend Coffee – the cock that'll keep you up all night!'

Colonel Ken

Smoky and the bandits

In Cambodia, a mate of mine had to go down to the docks to collect his containers full of supplies for his supermarket. We joined the convoy under armed UN escort going down to the docks. We were delayed at the docks getting his materials released and missed the return convoy. I said, "Fuck it, let's just stay the night here," referring to the flood-lit car park. However, there was further trouble in Phnom Penh and his wife called to say he must come back immediately, not the next day.

So we headed back in his white car. We came to one roadblock. No problem. Then another, no problem. But we're stopped at a third … a very professional-looking roadblock with logs and trees across the road and, pointing down at us, an array of rocket-launchers, AK-47s, etc. Fuck! Pointing to his white car, my friend says, "UN! UN!" He pulled out a piece of paper – actually an invite card to a UN cocktail piss-up – and pointed to the well-recognised logo, shouting "UN! UN!" This seemed to count for nothing. Oh shit. I pulled out a pack of cigarettes … if I'm gonna die I may as well have one last smoke.

"Smoke, my friend?" I offer them through the window. Aah, that's more like it. Smiles all round, guns and rocket-launchers lowered. We enjoyed a cigarette together before the obstacles were removed from the road and we were waved through.

Horse play

In the Philippines, this American guy was known to be a strong fighter and few would dare take him on. One day, he lost his temper and punched this horse, breaking its neck with a single blow. He was put in jail for his troubles and made to buy a new horse for the Filipino owner. This was long before the exact same scene appeared in the movie Blazing Saddles.

Flare game

We used to sail a lot between Singapore and Malaysia in the days when piracy was really rampant. It didn't stop us going on weekend trips, but we were alert. One night I was at the helm and we had a bunch of our wives up on deck sipping wine and G&Ts. The rest of the guys were downstairs playing cards or something. I noticed a grey craft approaching us out of the dark. Worse still, it had no lights on whatsoever.

I told all the ladies to go down below and send the guys up for a show of strength. At the same time I got out the boat's emergency flare gun and held it at my side just out of sight.

The boat drew nearer, checking us out. We just stared them down. Closer they came. I put my finger on the trigger ready to blast a flare straight into the cabin of their boat. It was our only hope. Closer again. Just as I was about to act, their boat pulled away. A close shave. Then all the guys let the air out of their chest.

Gelly fish

I was visiting a friend up in Chiangmai on his farm. Many beers were consumed before he suggested some fishing. We went down to the lake and hopped into his boat, a bamboo raft. Halfway out I said, "Where are the rods?" With that, he leant over, opened a big black box and produced five sticks of dynamite. We spent the next hour or so scooping up our fish.

Dead meat

Visiting a friend's farm in the Philippines at Christmas, they had a nice dam there. "Too bad we don't have any fishing rods," I said.

"Never mind," he said, pulling out a 9mm pistol. He proceeded to shoot about half a dozen fish, which floated to the surface, and went straight on to the barbecue. *Sarap!* (delicious!)

Friends in low places

After the Vietnam War, the waters of Thailand were filled with Vietnamese refugee boats heading south. Many of them were intercepted, raped, pillaged, plundered and sunk by Thai pirates. X had been demobbed from the military and was stationed in Thailand but was somehow given permission to keep his automatic weapon, and felt he had to do something to protect the innocent Vietnamese 'boat people'.

Out on his boat one day, he opened fire on a boat of Thai pirates with this weapon, spraying it with bullets and all but blowing it out of the water. He dragged the leader on board his boat and was dunking this guy into the water to teach him a lesson.

Big mistake! Turns out this guy was the son of a sugar tycoon from Songkla with all sorts of connections in the right places … especially in the underworld. X had to lie low for a number of years outside of Asia before he felt it was safe to return.

The pretzel position

I have studied *Tai Qi* in England, so the possibility of both seeing it and practicing it in China excited M (my wife) and I when we went on a tour of Guangdong province. One morning, in Zhou Xing, we escaped from the guide early in the morning and went to the park to try our *Tai Qi*. We got a little way into our form, when several locals came to watch. One particular woman came and observed very closely, and started taking notes! I managed to engineer a finish, as my form fell apart. We persevered to the very end, completing both sides of the Yang 54 step under this close scrutiny. By the end, my movements had lost all the fluidity that *Tai Qi* is supposed to display, and I was shaking with stress. M, however, managed to keep completely calm and in control.

The guide later that morning told us all how if we had got up early we could have seen the local people practicing the strange art of Chinese *Tai Qi*. If only he had known he could have seen something a darn sight stranger!

Importing expertise

When I went to Shanghai with my Chinese girlfriend, J, I thought it would be good to practice my *Tai Qi* skills. She had never studied *Tai Qi*, but was keen to learn, so I took her out to the park near where we were staying, and started to teach her some simple moves. It is hard to describe the astounded inquisitive looks we got from some local people out ballroom-dancing in the morning air, when they saw me (a *gweilo*) instructing her. J told me that some of them were saying how they could not understand how she should be learning from a foreigner, so I must be a great master!

Made a monkey out of me

I was in Hangzhou, having finished work at a customer site in a side street, waiting with two Chinese colleagues for a taxi back to our hotel. We were all three dressed in short-sleeved shirts. While we were waiting a small boy came up to us, eyed me very strangely, and then came up to me gingerly and started to stroke my rather hairy forearm. He was clearly fascinated by this, and continued for a minute or two while I worked out how I should react to this. Eventually one of my colleagues talked to the boy, who then went away. He explained to me that the boy had never seen a European before, and was trying to work out if I was human or some sort of strange animal! He said that in China they call it 'Ape's Hair Arm'.

Hair today, gone tomorrow

I was in Taipei one Saturday morning, and decided it was time to get a haircut. So when I came to a barber's shop in a small side street, in I went and sat down. The man in the shop immediately understood and gave me a very presentable haircut. He then noticed my fairly hairy chest and, filled with fascination at this strange phenomenon, started to cut that too!

Sunken hopes

We had gone diving off Puerto Gallera in the early 80s and came across some amazing artefacts on the seabed. They were obviously relics from a shipwreck, although the ship itself had long since rotted away. Excitedly, we helped ourselves to all the good stuff we could find. Then we did the proper thing and notified the authorities of our find. They planned to send a diving team down, but a typhoon came roaring through, making the waters inaccessible for the next six weeks. Meantime, we had gone up to Hong Kong to sell our treasure ... which turned out to be Ming Dynasty crockery but which fetched only several hundred dollars or up to a thousand bucks per piece. Not exactly retirement money.

Returning to the dive site, we were really pissed off to find that the heavy seas caused by the typhoon had unearthed the site even further, exposing the really good stuff. We could only watch and wonder as the appointed divers brought up loads and loads of real Ming Dynasty treasures.

Just like grandma used to cook it

Have you every noticed the absence of birds and bird songs in Hanoi? Every morning locals armed with air-guns swarm the streets hunting for inexpensive supplements to their diet.

Engaged in my many official and unofficial outings with the native counterparts, I came up with a party game to find and call out a particular species a Vietnamese would definitively refuse to eat! Bugs, vermin, birds, you name it we tried everything. Whenever I thought we finally got a winner, one of the folks would suddenly 'remember' having heard of somebody who'd eaten that particular 'endangered species' with some special sweet-sour sauce preparation, or together with some *nuoc mam* (fish sauce).

After many years I concluded that everything crawling, flying, and all two- or four-legged things, would eventually end up in the pot ... with the possible exception of chairs and tables!

Like a good wine

Following an early, but heavy, business drinking dinner at Pattaya, I wasn't in the mood to return straight back to my wife in Bangkok … especially after being provided with a perfect alibi for a night out. But Pattaya appeared too busy and uninviting that particular evening and I decided to head home. The ride to Bangkok was uneventful thanks to the slow driving mode selected to suit my state of intoxication.

What to do for relaxation and sobering up? The obvious choice was one of the better massage parlours but, since it was already closing in on midnight, the choice of ladies available at that time was not too impressive. Ready to leave, the manager approached me, heavily lobbying the services of a girl who looked to be well past her best years. Finally I gave in, and I walked off with this short, elderly bird.

She turned out to be an absolute expert in her own right, not surprising considering her age (40-some?) and experience. She asked me to call and invite one of her friends (another massage girl from downstairs) to help her massage 'my big frame'. Pissed as I was, I gave in. The second one – surprise, surprise! – turned out to be even older than the first girl. I didn't dare to open my eyes for the two hours I was being 'serviced' but it was, I must admit, the absolute best time of my life.

Don't tell anybody that my current Thai wife is only 21 years old …

Princess of darkness

I was staggering home to my hotel up Tanglin Road in Singapore, and was feeling a little worse for wear having spent the last few hours in I-can't-remember-how-many bars in Orchard Towers. Suddenly, from behind a tree, a large Indian 'girl' confronts me with "100 dollars for a blow job."

"That's a lot of money," I said, trying to focus my eyes on this vision of splendour.

"I am very good," said the vision. Now good, to me, is someone with the awesome ability of being able to suck a golf ball through 40 feet of garden hose. Somehow, in this case, I couldn't see it.

"See this," I said, holding up my right hand, "It's free. And this," I said, holding up my left hand, "if I paint the nails, it feels like someone else." At this point the Indian beauty disappeared back into the darkness.

Flaming hell

At a Christmas party in 1970 at the Selangor Club, Kuala Lumpur, the party was in full swing late at night when there was a strong smell of smoke, followed by the sight of leaping flames. A short-circuit in the kitchen had started the fire and it had spread from there, trapping the staff who were saved only by breaking through at the back and sending a small guy in to rescue them and lead them out. We ourselves evacuated (not before I'd grabbed my beer of course!) and stood on the *padang* out the front watching the fire spread from the kitchen area to the main wing. The fire brigade arrived and sprayed the roof, the weight of the water just helping to collapse it. Fortunately, the wind changed and blew the fire back on itself, saving most of the building. A not so Merry Xmas!

When it rains it pours

There was once a massive flood in KL, Malaysia. I was making my way to the Selangor Club, but couldn't make it to that part of town. So I pulled in and parked in the personal parking space reserved for the Governor of the Bank of Negara, ie, a very big shot. The rain never let up and I wasn't able to retrieve my car for ten days due to the flooding. Where he parked in the meantime, I'm not sure, but luckily my car was still there and nothing came of it.

Dead weights and dead wood

One of the inevitabilities of sailing the world with a couple of thousand passengers on board, mostly elderly, is that some die. We averaged one a month and, I hasten to add, all from natural causes: usually heart attacks. If we were more than a couple of days from port, and a relative was on board, they were usually buried at sea. A brief ceremony at 6am on the after deck, senior officers in attendance, and the body in a canvas shroud under the Union flag. The ship was brought to a halt, and a couple of burly boatswain's mates lifted the plank, a 'w-o-o-s-h' and it was gone.

Except once when they had not weighted the sack properly, and it floated away a good distance before sinking. Luckily the widow had enough tears in her eyes not to notice.

However, we were approaching Yokohama, Japan, one day and a passenger, Mr X, died. We were only a couple of hours out, so burial at sea was not really an option. The surgeon certified death, the usual formalities were completed and the body landed ashore for cremation. We were in port for three days and, on the third day, the agent came into the Purser's Office with a small box wrapped in brown paper, tied with string and with wax seals.

"Could you sign for this and take it back to the UK."

"What is it?" I asked.

"Mr X."

It was still warm.

Chickened out

I had been bonking this lady from the Firehouse in Manila for years, and she was about to move to Australia to get married. She had to go back to her hometown in Zamboanga to get her baptismal certificate so she could get a passport, so I decided to join her for the trip. From Zamboanga we caught a ferry a couple of hours south. The next morning she was going off to the city hall and other government offices to attend to her paperwork. I said, "I'll come with you," and got ready to go. Her father pushed me back to the room.

"No, no … they shoot you like chicken!" Unknown to me, this was deep in Muslim rebel country. I stayed in the room, nervous and sweaty till she came back. Then we got the first ferry out of Zamboanga. I've never been so glad and relieved to see Manila.

My enemy's enemy must be my friend

I was visiting Hong Kong from Manila, and had two contacts to catch up with. I stayed with one, an old friend from my days as a rower, and had a great time making up for lost time. A few days later, I arranged to catch up with another mate of mine down at The Wanch pub. He asked where I was staying, so I told him with my old mate X. At the mention of that name, his jaw dropped and he started muttering aggressively, saying what a complete bastard he was.

The mate I was staying with was this guy's 'boss' – well, until two days earlier, that is, when he was fired from this big engineering project. I later mentioned this chance meeting to my host, who also started mutteringly darkly. Obviously still a raw nerve, so I never got to the bottom of it.

Big bang theory

One of the best New Year's Eves we've ever had was on Corregidor Island, off Manila. From 6am till the following afternoon, we had hired out one of the most famous historic islands in the world. We loaded up a ferry with ourselves, a whole bunch of whores, and an industrial quantity of fireworks. The coast guard had a problem with us transporting these, but one of our crowd had gone to school with this guy, so it was agreed they could be carried across on a separate boat.

So let me get this straight, Dave. You actually went in there to get a haircut?

And the fireworks? It was magic. Can you imagine setting off six-foot rockets, sometimes with three tied together. Talk about starting the New Year with a bang.

What a hide

An American friend of mine decided to become a Buddhist and did a tour as a novice monk. Part of his duty was to accompany an older monk, who spoke some English, to the morning alms bowl. Walking barefooted on country roads was not fun for the tender-footed American and he asked the older monk how he learned to do it. Without a word, the old man found a pile of fresh buffalo manure and waded right into it, liberally coating his feet. From there he stepped into the sand, which stuck to the manure, and walked on. Nature's own sandals.

Life is cheaper

There was a fight in a Manila street – a staring incident or some such –

and a Brit stepped in the middle to mediate. A Filipino guy stepped forward and said: "For 3,000 pesos we can have you taken out." With this the Brit berated him:

"It's people like you who spoil the market ... I can get it done for 1,000!"

Dead ringer

A European drug addict who had moved to Lamai, Koh Samui, ended up being really down and out and subsequently hung himself. Curiously his funeral was attended by a group of twenty *katoeys* ... and myself.

On yer bike, mate

On an island in Thailand is a gent who runs a motorbike shop. He is reputed to be the son a very prominent legal family in the UK ... as a 'remittance kid' they apparently pay him a lot of money to stay out of the country and in the tropics somewhere where he won't besmirch the family's name.

Hair-raising experience

While living in Thailand I had a relationship with a local girl, Y. She lived in a small house with her parents, three brothers, and two sisters. Their house was big enough, but still they shared a lot of rooms and bed space. This made sex much more exciting, for though all knew what went on beyond closed eyelids, no-one wanted to get caught.

One night we were caught in the mood so she went to get a bottle of moisturising lotion to help things along (as we didn't have any protection and decided to improvise by rubbing our bodies together, spoons-like). Eventually she says to me: "Hey, it stings." She said it again: "Stings! Stings! Stings! Ouch! Hot!"

I stopped. As soon as I stopped, the pain grabbed me by the balls. It really stung. I looked down at my quickly shrinking package. Red. Welted. Blistered. And hot. I curled up in a ball and Y ran for a cold cloth. I sat still, wondering how any moisturiser could have such an effect.

Two minutes later she arrived with the bottle and her two sisters, who proceeded to poke me and giggle. "Do you have any hair on your balls?" her sister asked, leaning over me holding up the cause of my discomfort ... a pink lotion bottle with 'Hair Remover' in small letters on the label.

McChromeDome

A poor expat Brit, having consumed too much alcohol one night, falls asleep at a party in Hong Kong. So, boys being boys, they decide to shave off all his hair. This results in the poor sod having to visit Jordan Market to buy a wig to cover his bald head.

Obviously the wig that he picked was so stupid that he stood out like a dickhead in the crowd. While sitting in McDonalds the whole restaurant kept looking and staring at him. One of his mates could take no more, grabbed the wig off his head and threw it across the restaurant. This is the only time that I have been in a crowded place of Chinese where they have all burst out in rapturous laughter. Needless to say the guy stayed bald gracefully.

Shooting his load

X (an Irishman) visits Saigon, and one of the tours is a trip to the Cu Chi tunnels from the Vietnam War. At the firing range, tourists are using AK-47 rifles to shoot at targets on a hill top at a cost of one dollar a bullet. All the marksmen are firing one shot individually from the rifle at the targets.

X asks for his magazine to be filled up, takes the rifle, holds his finger on the trigger and sprays the hill top with automatic gunfire, blasting anything in sight. He turns to the crowd of onlookers and tourists who are shocked in amazement and states: "That's the way we use AK-47s in Belfast!"

Signs of civilisation

In Bali many years ago, a public toilet for ladies carried this message: 'PLEASE DO NOT FLASH YOUR TAMPOONS'. Another sign at a nearby temple, which had obviously had one Australian visitor too many, said: 'PLEASE DO NOT WRECH OR PISS HERE!'

Average day in the field

I had achieved the pinnacle of middle-aged expat male life ... I was taking a young Asian beauty to the Hong Kong 7s to show the world that I had achieved success, power and money. But to add to the display I had to escort one of my friend's girlfriend to the Sevens ... no big deal except that he (married) and she are having a full-on affair and I'm to pretend that this girl is a friend of my girlfriend so that she can come and sit in our group, while my mate takes his wife.

An interesting experience when these two are making eyes at each other, and the wife is wondering what the hell is going on. At the same time my girlfriend, a rather quiet person who had just started going out with me and had only ever seen me go to and from work and being very conservative around the housing estate, is trying to come to grips with the fact that this male she has just started going out with is sitting at her side with a red wig on his head shouting till he is hoarse, at anyone that is willing to reciprocate. And on the other side of her is another mate of mine who is having a ménage-a-trois with his own Asian beauty and a blow-up sheep (no he is not a Kiwi but I believe he does have some Welsh blood in him).

Mistake number two for my girlfriend (assuming mistake number one was coming in the first place) was that she let her mobile phone ring: after saying 'hello' to her cousin I requested to speak to her, too. Well, the cousin had no idea what hit her, because the phone was promptly passed around the bay of spectators so that all and sundry got a chance to say 'hello' to her cousin, ask about the weather, describe the current game and in one case ask her out for a date ... in effect the one phone call ensured that my girlfriend's cousin made about 25 new friends. This little ploy was amusing (yes, after the initial shock even my girlfriend laughed) and it became even more humorous when one of our group from New Zealand happened to receive a call on his mobile from his son in Sydney, Australia. You guessed it ... this young man was promptly informed by about 40 supporters in and around our bay of their thoughts on NZ rugby, Australian prowess, NZ males' abnormal interest in sheep, and the fact he should be here. Well, he was almost as good as being in HK, as the phone call lasted several games.

So what happened in the end? My mate number one ended up with the lover (the wife wasn't that naive), the Kiwi went home to work off his phone bill (and the son watched the games on the TV replay at a cheaper rate), my mate number two decided the blow-up sheep was a better partner than his girlfriend, the cousin is still waiting for the 'date' to call back (men are bastards), and I became a father (work that last one out for yourself but, needless to say, I won't wear the red wig again as it was just too erotic!).

The bottom line

In Jakarta, one of our colleagues goes to the loo and re-emerges some time later. "That was the most expensive shit I've ever had," he said. Explaining to his friends, he said he had Bali Belly and there was no toilet paper. "I started with 100 rupiah notes, and graduated reluctantly to the 5000s." Afterwards he deposited the whole sordid mess into a bin. We bet they would re-surface as legal tender within a matter of days.

Bear naked

During my stay in Hong Kong, my son (aged seven) visited me for Christmas. One day we were walking through Wanchai in the 'wrong' neighbourhood. We were passing the Panda Bar (a-go-go) and I told my son, a real animal lover, that inside the bar real pandas were dancing. He looked at me with the thought of having a not-too-clever father and said to me: "No papa, you don't understand … those are not real pandas, those are people dressed as pandas."

If you have a good story about living in or travelling through Asia email The Editor at hardshipposting@hotmail.com or fax 612-9499-5908. We'll find a space for it somewhere, even if we have to invent a category!

A few words about the Hardship Posting team.

Stu Lloyd (Editor)

The short story goes something like this: conceived in California, born in Zimbabwe, raised in South Africa, emigrated to Australia, transferred to New Zealand, posted to Hong Kong, relocated to Singapore, moved back to Australia.

Stu is a full-time writer/journalist and oral historian who specialises in travel, colonial history and lifestyle writing.

He spent over 12 years living in Hong Kong and Singapore, and continues to travel extensively to all corners of Asia and, indeed, the world.

He is a graded karate exponent and a degraded Hashman.

Colonel Ken Oathe (Narrator)

Col Ken is an Old Asia Hand, having first arrived in South East Asia in 1968. Since his retirement from active military life, we can divulge (as the relevant statutes and classifications have now expired) he has been Defence Attache and First Secretary (nudge, nudge, wink, wink!) at a number of embassies in the region

He now lives in Koh Samui, Thailand, where an unusually large household staff – notably all female with the exception of his Gurkha driver/bodyguard – attend to his daily whims. You can email the Colonel directly at *ColonelKen@hotmail.com*

Hugh Harrison (Cartoonist)

A relentless rolling stone with an audacious appetite for life and protean talents, Hugh's 50-year quest to see what's over the next hill has taken him to every corner of the globe, working along the way at a hundred different jobs as diverse as farmhand, fishing guide, train driver, talk show host, miner, musical director, pilot, producer, illustrator, impressario…the list goes on. Last seen shooting commercials in Rwanda, Hugh has a wife, daughter and son living in northeast Thailand. He can be reached through his website at www.hhdesign.intl.biz or hughchi@asia.com.

"Keep 'em coming!"
*Contributors wanted NOW for the next
volume of Hardship Posting.*

The editor is currently hard at work producing the next volume of 'Hardship Posting' so get your stories in to us at soonest if you want fame, fortune and immortality (OK, so nought out of three ain't bad!).

You don't have to be an expert writer, because – believe you me – The Editor will edit and re-write submissions for length, grammar and content anyway. Some tips:

● Make it around 150-200 words long. (Only go longer if the story needs to dramatically unfold).

● Make it short, sharp, to the point. And amusing. Or amazing.

● Submit as many as you want – there is no limit.

● Put your name and contact details together with the story.

● Indicate which category you think it belongs to, ie Police, Airports, etc.

● All contributions accepted will have their writer's name printed in the Acknowledgements section of the book, not alongside their individual stories, for anonymity.

● Individual contributors reserve the copyright of their own original contribution, so may use it elsewhere. However, all contributions must be original works and free of libel and slander.

● All published contributors will receive an autographed copy of the volume in which their work appears as full and final compensation for their submission. Discounts on further copies may also be extended.

It's that simple! Just send them in whenever you remember an episode, or whenever you find yourself in an amusing or amazing situation in Asia. If you know of others that have great true tales of expat misadventure in Asia, get them to contact us. Or let us know who they are and we'll contact them.

*Send your stories today to The Editor at hardshipposting@hotmail.com
or fax Australia 612-9499-5908. Our operators are standing by!*

Join our online expat community at
www.hardshipposting.com

for more mayhem and misadventure, laughs, new stories, freebies, travel trials and tribulations, and over 500 useful and interesting links to expat sites.

Ladies and genitals, bastards and bargirls,

Join me on our website for a bunch of great stuff. I've got nothing better to do than keep you posted with what's going on around Asia. So sign up for the 'Friends of Colonel Ken' (F*CK) club immediately, if not sooner.

You'll get:

● A regular "Debriefing Asia" newsletter, with my cynical observations of news items in Asia, jokes, relevant new web links, and sneak previews of the latest stories of misadventure

● special discounts on Hardship Posting books and merchandise

● special offers from those in our club, such as bars, hotels, mobile phones, travel, moving companies or whatever dodgy goods or services they provide! (and free links to your homepage or relevant site)

● invitations to join the Colonel for some fun and games when he comes to your city/town/remote outpost

● and, mainly, a sense of belonging to a group of like-minded individuals that enjoy living life in Asia to the fullest

Of course, it's all FREE, as I know you highly-overpaid cheapskates would never actually pay for any of this frivolity out of your own pockets. (Of course, if you want to advertise to a large expatriate audience – numbering conservatively in the high millions or perhaps even low billions – then we're all ears too!)

It's more than a website – it's a way of life!

Cop you later.

Colonel Ken